Human Computer Interaction and Emerging Technologies:
Adjunct Proceedings from the INTERACT 2019 Workshops

Edited by
Fernando Loizides, Marco Winckler,
Usashi Chatterjee, Jose Abdelnour-Nocera
and Antigoni Parmaxi

Cardiff | Gwasg
University | Prifysgol
Press | Caerdydd

Published by
Cardiff University Press
Cardiff University
PO Box 430
1st Floor, 30-36 Newport Road
Cardiff CF24 0DE

https://cardiffuniversitypress.org

First published 2020

Cover design by Hugh Griffiths

Cover image by Easy Conferences Ltd.

Print and digital versions typeset by Siliconchips Services Ltd.

ISBN (Paperback): 978-1-911653-09-7
ISBN (PDF): 978-1-911653-13-4
ISBN (EPUB): 978-1-911653-10-3
ISBN (Kindle): 978-1-911653-11-0

DOI: https://doi.org/10.18573/book3

The full text of this book has been peer-reviewed to ensure high academic
standards. For full review policies, see https://www.cardiffuniversitypress.org/
site/research-integrity/

Suggested citation: Loizides, F., Winckler, M., Chatterjee, U.,
Abdelnour-Nocera, J. and Parmaxi, A. (eds.) 2020. *Human Computer
Interaction and Emerging Technologies: Adjunct Proceedings from the
INTERACT 2019 Workshops*. Cardiff: Cardiff University Press. DOI: https://
doi.org/10.18573/book3. License: CC-BY 4.0

To read the free, open access version of this book
online, visit https://doi.org/10.18573/book3 or
scan this QR code with your mobile device:

Contents

Foreword

The 17th IFIP TC13 International Conference on Human-Computer Interaction, INTERACT 2019, took place during September 2–6, 2019, in Paphos, Cyprus. This conference was held at the Coral Beach Hotel Resort. The conference was co-sponsored by the Cyprus University of Technology and Tallinn University, in cooperation with ACM and ACM SIGCHI.

The conference falls under the responsibility of the International Federation for Information Processing (IFIP) which was created in 1960 under the auspices of UNESCO. The Technical Committee 13 (TC13) of the IFIP aims at developing the science and technology of human-computer interaction (HCI). TC13 has representatives from 32 countries, 2 international organizations, apart from 14 expert members and observers. TC13 started the series of the INTERACT conference in 1984. These conferences have been an important showcase for researchers and practitioners in the field of HCI. Situated under the open, inclusive umbrella of the IFIP, INTERACT has been truly international in its spirit and has attracted researchers from several countries and cultures. The venues of the INTERACT conferences over the years bear a testimony to this inclusiveness. INTERACT 2019 continued the INTERACT conscious efforts to lower barriers that prevent people from developing countries to participate in conferences. Thinkers and optimists believe that all regions of the world can achieve human development goals. Information and communication technologies (ICTs) can support this process and empower people to achieve their full potential. Today ICT products have many new users and many new uses, but also present new challenges and provide new opportunities. It is no surprise that HCI researchers are showing great interest in these emergent uses. INTERACT 2019 provided a platform to explore these challenges and opportunities, but also made it easier for people from developing countries to participate. Like its predecessors, INTERACT 2019 aimed to bring together high-quality research. As a multidisciplinary field, HCI requires interaction and discussion among diverse people with different interests and backgrounds. The beginners and the experienced, theoreticians and practitioners, and people from diverse disciplines and different countries gathered together in Paphos to learn from each other and to contribute to each others' growth.

We thank all the authors who chose INTERACT 2019 as the venue to publish their research, all the reviewers and the INTERACT 2019 accepted and ran 9 workshops out of the submissions. From these workshops papers were published in this volume, under the categories of Designing for Aging People, Challenging Misinformation: Exploring Limits and Approaches, Socially-AcceptableHCI: Social Acceptability of Emerging Technologies and Novel Interaction Paradigms, User Experiences and Wellbeing at Work, Human(s) in the Loop Bringing AI HCI, Handling Security, Usability, User Experience and Reliability in User-Centered Development Processes, Pushing the Boundaries of Participatory Design, HCI Challenges in Human Movement Analysis.

We would particularly like to thank Cardiff University Press for giving us the means and their support in publishing these works. We hope that this volume will inspire, benefit and change the world for the better.

Fernando Loizides
Marco Winckler
Usashi Chatterjee
Jose Abdelnour-Nocera
Antigoni Parmaxi

SECTION 1

Designing for Aging People

A Storytelling-based Approach to Designing for the Needs of Ageing People

Elena Comincioli and Masood Masoodian

School of Arts, Design and Architecture, Aalto University, Finland

elena.comincioli@aalto.fi, masood.masoodian@aalto.fi

Abstract

Identifying users' needs is the basis of many design methodologies centred around a *problem-solution* approach. Ageist views of designers and older adult users themselves, however, negatively affect the use of existing methods for identifying their needs. In this paper, we describe an alternative approach to designing for older adults' needs based on storytelling. We introduce a method which uses a set of visual cards to allow older adult participants to tell their stories in co-design workshops. These stories can then be used to identify their needs.

Keywords

Design for ageing · design without ageism · human centred design · storytelling · visual cards · user needs

---

How to cite this book chapter:

Comincioli, E. and Masoodian, M. 2020. A Storytelling-based Approach to Designing for the Needs of Ageing People. In: Loizides, F., Winckler, M., Chatterjee, U., Abdelnour-Nocera, J. and Parmaxi, A. (eds.) *Human Computer Interaction and Emerging Technologies: Adjunct Proceedings from the INTERACT 2019 Workshops.* Pp. 3–12. Cardiff: Cardiff University Press. DOI: https://doi.org/10.18573/book3.a. License: CC-BY 4.0.

1 Introduction

Despite the ageing world population, ageism is so prevalent in our modern societies that it even affects the older adults' views of themselves [4]. As such, ageist stereotypes and prejudices also negatively influence design practices. Many designers who use design methods based on a *problem-solution* approach often end up viewing ageing itself as a source of problems which require design solutions, leading to ageist attitudes when designing for older people [5].

In a problem-solution approach, designers aim to identify and address the needs of potential users. This idea of design as a discipline which investigates the needs of people was originally proposed by Munari [13]. In an attempt to clarify the role of designers by looking at the process of design, and comparing it with artistic practice, Munari suggests that designers proceed using creativity, while artists use fantasy—by which Munari considers creativity as a problem-solving task. Similarly, Papanek [14] stresses that the role of the designer is to focus on the needs of people rather than their desires.

These days, the idea that design must address users' unmet needs is so pervasive that the design output is considered to be successful if it merely satisfies the users' needs. It is, therefore, not surprising that the quest to investigate users' unmet needs has become the goal of many conventional design processes, methods and tools.

In this paper, we propose that addressing the needs of ageing people using a hierarchy of needs—in which some needs are considered higher than others — is less than satisfactory. The ageist attitudes of designers and older users themselves, limits what is considered as reasonable or expected needs that could then be addressed through the resulting design solutions. We discuss an alternative approach to designing for the needs of ageing people using storytelling, and introduce a method using visual cards for creating and narrating stories by older adult participants in co-design workshops.

2 Human Needs

In his now much referenced Theory of Human Motivation [11], Maslow presented his Hierarchy of Needs (HON), according to which people have certain needs, and some needs (e.g., physiological) are more primitive than others (e.g., social). This HON model is usually presented as a five-level pyramid, in which it is assumed that the higher-level needs are only considered by people, once their lower-level needs have been met. According to McGregor [12], "The man whose lower-level needs are satisfied is not motivated to satisfy those needs. For practical purposes they exist no longer." Similarly, Chapman [3] suggests that, "In the comfortable developed world, the satisfaction of physiological needs, and safety and security needs is practically a given. This concentrates remaining human need within the other three levels; therefore, developed world consumer motivation is primarily driven by social, ego and self-actualizing need."

Despite its widespread acceptance and use, HON has come under some scrutiny in recent years. Bridgman et al. [1] argue that Maslow never intended HON to be represented has a pyramid, and that this representation is problematic because it implies an elitist interpretation of human needs—i.e., it assumes that fewer people have the higher-level needs than those with lower-level needs, and that, as mentioned, a person can experience the desire to fulfil a higher-level need only when a lower-level one is satisfied. Bridgman et al. highlight that according to Maslow, most people *"are partially satisfied in all their basic needs and partially unsatisfied in all their basic needs at the same time"*, and that *"any behaviour tends to be determined by several or all of the basic needs simultaneously rather than by only one of them"* (quoted from Maslow). Based on this, Bridgman et al. propose that a ladder representation of HON is more appropriate than a pyramid one [1]. They also suggest that, "The ladder [representation] also attenuates the most common misrepresentation of the HON: that people occupy only one level at any particular time... Moreover, a ladder better de-notes movement both up and down the hierarchy, another overlooked feature of Maslow's theory." [1].

3 Design™ing for Needs

As mentioned earlier, in a problem-solution approach, identifying and addressing users' needs is critically important for guiding the design process. In this approach, when a pyramid representation of human needs it adopted, certain needs are considered more important than others to address—with some needs not being considered at all.

This is a particularly relevant issue to consider in designing for older adults, when designers can often dismiss *higher-level* needs as not being relevant or essential. For instance, it has been noted that "Much less attention has been given to the support of meaningful social activities and pursuits for seniors that are not tied directly to subsistence-based concerns—such as ignoring the fact that seniors also seek support for meaningful engagement in terms of entertainment, recreation and social connectedness." [2]. As we have pointed out in the introduction, prejudices and stereotypes concerning old age can influence how the needs of older adults in designing for them.

In this paper, we propose that if a ladder representation of HON is used to guide the design process, instead of a pyramid one, this would allow the attention of the designers to be focused on all, or any, of the users' needs, rather than focusing only on some needs (usually the lower-level ones) at the expense of other needs (usually the higher-level ones). In this ladder representation, while some needs are higher than others, as shown in Fig. 1, all needs are equally important to the users.

Fig. 1: Representation of Maslow's Hierarchy of Needs as a ladder, in which a person has needs at different levels.

In this open approach, however, when all user needs are equally important, it can become challenging to start and proceed with the design process, in which design choices need to be made somehow. Therefore, alternative design processes must be adopted and suitable design methods need to be devised to allow identifying user needs more effectively at all levels.

4   Designing for Empathy

Design empathy is considered important for better understanding users and identifying their unmet needs. For example, according to IDEO [9] empathy is the key to identifying the unmet needs of the target users of design outcomes, and as such, IDEO provides designers with examples and a set of tools for achieving better empathy with users.

When using empathy in the design process, however, it is important to keep in mind that complete empathy is nearly impossible to achieve, and that for instance, our human feelings and perceptions are often different from those of others—as Decety and Ickes point out, "there is no way that Person A can verify that the experience he has when he sees red is the same experience that Person B has when she sees red." [6]. Similarly, while the use of wearable simulators, such as glows or suits that mimic a body impairment, can be used to trigger a certain degree of empathy in the wearer, it is important to remember that such simulators need to be considered mediators of particular experiences (e.g., opening the lid of a jar with reduced hand mobility) rather than tools that can fully enable having another human's experiences [10]. As Decety and Ickes further note, the risk is to "over project—to view ourselves

as more representative of other people in specific respects than we really are."
[6]. Therefore, tools that trigger empathy should be used as mediation tools
between designers and users, and not as substitutes for other design methods
of interaction between them.

There is emerging evidence that storytelling-based methods are particularly
useful for triggering empathy. Villalba et al. [15] describe a case example of the
use of this method to trigger empathy and foster discussions with users. In their
example, teams were "invited by the facilitator to create a character... [and] to
give the character a name and a back-story". In this case the story was invented,
and was just partially based on the abilities, desires or interests of the participants themselves. However, Villalba et al. [15] note that when storytelling is
carried out with the actual users' stories, the outcomes are more meaningful
and less predictable. This underlines the need for storytelling to be fully related
to users' real lives and their own experiences.

5 Storytelling using Visual Cards

We have been developing a storytelling method using visual cards to empower
older adult users in co-design teams to better express their needs and trigger
more empathy in the designers. This method has emerged from a workshop we
held with a design team, as a way of investigating the emotional reactions of
older users to design topics and themes being investigated. In developing the
method, we took several challenges into consideration:

- Overcoming ageism in designers and older users themselves who are participating in the co-design process.
- Empowering all the older user participants during the co-design process.
  We have noted that the most vocal participants are not always going to be
  the most active ones during the design process. Therefore, it is essential to
  make sure that the less vocal participants are also empowered to take part
  in the co-design process.
- Finding a way to assess the emotional responses of the older user participants to the design topics, in order to have a better idea of what their needs
  and desires are.
- Improving the clarity of the design process proposed by the designers to
  older users participating in the co-design process.

5.1 The Visual Cards

The images presented on the visual cards should be decided in consultation
with the designers. We suggest following the instructions presented in the
"Cards" method by IDEO [9], in the "Field guide to Human Centered Design",

which ask designers to "Make your deck of cards for the card sort. Use either a word or a picture on each card, but whatever you select, make sure that it's easy to understand. Pictures are a better choice if the person doing the Card Sort speaks another language or cannot read."

For example, in our first trial of this method, the idea was to test the core motivations and values of the proposed design project—which was to grow food in a local neighbourhood setting in Finland. We decided to test the concept of presenting a simplified service design journey, and mimicking all the steps that the participants would need to follow to grow food in an urban neighbourhood in Helsinki. For this project we designed the following sets of visual cards:

1. **Plants, locations and soil cards:** We looked at traditional Finnish recipes, making sure to include recipes from all the different seasons of the year. On the visual cards, we included images of the ingredients, various places to grow the ingredients, different location to grow the plants (e.g., urban and rural locations), and different kinds of soils to be used when growing the plants.
2. **Emotion cards:** To investigate the emotional reaction of the participants to the overall service design journey we created a set of visual cards with pictures of people from different age groups, each depicting a vague emotional state, as identified by Ekman [7].
3. **Word cards:** We created a set of cards each with a basic emotion word in Finnish. In addition, we also provided blank cards for the participants to write their own emotion words.
4. **Rating card:** We created a rating card using a version of the Geneva Emotional wheel [8], for the participants to rate their level of valence/arousal for their selected emotions.

5.2 The Storytelling Workshop Method

We have developed a storytelling workshop method which uses the above set of visual cards to investigate the needs of older adults in a design project. The aim is to preserve the individual voice of each person, assess the level of expertise and engagement of each person, and assess the emotional involvement of each person in the process. The cards are in the shape of a square to facilitate free association between them, and to avoid a suggestion of hierarchical order.

In the case study project, for which the above set of cards were created, we held a 2-hour workshop with a group of older adults and the design team, and followed these phases:

1. **Introduction and warm-up** *(45 minutes)*: the design team welcomed the participants to a communal meeting room, which was an intimate and friendly space usually used for community meetings. The design team then proceeded to offer coffee and food to the participants while presenting the aims of the design project. The participants then introduced themselves, explained in detail the reasons for their participation, and the wishes they had for the future of their community. Once the presentations were concluded, the design team described the visual cards method and proceeded to the next phase.

2. **Cards selection** *(30 minutes)*: the rules that need to be followed are simple, and the method has been designed to be intuitive and easy to follow. The participants were presented with different set of cards, and asked to choose the cards in response to a request or a question that was posed to them. Once the participants have chosen their cards, the remaining cards are removed, and this step is repeated with the next set of cards (as shown in Fig. 2). For the first set of cards, the participants were asked to choose the recipe they like the most, and then were presented with the card for the ingredients, plants, locations, and soil to choose from. For the second set of cards, they were asked to choose emotions associated with the growing process. The participants were then asked to choose a word card (from the third set, or wrote their own) that described their selected emotion card, and rated their level of emotion using a rating card (from the fourth set). Once the cards selection was completed (e.g., see Fig. 3) each participant proceeded to the next phase.

3. **Storytelling** *(30 minutes)*: each of the participants were asked to tell a real-life story associated with their selected cards. After hearing all the stories, the workshop moved to the next phase.

1. The designer places the cards on the table.

2. Participants select the cards they want.

3. The designer removes the cards not selected.

Fig. 2: The process followed for each set of cards in the card selection phase.

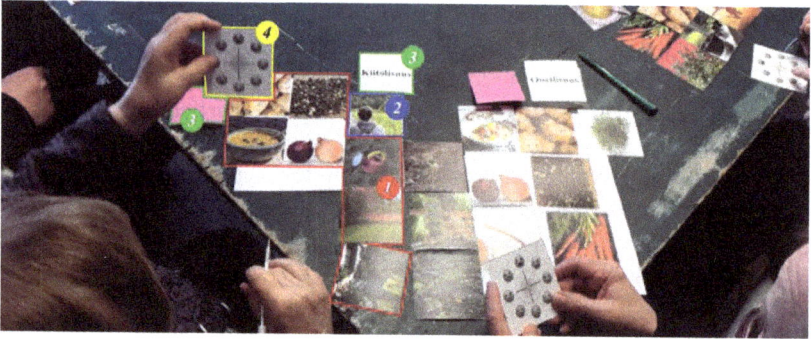

Fig. 3: The visual cards selected by a group of older participants to narrate their story. Some of the visual cards in each of the 4 categories have been marked in this image.

4. **Debrief** *(15 minutes)*: the participants were invited to reflect on the possible next steps of the design project in an open discussion.

After the workshop we analysed the stories told by the workshop participants. In this case we noticed how the initial need identified by the design team was misplaced. The older user participants were more interested in the idea of building a common vegetable garden rather than cultivating food in their private spaces. Furthermore, the participants were interested in how this project could provide a common social activity rather than producing food. They associated the idea with one they were familiar with—*talkoopäivä*—a celebration promoting the Finnish tradition of doing things together.

6 Conclusions

In this paper, we have proposed an alternative approach to considering ageing peoples' needs during the design process, which requires addressing their needs at all levels, rather than primarily focusing on the lower levels of their hierarchy of needs.

To address this, we have developed a storytelling-based method using visual cards to assist meaningful participation of older users in a co-design process. Our initial trials of this method in a series of workshops with older adults in Finland has shown promising results in allowing designers to investigating the unmet needs of older adults.

We are currently planning to further test this method with other participants living in different urban communities. Our aim is to investigate how emotions can be used as a way of identifying older users' needs, and eliminating ageism-related influences in co-design processes.

References

1. Bridgman, T., Cummings, S., Ballard, J.: Who built maslow's pyramid? A history of the creation of management studies' most famous symbol and its implications for management education. Academy of Management Learning & Education **18**(1), 81–98 (2019), https://doi.org/10.5465/amle.2017.0351
2. Burns, L., Masoodian, M.: Storytelling: A medium for co-design of health and well-being services for seniors. In: Clua, E., Roque, L., Lugmayr, A., Tuomi, P. (eds.) Proceedings of the IFIP International Conference on Entertainment Computing. pp. 349–354. Springer (2018), https://doi.org/10.1007/978-3-319-99426-0_43
3. Chapman, J.: Emotionally Durable Design: Objects, Experiences and Empathy. Routledge (2012)
4. Coughlin, J.F.: The Longevity Economy: Unlocking the World's Fastest-Growing, Most Misunderstood Market. PublicAffairs (2017)
5. Dankl, K.: Design age: Towards a participatory transformation of images of ageing. Design Studies **48**, 30–42 (2017), https://doi.org/10.1016/j.destud.2016.10.004
6. Decety, J., Ickes, W. (eds.): The Social Neuroscience of Empathy. MIT Press (2011)
7. Ekman, P.: An argument for basic emotions. Cognition and Emotion **6**(3–4), 169–200 (1992), https://doi.org/10.1080/02699939208411068
8. van Gorp, T., Adams, E.: Design for Emotion. Morgan Kaufmann (2012)
9. IDEO.org: The Field Guide to Human-Centered Design. IDEO.org/Design Kit (2015)
10. Kullman, K.: Prototyping bodies: A post-phenomenology of wearable simulations. Design Studies **47**, 73–90 (2016), https://doi.org/10.1016/j.destud.2016.08.004
11. Maslow, A.H.: A theory of human motivation. Psychological Review **50**(4), 370–396 (1943), https://doi.org/10.1037/h0054346
12. McGregor, D.: The Human Side of Enterprise. McGraw-Hill (1960)
13. Munari, B.: Artista e designer. Universale La Terza (1971)
14. Papanek, V.: Design for the Real World: Human Ecology and Social Change. Academy Chicago Publishers, 2nd edn. (1985)
15. Villalba, C., Jaiprakash, A., Donovan, J., Roberts, J., Crawford, R.: Testing literature-based health experience insight cards in a healthcare service co-design workshop. CoDesign, pp. 1–13 (2019), https://doi.org/10.1080/15710882.2018.1563617

Breaking Interaction Barriers: Monitoring Elderly in Natural Settings Exploiting Everyday Objects

Marina Buzzi

IIT-CNR, via G. Moruzzi, 1 56124 Pisa

marina.buzzi@iit.cnr.it

Abstract

The European population is aging steadily. As a consequence neurodegenerative pathologies are becoming widespread, impacting heavily on social costs, so it is important to support independent living as long as possible, especially in the healthy elderly.

This paper proposes an idea for advancing current monitoring technologies by breaking down the current paradigm and exploiting augmented everyday objects. Monitoring and behavior analysis can be exploited as triggers for motivating behavior changes in an elderly person. Thanks to progress in Internet of Things (IoT) and Artificial Intelligence (AI) one scenario is described to illustrate the proposed design concept. With a collaborative multidisciplinary effort, this view could be fast become a reality.

Keywords

Elderly · Disability · IoT

How to cite this book chapter:

Buzzi, M. 2020. Breaking Interaction Barriers: Monitoring Elderly in Natural Settings Exploiting Everyday Objects. In: Loizides, F., Winckler, M., Chatterjee, U., Abdelnour-Nocera, J. and Parmaxi, A. (eds.) *Human Computer Interaction and Emerging Technologies: Adjunct Proceedings from the INTERACT 2019 Workshops*. Pp. 13–22. Cardiff: Cardiff University Press. DOI: https://doi.org/10.18573/book3.b. License: CC-BY 4.0.

1 Introduction

More than 25 years ago, Mark Weiser's vision greatly influenced research on ubiquitous computing, foreseeing that "the most potentially interesting, challenging and profound change implied by the ubiquitous computing era is a focus on calm." [1]. Imagining that computers would be everywhere, surrounding us in the environment, in our bodies, and in everyday objects, Weiser suggests that it is better to not be overburdened in our lives. His vision of calm technology is an image of a world that is quiet and comfortable, where we are always aware of what is happening around us, what is going to happen and what has just happened. Information would effortlessly emerge when needed and smoothly disappear from our attention [2].

In recent years, many researchers have focused on how to promote physical activity among people with cognitive impairment. Our target group includes fragile individuals such as people with disability and the elderly. A technology's invasiveness impacts on interaction. When technology is embedded and hidden within the object, its use becomes natural and simple, since no interaction is required. The idea is to modify every object which the person habitually uses in their routine activities. In the following we offer three scenarios illustrating the proposed design concept. Any technology issues still present today could be easily overcome in the near future.

Designing for the elderly as well as for persons with disability may require modifying the interaction protocol. Instead of creating new interfaces that require familiarizing oneself and becoming proficient with new objects and their apps, the design concept is to use everyday objects to collect user data, maintaining the usual interaction and not disturbing the user's routine by asking then to learn new competences.

Maintaining independence is fundamental as we age. The ability to perform personal care is one of the skills we learn early and maintain later in life; gestures become automatic day after day. This paper, in accord with Weiser's vision, proposes using ICT technology in an unobtrusive setting in order to monitor older people in their natural environment, without changing the surrounding environment or their interaction habits.

This paper is organized into four sections. After this introduction, section 2 introduces related work. In section 3 principles driving the proposed design concept are illustrated, discussing a scenario. Last, a discussion suggesting future research directions ends the paper.

2 Related Work

Age can degrade our physical and cognitive abilities either suddenly or progressively. Neurodegenerative pathologies such as Alzheimer's disease (AD) are receiving worldwide attention due to the enormous burden it places on families, health costs, and the prospect of a steadily increasing number of affected adults over the next few years [3]. IoT can help people prolong their autonomy over time. This reduces the cost of assistance, and improves the lives of the elderly and their relatives.

Dementia tests are usually a series of trials for evaluating personal abilities including memory, attention, logic, language, orientation. However these tests have usually been performed after the first signs of dementia are detected by relatives and/or clinicians. Early diagnosis could facilitate the introduction of cognitive training as well as drug therapy to control disease progress. Since events such as moving to a new home can disorient an elderly person, and accelerate or trigger the degeneration process, it is very important to keep the person in their own home, and independent as long as possible.

Technology has an increasing role in supporting people with disabilities and the elderly in everyday life. A useful overview of smart technologies and objects for assisting people with disability is offered by [4]. Sensors and RFID technology have been extensively applied to assist people with disability. Some examples include the smart cane for blind persons, and GPS-equipped shoes for persons in the early stage of Alzheimer [5].

For instance, RFID paths have been created to assist visually impaired people in walking autonomously. A smart cane equipped with an RFID reader facilitates orientation and provides information: vocal messages for directions and information about close artifacts, or services (shops, metro, etc.) [6]. Thanks to ultrasonic sensors and an obstacle detection system, a sound alert goes off if the person is leaving the main path, in order to prevent falls near the edge of the sidewalk [7]. The RFID cane reads data on the RFID tag, i.e., the tag's unique identifier, and transmits it via network to the server application. The person can also interact naturally, using their voice to specify their destination [8]. Moreover, smart shoes equipped with sensors to detect obstacles at a greater distance (more than half a meter ahead) are proposed in [9].

All this research focuses on enhancing and maintaining an individual's autonomy. This is very important for people with disability and also for the elderly. Old people wish to live in their own homes [10]. Nearly 40% of the elderly population worldwide live independently. In Northern Europe more than 90% of older persons live independently, while less than 60% in Southern Europe. In developed countries about 75% of elderly people live independently [11].

A UK survey revealed that old people worry more about losing their independence (49%) than about dying (29%). Similar results also emerged in a US study [12]. Moreover, losing independence was considered a bigger and more relevant issue than financial problems. In this view, one's own home is the central point for ensuring independence, health, and social inclusive activities. By exploiting technology it is possible to offer a vast range of usable services matching the needs of older people in order to combat isolation, loneliness, and related physical and mental decline [13, 14]. Also, elderly people with neurological disability declare that their priority is to lead an independent life at home [15].

Literature indicates many technologies for monitoring elderly or fragile users smoothly in a domestic environment, including sensors, video cameras, RFID systems and smart devices connected to the Internet. A smart TV, which runs an operating system, is able to connect to the network, and to execute a web app. By exploiting these very familiar objects, it possible to deliver care services and support the elderly in their autonomy. The iNeighbour TV project, for instance, exploits a smart TV to promote healthcare and social interaction among seniors, their relatives, and caregivers. Delivered services include: meteo info, medication reminder, events planning, audio/video calls, read SMS and email messages. In addition, the app monitors the user by keeping track of the user's TV use. When a significant variation occurs it triggers an alert to caregivers [16].

Another example is the COACH project, which collects data acquired by video camera and sensors for monitoring persons who have difficulty completing everyday tasks, such as dressing or washing. Starting from collected data it is possible to infer user actions and capabilities and send appropriate messages to motivate the behavior change [17].

Progress in technology makes it possible for smart objects to interact autonomously and be able to establish relationships and shape 'social networks' of objects (Social IoT) [14, 18]. The Socialize project for instance, exploits SIoT components including smart TVs, environmental sensors, and wearable devices (Smartwatches) to smoothly monitor and analyze user activities involving both personal and environmental parameters, under the supervision of doctors, relatives, and caregivers [19].

Recently Sawyer et al. discuss a set of challenges posed by dementia monitoring systems [20]. Specifically, Cognitive Assistive Technology (CAT) aims at monitoring and supporting people with cognitive deficits. Recent evidence suggests that spatial navigation is emerging as an important parameter in detecting preclinical signs of Alzheimer's disease: "spatial deficits, in particular related to way finding, are present in preclinical AD long before episodic memory symptoms emerge" [3].

Participative design with end users, and specifically with people with disability, can enhance the smart objects' usability and also lead to new ideas and innovative artifacts [21]. Everyday smart objects include a number of wearable devices such as smart watches, bands, and glasses. Withings has introduced a smart hairbrush to monitor the health status of one's hair. Figure 1 shows the smart brush, which thanks to the sound of hair, and the number and types of brush movements is able to evaluate the health condition of one's hair via an associated app.

However the potential of the Hair Coach that analyzes sounds could be further exploited by analyzing movements (thanks to an accelerometer and gyroscope) for monitoring elderly persons who are still in good health, in order to prolong their independent life, as discussed in the following section.

Detecting dementia at an early stage can help improve the quality of life, reducing side effects such as depression. Cognitive and drug therapy could be less effective when the damage to the brain becomes severe [20].

Fig. 1: Withings Kerastase smart hair brush and its Hair Health app (source: www.loreal.com).

Games such as a join-the-dots game [22] or card selection in game boards [23] can be exploited to gather assessment data. By measuring many parameters, including task completion time, latency time, mouse/pad/finger movements it is possible to evaluate the person's attention, executive functions, perception, and motor abilities, and compare them with reference performance values [24]. Monitoring user interaction with a digital game allows one to detect cognitive deficits. However if the user feels (s)he is undergoing a form of examination, this might impact on the results [20].

Since not all older people are interested in videogames, nor are they always able to describe their condition to the doctor or perform the classic tests, observation and analysis of movements and times in their interaction with everyday objects could be an interesting alternative to investigate.

This paper aims to stimulate discussion about these relevant topics. The idea is to sensorize everyday objects and analyze a vast amount of data coming from these distributed devices, which would enable a cooperative intelligence to enhance services in many aspects of everyday life (personal care, dental hygiene, movement, psychological wellness, prevention). This hypothesis needs to be validated in order to be accepted or discarded via a prospective study, by building operative prototypes and collecting data from a significant number of users.

3 The Everyday Smart Object Conceptual Model: a Scenario

An elderly woman is progressively losing some cognitive ability. Let us suppose that she can be rated in the middle of the Clinical Dementia Rating (CDR) scale (0, 0.5, 1, 2, 3 values), i.e., Mild 1 [25]. At this stage the person exhibits some difficulties: a) Moderate memory loss (especially for recent events). b) Moderate difficulty with time relationships; may have geographic disorientation. c) Moderate difficulty in handling problems, similarities, and differences. d) Unable to function independently in social activities (though appears normal to casual inspection). e) Mild impairment of function at home (more difficult chores, hobbies and interests abandoned). However it is important to observe that she is still able to carry out personal care but requires prompting, i.e., needs to be stimulated to perform personal care activities.

The idea is to exploit smart everyday objects to empower the individual. Smart Objects can collect and transmit data to a cloud system and thanks to artificial intelligence algorithms and natural interfaces (offering vocal and touch interaction), the processed data can provide feedback to users, through the smart object itself or via an associated smartphone app. Combining behavioral science and persuasive techniques the smart object can become a persuasive tool to keep the person's behavior positive as long as possible (in this case personal care abilities).

Let us introduce a scenario illustrating this concept. Martin is a 10-year-old boy who owns a personal smartphone. At the 80th birthday of his grandmother, Martin and his family give her a smart hairbrush and a smart toothbrush. He controls his grandmother's data via an app on his smartphone. When the app shows an alert, revealing no personal care activities have been performed by the grandmother, he sends her a video message to stimulate her to perform these activities.

Moreover, the collected data are aggregated and graphs are visible on a dashboard to summarize activities trending during the week, month and year. If a threshold is reached, an alarm is sent to her doctor who decides on the next care steps (see Fig. 2). Specifically exploiting AI and neural algorithms, it is possible to collect usage data in a preliminary training session in order to create a model of how the woman uses her hairbrush and toothbrush. Thus, over time when this model is breaking down, an alert is automatically activated, for instance:

- If the woman does not use the smart objects, an alert is sent to relatives, to check on the cause (sickness, fall, and so on).
- If the woman uses the smart objects but she is now unable to match their usage models over time (change in movements), an alert is sent to a clinician (her doctor).

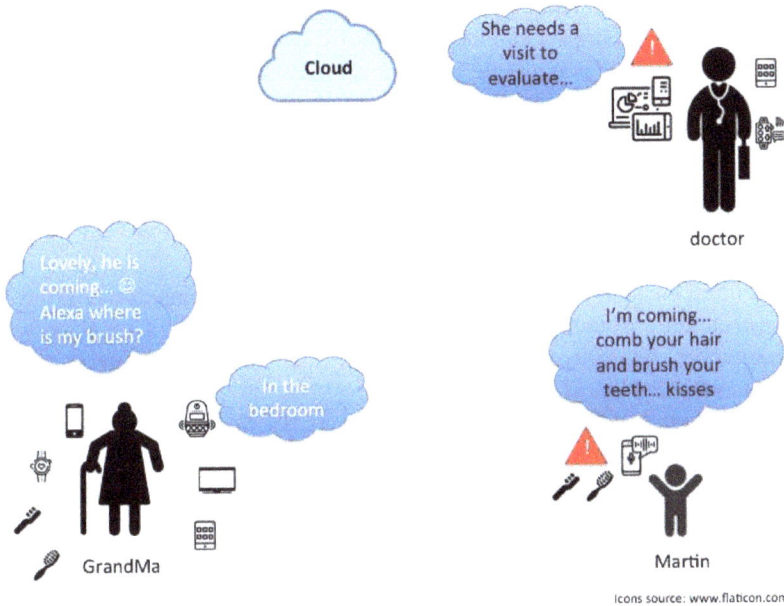

Fig. 2: Technology-enhanced care by IoT and ICT. Martin acts as his grandmother's coach. The doctor monitors main behavior changes over time.

However, bald men do not use hairbrushes, so it is crucial to design other smart objects of daily interaction. To brush one's teeth is the most frequent task performed every day. The idea is similar to the previous one: to learn the brushing patterns of the users and facilitate early detection of anomalies.

Other application fields are possible. Consider for instance children with low functioning autism, who are rigid, making dental hygiene a challenge for them. The idea is to add a micro-camera incorporated in the middle of the toothbrush to provide dental images. Lighting the oral cavity, images could be acquired and transmitted to the cloud system. Older persons can become lazy, so if the system detects some potential problem, an alert could be triggered to them and to relatives.

4 Discussion

Everyday objects can offer unexpected benefits, due to their frequency of use and the user's habits. For instance, they can help monitor the status of fragile users regarding their dental care.

An unexplored potential of IoT is mature for experimentation. Monitoring healthy parameters, tools and procedures while avoiding errors is an important emerging research field. When interfaces are dissolved inside objects the interaction is not impacted, but is maintained as usual and events or data are exploited to trigger actions and to enhance user services (context-aware intelligent services). Everyday objects can be adapted to enhance care and improve life for the elderly.

An interesting research question is whether the technology can be exploited to facilitate a diagnosis. For instance, can a change in trajectories (showing unstable movements or tremors for instance) discover early pathologies such as Parkinson's or Alzheimer's or other neurodegenerative pathologies? When something changes in these repetitive gestures it might signal body changes. These conditions could easily be detected if the software is first trained with persons with neurodegenerative diseases (to catch anomalous patterns and be able to predict a disease's onset).

This research field is extremely interesting since unobtrusive technologies might help make care more efficient, and diagnosis more precise, recognizable by data patterns. Possibly, the more data from different individuals could be analyzed, the more accurately the algorithms can learn to detect the individual's anomalous patterns.

A multidisciplinary team applying a co-design approach involving end users and professionals such as psychologists, clinicians, engineers, sociologists and HCI experts may be the key to revealing the full potential of ICT-enhanced solutions for everyday life and independence. Imagining the future of everyday objects can break down current interaction schemes and barriers, enabling monitoring of the elderly in a natural setting.

References

1. Weiser, M. Ubiquitous computing. *Computer*, (10), 71–72 (1993).
2. Rogers, Y. Moving on from weiser's vision of calm computing: Engaging ubicomp experiences. In *International conference on Ubiquitous computing* (pp. 404–421). Springer, Berlin, Heidelberg (2006).
3. Coughlan, G., Coutrot, A., Khondoker, M., Minihane, A. M., Spiers, H., & Hornberger, M. Toward personalized cognitive diagnostics of at-genetic-risk Alzheimer's disease. *Proceedings of the National Academy of Sciences*, 116(19), 9285–9292 (2019).
4. Domingo, M. C. An overview of the Internet of Things for people with disabilities. *Journal of Network and Computer Applications*, 35(2), 584–596 (2012).
5. Wan, L., Müller, C., Randall, D., & Wulf, V. (2016). Design of A GPS monitoring system for dementia care and its challenges in academia-industry project. *ACM Transactions on Computer-Human Interaction (TOCHI)*, 23(5), 31.
6. Saaid, M. F., Ismail, I., & Noor, M. Z. H. Radio frequency identification walking stick (RFIWS): A device for the blind. In *2009 5th International Colloquium on Signal Processing & Its Applications* (pp. 250–253). IEEE (2009).

7. Martin W, Dancer K, Rock K, Zeleny C, Yelamarthi K. The smart cane: an electrical engineering design project. In: Proceedings of ASEE north central section conference. Michigan, USA (2009).

8. Shiizu Y, Hirahara Y, Yanashima K, Magatani K. The development of a white cane which navigates the visually impaired. In: Proc. of the 29th annual international conference of the IEEE engineering in medicine and biology society (2007).

9. Zhang J, Lip CW, Ong SK, Nee A. A multiple sensor-based shoe-mounted user interface designed for navigation systems for the visually impaired. In: Proceedings of the fifth annual ICST wireless Internet conference (WICON). Singapore (2010).

10. Al-Shaqi, R., Mourshed, M., & Rezgui, Y. Progress in ambient assisted systems for independent living by the elderly. *SpringerPlus*, 5(1), 624 (2016).

11. UN, World Population Ageing 2013. https://www.un.org/en/development /desa/population/publications/pdf/ageing/WorldPopulationAgeingReport 2013.pdf

12. Mangoni, A. A. Geriatric medicine in an aging society: up for a challenge? *Frontiers in Medicine*, 1, 10 (2014).

13. Shikder, S. H., Mourshed, M., & Price, A. D. Luminaire position optimisation using radiance based simulation: a test case of a senior living room. (2010).

14. Atzori, L., Iera, A., & Morabito, G. From" smart objects" to" social objects": The next evolutionary step of the Internet of things. *IEEE Communications Magazine*, 52(1), 97–105 (2014).

15. Chan, M., Campo, E., Estève, D., & Fourniols, J. Y. Smart homes—current features and future perspectives. *Maturitas*, 64(2), 90–97 (2009).

16. de Abreu, J. F., Almeida, P., Afonso, J., Silva, T., & Dias, R. Participatory design of a social TV application for senior citizens–the iNeighbour TV project. In *International Conference on ENTERprise Information Systems* (pp. 49–58). Springer, Berlin, Heidelberg (2011).

17. Hoey, J. Boutilier, C. People sensors decisions: Customizable and adaptive technologies for assistance in healthcare, *ACM Trans. on Interactive Intelligent Systems*, 2(4), pp. 1–36, 2012.

18. Atzori, L., Iera, A., Morabito, G., & Nitti, M. The Social Internet of Things (SIoT)–when social networks meet the internet of things: Concept, architecture and network characterization. *Computer networks*, 56(16), 3594–3608 (2012).

19. Miori, V., Russo, D., & Ferrucci, L. Supporting Active Aging Through A Home Automation Infrastructure for Social Internet of Things. Advances in Science, Technology and Engineering Systems Journal 3(4), 173–186 (2018).

20. Sawyer, P., Sutcliffe, A., Rayson, P., & Bull, C. Dementia and social sustainability: challenges for software engineering. In *2015 IEEE/ACM 37th IEEE International Conference on Software Engineering* (Vol. 2, pp. 527–530). IEEE (2015).

21. Frauenberger, C., Makhaeva, J., & Spiel, K. Designing smart objects with autistic children: Four design exposès. In *Proceedings of the 2016 CHI Conference on Human Factors in Computing Systems* (pp. 130–139). ACM (2016).

22. Hagler, S., Jimison, H. and Pavel, M. Assessing executive function using a computer game: Computational modeling of cognitive processes. IEEE Journal of Biomedical and Health Informatics, 18(4), pp. 1142–1152 (2014).

23. McKanna, J.A., Pavel, M. and Jimison, H. Unobtrusive monitoring of divided attention in a cognitive health coaching intervention for the elderly. Proc. American Medical Informatics Association Symposium, pp. 507–511, (2010).

24. Tong, T. and Chignell, M. Designing game-based cognitive assessments for elderly adults. Proc. 1st Int. Conf. on Gameful Design, Research, and Applications, pp. 127–130, (2013).

25. KAD, Knight Alzheimer's Disease Research Center. Clinical Dementia Rating Worksheet. https://knightadrc.wustl.edu/cdr/PDFs/CDR_Table.pdf, last accessed 2019/06/01.

A Value-sensitive Toolkit: Bringing Values into the Design Process when Designing for the Elderly

Mert Oktay[*,†] and Hanna-Liisa Pender[*,†]
[*]Tallinn University, Narva rd 25, 10120 Tallinn, Estonia
[†]Trinidad Wiseman, Akadeemia rd. 21, 12618 Tallinn, Estonia
merdo@tlu.ee, pender@tlu.ee
www.tlu.ee, www.twn.ee

Abstract

The paper gives and overview of developing a design toolkit for designers that would encourage them to keep the human values on the forefront, despite all the other constraints that need to be faced when designing new technologies. The toolkit was validated and refined in a series of workshops with designers and design students. The outcome of the work is a toolkit prototype that includes tools like design fiction, bootlegging and value review. It is intended to be used to compliment a human centred design process after user research to scaffold ideation and tackle design challenges related to aging in place and smart habitats for elderly.

Keywords

Value based design · design fiction · elderly · design methods

---

How to cite this book chapter:
Oktay, M. and Pender, H-L. 2020. A Value-sensitive Toolkit: Bringing Values into the Design Process when Designing for the Elderly. In: Loizides, F., Winckler, M., Chatterjee, U., Abdelnour-Nocera, J. and Parmaxi, A. (eds.) *Human Computer Interaction and Emerging Technologies: Adjunct Proceedings from the INTERACT 2019 Workshops.* Pp. 23–30. Cardiff: Cardiff University Press. DOI: https://doi.org/10.18573/book3.c. License: CC-BY 4.0.

1 Introduction

In the industry context, user research is an essential part of the whole design journey, however, after user research there is often relatively little attention on the ideation process. The solutions are in many cases technology driven with too many material constraints or the most doable ones in a short time period. There are numerous ideation tools, commonly used in industry context, that are focused on human values e.g empathy maps [1], value proposition maps [2]; however none of them aim for value-sensitive solutions. Even though these tools might be efficient to map user needs and desires; they do not guide designers to think about possible solutions. While the needs and values can be well-described, the tendency of design teams is still to choose the most obvious and quickly-doable solution. Thus, there is a room for an additional toolkit which leads designers to develop meaningful and value-sensitive design solutions.

The context of this study is a contemporary issue that worries the entire world, especially the Global North: the population aging. According to research of European Commission; a quarter of Europeans will be over 60 years of age by 2020. This situation brings with it some concerns related to elderly care and independence of the elderly. Thereby, aging in place term [8] which provides autonomy for elderly, becomes more and more popular [9]. Elderly prefer to remain in the comfort of their familiar and safe homes instead of moving to a geriatric care center [10] which might create a negative emotional impact, both on the elderly and their families. Smart home technologies could be useful to support and to enhance aging in place for the elderly, although, these technologies might create privacy issues because they mostly rely on constant monitoring [11]. Privacy is only one of the many human values that designers should take into consideration while creating more meaningful solutions for the elderly. We are seeing more and more smart solutions that aim to support independent living for elderly whos physical and mental abilities are declining. These are for example smart habitats that involve constant medical monitoring of people's health. Technology is reaching for the most intimate spheres of human existence. That is why, it is crucial to consider the non-functional aspects of new technologies, when designing them. By empathizing with the user and designing from their perspective, designers can create solutions that people are more likely to adopt and appreciate. There are several studies [12, 13] focused on design values to use while designing for the elderly, however, they are not structured and formulated to be a guideline that would support designers, especially in industry context where designers need to often account with very limited time. Therefore a ideation toolkit for designers is proposed, that aims to endorse value based design for elderly. This paper gives an overview of developing a such toolkit and the lessons learned during the process.

2 Method

Research Goal: The goal of this research was to develop a value-sensitive design toolkit that would help to design for the elderly. To achieve these goals, two main research questions were selected as starting points.

[RQ1] What are the main design principles and values when designing for elderly?

The first step of the research was identifying design values that are used when designing for elderly. A systematic literature review was selected as method to identify the main design principles and how the value-sensitive concerns are addressed today when designing technology for the aging people.

[RQ2] How can the design values be meaningfully conveyed into the design process with the help of a design toolkit?

To answer this research question, research through design approach was adopted as the overall methodology. For achieving the goal, designing a meaningful and useful value-sensitive design toolkit that can be used to emphasize values when designing for elderly, an iterative approach was used. The proposed design toolkit prototype was refined in workshops with the help of designers and design students. Four ideation workshops were conducted in order to evaluate and improve the design toolkit.

Since research through design also asks researchers to investigate the speculative future, probing on what the world could and should be [3], this methodology suits this study in which a critical approach was adopted by practicing design fiction.

3 Developing the design toolkit

3.1 Literature review to map the values used in designing for elderly

A literature review was conducted to gain an overview of state of the art in designing for elderly care related challenges. 80 research papers were examined from ACM Digital Library. The systematic literature review consists of independent aging for the elderly and our keywords were elderly, elderly care, aging in place, elderly independence, smart homes for elderly, e lderly monitoring. The oldest publication included in the corpus was from 2005, the newest from 2018. All the papers were reviewed using the quick and dirty method [14]. Papers that addressed value-sensitive concerns e.g privacy issues became prominent. Thereby, papers addressing the value-sensitive concerns in the context of the independent aging, and the ones that give example use cases of smart home technologies in the aging in place context received the highest interest rating. A qualitative content analysis was conducted on 32 papers that received the highest interest ratings in the first part of the study. Strongly accentuated values that designers tend to take into account while designing for the elderly were mapped and categorized in five groups: autonomy, social inclusion, privacy, trust, and dignity.

3.2 The initial prototype

A toolkit prototype was proposed for designers to integrate value based approach into the ideation process. Design fiction [5, 6] and Bootlegging technique [7] were chosen for the initial design toolkit prototype, based on reviewing a number of design tools and methods. Five design fiction scenarios were written about the context of independent aging supported by technology. The aim of the scenarios was to push readers to think about possible unexpected effects of handing control into smart systems. Design fiction was also expected to encourage critical thinking and to provoke a discussion around the values by presenting possible negative or ambiguous outcomes.

Another component of the proposed toolkit was Bootlegging technique [7] which is a brainstorming technique that provides an opportunity to explore promising ideas as unexpected juxtapositions. It is a fast paced tool for ideating that is helpful for thinking out of the box and come up with unexpected ideas which might be meaningful and might have a design potential.

3.3 Refining the toolkit in ideation workshops

The toolkit was iteratively refined in four ideation workshops. The workshops took place over three weeks.

First workshop. The participants were seven design students from two different universities and six different nationalities. First workshop started with participants reading the design fiction scenarios to make them familiar with the context and to hint how the lack of values might be uncomfortable for the users. They were prompted to identify the values in the scenarios and to write them onto post-it notes to use during the following Bootlegging session. The Bootlegging categories were activities, technologies and values. Participants filled the other two categories with relevant content in short brainstorming sessions by writing the technologies and activities on post-it notes. They combined random items from different categories to come up with unexpected juxtapositions and used dot-mocracy (democratic voting within teams) to identify the most promising ideas to develop further. Observing the workshop demonstrated that the values identified from the scenarios were too ambiguous for the participants they had difficulties agreeing on the meanings of the values and some of them seamed to be overlapping. This motivated us to provide value cards with short definitions of the values for the next edition of the workshops.

Second workshop. The participants of the workshop were 7 design professionals from a UX consultancy. The main goal was testing the value card set. 18 values were printed out with short descriptions. The structure of the workshop was the same, except that in addition to values identified and discussed from the design fiction scenarios, the participants also received the value cards for Bootlegging. The second workshop demonstrated that at this point we had too many different value cards that were difficult for the participants to categorize and use. Another development in the second workshop was that the participants used the value cards after the ideation process to review their ideas and refine them. This step was included into the structure of the next workshops as value review. The review enabled to extend the design idea and integrate multiple values. In addition, a value map was composed for the next workshop to categorize and explain the value cards and the relations between them.

Third workshop. The participants of the workshops were three design students. The goal of the third workshop was testing the main structure of the workshop that now included value-reviewing as well as the value map. The participants found the review session relevant and helpful for elaborating their design ideas and integrating more values. However, they could not relate to the categories on the provided value map. Thus, to understand how designers perceive the values, a card sorting method was applied online after the workshop. Nine participants form the three conducted workshops participated in the card sorting. The result of card sorting enabled to divide the values in three very broad categories: core values, values related to social needs and nice to have values. For the next edition, the values were categorized accordingly and printed on one value list with values on one side and definitions on the other side of the list.

Fourth workshop. The participants of the last workshop were four design students. The goal of the workshop was testing the value-reviewing session with the categorized value lists. The list was perceived as a useful tool for extending the design ideas and integrating more values to the concept.

4 Results: a value sensitive toolkit

The result of the described research through design process is an ideation toolkit for designers, that aims to endorse value-based design of smart habitats for elderly. The work also provides an overview of the tool development process for reflective purposes. The design toolkit comprises of detailed instructions on design fiction, bootlegging and value review and offers a compact and efficient framework to tackle design challenges related to aging in place and smart habitats for the elderly. The design toolkit has four main steps:

1) **Design Fiction Scenarios.** The first session is composed of a design fiction set which contains 5 design fiction scenarios that focuses on the issues that the elderly face when living in their smart homes. The main goal of this step is activating inspiration and critical thinking.

Fig. 1: The design toolkit prototype and instructions.

2) **Bootlegging Session.** The second step is a brainstorming technique called Bootlegging and it provides an opportunity to explore promising ideas as unexpected juxtapositions. This technique has been modified to bridge ideation with previous user research and to keep focus on the values when ideating design ideas.

3) **Developing a design concept.** The third step is developing a design concept as a team; the design concept is developed based on one of the bootlegging combinations from the previous step. In this session, the participants are expected to generate ideas and solutions through desired format such as sketching, prototyping, enacting, etc. and create a design concept in order to support aging in place.

4) **Value reviewing.** As the last step in ideation, a value list is distributed to the teams to review their design concept. The goal of this step is to include more values to their design concept and to refine and extend the idea. The mapped value list is intended to be used as a prompt for discussion and kept nearby also for the later design and development phases in the project.

5 Discussion and future work

This process has shown that designers can enhance the design solutions by improving the ideation session within the design process and come up with more value-driven ideas using the proposed design toolkit. The qualitative data gathered from the participants of the study has shown that starting with a critical point of view and practicing Bootlegging technique are forming a promising way to develop creative ideas. The value-review phase provides a value list as a discussion starter to further extend the idea and include a broader range of values. The toolkit development was not related to an actual design project. As future work we would like to keep refining it in the context of an human centered design project where the toolkit could build on conducted user research.

References

1. David Siegel and Susan Dray. 2019. The map is not the territory: empathy in design. Interactions 26, 2 (February 2019), 82–85.
2. Osterwalder, A., Pigneur, Y., Bernarda, G., Smith, A. (2014). Value proposition design: How to create products and services customers want. John Wiley, Sons.
3. Zimmerman, J., Forlizzi, J., Evenson, S. (2007, April). Research through design as a method for interaction design research in HCI. In Proceedings of the SIGCHI conference on Human factors in computing systems (pp. 493–502). ACM.
4. Zimmerman, J., Forlizzi, J., Evenson, S. (2007, April). Research through design as a method for interaction design research in HCI. In Proceedings of the SIGCHI conference on Human factors in computing systems (pp. 493–502). ACM.
5. Lindley, J., Coulton, P. (2015, July). Back to the future: 10 years of design fiction. In Proceedings of the 2015 British HCI Conference (pp. 210–211). ACM.
6. Bleecker, J. (2009). Design Fiction: A short essay on design, science, fact and fiction. Near Future Laboratory, 29.
7. Holmquist, L. E. (2008, October). Bootlegging: multidisciplinary brainstorming with cut-ups. In Proceedings of the Tenth Anniversary Conference on Participatory Design 2008 (pp. 158–161). Indiana University.
8. Marek K, Rantz M (2000) Aging in place: a new model for longterm care. Nurs Admin Q 24(3): 111
9. AARP. (2005). Beyond 50.05: A report to the nation on livable communities: Creating environments for successful aging.
10. Birnholtz, J., Jones-Rounds, M. (2010, April). Independence and interaction: understanding seniors' privacy and awareness needs for aging in place. In Proceedings of the SIGCHI Conference on Human Factors in Computing Systems (pp. 143–152). ACM.
11. Altendorf, A and Schreiber, J. Assistive Technology in Dementia Care: Methodological Issues in Research Design. Journal of Assistive Technologies 9, 1 (2015), 3847.
12. Little, L., Briggs, P. (2009, June). Pervasive healthcare: the elderly perspective. In Proceedings of the 2nd International Conference on Pervasive Technologies Related to Assistive Environments (p. 71). ACM.
13. Denning, T., Borning, A., Friedman, B., Gill, B. T., Kohno, T., Maisel, W. H. (2010, April). Patients, pacemakers, and implantable defibrillators: Human values and security for wireless implantable medical devices. In Proceedings of the SIGCHI Conference on Human Factors in Computing Systems (pp. 917–926). ACM.
14. Yi, J. S. Qndreview: Read 100 chi papers in 7 hours. In CHI 14 Extended Abstracts on Human Factors in Computing Systems, CHI EA 14 (New York, NY, USA, 2014), 805814. ACM.

The Sailboat Exercise as a Method for User Understanding and Requirements Gathering

Paula Alexandra Silva

Department of Informatics Engineering | Centre for Informatics and Systems (CISUC), University of Coimbra, Coimbra, Portugal paulasilva@dei.uc.pt

Abstract

To design digital products and services that truly empower end-users requires that design and development teams involve end-users early and throughout the design process. However, regardless of the wealth of methods available to Human-Computer Interaction designers, to identify tools that are both intuitive to use and allow for the active engagement of end-users, namely though co-design activities, is hardly ever easy. To identify a simple and straightforward method can be challenging especially when the end -user group are older adults. This paper proposes an adaptation of an exercise, traditionally used in agile retrospectives – the sailboat exercise – here modified and tailored to be used as a co-design generative tool for user understanding and requirements gathering. In short, the method leverages the analogy of a sailboat, and its surrounding factors, and combines it with a set of prompt questions, to create a shared understanding between the end-users and the members of the design team and to support identification of users' goals, desires, challenges and frustrations.

Keywords

User research · Co-design · Participatory design method

How to cite this book chapter:

Silva, P.A. 2020. The Sailboat Exercise as a Method for User Understanding and Requirements Gathering. In: Loizides, F., Winckler, M., Chatterjee, U., Abdelnour-Nocera, J. and Parmaxi, A. (eds.) *Human Computer Interaction and Emerging Technologies: Adjunct Proceedings from the INTERACT 2019 Workshops.* Pp. 31–42. Cardiff: Cardiff University Press. DOI: https://doi.org/10.18573/book3.d. License: CC-BY 4.0.

1 Introduction

Including end-users in the design process allows for effective requirements gathering and increases both user satisfaction and the level of acceptance of the final design [1]. Therefore, it is key to practice a co-design approach, if aiming at novel [2], differentiated and inclusive solutions [3] and at designing digital products and services that do not fail to be adopted when market ready [2, 4].

Users are experts of their own experience [3] and as such, potential end-users should actively contribute throughout the design process as domain experts, working in cooperation, as equal partners, with the design team [5]. This generally involves engaging in a number of collaborative activities, the so-called 'generative tools' [5] or 'tools for conversation' [6], that allow users and stakeholders to dialogue and contribute their views, insights, and feedback.

User involvement is important throughout the design process (Fig. 1), at all stages, but it is vital in earlier phases. The specification of the context of use and of the user requirements are the first phases of human-centred design [7], thus impacting all sub sequent phases of the design of digital products and services.

From interviews, questionnaires, and focus groups to diary studies, photovoice, and workshops, there are many methods that can be used with the purpose of developing an understanding of the user and the context of use and for gathering and specifying user requirements (for methods descriptions refer to [8–11]). However, when designing with older adults, several adaptations may be required, ranging from simple communication and language adjustments to the need for meeting older adults at their own home [11–13]. Furthermore, especially when referring to the design of interactive systems, negative experiences, attitudes, assumptions, and preconceptions of both older adults and design teams regarding older adults and technology may get in the way, adding to the challenge of doing user research with this user group [11]. Design teams need to be creative and resourceful, carefully choosing and/or developing methods and tools that are both straightforward to use, requiring minimal instructions, and that enable 'conversations', around which user needs are made explicit from which key design insight can be gathered [6].

Fig. 1: User-centered design process, adapted from ISO 9241-210:2010 [7].

This paper introduces a modified version of the sailboat exercise, traditionally used in agile retrospectives [14], as a method for user understanding and requirements gathering that supports the process of making user goals, desires, challenges and frustrations explicit, while still keeping this process easy to understand and use. The following sections provide a concise background on the origins of the method and present its modified version. The paper then provides instructions for facilitation and elaborates on the specific value of the exercise.

2 The Sailboat Exercise

2.1 Original Version of the Sailboat Exercise

The sailboat exercise is credited to Ben Linders [15] and is commonly used by agile teams applying scrum processes. In the scope of agile retrospectives, "a retrospective is a regular meeting during which the team reflects on how team members work together and considers ways to improve that process, based on lessons from recently completed work." [14]. These meetings take place at the end of each cycle or iteration and are meant to create a platform for discussion and reflection on the team's successes and failures. In this process, the team identifies what went well, so that such aspects are repeated, and what failed, so that the team learns from what went wrong and sets out improvement strategies. All team members are invited to participate and contribute feedback. At the end of a retrospective, the team creates an action plan for addressing improvements, listing the next steps and assigning e ach step an owner, date, and priority level; subsequently the action plan is made available to all [14].

When using the sailboat exercise, a picture of a sailboat (Fig. 2) is used to facilitate the meeting discussion. Although a retrospective does not necessarily need to use the sailboat exercise, by using the analogy of the sailboat, it is easier for a team to relate to what is working well, propelling them forward, and what is holding them back.

2.2 Modified version of the Sailboat Exercise

Retrospectives have been used by product design teams (e.g. when launching a new product), user experience design teams (e.g. when introducing a new method), and leadership teams (e.g. when implementing a new company initiative or strategic plan) [14]. Here the sailboat exercise is proposed as a tool to engage end-users, and other stakeholders involved in the design process, in a shared activity that aims at supporting the elicitation of user requirements. This method has been used as part of codesign training workshops for non-designers [16]. The next section describes the structure of the proposed modified version of the method.

The sailboat exercise

The boat / trade winds.   The sun / land

The anchor   The ocean rocks

Fig. 2: Sailboat exercise support sheet.

Structure of the Method. While the original version of the sailboat exercise is intended for reflecting on a team's performance, in this article, the sailboat exercise is proposed as a method for understanding end-users and elicitation of their goals, desires, challenges, and frustrations. Additionally, while in its original version, the sailboat exercise is mainly directed at identifying plusses and minuses within the team's processes, this article proposes that all four sailboat surrounding factors – Boat/Trade Winds; Sun/Land; Anchor; and Ocean Rocks—are used to truly harness the full potential of the sailboat analogy. Specifically, it is proposed that:

– The *Boat/Trade Winds* factor is linked to user *Goals*, i.e. aspects of an experience that are currently available, working well, and allow the user to achieve her/his goals, e.g. the convenient bus stop outside her/his apartment door;
– The *Sun/Land* factor is linked to user *Desires*, i.e. anything that allows for a perfect effortless experience to become a reality, e.g. a 24/7 chauffeur;
– The *Anchor* factor is linked to user *Frustrations*, i.e. any personal circumstances that are holding a person back or creating difficulties, e.g. the persistent pain of a past hip fraction;
– The *Ocean Rocks* factor is linked to user *Challenges*, i.e. any external factors that are creating obstacles, e.g. a bus that is not prepared for wheelchair users to hop on, or the absence of bike lanes in the area.

In addition, it is proposed that the sailboat analogy is complemented by four sets of prompt questions, each associated to one of the sailboat

Sailboat exercise: prompt questions

The boat / trade winds
- What's working well at the moment?
- Anything that helps achieving your goal.
- Things, skills, qualities currently available.

The sun / land
- What would the truly perfect experience look like?
- What are you striving towards?
- Things, qualities, features that would create/contribute to an ideal, desirable situation.

The anchor
- What's holding you back?
- Aspects and/or situations, which are making things difficult, slowing you down.

The rocks
- What obstacles hold outside which are preventing you from achieving our goal?
- Problems you find along the way.

Fig. 3: Sailboat exercise prompt questions.

surrounding factors (Fig. 3). The prompt questions are meant to assist in the elicitation of beneficial and/or detrimental experiential aspects, by triggering participant to make them explicit. The prompt questions further intend to facilitate communication and reasoning while adding focus and direction to the exercise. Other methods have also used prompt questions to facilitate design-related processes [17].

Table 1, column 'Procedures', describes the steps involved in conducting a session with the sailboat exercise. Once all steps are completed, each group should have produced a list of items, organized under four categories, identifying the top three items to prioritize.

How the Method Fits in the Design Process. At the end of a sailboat exercise session, the design team collects the outcomes from all groups and reorganizes the results, by grouping similar or duplicate ideas together creating an aggregated list. Once this list exists, it is possible to create a list of user interface specifications, by converting user produced materials into a formal list of user interface design requirements and specifications. It is important not to lose track of the items identified, and negotiated by the team, as most relevant, as these are likely to indicate the features that should be core in the product or service to be developed. Thus the outcomes of the Sailboat exercise make an important contribution to informing the design, in particular phases 2 and 3 of the design process (Fig. 1). From the aggregated list of requirements and specifications, it is possible to proceed to the ideation phase in which design solutions are prototyped and produced.

Table 1: The sailboat exercise list of procedures and preparation guidelines.

Preparation	Procedures
Total number of participants: 16–20	**Part 1 – Starting off (20 minutes):**
Number of participants per group: 4–8	– Present the design brief.
Time: 90–180 minutes; length will vary with level of complexity of the design brief and participants' skills.	– Explain how the method works, clarifying what the trade wind, anchor, rocks, and sun mean and the purpose of the prompt questions.
Room and materials:	– Name (or ask each group to) a rapporteur.
– Reserve a quiet and comfortable room that allows for discussion, writing, and privacy.	– Ask each participant to write down her/his name on her/his A4 sailboat worksheet.
– One A4 print out of the sailboat worksheet per participant.	– Ask the rapporteur to write group name, number or letter on their A3 sailboat page.
– One A3 print out of the sailboat worksheet sheet per group.	
– One set of small sized post-its (ideally in diverse colors, each assigned to a different category: goals, desires, challenges, and frustrations) per participant, for each to write down ideas.	**Part 2 – Individual sailboat (10 minutes):**
– Pens and pencils for each participant.	– Have each participant record her/his goals, desires, challenges, and frustrations, by writing them down directly on the A4 sailboat worksheet or by using post-its.
– Four sets of five sticky dots/stars per participant, for voting.	– Have each participant present her/his ideas to the team.
– Give each group a name, number or letter.	
– Printout of the group name.	**Part 3 – Group sailboat (30 minutes):**
– Printout of the design brief/context.	– As each participant presents her/his ideas, the rapporteur records them on the group A3 the sailboat worksheet (alternatively participants can simple move in the post-its they previously used).
– Printout of the prompt questions.	
Optional	
– Printout of 'motivate to action' statements.	
– Printout of rules for ideation per group.	– Once contributions are gathered and grouped by category, have the team discuss the results and agree on which ideas are most relevant.
– Printout of rules for discussion.	
Before the session starts:	– In case there is a large number of ideas and the group does not naturally come to consensus, invite participants to use the five sticky dots and vote for the three ideas they would most like to see prioritized.
– Develop a clear description of the design challenge, stating the design domain and challenge the participants will work on.	
– Remember to prepare and collect informed consent from all participants.	**Part 4 – Debriefing (30 minutes):**
– You may wish to bring a soundtrack (there are plenty available online, some even	– Allow each team to present the results and speak about their list to all participants.
– with a timer) to play in the background as participants go through the steps of the exercise.	

Preparation	Procedures
Total number of participants: 16–20	**Part 1 – Starting off (20 minutes):**

– *In room*:
  – Form (or ask participants to) the teams, assigning profiles evenly, if stakeholders are in the room.
  – Observe the participants and check if anyone needs help writing, reading, hearing, etc.
	– Keep it brief and genuine, but make sure to acknowledge participants' contributions and express thanks.
	Important to keep in mind during session:
	– Remind participants there are no right or wrong answers.
	– When debriefing, distribute available time evenly across participants and teams.
	– As a facilitator, remember to keep a low profile; the same applies to any helpers.
	– Capture all notes and make photos of the session and the materials created.

In this process, the *Boat/Trade* Winds or user *Goals* are features the design team will want to keep; the *Sun/Land* or user *Desires* consist of opportunities for improvement; the *Anchor* or user *Frustrations* are likely to correspond to aspects the design needs to accommodate for; and the *Ocean Rocks* or user *Challenges* represent factors that need to be resolved and could give the product or service a strategic advantage.

Planning for and Facilitating a Session with the Sailboat Exercise. Similar to other methods, when planning for a session with the sailboat exercise, preparing and clarifying both the session's activities and the design brief is essential.

Essentially the design brief should: i) clarify the design domain, i.e. the broad area in which the group is going to work, and ii) concisely describe the design problem or challenge that is going to be addressed. The design domain and design challenge should be written in a clear, concise statement[1]. During the session this statement should be visible and it is recommended that the facilitator complements the written statement with examples and further details. In addition to the design brief, the facilitator should arrange for a suitable venue in which to conduct the exercise and for various supplies (for a full list of requirements please refer to the column 'Preparation' in Table 1).

3 The Value of the Sailboat Exercise

The design of digital products and services which meet user needs and are accepted when market-ready, demands careful consideration of end-users' needs and their active involvement in the design process [1, 2]. In this

---

[1] An example of a possible statement could be 'Getting places, when I can no longer drive'.

context, it is important to create opportunities for collaboration, communication, and exchange, which can spur design knowledge. The sailboat exercise allows for the active engagement of end -users and can be easily adapted to different audiences and design problems. In addition to being adaptable across different contexts, the sailboat exercise has several other benefits, which are discussed in the following three sections.

3.1   A tool participants relate to immediately

One of the advantages of the sailboat exercise stems from its simple analogy. To establish a parallel between the impact of goals, desires, frustrations and challenges on user experience and the impact of the four factors—Boat/Trade Winds, Sun/Land, Anchor, Ocean Rocks—on a sailboat is simple and straightforward. This makes it easy to create a shared understanding about the activity and to rapidly engage in a conversation where users are able to relate to goals, desires, frustrations, and challenges, without requiring long and complex explanations.

3.2   A tool that allows for different stakeholders to be involved

All types of stakeholders, from older adults to formal or informal caregivers can be invited to participate in a sailboat exercise session. This means that the design team can simultaneously collect needs from the different stakeholders, while still having each participant making her/his own individual needs explicit (Part 2 of the method). In Part 3, the full potential of the method is harnessed, when the participants, as a team, negotiate and make decisions on what requirements should be prioritized to create one single list. This allows the design team to gain an understanding of the diverse requirements of (related) users and their complete context of use, providing a more accurate representation of the context. To involve the different stakeholders in eliciting and negotiating requirements has been identified as key in projects that aim to be innovative [18].

3.3   A tool that allows for easy follow-ups

A Human-Computer Interaction (HCI) design process is iterative. This means that an HCI design team may need to revisit design requirements throughout the design process and that multiple meetings to review requirements may be necessary. Repeating or carrying out multiple data gathering sessions also helps to ensure accurate interpretation. Users may not be used to articulating their needs and may use or assign meaning to terms differently from how those terms are used in design fields; therefore, it is important to review each session and check interpretations with users/stakeholders to ensure clarity.

4 Conclusions

To design appropriate digital products and services it is vital to understand end -users and to grasp what they want to do with the products/services as well as the environments in which the products /services will be used. This paper introduced the sailboat exercise as a method for improving understanding of end -users and the contexts in which they are immersed. The exercise can be facilitated by designers with end -users/stakeholders at the early stages of HCI design processes. The proposed method demonstrates potential for aiding with the important task of user requirements gathering—it is flexible, requires little to moderate preparation and is accessible in form and content for a variety of people. As reported in [16], the method has been successfully used to assist requirements gathering of Active and Assisted Living systems, but in the future it would be interesting to experiment how it performs in other domains.

Acknowledgments

This research was developed with the support of the Research Program "CeNTER-Community-led Territorial Innovation" (CENTRO-01-0145-FEDER-000002), funded by Programa Operacional Regional do Centro (CENTRO 2020), PT2020. Many thanks also to Leah Burns, Aalto University, for the suggestions on the manuscript.

References

1. Kujala, S.: User involvement: A review of the benefits and challenges. Behaviour & Information Technology. 22, 1–16 (2003). doi:10.1080/01449290301782
2. Trischler, J., Pervan, S.J., Kelly, S.J., Scott, D.R.: The Value of Codesign: The Effect of Customer Involvement in Service Design Teams. Journal of Service Research. 21, 75–100 (2018). doi:10.1177/1094670517714060
3. Co-Create Project: Co-Create Essentials. (2019)
4. Wherton, J., Sugarhood, P., Procter, R., Hinder, S., Greenhalgh, T.: Co-production in practice: how people with assisted living needs can help design and evolve technologies and services. Implementation Science. 10, 75 (2015). doi:10.1186/s13012-015-0271-8
5. Sanders, E.B.-N., Stappers, P.J.: Co-creation and the new landscapes of design. CoDesign. 4, 5–18 (2008). doi:10.1080/15710880701875068
6. Sanders, E.B.-N.: Generative Tools for Co-designing. In: Scrivener, S.A.R., Ball, L.J., and Woodcock, A. (eds.) Collaborative Design. pp. 3–12. Springer London, London (2000)

7. ISO 9241-210:2010(en), Ergonomics of human-system interaction—Part 210: Human-centred design for interactive systems, https://www.iso.org/obp/ui/#iso:std:52075:en

8. Preece, J., Sharp, H., Rogers, Y.: Interaction Design: Beyond Human-Computer Interaction. Wiley, Chichester (2015)

9. Farrell, S.: UX Research Cheat Sheet, https://www.nngroup.com/articles/uxresearch-cheat-sheet/

10. Rohrer, C.: When to Use Which User-Experience Research Methods, https://www.nngroup.com/articles/which-ux-research-methods/

11. Eisma, R., Dickinson, A., Goodman, J., Syme, A., Tiwari, L., Newell, A.F.: Early user involvement in the development of information technology-related products for older people. Universal Access in the Information Society. 3, 131–140 (2004). doi:10.1007/s10209-004-0092-z

12. Silva, P.A., Nunes, F.: 3 × 7 Usability Testing Guidelines for Older Adults. In: MexIHC 2010 (2010)

13. Dickinson, A., Arnott, J., Prior, S.: Methods for human–computer interaction research with older people. Behaviour & Information Technology. 26, 343–352 (2007). doi:10.1080/01449290601176948

14. Krause, R.: UX Retrospectives 101, https://www.nngroup.com/articles/uxretrospectives/

15. Gonçalves, L.: Run the Sailboat Agile Exercise or Sailboat Retrospective, https://medium.com/@lgoncalves1979/sailboat-exercise-sailboat-retrospective-4893ca6b5fd3, (2017)

16. Silva, P.A., Daniel, A.D.: Training Non-Designers in Co-Design Methods through an Active Assisted Living Interactive Workshop. In: Human-Computer Interaction – INTERACT 2019. Springer International Publishing. (2019)

17. Silva, P.A.: BadIdeas 3.0: A Method for Creativity and Innovation in Design. In: Proceedings of the 1st DESIRE Network Conference on Creativity and Innovation in Design. pp. 154–162. Desire Network, Aarhus, Denmark (2010)

18. Fitzpatrick, G., Malmborg, L.: Quadruple Helix Model Organisation and Tensions in Participatory Design Teams. In: Proceedings of the 10th Nordic Conference on Human-Computer Interaction. pp. 376–384. ACM, New York, NY, USA (2018)

SECTION 2

Challenging Misinformation: Exploring Limits and Approaches

Misinformation and User-Generated content: Applying participatory journalism practices in fact-checking

Theodora Saridou[*], Theodora Maniou[†]
and Andreas Veglis[*]

[*]Media Informatics Lab, School of Journalism & Mass Communication, Aristotle University of Thessaloniki, 54124, Thessaloniki, Greece
[†]Department of Social & Political Sciences, University of Cyprus, L. Panepistimiou, 2109, Ag-lantzia, Nicosia, Cyprus
maniou.theodora@ucy.ac.cy

Abstract

In the evolving news media landscape, the proliferation of user-generated content in online news outlets and social media platforms has triggered changes in traditional processes and relationships. However, the coexistence of professional and amateur content raises a wide range of matters. Misinformation is one of the main problems faced by media organizations during the exploitation of huge amounts of data. In order to ensure the quality of the content, journalists use control methods and perform fact-checking not only on their own, but also by engaging users. By offering an examination of key issues arising from UGC research, this article seeks to focus on the application of participatory practices in fact-checking. In addition to more traditional methods, the web-based platform of Truly Media, which supports collaborative verification, is used as a case-study.

How to cite this book chapter:
Saridou, T., Maniou, T. and Veglis, A. 2020. Misinformation and User-Generated content: Applying participatory journalism practices in fact-checking. In: Loizides, F., Winckler, M., Chatterjee, U., Abdelnour-Nocera, J. and Parmaxi, A. (eds.) *Human Computer Interaction and Emerging Technologies: Adjunct Proceedings from the INTERACT 2019 Workshops*. Pp. 43–48. Cardiff: Cardiff University Press. DOI: https://doi.org/10.18573/book3.e. License: CC-BY 4.0.

Keywords

Participatory Journalism · Fact-checking · Truly Media · Verification · User-Generated Content

1 Introduction

Over the recent decades, the predominance of user-generated content (UGC) in journalism has generated wide academic and entrepreneurial interest, since it has led to fundamental changes both in the news production process and in the journalists' relationship with the audience. Mainly in the form of text, photos, video and graphics [3], users' material is often invited and adopted by media organizations, which integrate non-professional contributions in their daily work routine, either directly or indirectly [14, 15]. Thus, part of the citizens' activity takes place inside the walls of the established media outlets, where professional journalists and amateur users co-produce news within a mainstream platform in a participatory journalism context [2].

At the same time, news creation and dissemination is also shaped by the vast amounts of content that are dynamically produced on social media platforms. Networked media technologies are extending the ability of users to create and receive personalized news streams with social media becoming central to the way people experience news [10]. Instead of actively choosing to visit a news website or explicitly searching for a news topic, now news is passively found in posts shared from friends, family or news sources that users follow [4]. Journalists, on the other hand, use social networks to check on the activity of other news organizations, to look for breaking news events, find ideas for stories, keep in touch with their audience and gather information [28, p. 853].

As news becomes more social, journalists have to develop their skills and use digital tools in the service of tracing information, forensic examination, UGC dissemination and verification [11, 27]. Apart from traditional methods, though, part of the collection, management and validation is sometimes based on semantic web services. However, such methods are not widely adopted by organizations mainly due to problems related to the fragmented confrontation of the various cases and the maturation of the semantic technology [22].

2 The need for fact-checking

The challenge of exploiting a world of data stemming from a variety of sources is therefore posed to media organizations, as the incorporation of UGC often provokes threats to the ethical and legal established modus operandi [21, 24]. At times of economic uncertainty, hyper-competition and diminishing accountability levels, when convergence is used as a cost-effective strategy fostering low-cost and spreadable news production [23], the hectic pace of news production process enhances the need of continuous monitoring and effective management.

Participatory spaces, however, are also considered vulnerable to the excessive use of inappropriate language, flaming, stereotyping, superficial discourse, hateful messages and incivility [8, 17, 20]. Research reveals that the potential for dark participation – ranging from misinformation and hate campaigns to individual trolling and cyberbullying is enormous, not only in comment sections controlled by the media themselves, but also on non-proprietary platforms, like Facebook, Youtube, Instagram or Twitter, where the negativity and toxic atmosphere can be equally bad and the deliberative quality is even lower [19]. The spreading of fake news, disinformation and conspiracy theories in UGC are forms of deviances as well, while malicious 'pseudo-users', troll armies and social bots have jarred confidence in even the fundamental assumption that user interaction is interaction with users [9].

In 2014, The Guardian publicly announced that a high number of strategically placed, manipulative pro-Russian user posts was detected in their comment sections. In a form of covert political propaganda, these 'participators' aimed to influence the Western public and (potentially) the journalists and there was evidence that linked these posts to the Russian government or at least their support groups [19]. Misinformation and propaganda can also take the form of hate campaigns that attack specific groups or individuals that symbolize these groups [18], while misinformation is also spread via social networks and short messaging services.

3 Participatory practices for fact-checking

In order to monitor UGC, media organizations utilize tools and build platforms which enable them to obtain, sort and disseminate news [12]. When pre-moderation is employed, journalists check every piece of UGC before published, achieving an adequate level of security, however not without high consumption of financial, human and time resources [24]. On the other hand, during post moderation, comments are first published and professionals intervene if a reason occurs; such techniques are nearly always accompanied by mandatory registration where users submit personal information in order to be accredited as commenters [24, p. 109], contributing in this way in the formation of hybrid salience [16].

In some cases, users are allowed to participate in the moderation process as well. When organizations apply reactive moderation, posts are checked only after the moderator receives an alert from a user [1]. Similarly [13], describe how the website 'Slashdot' distributed the moderation system to its user base: users achieved 'karma' (as the website itself describes it) through several activities. Each posted comment had a current score, from −1 to +5. Users increased or decreased this score and chose from a list of descriptions, such as 'off topic', 'troll', 'insightful', 'funny' or 'overrated'.

Except for concerns regarding resources, the individual moderation decision is also affected by newsroom routines, media organizations for which journalists work, the societal institutions and social system in which they operate, their personal experiences or even gut feelings [5, p. 60]. At the same time, although semantic technologies can help towards the direction of the simplification of UGC exploitation, such practices are not largely spread apart from several heterogeneous tools and applications. Moreover, it is noticed that tools and applications used by media organizations in UGC-driven platforms rely mostly on the integration with services provided by third parties, while professional journalists are still involved in many stages of the process [22, p. 286]. In a similar vein [26], argue that in the context of semantic web services it is hardly imaginable that isolated applications are able to serve successfully the users' ever growing requirements since the information normally available to human decision makers continues to grow beyond human cognitive capabilities. The rapid growth of such services also poses challenges on the field of interactions, for instance on social aspects connected with automatic transactions, especially the issue of trust within service discovery and composition [26].

In order to verify content, professionals often use web-based platforms or tools developed in collaborative projects which aim at finding and organizing information produced in social media and elsewhere. Truly Media (http://www.truly.media), for example, is a collaboration platform developed to support journalists and human rights workers in the verification of digital content, such as material residing in social networks. In order to address the misinformation ecosystem and what is often referred to as fake news, it supports its users to collaboratively assess the validity and accuracy of UGC that is distributed and shared via various means and networks. Based on the three main steps of detection, organization and verification, Truly Media applies a fully participatory practice in fact-checking. First, it provides to users the tools in order to find content from a variety of sources and bring all pieces of data together in one collection. Participants can afterwards organize their content and share their work and findings in real time with their colleagues. Finally, real-time collaborative verification is supported, through the exploitation of internal and third party tools.

4 Conclusion

The constantly produced UGC both in news websites and social media necessitates a thorough handling by media organizations. Fact-checking holds the leading position in struggling against misinformation and a long series of occurring problems. Participatory journalism can be an ally in this direction, mostly via platforms that reinforce collaboration between journalists and users and provide the tools for verifying the authenticity of the available information.

Overall, participation agitates not only the well-known notions of news production and consumption, but also traditional work practices as well. Gatekeeping turns to gatewatching [7] or even gateopening [6] and journalists do not define, but observe the information flow stemming from a variety of sources, receive UGC and construct a final product. It can thus be considered that users' involvement in fact-checking supports the core value of participatory journalism.

References

1. ABC (2014), Moderating user generated content-Guidance Note, http://about.abc.net.au/reports-publications/moderating-user-generated-content-guidance-note/, last accessed 2019/4/20
2. Aitamurto, T.: Balancing between open and closed: Co-creation in magazine journalism. Digital Journalism, 1(2), 229–251 (2013).
3. Anderson, P.: What is Web 2.0? Ideas, technologies and implications for education. Technology & Standards Watch, 1(1), 1–64 (2007).
4. Bentley, F., Quehl, K., Wirfs-Brock, J., & Bica, M.: Understanding online news behaviors. In CHI Conference on Human Factors in Computing Systems Proceedings, Glasgow, Scotland: ACM, New York. doi: https://doi.org/10.1145/3290605.3300820 (2019).
5. Boberg, S., Schatto-Eckrodt, T., Frischlich, L., & Quandt, T.: The moral gatekeeper? Moderation and deletion of user-generated content in a leading news forum. Media and Communication, 6(4): 58–69 doi: https://doi.org/10.17645/mac.v6i4.1493 (2018).
6. Boczkowski, J. B.: Digitizing the news: Innovation in online newspapers. Cambridge, MA: MIT Press (2005).
7. Bruns, A.: The active audience: transforming journalism from gatekeeping to gatewatching. In C. Paterson, & D. Domingo (Eds.), Making online news: The ethnography of new media production (pp. 171–184). New York, NY: Peter Lang (2008).
8. Coe, K., Kenski, K., & Rains, S. A.: Online and uncivil? Patterns and determinants of incivility in newspaper website comments. Journal of Communication, 64 (4): 658–679. doi: https://doi.org/10.1111/jcom.12104 (2014).
9. Frischlich, L., Boberg, S., & Quandt, T.: Comment sections as targets of dark participation? Journalists' evaluation and moderation of deviant user comments. Journalism Studies, (latest articles). doi: https://doi.org/10.1080/1461670X.2018.1556320 (2019).
10. Hermida, A., Fletcher, F., Korell, D. & Logan, D.: Share, like, recommend. Journalism Studies, 13 (5–6): 815–824. doi: https://doi.org/10.1080/1461670X.2012.664430 (2012).
11. Johnston, L.: Social news=Journalism evolution? Digital Journalism, 4 (7), 899–909, doi: https://doi.org/10.1080/21670811.2016.1168709 (2016).
12. Katsaounidou, A., Dimoulas, C., & Veglis, A.: Cross-media authentication and verification: Emerging research and opportunities. Hershey, PA: IGI Global. doi: https://doi.org/10.4018/978-1-5225-5592-6 (2018).
13. Lampe, C., & Resnick, P.: Slash(dot) and burn: Distributed moderation in a large online conversation space. In E. Dykstra-Erickson, & M. Tscheligi

(eds.), Proceedings of ACM CHI 2004 Conference on Human Factors in Computing Systems (pp. 543–550). Vienna, Austria: ACM New York (2004).

14. Maniou, T., & Veglis, A.: 'Selfie Journalism: Current Practices in Digital Media. Studies in Media and Communication, 4 (1), 11–118, doi: https://doi.org/10.11114/smc.v4i1.1637 (2016).

15. Maniou, T., Panagiotidis, K., & Veglis, A.: The Politicization of Selfie Journalism: An empirical study to Parliamentary Elections. International Journal of E-Politics, 8 (2), 1–16, doi: https://doi.org/10.4018/IJEP.2017040101 (2017).

16. Maniou, T., & Bantimaroudis, P.: Hybrid Salience: Examining the role of traditional and digital media in the rise of the Greek radical left. Journalism, doi: https://doi.org/10.1177/1464884918796587 (2018).

17. Manosevitch, I.: User generated content in the Israeli online journalism landscape. Israel Affairs, 17 (3): 422–444. doi: https://doi.org/10.1080/13537121.2011.584670 (2011).

18. Quandt, T., & Festl, R. Cyberhate. In P. Rössler (ed.), The international encyclopedia of media effects (pp. 336–344). Malden: Wiley-Blackwell (2017).

19. Quandt, T.: Dark participation. Media and Communication, 6 (4): 36–48. doi: https://doi.org/10.17645/mac.v6i4.1519 (2018).

20. Santana, A. D.: Virtuous or vitriolic. The effect of anonymity on civility in online newspaper reader comment boards. Journalism Practice 8 (1): 18–33. doi: https://doi.org/10.1080/17512786.2013.813194 (2014).

21. Saridou, T., & Veglis, A.: Participatory journalism policies in newspapers' websites in Greece. Journal of Greek Media and Culture, 2 (1): 85–101. doi: https://doi.org/10.1386/jgmc.2.1.85_1 (2016).

22. Saridou, T., Panagiotidis, K., Tsipas, N., & Veglis, A.: Semantic tools for participatory journalism. Journal of Media Critiques, 4 (14): 281–294. doi: https://doi.org/10.17349/jmc118221 (2018).

23. Saridou, T., Spyridou, L. P., & Veglis, A.: Churnalism on the rise? Digital Journalism, 5(8), 1006–1024. doi: https://doi.org/10.1080/21670811.2017.1342209 (2017).

24. Singer, J. B., Hermida, A., Domingo, D., Heinonen, A., Paulussen, S., Quandt, T., Reich, Z., & Vujnovic, M.: Participatory journalism. Guarding open gates at online newspapers. West Sussex, UK: Wiley-Blackwell (2011).

25. Truly Media, http://www.truly.media/, last accessed 2019/4/20

26. Vargas-Vera, M., Nagy, M., Zyskowski, D., Haniewicz, K., & Abramowicz, W.: Challenges on semantic web services. In M. Cruz-Cunha, E. F. Oliveira & A. J. Tavares (Eds.). Handbook of research on social dimensions of semantic technologies and web services (pp. 25–48). Hershey, PA: IGI Global. doi: https://doi.org/10.4018/978-1-60566-650-1

27. Veglis, A.: Education of journalists on ICTs issues and opportunities. Journal of Applied Journalism & Media Studies, 2 (2): 265–279. doi: https://doi.org/10.1386/ajms.2.2.265_1 (2013).

28. Weaver, D. H., & Willnat, L.: Changes in U.S. Journalism. Journalism Practice, 10 (7): 844–855. doi: https://doi.org/10.1080/17512786.2016.1171162 (2016).

Navigating through real and fake news by using provenance information

Bianca Rodrigues Teixeira and Simone D. J. Barbosa

Department of Informatics, PUC-Rio R. Marques de Sao Vicente,
225, Rio de Janeiro, RJ 22451-900, Brazil
bteixeira@inf.puc-rio.br, simone@inf.puc-rio.br

Abstract

With the large number of internet users today, fake news and misinformation become more and more visible online, especially through social media platforms. Users' belief in online information and news is related to trust in the information sources. To prevent the dissemination of fake news and misinformation online, trust can be supported by provenance information in online publications. We use the OurPrivacy conceptual framework to illustrate a way in which provenance can be used to help users define their trust in artifacts posted online. We also discuss the possibility to filter artifacts by only viewing trusted sources of information.

Keywords

Provenance · Trust · Fake News · Privacy · Conceptual Framework

---

How to cite this book chapter:
Rodrigues Teixeira, B. and Barbosa, S.D.J. 2020. Navigating through real and fake news by using provenance information. In: Loizides, F., Winckler, M., Chatterjee, U., Abdelnour-Nocera, J. and Parmaxi, A. (eds.) *Human Computer Interaction and Emerging Technologies: Adjunct Proceedings from the INTERACT 2019 Workshops.* Pp. 49–56. Cardiff: Cardiff University Press. DOI: https://doi.org/10.18573/book3.f. License: CC-BY 4.0.

1 Introduction

Internet users are everywhere. Around the globe, smartphone ownership rates are rising fast [12], especially in developing countries in which mobile phones used to be considered a luxury. Because of the large amounts of active internet users, it is safe to say that fake news or misinformation online is more dangerous than ever. Although trusted organizations attract more direct traffic [13], Allcott and Gentzkow performed a study on the 2016 United States presidential election and found that 13.8% of news and information was accessed on social media [1]. More recently, in a study with 174 participants, Bentley et al. found that 16% of all news sessions started from social media [2]. The shareability of fake news in social media is massive, and in a recent survey, 37% of the respondents admitted having "come across a news story, believed it to be true, then later realized that it was either exaggerated, inaccurate or blatantly false" [6]. Moreover, people may remember fake news better than traditional news [3].

Besides social media, messaging mobile applications, such as WhatsApp, with over one billion active users [5], provide a great platform for the dissemination of all kinds of information, including misinformation. This issue is so well known that, on their Frequently Asked Questions page, WhatsApp provides tips to help prevent the spread of rumors and fake news [16]. They include a brief explanation of their *"Forwarded"* feature, which indicates whether a message has been forwarded to the user. This could mean that the person who sent it may not have written it, and thus the receiving end should double check the facts.

Lazer et al. discussed potential interventions for controlling the flow of fake news, dividing them into two categories: individual empowerment and algorithms [11]. The former includes mostly fact checking and researching as a means to confirm the information, whilst the latter regards automatic detection of untrustworthy sources. The authors suggest that social media platforms could provide a sort of "seal of approval" for certain sources, which then would be used to sort and rank the content the users would then consume.

In the following section we discuss some of the trust and provenance aspects of information shared online. Next, we propose to use a conceptual framework to help contain the flow of fake news. Finally, we provide a conclusion and propose next steps.

2 Provenance and trust

Gil and Artz define content trust as "a trust of judgement on *a particular piece of information* in a given context" [7]. It is a subjective judgment, and two people may have opposite opinions on whether they trust a piece of information. This generates a problem when it comes to actual false information. It is not possible to control whether someone will believe what he/she reads online, and often people believe without questioning. In particular, older adults are more likely to believe false information than young adults, consciously recollecting false statements as true [3, 8]. Therefore, although there are indeed internet users who may believe false information more often than other users, it is still important to lower trust on fake news or misinformation.

Wang and Mark performed a study in 2013 comparing trust in official media and in citizen media in China [15]. Official media comprises companies run or influenced by the state, with professional journalists, and citizen media is media posted and disseminated by citizens in social media. They found two contrasting groups of respondents, Traditional (high trust in official, low trust in citizen media) and New Generation (low trust in official, high trust in citizen media). The authors hypothesize that this difference in behavior could be due to political views, or due to the social media adoption by the New Generation group, earlier than the Traditional group, which can lead to familiarity and then trust in citizen media.

In a similar study, Hermida et al. found that 37% of news consumers tend to trust and prefer content curated by professional journalists over user-generated content, but 44% of respondents were unsure [9]. Ultimately, on specific pieces of information, this uncertainty will result in either trust or not trust.

Gil and Artz listed 19 factors that influence content trust [7]. In this paper, in order to help users make a decision on trust, we focus on *provenance*. Provenance, in this context, can be defined as the source and date of a piece of information, such as a news outlet. News articles that are purposefully created as fake news usually are not originated from a source with respectful journalistic reputation, so their provenance may not generate trust on the reader.

The provenance of a piece of information has a direct effect on trust [6], which then defines whether a reader believes in it or not. When a news article is shared on social media, the provenance is easily identified by experienced users via the URL of the source website. However, when the information shared does not contain a clear source, the users have to do research and fact check it themselves, but this requires some skepticism from their part.

Content trust can also be established by having a "trust chain". One may not trust a specific piece of information published by an untrusted source A, but if a previously trusted source B states that it trusts A's publication, then one can then start trusting A [10].

In the next section, we discuss the use of a conceptual framework called OurPrivacy in the context of using provenance information to create – or not – trust in information shared online.

3 OurPrivacy

OurPrivacy is a conceptual framework to characterize what privacy is in the context of social networks and how privacy rules can be expressed [14]. Each piece of information is modelled as a nanopublication,[1] which comprises three basic elements: the assertions, the provenance, and the publication information. The assertions are related to the content of the nanopublication, *i.e.*, the semantic information it represents. The provenance is considered metadata about the assertions: it contains information about how to assertions came to be. Finally, the publication information is metadata about the nanopublication as a whole. In the context of a social network, it contains information about the user who actively posted the nanopublication, whereas the provenance information regards where the information (assertions) actually came from.

By modeling social media artifacts as nanopublications, the provenance information can be used as a means to establish trust in that artifact. Having this information readily available, since it is tied to the content of the artifact, the user can use it to determine whether he/she trusts it or not.

OurPrivacy also allows users to create privacy rules. A privacy rule can reference the content (assertions), provenance or publication information of an artifact. For instance, John Stuart can specify a rule that states that he only wants to access artifacts that have BBC or CNN listed as their provenance. He can also set a rule that prevents his grandmother from viewing his publications about politics, maybe because he tends to use sarcastic tones and knows his grandmother would take his words literally.

The OurPrivacy framework allows for customization of rules about virtually any type of artifact, since we consider that the assertions would contain complete semantic information, which would be supported by the provenance information. This model could be used as a way to help control the dissemination of fake news or misinformation, by using the provenance information as a type of filter.

Besides being able to create rules in a top-down fashion, as stated above, we can also envisage using fake news detectors, such as XFake [17], to inform our decisions on which rules to create, thus also supporting a bottom-up process for creating rules.

The "trust chain" mentioned in the previous section can also be tracked using OurPrivacy in a network of artifacts. As an example, we have a user U, an untrusted source A and a trusted source B. A's publications are generally not trusted by U, whereas B's are trusted. If B were to publish a claim, *i.e.*, generate a new artifact, about trusting A's publication, in the "provenance" element of the artifact there would be some information relating to A's original publication. Since B is citing A's publication in order to back it up, the provenance information should contain A's publication. Also, in the assertions, it should be stated that B trusts A's publication.

This way, the user U could also customize rules or browse the network looking for trusted sources that claim to trust the previously untrusted publication

---

[1] http://nanopub.org/wordpress/.

by A. The chain of claims regarding trust in other publications should be transparent for users to help make their decisions about trusting new sources.

By modeling social media using nanopublications as artifacts, as proposed in OurPrivacy, a change in paradigm is impending. In social networks today, it is common to have both the assertion and the publication information components. The provenance aspect would be a new element, and social media users would need to be aware of the change. Publications and news they consume would have the provenance information available, and people would learn to use it to make more informed decisions regarding trust and whether to disseminate the publication.

4 Conclusions

The information available on social media today is mostly unstructured, which makes it difficult to track and to navigate in. This helps with the propagation of fake news, which are posted and consumed every day, especially in social media and messaging applications. The general population tends to use social media without considering the impact of their publications. Sharing misinformation is not usually seen as a critical act, but in our view it should.

The OurPrivacy conceptual framework can be used as a model for a more transparent social media. By mapping artifacts as nanopublications, the provenance information is tied with the assertions contained in the artifact, and can help the user in knowing the source of the information. Although most publications in social media today do not contain clear sources and are not structured in a way that contains semantic information, perhaps in the future this shall be possible, and OurPrivacy could be used to model this network.

Trust in information online varies from person to person, but we can try to make it easier for users to make their decisions when defining their beliefs. By providing clear provenance information, or allowing users to filter through their networks, we can perhaps help decrease the proliferation of fake news and misinformation.

References

1. Allcott, H., Gentzkow, M.: Social Media and Fake News in the 2016 Election. Journal of Economic Perspectives. 31, 211–236 (2017). https://doi.org/10.3386/w23089.
2. Bentley, F. et al.: Understanding Online News Behaviors. In: Proceedings of the 2019 CHI Conference on Human Factors in Computing Systems. pp. 590:1–590:11 ACM, New York, NY, USA (2019). https://doi.org/10.1145/3290605.3300820.

3. Budak, C.: What Happened? The Spread of Fake News Publisher Content During the 2016 U.S. Presidential Election. In: The World Wide Web Conference. pp. 139–150 ACM, New York, NY, USA (2019). https://doi.org/10.1145/3308558.3313721.

4. Chen, Y.: Unwanted Beliefs: Age Differences in Beliefs of False Information. Aging, Neuropsychology, and Cognition. 9, 217–230 (2002). https://doi.org/10.1076/anec.9.3.217.9613.

5. Constine, J.: WhatsApp hits 1.5 billion monthly users. $19B? Not so bad., http://social.techcrunch.com/2018/01/31/whatsapp-hits-1-5-billion-monthly-users-19b-not-so-bad/.

6. Flintham, M. et al.: Falling for Fake News: Investigating the Consumption of News via Social Media. In: Proceedings of the 2018 CHI Conference on Human Factors in Computing Systems. pp. 376:1–376:10 ACM, New York, NY, USA (2018). https://doi.org/10.1145/3173574.3173950.

7. Gil, Y., Artz, D.: Towards content trust of web resources. Journal of Web Semantics. 5, 227–239 (2007). https://doi.org/10.1016/j.websem.2007.09.005.

8. Grace, L., Hone, B.: Factitious: Large Scale Computer Game to Fight Fake News and Improve News Literacy. In: Extended Abstracts of the 2019 CHI Conference on Human Factors in Computing Systems. p. CS05:1–CS05:8 ACM, New York, NY, USA (2019). https://doi.org/10.1145/3290607.3299046.

9. Hermida, A., Fletcher, F., Korell, D., Logan, D.: Share, Like, Recommend: Decoding the social media news consumer. Journalism Studies. 13, 815–824 (2012). https://doi.org/10.1080/1461670X.2012.664430.

10. Laufer, C., Schwabe, D.: A Framework to Support the Trust Process in News and Social Media. In: Proceedings of the Workshop on Semantic Web for Social Good co-located with 17th International Semantic Web Conference (ISWC 2018). Monterey, CA, USA (2018).

11. Lazer, D.M.J., Baum, M.A., Benkler, Y., Berinsky, A.J., Greenhill, K.M., Menczer, F., Metzger, M.J., Nyhan, B., Pennycook, G., Rothschild, D., Schudson, M., Sloman, S.A., Sunstein, C.R., Thorson, E.A., Watts, D.J., Zittrain, J.L.: The science of fake news. Science. 359, 1094–1096 (2018). https://doi.org/10.1126/science.aao2998.

12. Poushter, J.: Smartphone Ownership and Internet Usage Continues to Climb in Emerging Economies | Pew Research Center, https://www.pewglobal.org/2016/02/22/smartphoneownership-and-internet-usage-continues-to-climb-in-emerging-economies/, (2016), last accessed 2019/04/20.

13. Taneja, H., Yaeger, K.: Do People Consume the News They Trust? In: Proceedings of the 2019 CHI Conference on Human Factors in Computing Systems. pp. 540:1–540:10 ACM, New York, NY, USA (2019). https://doi.org/10.1145/3290605.3300770.

14. Teixeira, B., Schwabe, D., Santoro, F., Baião, F., Campos, M.L., Verona, L., Laufer, C., Barbosa, S.D.J., Lifschitz, S., Costa, R.: Privacy and Transparency within the 4IR: Two faces of the same coin. In: Proceeding of FATES on the Web, co-located with The Web Conference '19., San Francisco, CA, USA (2019).
15. Wang, Y., Mark, G.: Trust in Online News: Comparing Social Media and Official Media Use by Chinese Citizens. In: Proceedings of the 2013 Conference on Computer Supported Cooperative Work. pp. 599–610. ACM, New York, NY, USA (2013). https://doi.org/10.1145/2441776.2441843.
16. WhatsApp FAQ - Tips to help prevent the spread of rumors and fake news, https://faq.whatsapp.com/en/26000216/?category=5245250, last accessed 2019/04/20.
17. Yang, F. et al.: XFake: Explainable Fake News Detector with Visualizations. In: The World Wide Web Conference. pp. 3600–3604 ACM, New York, NY, USA (2019). https://doi.org/10.1145/3308558.3314119.

Disinformation online: potential legal and regulatory ramifications to the right to free elections – policy position paper

Krisztina Rozgonyi

University of Vienna, 1090 Vienna, Währingerstrasse 29

krisztina.rozgonyi@univie.ac.at

Abstract

This paper provides an overview on the implications of digital information disorder to exercise the right to free elections. It suggests a need for public scrutiny and calls for action on the revision of rules on political advertising, on enhanced accountability of internet intermediaries, on strengthening quality journalism and empowerment of voters towards a critical evaluation of electoral communication. Furthermore, it considers the potential role and involvement of national regulators and of the judiciary in law enforcement and regulation.

Keywords

Information disorder · the right to free elections · accountability of online platform providers'

How to cite this book chapter:

Rozgonyi, K. 2020. Disinformation online: potential legal and regulatory ramifications to the right to free elections – policy position paper. In: Loizides, F., Winckler, M., Chatterjee, U., Abdelnour-Nocera, J. and Parmaxi, A. (eds.) *Human Computer Interaction and Emerging Technologies: Adjunct Proceedings from the INTERACT 2019 Workshops.* Pp. 57–66. Cardiff: Cardiff University Press. DOI: https://doi.org/10.18573/book3.g. License: CC-BY 4.0.

1 Information disorder and its (potential) impact on elections

The internet has, to a large extent, changed political campaigning. Major political events in 2016 in the United Kingdom and the United States of America, namely the Brexit referendum and the presidential election respectively, pointed to several potentially critical defects in the regulatory regimes governing political campaigning online. The enforcement of rules and regulations on paid advertising was limited; voters' personal data were collected and processed for election purposes without their consent and in lack of legal entitlement; political communication was channeled to unregulated social media platforms without safeguards in place on fair media coverage. Moreover, digital content production and dissemination on social media exposed citizens to disinformation, including propaganda-driven falsified news. These implications fundamentally challenged the established institutions and principles of regulation of election communications [1] and interfered with democracy in distorting public and informed discourse of the electorate. The erosion of the watchdog-function of traditional media and a general loss in trust in such media accompanied this process.

The combined effects of these changes led to the stage of information disorder [2], making possible the spread of false and/or harmful information on an unprecedented scale without effective control or countering. This was reached as a consequent change in media consumption practices with social media becoming one of the primary sources of news across the world [3]. Social media platform operators, a type of internet intermediary,[1] give access to and host content, facilitating its creation and sharing among their virtual networks and communities. Such platform operators acquired control over the flow, availability, findability and accessibility of information and other content online whereby users "discover" content rather than search for specific information. By now, a serious shift in the influence of internet-based channels of electoral communication has reached a tipping point in terms of immediacy and power [4] and dominance [5]. Citizens thus depend to a large extent on

---

[1] The term 'internet intermediaries' refers to the operators of online media platforms, of search engines, social networks and app stores [15]. According to the Council of Europe's Recommendation CM/Rec(2018)2 on the roles and responsibilities of internet intermediaries, these players facilitate interactions on the internet between natural and legal persons by offering and performing a variety of functions and services. Some connect users to the internet, enable the processing of information and data, or host web-based services, including for user-generated content. Others aggregate information and enable searches; they give access to, host and index content and services designed and/or operated by third parties. Some facilitate the sale of goods and services, including audio-visual services, and enable other commercial transactions, including payments.

the social platforms' content moderation and amplification policies, and the algorithms designed for maximum engagement and exploitation of network effects. It is this unexplored context within which the deeply rooted, but newly re-loaded nature of human communication plays out. People are more likely to share untrue news especially if they were to trigger emotions. There is an agreement in the academic community that the spread of misinformation was not to be blamed on algorithms [6] or robots, but on humans who were eager to spread it [7]. And this vulnerability served the aims of many acting with the intent of harmdoing.

Governments, the military and political parties engaged cyber troops committed to manipulating public opinion over social media benefitting such communicative patterns. Organized interventions emerged first in 2010 and affected at least 30 countries by now [8–9]. Social media platforms and search engines [10] were the main targets of manipulations potentially skewing the election results in favor of a particular political option. Meanwhile, these incidents were only partially countered by the media. News consumption via social media cut out to a large extent journalism from its established gatekeeper position supported by editorial practices, ethical obligations and regulatory frameworks. Also, policy-makers, governments and civil society alike had to face the reality of their limited potential enforcing existing laws on electoral campaigns and regulations of political advertising on the internet across jurisdictions. This environment potentially undermines the exercise of the right to free elections and creates considerable risks to the functioning of a democratic system.

2 The positive obligations of the State ensuring the right to free elections: what role for public scrutiny and which measures to apply?

Within Europe, under the Convention for the Protection of Human Rights and Fundamental Freedoms as interpreted by the European Court of Human Rights, States have an obligation to secure the right to free elections enshrined in Article 3 of Protocol No. 1 to the Convention. The right to free elections incorporates the right to vote and the right to stand for election. Moreover, it also entails a positive obligation of the States to ensure conditions under which people can freely form and express their opinions and choose their representatives which is of utmost relevance to the (un)disrupted communicative context of elections. Furthermore, the right to freedom of expression (Article 10) and of election are intertwined as reaffirmed by the Court in stating, that "free elections and freedom of expression, particularly freedom of political debate, together form the bedrock of any democratic system".[2] We should then consider

---

[2] Bowman v the United Kingdom App. no. 24839/94 (ECtHR, 19 February 1998), para 42.

what necessary and possible steps are to be taken in safeguarding a democratic electorate in the age of information disorder.

2.1 Legislative interventions by the State and regulatory oversight

After a decade of liability by 'safe harbors'[3] provided to intermediaries all around the world, the policy discourse shifted to 'intermediary responsibility' along with an overall move towards incentivizing intermediaries private ordering online [11]. There is a wide consensus on the limits of such responsibility: platform providers should not be responsible for third-party content but for administering their platform rules [12] thus securing a safe and undistorted sphere to public debate. This duty would entail inter alia protection of users' personal data and of privacy and provision of non-disturbing channels to receive and impart information. Depending on national contexts this is to trigger legislative and regulatory interventions and new approaches to public scrutiny. The revision of rules and regulations on political advertising is of priority here. The equal and fair access of political parties to campaign through social media requires updating of broadcasting quotas and the introduction of new measures covering internetbased media. Campaign spending limits and sources of funding are to be effectively enforced with the broadening scope of communication channels covered by the relevant legislation and ensuring the monitoring capacities of national election bodies. Backstop options, such as immediate and effective intervention by public authorities, and the judiciary in case of breach of the law are of vital importance. The newly adopted French Bill on Combating the manipulation of information[4] is the first legislative example in this direction.

Protection of personal data of the electorate from misuse of microtargeting is the next area of public action. The fine-tuning of applicable laws according to national context should focus on enforceability. Within European Union member states the General Data Protection Regulation (GDPR) creates obligations on social media companies as joint data controllers to process personal data lawfully, fairly and transparently. However, the monitoring and enforcement competences of national data protection authorities needs further legislative backup and robust capacity enhancement.

The dissemination of disinformation and propaganda on online media platforms needs careful and narrowly tailored legislative design accompanied

---

[3] In the US laws such as Section 512 of the US Digital Millennium Copyright Act (DMCA) and Section 230 of the US Communications Decency Act (CDA Section 230), while in the European Union (EU) the E-Commerce Directive were to ensure exemptions to intermediaries from liability to third party user generated content.

[4] Loi du 29 juillet 1881 sur la liberté de la presse.

with vigorous regulatory oversight. Any laws adopted need to comply with international, European and national standards on freedom of expression which severely limit intervention options. Moreover, tempting solutions of the 'privatization of censorship' with general content monitoring obligations put on platform providers or outsourcing law enforcement to those operators, should not to be followed. The first law in force in Germany against dissemination of hate speech, of propaganda and of terrorist content[5] since 2018 that has left enforcement to social networks without in-depth public or judiciary control needs to be critically evaluated and its impact assessed. The newly published proposals on national legislative actions in the UK (UK Governments' Online Harms White Paper – April 2019)[6] or in in France (Interim Government Report May 2019)[7] should reflect on such assessments avoiding the incorporation of rules with detrimental effects.

2.2 Responsibility of platform providers and self-regulation

Online media platform providers came under various political and legislative pressure since the 2016 US and UK election (referendum) incidents. They have had to commit themselves to a new era of public enquiry. At the European Parliamentary hearing Mark Zuckerberg also admitted the need for regulation[8]. Hatred online and disrupted election procedures topped the political agenda, so online media platforms have adhered to selfregulatory measures

---

[5] Germany adopted in 2017 the Network Enforcement Act (Netzdurchsetzunggesetz, NetzDG) on setting reporting and removal requirements on social networks with regards to unlawful content. France passed a new law (LOI n° 2018-1202 du 22 décembre 2018 relative à la lutte contre la manipulation de l'information) at the end of 2018 on removal of "fake news" during election campaigns.

[6] See at https://www.gov.uk/government/consultations/online-harms-white-paper.

[7] Creating a French framework to make social media platforms more accountable: Acting in France with a European visionInterim mission report "Regulation of social networks – Facebook experiment" Submitted to the French Secretary of State for Digital Affairs May 2019.

[8] "I don't think the question is whether or not there should be regulation. I think the question is what is the right regulation … The important thing is to get this right," (Mark Zuckerberg at the EP hearing on 22 May 2018, see at http://www.europarl.europa.eu/news/en/press-room/20180522IPR04024/mark-zuckerberg-meeting-with-european-parliament-leaderstoday).

at least within the EU. First on combatting hate speech online[9] and next on countering election disorders. The Code of Practice on Disinformation[10] was to address legitimate calls to accountability in terms of enhancing transparency of spending for political advertising and shifting revenue streams away from sources of propaganda and disinformation.

This self-regulatory effort is in place since September 2018 and was to prevent interventions during the May 2019 European Parliamentary elections. The commitments made by the signatories focused on advert placements and avoiding the promotion of websites or adverts that spread disinformation; on clearly distinguished management of political and issue-based advertising from editorial content including transparency on sponsored content; on service integrity tackling fake accounts and improving transparency around the use of bots; and generally empowering users by making it easier to find trustworthy and diverse sources of news. In order to monitor progress, the European Commission has received monthly reports[11] on actions taken towards implementation of the commitments on electoral integrity. The reports indeed showcased several efforts made by platform providers on preventing election intrusions, and generally reducing disinformation. Yet, the true impact of such actions needs further analyses and independent assessment, especially with regards to potential chilling effects on communication.[12] Also, critics expressed concern about the lack of indicators while the Code was adopted;[13] measurable results need to be re-addressed for truthful evaluation of the self-regulatory regime.

---

[9] To prevent and counter the spread of illegal hate speech online, in May 2016, the Commission agreed with Facebook, Microsoft, Twitter and YouTube a "Code of conduct on countering illegal hate speech online". See at https://ec.europa.eu /info/policies/justice-and-fundamental-rights/combatting-discrimination /racism-and-xenophobia/countering-illegal-hate-speech-online_en.

[10] The Code of Practice on Disinformation as enshrined by the Communication from the Commission on tackling online disinformation: a European Approach. Brussels, 26.4.2018 COM(2018) 236 final. Signatories include some of the largest platform providers, such as Facebook, Google, Twitter, and Mozilla.

[11] See at https://ec.europa.eu/digital-single-market/en/news/fourth-intermediate -results-eu-code-practice-against-disinformation.

[12] It remained unclear on what accounts and according which standards content had been identified as "disinformation", nor due process guarantees were adopted ensuring appeal against such decisions.

[13] See the comments of the Sounding Board on the Code of Practice stressing that the Code "contains no common approach, no clear and meaningful commitments, no measurable objectives or KPIs, hence no possibility to monitor process, and no compliance or enforcement tool: it is by no means self-regulation, and therefore the Platforms, despite their efforts, have

Furthermore, meaningful civil society initiatives emerged such as the Global Disinformation Index to reduce disinformation. with a focus on the ad-tech industry[14] or the FactCheckEU of 19 European media outlets from 13 countries.[15] The contribution of such schemes to the policy debate needs to be assessed. The structural and de facto limitations of self-regulation as an effective tool to protect citizens' and of human rights should additionally inform the debate. The well-founded arguments of policy scholars on the need for critical study of self-(solo-)regulatory mechanisms [13] as well as detailed election media monitoring data analyses[16] are to guide such efforts.

Arguably the positive obligations of the State in ensuring the enjoyment of the right to free elections implies the enforcement of obligations imposed on platforms should not be left at the discretion of their providers. The representation of the public interest necessitates active involvement of public actors, such as regulators and the judiciary along with civic engagement. The securement of human rights, the balancing of freedom of expression with harm assessment needs to imply checks and balances fundamental in democratic contexts.

3 Further discussion

However, the extent and the manner of public interest involvement are neither straightforward, nor tested. There are no best or worst cases to be consulted. Previous regulatory models and organizational arrangements are as much restricting as they are enabling the creation of future scenarios. It is therefore the challenge for policy-makers, to academia and to civil society to cooperate and co-create an enabling environment safeguarding the basic tenets of democracy. Lessons are to be learned with an interdisciplinary approach and across sectors on the necessary skills and competencies [14], to methodological as well as logistical matters to such involvement. Collaborative and flexible

---

not delivered a Code of Practice." at https://ec.europa.eu/newsroom/dae /document.cfm?doc_id=54456.

[14] See at https://disinformationindex.org/wp-content/uploads/2019/05/GDI _Report_Screen_AW2.pdf.

[15] See at https://factcheckeu.info/en/.

[16] The upcoming elections in Ukraine in July 2019 could serve as a testbed for such research. Since the 2019 Presidential elections were already subject to high level international observations (see e.g. Council of Europe reports at https://www.coe.int/en/web/kyiv/-/which-candidates-do-ukrainian-media -favour-results-of-media-monitoring) with transparent methodological foundations (see at http://www.cje.org.ua/sites/default/files/library/FIN_ENG _Media%20Monitoring%20Methodology_Ukraine.pdf) it is to be expected that the next electoral process would also provide in-depth data for independent analyses.

intervention tools are to be developed with an overall participatory attitude. The globality, the pace and the rapidity of the environment under oversight requests responsible and responsive collaboration of all stakeholders involved.

References

1. Tambini, D.: Social Media Power and Election Legitimacy. In D. Tambini & M. Moore, Digital dominance: the power of Google, Amazon, Facebook, and Apple (pp. 265–293). Oxford University Press, New York (2018).
2. Wardle, C., & Derakhshan, H.: Information disorder: Toward an inter-disciplinary framework for research and policy making (No. REF. 162317GBR). Council of Europe, http://edoc.coe.int/en/media/7495 -information-disorder-toward-an-interdisciplinary-framework-for -research-and-policy-making.html, Strasbourg (2017).
3. Reuters Institute: Digital News Report 2019, https://reutersinstitute.politics .ox.ac.uk/sites/default/files/2019-06/DNR_2019_FINAL_0.pdf (2019).
4. Plaizier, C.: Micro-targeting Consent – A human rights perspective on paid political advertising on social media. University of Amsterdam, Amsterdam (2018).
5. Tambini, D.: Internet and electoral campaigns - Study on the use of internet in electoral campaigns – Council of Europe study, DGI(2017)11. Council of Europe Committee of experts on media pluralism and transparency of media ownership (MSI-MED), http://edoc.coe.int/en/internet/7614 -internet-and-electoral-campaigns-study-on-the-use-of-internet-in -electoral-campaigns.html, Strasbourg (2017).
6. Lazer, D. M. J., Baum, M. A., Benkler, Y., Berinsky, A. J., Greenhill, K. M., Menczer, F., … Zittrain, J. L.: The science of fake news. Science, 359(6380), 1094–1096 (2018).
7. Vosoughi, S., Roy, D., & Aral, S.: The spread of true and false news online. Science, 359(6380), 1146–1151 (2018).
8. Bradshaw, S., & Howard, P. N.: Troops, Trolls and Troublemakers: A Global Inventory of Organized Social Media Manipulation (No. Working paper no. 2017.12). Computational Propaganda Research Project by the Oxford Internet Institute, http://comprop.oii.ox.ac.uk/wp-content/uploads/sites /89/2017/07/Troops-Trolls-and-Troublemakers.pdf, Oxford (2017).
9. Freedom House: Freedom on the Net 2018: The Rise of Digital Authoritar-ianism, https://freedomhouse.org/report/freedom-net/freedom-net-2018 /rise-digital-authoritarianism (2018).
10. Epstein, R., & Robertson, R. E.: The search engine manipulation effect (SEME) and its possible impact on the outcomes of elections. Proceedings of the National Academy of Sciences, 112(33), E4512–E4521 (2015).

11. Frosio, G. F.: Why keep a dog and bark yourself? From intermediary liability to responsibility. International Journal of Law and Information Technology, 26(1), 1–33. (2017).

12. Bayer, J., Bitiukova, N., Bárd, P., Szakács, J., Alemanno, A., & Uszkiewicz, E.: Disinformation and propaganda – impact on the functioning of the rule of law in the EU and its Member States, European Parliament Policy Department for Citizens' Rights and Constitutional Affairs, Brussels (2019).

13. Milosavljević, M., & Micova, S. B.: Banning, Blocking and Boosting: Twitter's Solo-Regulation of Expression. Medijske Studije = Media Studies; 7(13), 43–58, Zagreb (2016).

14. Rozgonyi, K.: A new model for media regulation. Intermedia, 46(1), 18–23, http://iicom.org/images/iic/intermedia/april-2018/im-apr2018-vol46 -iss01_media-regulation.pdf (2018).

15. van der Noll, R., Helberger, N., & Kleinen-von Königslöw, K.: Regulating the new information intermediaries as gatekeepers of information diversity. Info, 17(6), 50–71 (2015).

Democratic Policy-making for Misinformation Detection Platforms by Git-based Principles[1]

Oul Han[*], Ipek Baris[*], Akram Sadat Hosseini[*], Sarah de Nigris[*] and Steffen Staab[*,†]

[*]Institute for Web Science and Technologies (WeST),
University of Koblenz, Germany han@uni-koblenz.de,
ibaris@uni-koblenz.de, sadathosseini@uni-koblenz.de,
denigris@uni-koblenz.de, staab@uni-koblenz.de
[†]Web and Internet Science Group (WAIS), University of Southampton,
United Kingdom

Abstract

Combating misinformation is a challenging task due to the fact that misinformation evolves in content and strategy. We describe the challenges of this task and propose a git-based framework for collaborative and open policy-making against ever-evolving misinformation. We present the setup for future test-runs where users receive tasks that conduct the core functions of git-based policy-making against misinformation.

Keywords

Co-creation · Git · policy development · open governance · misinformation

---

[1] Supported by EU-Project Co-Inform under grant agreement No 770302.

How to cite this book chapter:
Han, O., Baris, I., Hosseini, A.S., de Nigris, S. and Staab, S. 2020. Democratic Policy-making for Misinformation Detection Platforms by Git-based Principles. In: Loizides, F., Winckler, M., Chatterjee, U., Abdelnour-Nocera, J. and Parmaxi, A. (eds.) *Human Computer Interaction and Emerging Technologies: Adjunct Proceedings from the INTERACT 2019 Workshops*. Pp. 67–74. Cardiff: Cardiff University Press. DOI: https://doi.org/10.18573/book3.h. License: CC-BY 4.0.

1 Introduction

Misinformation in online media is a broad term to design deceitful content, such as disinformation (i.e. fake news), rumors, manipulated content, authentic material used in the wrong context [6]. While misinformation in general may not be driven all the time by the intent to deceit, disinformation has indeed such aim [2].

Under any form, however, misinformation undeniably poses a threat, as this content can maliciously manipulate peoples beliefs and their decisions, carrying thus a social impact. For example, misinformation about the refugee crisis affected how citizens view refugees and their attitudes towards national and European Union politics [1]. Countering the instrumental use of misinformation to manipulate the public opinion is a multifaceted challenge: policy design to this end spreads on many levels, starting from the very definition and detection of misinformation to the regulation of online platform users' behaviour. Thus, our contribution revolves around the following research question: **How to improve platform-internal management policies against misinformation that is spread by users of diverse backgrounds, which negatively affects all platform users?**

Online platforms, such as Twitter and Facebook, provide, indeed, the natural environment for the aforementioned challenge and many, if not all, of them have already undertaken such task of policy design after having been a fertile substrate for misinformation diffusion. For example, Facebook has a section called "community standards" which lay out common policies.[2] It includes a dedicated paragraph on how they will combat the spread of false news on their platform, and lists a number of methods by which they seek better regulation. Stated among these methods are the disruption of economic incentives for spreading misinformation, using machine learning for false news detection, and integrating third-party fact-checkers. Other comparable platforms list their policies for the management of platform users and misinformation in similar format, which is the result of centralized policy-making by a closed minority of platform managers, developers, and governments.

However, this top-down approach is the dangerous Achilles' heel of such policies: We argue that, to target and effectively manage the diverse types of misinformation via democratic participation (i.e. "acts that are intended to influence the behavior of those empowered to make decisions" [5, p. 53]), the policy design process should be a decentralized and collaborative one, to allow the open inclusion of platform users, instead of being opaquely determined by a small group of experts in public or private sectors.

Thus, in this position paper, we propose a git-based framework to enable such collaborative and flexible policy-making, which we describe in Sec. 3.1. Moreover, we propose is Sec 3.3 how this framework could be tested by users, who will be given initial policies and specific tasks that relate to the further development of policies according to their wants and needs.

---

[2] https://www.facebook.com/communitystandards/false_news/.

2 Related Work

Governments and public institutions are using Git-based frameworks for open co-creation of computer code as well as codified text (laws and policies). Audrey Tang, the current Digital Minister of Taiwan and civic hacker, provides git repositories for open government tools with the call to "fork the government".[3] The NYU GovLab's Project CrowdLaw[4] seeks to involve collective intelligence in every stage of lawmaking, and mentions more than two dozen examples worldwide where governments use the Internet to involve citizens for proposing legislation, drafting bills, monitoring implementation, and supplying missing data.

Some even go further and ask: "What if anyone could write amendments to existing laws, or even entirely new laws and propose them to Congress (or lobby their Congressperson to introduce it) using pull requests?"[5] This idea is already nearly fully implemented: San Francisco laws,[6] the White House Open Data policy,[7] and government agency services[8] are forkable. These and more repositories by official government institutions around the world are listed in the Government GitHub Community.[9] 10k active government users were reported in 2014 with steep trend[10]. Studies provide user and satisfaction surveys with usage statistics that imply that git-based co-creation of textual policy (as opposed to software code) is useful for general collaboration [3–4].

In addition but also in contrast, we highlight a specific application area for git-based co-creation of textual policy *against multi-medial and multi-lingual misinformation on online platforms*. We argue that git-based co-creation of textual policies makes immediate sense for the case of platform policy for antimisinformation, because online platforms merge the application area (the Internet and its information environment) with the target of policies (online misinformation), which differs from the online co-creation of offline laws. Additionally, the national and contextual diversity of misinformation is its largest challenge and is well addressed by branching out policies across authors from various backgrounds.

In open co-creation, most likely complications are: The higher the openness, the freedom to co-create is higher, and the risk of disagreement between users

---

[3] http://g0v.asia/.

[4] http://www.thegovlab.org/project-crowdlaw.html.

[5] https://blog.abevoelker.com/gitlaw-github-for-laws-and-legal-documents-a-tourniquet-for-american-liberty/.

[6] https://github.com/SFMOCI/openlaw.

[7] https://project-open-data.cio.gov/.

[8] https://github.com/cfpb/transit_subsidy/pull/1#commits-pushed-323f076.

[9] http://government.github.com/community/.

[10] https://github.blog/2014-08-14-government-opens-up-10k-active-government-users-on-github/.

is higher regarding **a) which misinformation to regulate how** and **b) how to regulate co-creating users in the case where subjective views collide**.

3 Organizing policy-making against misinformation

Our approach proposes a decentralized and horizontal git-based framework for misinformation policy-making in an online platform. We describe functions, examples, and the testing setup.

3.1 Git-based functions

If the creation of policies does not involve platform users, policies will lag behind real misinformation, or miss blind spots that are outside the range of expertise, cultural familiarity, or linguistic barriers of a closed, centralized minority of policy-makers. Moreover, the centralization of such policy-design by a minority can pose a potential threat to the freedom of speech, as it would be in charge of discerning what is misinformation and what is not.

In this view, the native functions of git[11] allow to bypass such limitations, implementing decentralized and democratic policy-making through the following actions:

– **Version control** enables tracking changes of the project/written code, which can be a set of written misinformation management policies.
– **Push** is used for updating a project, and **pull** is used for accepting changes in a project. These functions enable developers to work collaboratively while users can develop policies with complete freedom, while remaining connected to the updated version of the original root, with the option to communicate or merge at any time.
– **Clone** copies an existing project into a freely modifiable copy of the project.

This gives flexibility to developers for working on the project in their own server. This functionality can be applied for an open and decentralized development of misinformation management policies. If clone is utilized by users from different backgrounds, the handling of misinformation can differ by culture and country's specific regulations (i.e it is likely that offensive content will be different and/or unexpected within cultures, or nations).

3.2 Example Usecase

An initial and generic example policy could be: "We inspect posts that contain hate speech against minorities". A user finds that some posts are not against

---

[11] https://git-scm.com/docs/.

minorities but are satirical (e.g. in liberal left-leaning satire), and decides that the policy needs conditions. Hence, she suggests the following revision: "We inspect posts that contain hate speech against minorities, if the hate speech is not irony". Another user still finds flaws in this formulation, because in his resident country, this sort of satire does not exist. Now, he and any other users may either suggest revisions, or develop their own version that fits their own information environments, national and cultural conflicts, or linguistic traits.[12]

The above example policy-making process starts from initial policy, then is followed by specification by user A, which is followed by further specification by user B. Additionally, user B forks the policy for further modifications that diverge from the original specifications. This entire process is facilitated by git-based principles and Github-based social interactions for deciding platform policies that manage both **misinformation content** and **user regulation** (e.g Figure 1.)

3.3 Setup of the testing environment

We provide the environment for test users by setting up a Git-based social media platform. For trials, we provide initial platform policies. Each policy has its own folder for separate development. In this framework, policies are not just written but developed. The participants of our trials are stakeholders of different backgrounds (e.g occupation, age, culture). We ask the participants to perform following actions:

– Create national versions of policies
– Creating/editing policies on main repository
– Discussion for better misinformation coverage by policies
– Clone main repository and make revision for desired policy
– Offer revised suggestions by push/pull requests
– Accept revised suggestions by moderator pull
– Discuss the role of moderator, then create a policy for moderators

A git-based framework presents the codification of policies as a collaborative coding project. In order to increase the accessibility for users to the git based framework, we rename git-specific-functions with terms that describe their policy-specific function. Table 1 shows our suggestions and maps each function to democratic effects with positive and negative implications.[13] Additional GitHub-native functions are shown that relate to graphical interfaces and user interactions.

---

[12] All policies are automated by the platform, which performs machine readable rules, such as: "In the event of a post containing a word from this list of hate speech, alert this user".

[13] https://www.opengovpartnership.org/glossary.

Fig. 1: Git-based platform where users edit and discuss misinformation policies.

Finally, we will conduct data analytics on the resulting policies and satisfaction survey on user experiences. Test runs should yield two levels of policy: **misinformation content and user management**.

1. Misinformation content
   – Which contents of misinformation and which handling actions were covered by the users?
   – Was the process of developing policies more interactive in cases of agreement or disagreement?

Table 1: Mapping the name of git-based (and GitHub-only) functions to policymaking

Git	Policy-making function	Democratic effect (positive/ negative implication)
software code moderating version control	policy moderate track-policy	transparency (information/ too much information)
blame commit merge	whose-idea contribute finalize	accountability (shared control/need for control)
clone push pull diff branch	take update accept difference localize-policy	public engagement (inclusiveness/conflicting perspectives)
GitHub-only discussion issue report	discussion suggest-policy	public engagement (discussion/failure of agree)

    – How were discussions resolved at disagreement over defining and handling misinformation?

2. User management
    – What is the best policy for electing and managing moderators?
    – What is the best policy for managing conflicting views in the process of defining policies?

4 Conclusion

This position paper proposes git-based framework for developing platform policies on misinformation in a decentralized and collaborative way. We introduce the benefits of git for misinformation policy-making for platforms, and suggest a methodology for testing the requirements. As future work, we will evaluate the outcomes by feedback rounds and conduct data analysis on users interactions.

References

1. Bartsch, M., Clau, A.: The Case of the Murdered Goats: Exploring Germany's Far-Right Rumor Mill. Spiegel Online (Jan 2016), https://www.spiegel.de /international/germany/far-right-misinformationstokes-anti-refugee -sentiment-a-1070413.html
2. Golbeck, J., Mauriello, M., Auxier, B., Bhanushali, K.H., Bonk, C., Bouzaghrane, M.A., Buntain, C., Chanduka, R., Cheakalos, P., Everett, J.B.,

et al.: Fake news vs satire: A dataset and analysis. In: Proceedings of the 10th ACM Conference on Web Science. pp. 17–21. ACM (2018)

3. Longo, J., Kelley, T.M.: Github use in public administration in canada: Early experience with a new collaboration tool. Canadian Public Administration 59(4), 598–623 (2016)

4. Mergel, I.: Open collaboration in the public sector: The case of social coding on github. Government Information Quarterly 32(4), 464–472 (2015)

5. Verba, S.: Democratic participation. The Annals of the American Academy of Political and Social Science 373(1), 53–78 (1967)

6. Wardle, C.: 6 types of misinformation circulated this election season. Columbia Journalism Review 18 (2016)

DisMiss False Information: A Value Matter

Alisson Puska[*], Lara Piccolo[†] and Roberto Pereira[*]

[*]Federal University of Parana, BR
aapuska@inf.ufpr.br; rpereira@inf.ufpr.br
[†]The Open University, UK
lara.piccolo@open.uc.uk

Abstract

The popularization of social media and the increasing consumption and dissemination of information online rise the concerns on the possible impacts of disinformation on a global scale. Although relevant progress to tackle disinformation online has been made recently, the problem seems to be still growing in space and complexity, affecting different aspects of the society, from personal relationships to entire democratic systems. In this position paper, we argue for the need to understand and approach disinformation and misinformation as a sociotechnical phenomena in cultures mediated by information and communication technology, in which both universal and specific values influence the way people experience the problem. A sociotechical perspective aware of the cultural influence can inform technical developments of user interfaces and algorithms, as well as the preparation of educational content in a more systemic and socially responsible way.

Keywords

Disinformation · Misinformation · Social media · Human-computer Interaction · Values · Culture

---

How to cite this book chapter:
Puska, A., Piccolo, L. and Pereira, R. 2020. DisMiss False Information: A Value Matter.
In: Loizides, F., Winckler, M., Chatterjee, U., Abdelnour-Nocera, J. and Parmaxi, A.
(eds.) *Human Computer Interaction and Emerging Technologies: Adjunct
Proceedings from the INTERACT 2019 Workshops.* Pp. 75–80. Cardiff: Cardiff
University Press. DOI: https://doi.org/10.18573/book3.i. License: CC-BY 4.0.

1   Disinformation and misinformation on social media

Mobile computing, social media and social application have connected people and made all sort of information available as never before. By boosting the access to information and social interactions, applications such as Facebook and WhatsApp have become key to foster digital literacy and education, including in countries where social and economic inequalities are still prominent. However, if on the one hand social media and social applications have contributed to democratize the access to information and communication technology (ICT), on the other hand they are favouring misinformation and disinformation spread, catalyzing social and cultural changes sometimes with hard and undesirable consequences.

Disinformation can be characterized as information intentionally created to trigger, mislead or generate decision errors, manipulate belief systems of individuals and deceive humans [1]. Online, disinformation is used for cognitive hacking [2], in social engineering and human-factors exploitation schemes, to persuade individuals to fall into targeted attacks like spear phishing and malware installation [3–4] or in the creation and dissemination of "false news" and hoaxes [5]. Misinformation, in turn, can be defined as misrepresented information that causes confusion and are not always intentionally created [1]. Despite the differences, both disinformation and misinformation are harmful and challenging. As a matter of simplification, in the remainder of this paper the term disinformation will refer to both.

The spread of disinformation against vaccines have reduced the results of public health programs to immunize citizens, and some diseases such as yellow fever, measles and poliomyelitis, which have been under control for decades, started infecting people again and causing deaths [10]. For example, in Brazil, India and Mexico, social applications have been used to disseminate vicious rumors that led to barbaric deaths of innocent victims [11–12] and to influence elections [12–13].

Although some progress has been made to stop disinformation spreading recently, the impact of disinformation seems to be reaching extreme levels, affecting relationships, freedom of expression in personal and professional domains, and threatening democratic systems. In this position paper, we argue that disciplinary approaches are not enough to deal with the complexity of disinformation spread and impact, and point out to the need for understanding and approaching disinformation as a sociotechnical phenomena in cultures mediated by information and communication technologies (ICTs). In ICT cultural contexts, both universal and specific values influence the way people perceive disinformation, react to it (or not), consume and spread it. Such a sociotechnical and cultural perspective can help us to deal with the problem in a systemic way, being able to design technical solutions and promote information literacy in a more socially responsible way.

2 Values and culture matter!

Different countries, regions or even social groups may have their own ways to establish communication, which includes the communication process meta-factors and how they perceive and appropriate received messages. Social media mediated communication is not apart from this sociocultural influence. Human values, social and economic conditions, educational level and different cultural traits seem to both affect and be affected by the way people use social applications to communicate with each other, produce, share and consume information, also online. Therefore, we argue that any initiative to tackle the disinformation problem must understand their consumption and dissemination as a sociotechnical phenomena in a society increasingly mediated by ICT. By a sociotechnical phenomena we mean that technical systems design, human processing capabilities, socioeconomic conditions, human values and cultural aspects must be understood and considered as intertwined to each other.

A recent social political event in Brazil related to formal education illustrates this view. Recently, Brazilian universities are suffering from funding cuts and political persecution. Political instability has caused the cuts of US$2.1 billion and the cancel of thousands masters and PhD scholarships. These policy measures were accompanied by a strong production movement and sharing of disinformation in social media, apparently with the aim of undermining social support to universities. Since Brazilian government announced funding cuts, a wave of disinformation against public universities has been flagged. According to "Aos Fatos", a monitoring tool developed at UFMG (Federal University of Minas Gerais), the sharing of nude student image in 350 WhatsApp groups monitored by the tool grew by at least 950% in 24 hours after the cuts. Most of the shared content used images and recordings to demoralize Brazilian universities and their students to support the cuts made by the government, showing naked students in random contexts, years and situations as if they were a current and common routine in universities [14–15]. In addition, title of dissertations and theses on gender and sexuality were shared without situating the content, using photos from other contexts and public, including other countries.

The same piece of information can be used to build perspectives of two opposite ideas that appeal to the subjectiveness of individual interpretation, triggering different perception and consequent behaviors on judging claims, as indicated in [7–9]. By omitting the original context in which the images were captured and by omitting or modifying details about the research, the content have a potential to deceive the reader by distorting or ignoring the intended meaning and purpose of images and pieces of research. This kind of action put in check the social media democratizing potential, promoting skepticism and outrage behaviors.

This example evidences three different dimensions that must be addressed when dealing with disinformation. The first dimension is related to people's *culture and values:* the content explored nudity going against religious values, as they are very appealing to a considerable part of the Brazilian society. In Brazil, WhatsApp groups are popular among families to get in touch and share news about their lives, jokes, etc., and have become a source for disinformation as family members, usually the older and less educated, tend to disseminate any appealing content as if it was ultimately true [13]. When the information touch something valuable for people, they seem more prone to assume the information is true as if the information carry authority per se and is beyond justification [6].

The second dimension is related to *formal education and authority*. Public universities usually have very competitive and difficult admission process for students and are not able to cope with the demand of a country with more than 200 million people. So most Brazilians have never had the opportunity to experience the environment of a university. Therefore, universities are a distant reality for the majority of Brazilians, especially the least privileged one. Therefore, people are easily influenced to believe lots of public money is being wasted by universities inefficient researches and immoral events instead of being applied for high quality education. As there is a lack of trust in formal authorities to whom people may resort to get verified information from, and as people seem to give credibility to controversial content or to content that agrees with their previous beliefs, social platforms (e.g., WhatsApp) end up becoming a source of authority that certificates the information quality itself.

The third dimension is related to *technical issues* that range from software requirements to user interface and legal norms. WhatsApp is an example of a widespread application digitally including a considerable part of population in Brazil. The application can be used in simple and cheap smartphones and is accessible to most of people, even those still not very familiar with technology. It is very easy to disseminate any content through WhatsApp. However, the application does not support any sort of verification of the information quality, as the authorship of content or history of the content in the platform. For marketing purposes, mobile carriers usually do not restrict data consumption for social media applications such as WhatsApp and Facebook, but they do charge the access to other services online. Hence, people receive unlimited content in their social media groups having no means to check the content in another source, search for additional information, or even report the content to other organization than the application itself. The soil for spreading disinformation becomes fertile!

The three dimensions mentioned above: culture and values, formal and authority, and technical issues are contextually dependent. The cultural characteristics of a people, the values they share and the beliefs they hold heavily influence the way they understand and use social media. The socioeconomic conditions of people and the formal system that regulates and guides their life also play an important role. Finally, the technical system used by people, its interface, underlying structure and algorithms will favour certain behaviours while inhibiting others depending on the cultural context they are being used.

3 Towards a Research Agenda

Existing literature in Computer Science has focusing mainly on the technical dimension of the problem paying little attention to the cultural and formal ones. Although there is no arguments against the need for technical advancements to stop disinformation spreading, starting by focusing on technical aspects in isolation may not be the most effective way. Technical advancements must be made grounded on the knowledge we gather from understanding the sociocultural context where people live, from understanding their values, preferences, needs, social norms, behavioral patterns, beliefs and demands.

Before introducing technical innovations to social groups to tackle misinformation spreading, we suggest a sociocultural contextual analysis considering, for example, whether people have access to resources and knowledge to critically evaluate pieces of information, for example, whether there are external factors or socioeconomic conditions pressuring for disseminating certain positions and intentions. In particular, investigate whether and how values and culture influence people judgement of information quality and veracity [16], which are open questions on the literature. Only starting by understanding a context and the people living in it we can grasp the particularities of their problems and design good solutions for them.

References

1. Tudjman, M. Mikelic, N. (2003). Information science: Science about information, misinformation and disinformation. Proceedings of Informing Science+ Information Technology Education, 1513–1527.
2. Cybenko, G., Giani, A., Thompson, P. (2002). Cognitive hacking: A battle for the mind. Computer, 35(8), 50–56.
3. Caputo, D. D., Pfleeger, S. L., Freeman, J. D., Johnson, M. E. (2014). Going spear phishing: Exploring embedded training and awareness. IEEE Security Privacy, 12(1), 28–38.
4. Nguyen-Vu, L., Park, J., Chau, N. T., Jung, S. (2016, January). Signing key leak detection in Google Play Store. In 2016 International Conference on Information Networking (ICOIN) (pp. 13–16). IEEE.
5. Bazan, S. (2017). A New Way to Win the War. IEEE Internet Computing, 21(4), 92–97.
6. Nickerson, R. S. (1998). Confirmation bias: A ubiquitous phenomenon in many guises. Review of general psychology, 2(2), 175–220.
7. Evans, J. S. B. (1989). Bias in human reasoning: Causes and consequences. Lawrence Erlbaum Associates, Inc.
8. Kerr, N. L., MacCoun, R. J., Kramer, G. P. (1996). Bias in judgment: Comparing individuals and groups. Psychological review, 103(4), 687.

9. Tversky, A., Kahneman, D. (1974). Judgment under uncertainty: Heuristics and biases. science, 185(4157), 1124–1131.

10. BBC, https://www.bbc.com/news/health-46387167. Last accessed May 2019

11. BBC, https://www.bbc.com/news/world-latin-america-46145986. Last accessed May 2019

12. BBC, https://www.bbc.com/news/world-asia-india-47797151. Last accessed May 2019

13. Folha, https://www1.folha.uol.com.br/amp/poder/2019/05/2-em-cada-3 - receberam-fake-news-nas-ultimas-eleicoes-aponta-pesquisa.shtml. Last accessed May 2019

14. AosFatos, https://aosfatos.org/noticias/meme-que-critica-manifestacoes-pela-educacao-usa-fotos-de-protestos-antigos/. Last accessed May 2019

15. AosFatos, https://aosfatos.org/noticias/foto-de-faixa-com-fora-bolsonaro -e-liberdade-para-lula-de-marco-nao-de-ato-pela-educacao/. Last accessed May 2019

16. Rieh, S. Y. (2002). Judgment of information quality and cognitive authority in the Web. Journal of the American society for information science and technology, 53(2), 145–161.

SECTION 3

Socially Acceptable HCI: Social Acceptability of Emerging Technologies and Novel Interaction Paradigms

On Social Acceptance of UI Intervention Mechanisms on Posting and Reading Comments on Online News

Joel Kiskola, Thomas Olsson, Heli Väätäjä,
Veikko Surakka and Mirja Ilves

Tampere University, Kalevantie 4, 33014 Tampereen yliopisto, Finland
joel.kiskola @tuni.fi, thomas.olsson @tuni.fi, heli.vaataja @tuni.fi, veikko.
surakka @tuni.fi, mirja.ilves@tuni.fi

Abstract

Issues in the discussion culture in social media call for new approaches to improve, for example, the practices of commenting online news articles or similar public content. Our ongoing research aims to design and develop user interface mechanisms that could automatically intervene the reading or commenting experience in order to enhance emotional reflection and thus improve online behavior. While this aim might seem desirable, it is a conundrum where the solutions need to carefully balance various requirements and values. For example, automatic moderation of the messages might violate the fundamental right to freedom of opinion, and computationally tampering the intimate act of human communication might feel inappropriate. This paper discusses various issues from the perspectives of social acceptance and ethics by presenting three seemingly effective, yet problematic design explorations. Following the ideology of critical design, we contemplate how the design conventions in social media could be changed without introducing adverse behavioral consequences.

How to cite this book chapter:
Kiskola, J., Olsson, T., Väätäjä, H., Surakka, V. and Ilves, M. 2020. On Social Acceptance
of UI Intervention Mechanisms on Posting and Reading Comments on Online
News. In: Loizides, F., Winckler, M., Chatterjee, U., Abdelnour-Nocera, J. and
Parmaxi, A. (eds.) *Human Computer Interaction and Emerging Technologies:
Adjunct Proceedings from the INTERACT 2019 Workshops*. Pp. 83–90. Cardiff:
Cardiff University Press. DOI: https://doi.org/10.18573/book3.j. License: CC-BY 4.0.

Keywords

Emotion Regulation · Critical Design · Social Media

1 Introduction

In both the academic community and public discourse, we have recently seen heated discussions on how the various services have detrimentally affected the communication culture. Issues like social media rage, hate speech [5] cyberbullying, and increased polarization of the opinion sphere [6] could be considered as side effects of using digital media as the channel for public discourse and opinion exchange. However, the processes and reasons behind these symptoms are much deeper than people misbehaving in such digital communication services.

We suggest that the symptoms result from processes related to emotions and emotion regulation. The ability to regulate one's emotions and mood is a necessity practically for every area of life [4] but has been found to be challenging in technology-mediated textual communication. Emotions are widely expressed in textual format in digital media environments, such as social media services, online communities, and commenting threads of journalistic content, but it has been argued that the lack of nonverbal cues in textual communication deteriorates the ability to control emotions and empathize with other people [10]. Thus, we should better understand how emotions actually function in such communication and develop mechanisms that help individuals to regulate emotions.

Emotion processes operate largely unconsciously. An example of this is the case of emotional mimicry. People tend to react automatically to other people's emotion expression stimuli so that when we see or hear others' expressions of joy or anger, for example, we tend to mimic them without being conscious of what we saw or heard [3–8]. Additionally, visually presented emotional words have been shown to evoke emotions. In digital media environments, it has been found that the conversation context, mood and other contextual factors can increase the probability of anyone writing uncivil comments [2].

Recent evidence shows that *affect labelling* (e.g., turning emotional cues into words) can attenuate emotional experiences and thus be one form of emotion regulation. Studies have shown that affect labelling does have significant effects on emotion related physiology, behavioral responding, and experiences. This is called as implicit emotion regulation because it does not require conscious intent to regulate emotional experience [9]. This type of process could be a potential option for unobtrusive emotion regulation in social media.

This challenging application area and research goal calls for critical thinking and systematic analysis of the existing UI mechanisms in computer-mediated communication. Consequently, we utilize *critical design* [1], which applies knowledge from social sciences and humanities for reflective design of artefacts, foregrounding the ethics of design practice, revealing potentially hidden agendas and values, and exploring alternative design values. Critical design has been argued to allow better understanding and shaping technologies that can lead to negative outcomes. Design artefacts are used to make consumers more critical about "how their lives are mediated by assumptions, values, ideologies, and behavioral norms inscribed in designs" [1].

Having said that, applying critical design to improve online discussion culture necessitates a careful analysis of the possible behavioral consequences of the developed UI mechanisms and how people could appropriate them in various ways, some of which might be detrimental. This position paper contributes a critical analysis from the viewpoint of social acceptance with regard to three preliminary and speculative concept designs. Rather than trying to theorize or define the notion of social acceptance, this paper identifies domain-specific risks and issues that could help doing so at the workshop.

2 Designs and Critique

2.1 On the Design Space/Design Principles

We subscribe to the idea of implicit *affect labelling* by Torre & Lieberman [9], that is, making the emotionally loaded elements in a message more explicit. Our designs for this expect a future where we have advanced methods of natural language processing and human-labeled training data for supervised machine learning.

These designs are three handpicked examples out of 50+ ideas, included here because they elicit different kinds of social acceptance issues. However, the designs share the principle that affect labelling is meant to be purely personal and not visible to others (other, remote users of the platform).

2.2 Design 1: Virtual Audience

In the Virtual Audience design, the user intends to read the comments to an article when they see an array of abstract, yet animated anthropomorphic figures with various facial expressions (see Fig. 1 left side). The facial expressions represent the emotional reactions present in the discussion. In addition, when one starts to write a comment, a similar visualization of the anticipated reactions (of different kinds of people) begins to form (see Fig. 1 right side).

The design attempts to solve the practical problem that to understand how people feel about an article and the comments requires carefully reading the comments. The emotional reactions are summarized to give a sense of a

Fig. 1: Left: A virtual audience showing emotional reactions present in the discussion would appear on top of the comment section. Right: Anticipated reactions to user's writing.

live audience. The more specific critical design principles that the design utilizes include:

• Humanization of text that could otherwise seem impersonal.
• Social pressure: people generally want to produce positive emotions in others.
• People are wired to look at human faces.
• Ambiguity in how the facial expressions come about.
• Exaggeration of facial expressions and contrasts between the expressions.
• Gentle satire: imitating opposite emotional reactions to texts, to ridicule people.

The design introduces several potential issues of social acceptability and ethics. (1) The virtual audience may feel like an actual audience and this may evoke more real life like normative behavior in the digital environment. (2) The virtual audience may highlight or greatly increase the impact of the first comments; hence, the first commenters may feel that their comments are given a disproportionate amount of attention by the virtual audience. (3) Users might start to optimize their comments to reach positive audience reactions; alternatively, some users might be provoked to opposite behavior. (4) The virtual audience, being an easily observable UI element, may enable collocated people to judge the quality of a commenter's writing. (5) The virtual audience might become a key element of the public image of a certain digital platform or news broadcaster, which might contradict with how they want to be seen. Furthermore, some commenters might be considered as obedient or disobedient, affecting their public image.

2.3 Design 2: Emotion Symbols

The Emotion Symbols design mimics the convention of giving certain reactions to posts, but approaches this by explicating one's emotional reaction to a message. While Fig. 2 displays only three types of labels (a general positive reaction, "this is explosive" and "loving this"), the vocabulary of labels could be very

Fig. 2: Left: Users rate comments for their emotional qualities and the system calculates percentages of ratings for comment threads and individual comments. Right: The system predicts what kind of emotional reactions the comment would elicit.

broad. The users can rate the comments by clicking the symbols. In addition, when a user is writing a comment, they will see the symbols and percentages change based on what they write, according to the system's prediction on what kind of emotional reactions the comment would elicit.

The design attempts to solve the problem that there is no explicit information on the emotional content of the comments. It proposes to explicate the emotional quality of each comment and comment thread in a quantified way to help to select which comments or threads to read. Other principles that the design utilizes include:

- Playfulness: the symbols chosen to represent emotions (e.g., hearts and bombs) are visually playful.
- Gamification: e.g., users may try to get hearts or bombs.
- Ambiguity: leaving room for interpretation on what contributes to the percentages, which can encourage people to reflect on the messages they create.

The social acceptability and ethical issues include, for example, the following. **(1)** The commenter may feel that this design increases the risk that they will be bullied. Getting "bombed" or assigning other labels introduces new mechanisms of giving feedback, which might affect self-esteem. **(2)** Related to quantification, some may find it questionable that the nuanced and highly subjective semantics in their comments are reduced into numbers. As Lucy Suchman warns, any form of categorizing bears the risk of politicizing, with which minds can be formed and opinions made [7]. **(3)** While writing, it can feel awkward that an algorithm defines the *value* of the comment. **(4)** Related to the previous, some users may try to "game the system" and try to maximize or minimize the metrics. This provides a new potential reason for writing comments, which undermines the primary communicative purposes of writing comments.

2.4 Design 3: Regretting one's choice of words

In the Regret design, user 1 has just published a comment and they are looking at it. Then they see a notification on their comment that allows regretting one's words (see Fig. 3, left). Alternatively, the user 1 may regret after seeing what kind of a mess their comment caused. It is noteworthy that only the user sees the notification and only after clicking the regret button the other users see this as an extra label (Fig. 3, right).

The design attempts to solve the problem that there are no quick and easy ways for a commenter to regret what they wrote or how they placed their words; editing a published comment requires more skill and effort, and deleting one's comment entirely might not be desirable either. In other words, the design introduces a light-weight way for a user to notify others that they are not happy with their comment either, for example, to help resolving heated discussions. More specific principles include:

- Surprise: if the user does not realize their comment is controversial, notification by the system will surprise them. Moreover, regretting can be surprising to other users.
- Implying that messages should not be read too literally.
- Drama: it can be thought to be dramatic when someone regrets what they said.
- Social conventions: regretting is a universal behavioral pattern related to forgiveness.
- Gamification: the design adds cost-benefit calculation to the discussion, making it more game-like; and the regret notification is "armor" against criticism.

The potential social acceptability and ethical issues include the following. (1) Users may consider regretting like this to be too easy to be counted as real regretting. (2) Some users might start writing more thoughtlessly than before, thinking, "you can regret it later, right?" The discussion might start resembling more synchronic communication, however, without the benefits of the multimodal face-to-face channel. (3) The system might feel patronizing and awkward in some cases (presuming it lacks "common sense" and does not recognize that strong language is sometimes ok).

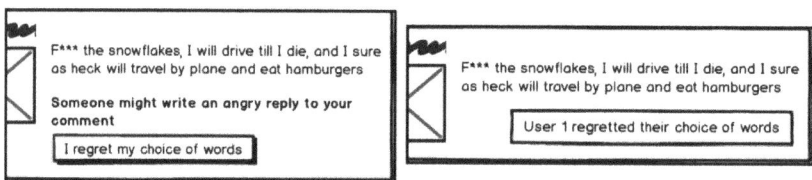

Fig. 3: Left: User is given a chance to regret one's choice of words after publishing a seemingly uncivil comment. Right: User 2 sees a note that user 1 has regretted their words.

3 Discussion and Conclusions

We presented work-in-progress on UI designs that aim to improve emotional reflection in social media discussions. While our intention is to create ethically sustainable designs and to avoid compromising social acceptance, this preliminary analysis implies that identifying a design that is at the same time effective and sustainable is challenging. Each design has their pros and cons. We would gladly continue the discussion on problematizing the existing UI mechanisms in social media and the presented designs. A more thorough analysis of the potential ramifications could be implemented by, for example, reflecting on certain items in the human rights declaration by the United Nations (e.g., freedom of opinion and expression, peaceful assembly, free participation in cultural life). Various moral philosophical doctrines (e.g., starting all the way from Nichomachean Ethics by Aristotle, and other virtue ethics) would also provide insightful viewpoints. That said, while Critical Design is all about questioning various conventions, we argue that especially in this kind of application area something that should *not* be deliberately twisted are the ethical principles—they also shape people's perceptions of what kind of technology is acceptable.

References

1. Bardzell, J., & Bardzell, S. (2013). What is "critical" about critical design? Proc. of CHI '13. ACM, New York, NY, USA, 3297–3306.
2. Cheng, J., Bernstein, M., Danescu-Niculescu-Mizil, C., & Leskovec, J. (2017). Anyone can become a troll: Causes of trolling behavior in online discussions. In CSCW 2017, February 25–March 1, 2017, Portland, OR, USA.
3. Fischer, A., & Hess, U. (2017). Mimicking emotions. Current opinion in psychology, 17, 151–155.
4. Gross, J.J. (1998). The Emerging Field of Emotion Regulation: An Integrative Review. Review of General Psychology, 2, 271–299.
5. Guiora, A., & Park, E.A. (2017). Hate speech on social media. Philosophia, 45(3), 957–971.
6. Nelimarkka, M., Laaksonen, S.M., & Semaan, B. (2018). Social media is polarized, social media is polarized: towards a new design agenda for mitigating polarization. In Proceedings of the ACM Conference on Design Interactive Systems (DIS'18).
7. Suchman, L. (1993) Do Categories Have Politics? The language/action perspective reconsidered. Proc. of ECSCW '93. Springer, Dordrecht
8. Surakka, V., & Hietanen, J.K. (1998). Facial and emotional reactions to Duchenne and nonDuchenne smiles. International Journal of Psychophysiology, 29 (1), 23–33.

9. Torre, J.B., Lieberman, M.D. (2018) Putting Feelings Into Words: Affect Labelling as Implicit Emotion Regulation. Emotion Review, 10, 116–124.
10. Walther, J.B. (1993). Impression development in computer-mediated interaction. Western Journal of Communication (includes Communication Reports), 57(4), 381–398.

What Smartphones, Ethnomethodology, and Bystander Inaccessibility Can Teach Us About Better Design?

Eerik Mantere

Tampere University, Kalevantie 4, 33100 Tampere, Finland
Université de Bordeaux, 3 ter Place de la Victoire, 33076 Bordeaux, France
emantere@u-bordeaux.fr

Abstract

Smartphones, the ubiquitous mobile screens now normal parts of everyday social situations, have created a kind of ongoing natural experiment for social scientists. According to Garfinkel's ethnomethodology social action gets its meaning not only from its content but also through its context. Mobility, small screen size, and the habitual way of using smartphones ensure that, while offering the biggest variety of activities for the user, in comparison to other everyday items, smartphones offer the least cues to bystanders on what the user is actually doing and how long it might take. This 'bystander inaccessibility' handicaps shared understanding of the social context that the user and collocated others find themselves in. Added considerations and interactive effort in managing the situation is therefore required. Future design needs to relate to this basic building block of collocated interaction to not be met with discontent.

Keywords

Smartphones · Ethnomethodology · Collocated Interaction

How to cite this book chapter:

Mantere, E. 2020. What Smartphones, Ethnomethodology, and Bystander Inaccessibility Can Teach Us About Better Design? In: Loizides, F., Winckler, M., Chatterjee, U., Abdelnour-Nocera, J. and Parmaxi, A. (eds.) *Human Computer Interaction and Emerging Technologies: Adjunct Proceedings from the INTERACT 2019 Workshops.* Pp. 91–100. Cardiff: Cardiff University Press. DOI: https://doi.org/10.18573/book3.k. License: CC-BY 4.0.

1 Introduction and Background

In United States 81% owns a smartphone [1] and they are routinely used in the presence of others. How this impacts relationships with collocated others regularly hits the headlines [2–3]. Previous research suggests various negative effects. Smartphone use can be distracting and undermine the benefits of social interactions [4], which have previously found to be so crucial to psychological well-being [5]. Although often aiming for connection with distant others, interactions online do not provide the same sense of social support as collocated interactions [6]. Being distracted in collocated interactions due to smartphone use therefore seems like an ill-chosen trade-off.

An Australian dictionary jumped on the idea by coming up with a new word for the phenomenon. "Phubbing" is defined at their marketing campaign's website site as "the *act of snubbing someone in a social setting by looking at your phone instead of paying* attention" [7]. Researchers got on board with the term and phubbing has since been found to reduce communication quality and relationship satisfaction by reducing the feelings of belongingness and positive affect [8], make both phubbers and the phubbed to be more likely to see phubbing as an inevitable social norm [9], and be thought of as 'bad' by young people, even if they are doing it themselves [10]. "Partner phubbing" has further been found to reduce relationship satisfaction by creating conflicts over cell phone use [11] and cause depression in China for couples married more than seven years [12]. A validated scale to measure phubbing has also been developed [13] and the capacity to predict phubbing risk has been pursued by forming a model constituting of communication disturbances and phone obsession [14]. One should not then be surprised then that an article in the New York Times portrayed phubbing as if the term was developed by psychologists [15].

Not wanting to discredit the previous work, three points should be noted of their similar methodologies and the gap they fail to fill. First, though they study the social situation, they do not directly describe it, but rather produce second level constructs of it [16]. Research participants have produced numeric or verbal accounts of imagined or previously lived situations. These are then used to make a scientific account—now two levels distanced from the phenomenon they aim to depict. Second, when directly observing social situations, they rely on *a priori* chosen qualities of interaction. Researchers observing social behavior then code it in regard to these qualities in order to use them as indicators in seeking relevance between them and general social categories like age or gender [25]. Third, none of them spring from a theoretical understanding of social action. Harold Garfinkel pointed out the problems of theories that rely on internalization of society's norms and found ethnomethodology (EM) to study how people themselves in everyday situations construct meaning and make and interpret social typifications as relevant. EM has quickly gained more and more ground as *the* theory of social action and has given birth to conversation analysis (CA), now considered the principal way to study verbal and nonverbal interaction alike [16–20].

Though EM/CA literature covers a wide range of interactive contexts, research on spontaneous individual smartphone use in social situation is practically non-existent. One of the most closely related EM/CA studies looked at how smartphone use while driving is interleaved with traffic light stops. Users were looking for moments when the affordances of the phone's interface co-constructed transition relevant places with the activities of the user. In these moments a possible shift in orientation between smartphone use and other activities is sequentially made most available. The regularity in which the interface makes these moments possible was considered a central theme in organizing multiactivity with smartphone use and other concurrent activities [21]. Another study of using public transport found gaze shifts away from the phone to be organized in relation to the sequential progression of the activity with the device. Beginning stages of phone use were suggested to be especially sequentially engaging but the methodology used and the level of granularity of the analyzes lacked the possibility to describe the interactive practices of in their sequential contexts [22].

A study focusing on the use of a map applications found people sequentially organizing their phone use with actions like unilateral stopping, turning, and restarting, while walking together in public places. Again, phone use was found to have its own sequential progression which, then was interleaved with that of the concurrent social activities of the physical environment [23]. The most relevant EM/CA work on smartphone use and collocated interaction addresses phone use in pubs [24]. It does introduce and explore the topic but does not exhaust neither a single episode of interaction, nor describe any putative practice taking place in various interactions, to a satisfactory degree from the point of view of CA. Similarly, it does not make real use of the theoretical offer of EM. I encourage looking at smartphone use in social situation with a viewpoint rooted in EM, and adding in CA analysis, in order to understand how phone use may be constructed as unacceptable, and to find inspiration for more socially acceptable design.

2 Social Theory and Indexicality

Goffman [25] defined the social situation as an *"environment of mutual monitoring possibilities, anywhere within which an individual will find himself accessible to the naked senses of all others who are 'present,' and similarly find them accessible to him."* All speaking and gesturing in face-to-face interaction takes place in the social situation and he emphasized the importance of the physical setting in any analysis of them. Even more than Goffman, Harold Garfinkel saw the context of interaction to be central in what the interaction itself means [16–18]. Let us consider the following example:

I'm sorry

The phrase seems to clearly convey an apology. We might imagine that the person uttering the words feels regretful and elucidate how each of the words, I – am – sorry, convey something that together constitute an apology. We might reflect on how it differs from the more casual "sorry 'bout that", and we might even say that this apologizing seems humble and empathetic. But what if we added a context:

I got my diploma from the University of Honolulu

I'm sorry

Now the phrase "I'm sorry" doesn't seem so kind. This example shows how the same practice of "apologizing" can be used to do different things—one of them teasing. As the immediate social context changes, the meaning of the action changes too. Before Garfinkel, 'indexicality' was considered as a character only of words like "this", "here" or "now"—words that point, or index, a context in acquiring their meaning. Garfinkel planned a series of breaching experiments to claim that actually all human action is understood as indexing the context it takes place in. If people encounter behavior that is not designed in relation to the commonly shared situation, they feel awkward and severely challenged in knowing how to proceed. Whatever is done, through words or otherwise, always gets interpreted through what is seen as the *shared understanding* of the situation that the action takes place in [16–18].

Garfinkel further proposed that this understanding was not only his, but people conducting their everyday lives actually orient to each other as *accountable* in entering social situations with the assumption that it is common knowledge [18]. This knowledge is not rooted in detached reflection of the deep nature of social action. He does not suggest that all members of society passed sleepless nights in understanding the core concepts of ethnomethodology. Rather, in interacting with one another, a general thesis of interchangeability of perspectives is at work. To put it simply, people assume that what they see as relevant in a situation is seen relevant by others in the same situation. This is crucial for being able to trust to the shared understanding of the social situation as "good enough" for interaction to be meaningful. If we could not trust that we and another person have at least "good enough" match in understanding what is going on, we could not trust that anything we say or do in the situation would be understood as we would like it to be understood.

3 Bystander Inaccessibility

The participants of a social situation who start to use a smartphone, to a large extent stop giving hints of the goals of their actions to collocated others. Others can less often than is the case with other devices, infer from the posture and movements of the user, or from the shape and state of the smartphone, what the user is currently doing. The lack of visual and auditive cues to the bystander, the mobility of the device, bigger amount of variation in the types of actions possibilitie, than is the case with any other device, and the varied temporal organizations of the different smartphone activities are responsible of keeping some crucial aspects about the smartphone user's activity hidden to the person in their immediate vicinity:

I. Phase of action (e.g. preparatory phase, execution phase, or being already close to terminating the action)

II. Category of action (e.g. entertainment, work, information seeking, or communication)

Not knowing what the activity of the smartphone user is, the other participants in the social situation are also in the dark about the "good enough" knowledge about nature of the situation as a whole. I call this bystander inaccessibility (BI). Imagine you want to ask something mundane of your partner, let's say, if she has gotten the mail. The mailbox is just outside, and you could easily check it yourself, but you would prefer not getting out of the house in vain. You see your partner sitting on the sofa, absorbed in their phone. Now if you would know that they are responding to an important work email, you might leave them alone and check the mail yourself. But if they were just scrolling a friend's Facebook feed, you might feel at ease to interrupt them. Being in the dark about the activity they are engaged in, you are also unable to know what your planned communicative action, "have you checked the mail?", would signify to them.

It works the other way around as well. This is exemplified in the following data excerpt. Clo and Liz are eating out and exchanging funny stories together with a friend.

Excerpt 1.
[overlapping speech]
>faster speech<
(0.9) silence in tenth of seconds
(.) noticeable silence of maximum 0.3 seconds
.mt smacking of the mouth
@transformed speech, e.g. when quoting someone@
°spoken silently°
the-the production of the word is halted suddenly
((comments))
((Clo is using her phone while talking))

64 Clo: [>Nii nimeonomaa<] (.) ja sit vielä se ku tota noin ni toi
         [>Yeah exactly<] (.) and then also that when you know that

65   (0.9).mt ((Clo stops typing and puts left hand to her face))

66   (0.2) ((Clo continues to gaze at the phone))

67 Clo: öö iskä >oli sillee< [@↑nii joo mä muistan kun Niina
         umm dad >was like< [@oh yeah I remember when Niina
68 Liz: [°mä katon ton-°
                            [°I'll check th-° ((picks up her phone))

Clo is starting to tell a story that continues the theme of previous stories that night. While doing this she pauses (line 65, 66) and utilizes filler words (lines 64–67) before actually getting the story going (line 67). Before her turn she was using her phone. While beginning the telling at line 67, she is still looking at it. Liz is listening, gazing at Clo, and sees all this taking place. While Clo is struggling while visibly distributing her attention between two activities—telling a story and using her phone—she is also putting Liz in a difficult position. Clo has already prefaced her story and gained a silent "permission" from the group to occupy a speaker position for a longer duration than normal, i.e. until the story is finished. Therefore other participants are normatively restricted to the position of recipient. When regardless of this, Clo still does not put her full attention to the activity of telling the story, and is faltering in beginning the story, the next activities, being indexical, connect in their meaning also to this event.

When Liz begins to use her phone at line 68, BI makes Clo unable to automatically see the type and the goal of Liz's phone use. In this context it therefore risks being interpreted as motivated by dissatisfaction with the haphazard way Clo begun her responsibilities as a storyteller. Considering Goffman's [26] face-work and the normative ways we protect the faces of ourselves, as well as other people from straightforward criticism, it is understandable that Liz chooses to counter this potentially face-threatening interpretation. She provides an account: "I'll check the" at line 68. Interestingly, she does not actually specify the activity she will commence with the phone, but in providing the account, she nevertheless hints that there is something to be "checked" and the reason for her staring to use the phone could be in this "checking", rather than in the faltering conversational performance of Clo. To conclude, as BI hides Liz's activity from Clo, Liz has to produce an account to circumvent this lack. Providing this account in a sequentially appropriate manner encumbrances a very limited resource in the context of being a recipient to verbal storytelling: audible speech.

Fig. 1: Respondents identified with the person speaking and rated A and B in random order.

BI -instigating technology (BI-tech) also makes it harder for collocated others to interpret responses, or lack of them, by a BI-tech user. Our study using role playing method and comic strips found most respondents more irritated when trying to unsuccessfully get the attention of a phone-using person, while no respondents evaluated the newspaper - condition as more irritating ($p < 0.001$). Furthermore, the written responses often included descriptions on being bothered by not knowing what the phone user was actually doing [27].

4 Conclusion

Designing socially acceptable technology should be informed by ethnomethodological study on the device's effect on social situation. What people do or do not accept is the way technology enters into the situation as part of the network of social activities. When engaged in technology use, a crucial aspect of it is that the activity is part of constituting the shared social reality that then gives meaning also to all the other activities of everyone else present in the situation. All their decisions to act or not to act are impacted by their understanding of what the technology use is about and whether they can trust that other participants see the situation similarly. There should be more work on design instigating affordances for collocated others to see, hear, or feel the nature of the technology use taking place in a social setting [28]. Crucially, I call for interdisciplinary work that benefits from EM/CA methodology to develop and test new prototypes. BI tech handicaps participants in social encounters. While people find ways to circumvent it, the plethora of research reporting dislike of smartphone use in social situation suggests they would prefer to avoid these challenges. Interactional work and designing non face-threatening actions takes effort, and people do not like to be forced to make effort.

References

1. Taylor, K., & Silver, L.: Smartphone Ownership Is Growing Rapidly Around the World, but Not Always Equally. Pew Research Center, (2019).
2. Ducharme, J.: "Phubbing" Is Hurting Your Relationships. Here's What It Is. TIME, (2018).
3. Molina, B.: Do smartphones keep us in or out of touch?: Devices often isolate, distract and disrupt acting with others. USA TODAY, (2017).
4. Dwyer, R. J., Kushlev, K., & Dunn, E. W.: Smartphone use undermines enjoyment of face-to-face social interactions. Journal of Experimental Social Psychology 78, 233–239 (2018).
5. Feeney, B. C., & Collins, N. L.: A New Look at Social Support: A Theoretical Perspective on Thriving Through Relationships. Personality and Social Psychology Review 19(2), 113–147 (2014).

6. Kim, J.-H.: Smartphone-mediated communication vs. face-to-face interaction: Two routes to social support and problematic use of smartphone. Computers in Human Behavior 67, 282–291 (2017).
7. Stop Phubbing Website, http://stopphubbing.com, last accessed 2019/3/22.
8. Chotpitayasunondh, V., & Douglas, K. M.: The effects of "phubbing" on social interaction. Journal of Applied Social Psychology 48(6), 304–316 (2018b).
9. Chotpitayasunondh, V., & Douglas, K. M.: How "phubbing" becomes the norm: The antecedents and consequences of snubbing via smartphone. Computers in Human Behavior 63, 9–18 (2016).
10. Aagaard, J.: Digital akrasia: a qualitative study of phubbing. AI and Society, 1–8 (2019).
11. Roberts, J. A., & David, M. E.: My life has become a major distraction from my cell phone: Partner phubbing and relationship satisfaction among romantic partners. Computers in Human Behavior, 54(Journal Article), 134–141 (2016).
12. Wang, P., Wang, X., Wang, Y., Xie, X., & Lei, L.: Partner phubbing and depression among married Chinese adults: The roles of relationship satisfaction and relationship length. Personality and Individual Differences 110, 12–17 (2017).
13. Chotpitayasunondh, V., & Douglas, K. M.: Measuring phone snubbing behavior: Development and validation of the Generic Scale of Phubbing (GSP) and the Generic Scale of Being Phubbed (GSBP). Computers in Human Behavior 88, 5–17 (2018a).
14. Guazzini, A., Duradoni, M., Capelli, A., & Meringolo, P.: An explorative model to assess individuals' phubbing risk. Future Internet 11(1), 21–34 (2019).
15. Roose, K.: Do Not Disturb: How I Ditched My Phone and Unbroke My Brain. New York Times (2019).
16. Garfinkel, H.: Studies in ethnomethodology. Prentice-Hall, Englewood Cliffs, N.J. (1967).
17. Goodwin, C.: Conversational organization: interaction between speakers and hearers. Academic Press, New York (1981).
18. Heritage, J: Garfinkel and Ethnomethodology. Polity Press, Cambridge (1984).
19. Hutchby, I., & Wooffitt, R.: Conversation analysis: principles, practices and applications. Polity Press, Cambridge (1998).
20. Mondada, L: Multimodal resources for turn-taking: pointing and the emergence of possible next speakers. Discourse Studies 2(9), 194–225 (2007).
21. Licoppe, C., & Figeac, J.: Gaze Patterns and the Temporal Organization of Multiple Activities in Mobile Smartphone Uses. Human-Computer 33(5–6), 311–334 (2018).
22. Figeac, J., & Chaulet, J.: Video-ethnography of social media apps' connection cues in public settings. Mobile Media & Communication 6(3), 407–427 (2018).

23. Laurier, E., Brown, B., McGregor, M.: Mediated Pedestrian Mobility: Walking and the Map App. Mobilities 11(1), 117–134 (2016).
24. Porcheron, M., Fischer, J., & Sharples, S.: Using Mobile Phones in Pub Talk. Proceedings of the 19th ACM Conference on Computer-Supported Cooperative Work & Social Computing, 1649–1661. ACM (2016).
25. Goffman, E.: The Neglected Situation. American Anthropologist 66(6), DEC–136. (1964).
26. Goffman, E.: Interaction ritual: essays on face-to-face behavior. Aldine, Chicago (1967).
27. Raudaskoski, S., Mantere, E., & Valkonen, S.: Älypuhelin ja kasvokkaisen vuorovaikutuksen muuttuvat käytänteet. *Sosiologia* (accepted for publication) (2019).
28. Ens, B., Grossman, T., Anderson, F., Matejka, J., & Fitzmaurice, G.: Candid Interaction: Revealing Hidden Mobile and Wearable Computing Activities. Proceedings of the 28th Annual ACM Symposium on User Interface Software & Technology, 467–476. (2015).

A Scenario Generator for Evaluating the Social Acceptability of Emerging Technologies

Hannah Meyer, Marion Koelle and Susanne Boll

University of Oldenburg, Oldenburg, Germany

hannah.meyer@uni-oldenburg.de, marion.koelle@uni-oldenburg.de, susanne.boll@uni-oldenburg.de

Abstract

In addition to functionality, usability and user experience, *social acceptability* is increasingly recognized as driver (or hindering factor) for the adoption of emerging interface technologies. In consequence, factors influencing *social acceptance*, the perception of technology usage in presence of other people – both, from the user's and the by-stander's points of view, has become of interest to researchers in Human-Computer-Interaction (HCI). *Social acceptance* does not only depend on the considered device, but also on design aspects, e.g., input and output modalities, and social context, e.g., usage location or the user's relationship to the bystanders. To investigate these factors, and how they interconnect, prior work made use of *scenario visualizations*, e.g., photographs, videos, or illustrations, whose creations is often time-consuming and labour-intensive. With **SAGE**, the Social Acceptability (Scenario) **G**enerator and **E**valuator, we present a tool that solves this issue by enabling semi-automatic generation of scenario illustrations for the purpose of evaluating the social acceptability of human-computer interfaces. Embedded into a website, **SAGE** facilitates evaluation, generation and export (download) of scenarios. Thus, it provides an infrastructure for online and offline scenario evaluation, which contributes to research efforts in the field of social acceptability of emerging technologies and novel interaction paradigms.

How to cite this book chapter:

Meyer, H., Koelle, M. and Boll, S. 2020. A Scenario Generator for Evaluating the Social Acceptability of Emerging Technologies. In: Loizides, F., Winckler, M., Chatterjee, U., Abdelnour-Nocera, J. and Parmaxi, A. (eds.) *Human Computer Interaction and Emerging Technologies: Adjunct Proceedings from the INTERACT 2019 Workshops.* Pp. 101–110. Cardiff: Cardiff University Press. DOI: https://doi.org/10.18573/book3.l. License: CC-BY 4.0.

Keywords

Social acceptability · social acceptance · understanding users · user study methods

1 Introduction

With the increasing ubiquity of human-computer interfaces, it becomes increasingly relevant that interface and interactions blend well into social context. As users may be noticed or even observed by other individuals who – consciously or unconsciously – wish to identify their attitudes, goals and intentions, interacting with devices in public can impact on the user's impression management and – in consequence – the *social acceptability* of the interaction [1]. Consequently, *social acceptability* in the context of technology usage comprises both, how other people perceive the usage of a technical device and how the user thinks that they do [2]. At the development of emerging technology, social acceptability should be taken into account as a crucial factor and source of potential problems.

1.1 Using Scenarios to Evaluate Social Acceptability

Prior work demonstrated that social acceptance of a user's interactions with an interface depends on the usage context and may be influenced by a variety of different factors. These include, for example, the view point [2–3], usage location [4–5], interaction modality [6–7], functionality [8–9] or appearance [10–11] of the device, user type [2, 12], audience [4] or usage purpose [3]. There are several options to test the influence of those factors on a user's or their bystanders' attitude towards using a technology. In any case, a study participant must be confronted with the situation to be assessed. In-situ studies may be used [9, 13–14], however, they often do not allow to set and control all variables of interest in the desired way. Thus, the presentation of visualizations of the considered situations, which we refer to as *scenarios*, has become a valid, and popular alternative.

Videos and Photographs Media which are frequently used to present scenarios are *videos* and *photos*. Since many interactions in scenarios include some kind of movement or sound, videos are a well suited presentation format for dynamic scenarios. They are used to investigate, for example, gesture based interaction [2, 4, 15–17]. On the other hand, they require time and effort to create, and the creation of additional videos later-on, e.g., after a study pretest, is prone to introduce confounding variables. In contrast, photographs are easier to administer, and it is easier to create a high number of variations (e.g., scenarios with one to many bystanders). For example, Lum et al. [18] investigated how the perception of humans is affected by the use of technology using photos of models wearing various devices. Recently, Schwind et al. [5] explored the social acceptance of virtual reality glasses in various situations, with varying locations, users and bystanders. While both approaches, *videos* and *photos* are beneficial to depict scenarios in a rather realistic way, they are also harder to control, and – as they require actors – can potentially introduce racial, cultural or gender bias. *Illustrations* This issue might be mitigated by using drawn, abstract pictograms – as e.g., proposed in Koelle et al. [3]. This kind of presentations allows to keep environments constant, and increase control over assumptions that are made about depicted persons and also leverages the ability to directly highlight the perspective from which the scenario shall be rated. A similar presentation technique is used by the "moral machine" [19, 20], a website which aims to support the decision making in autonomous cars by understanding social preferences. Pictured individuals are visually characterized by certain features as e.g. age, gender or fitness.

All of these approaches, *videos*, *photos* and – in particular – *illustrations* have the disadvantage that scenario visualizations are time-consuming and labour-intensive, in particular if many factors are compared to each other. With our work we provide a more efficient approach that allows to automatically create abstract scenario visualizations based on the *independent variables* a researcher want to investigate with regard to social acceptability.

1.2 Contribution Statement

This paper presents the development of SAGE – short for "Social Acceptability (Scenario) Generator and Evaluator" – an online tool to automatically generate scenario illustrations from various components, i.e. *independent variables* or *constants*. Our contributions are two-fold: first, SAGE allows to automatically generate and download customized scenarios for own research purposes. Second, SAGE enables browsing and evaluation of scenarios on the website. In the following, we present the tool's design process, and motivate the decision process as to which components should be included. In addition, we discuss existing questionnaires for the evaluation of social acceptance and motivate our selection. Finally, we will give an overview about the implementation and outline how we intend to evaluate the presented tool as part of our future research.

2 Concept Development

While we intentionally designed SAGE to be extensible in terms of components, we selected the components included in this first version based on prior work and expert interviews (N = 4) with researchers working on social acceptability issues with human-computer interfaces. Similarly, while scenarios created with SAGE could be used in conjunction with a variety of existing questionnaires, we decided for one set of questions for the current version. Subsequently, we outline and motivate our choices.

2.1 Selection and Visualization of Scenario Components

As aforementioned, there is a range of factors found by prior work to be influential on social acceptability. However, there is no indication about their actual relevance for future research. Thus, we conducted expert interviews to create an initial set of components to be included in SAGE. Note, that SAGE is constructed to be extendable – thus, the selected components do not necessarily represent a final choice. All interviewed experts were researchers in the field of Human Computer Interaction who published at least one paper covering social acceptability. Overall, we interviewed four experts (2 female), aged 31 to 42 ($\bar{x} = 35$, $\sigma = 5$) from Europe with 5 to 10 years of research experience in HCI. The experts indicated to have published 2 to 10 papers on social acceptability in HCI.

We conducted semi-structured interviews over Skype that were tied around the topics "Location", "User", "Interaction", "Bystanders" and "General Factors". In addition, the participants were asked to comment on candidate components derived from literature. Notes taken during the interviews were clustered and analyzed for main themes that we present subsequently:

1. Details about the user and the bystanders – such as gender, age, etc. – do influence the social acceptance. However, these are not part of interface design. Thus, those factors should be (and have been) investigated detached from technology usage and their examination is therefore not the focus of HCI. We excluded those details from the configuration options provided by SAGE.

2. Both the purpose of use and the interaction modality are exceedingly relevant for social acceptability, the device appearance is considered to play a minor part. This supports our selection of abstract device representations for SAGE. The interaction modality is one of the main components of SAGE.

3. Social context is more relevant for social acceptance than the spatial context. However, locations typically indicate social context and induce the relationships between bystanders and the user. Thus, location is included in SAGE, but could be understood as outline of social context.

From these results, we derived the components and specifications listed in Table 1. We focused on the social acceptability of mobile devices – computing devices small enough to be carried around.

We based the visualization of the components on the bikablo visual dictionaries [21–22] in order to use symbols that are proven to be as understandable as possible. We give an example of one automatically generated scenario in Figure 1.

Table 1: Scenario Components and their Specifications included in SAGE.

Component	Specifications
Device Kind	Smart Watch, Smart Phone, Smart Glasses, Smart Clothing, Electronic Tattoo, Smart Contact Lenses
Interaction Modality	None, Speech, Arm Gesture, Hand Gesture, Touch of Device
Usage Location	Neutral, Home, Pavement, Public Transport, Restaurant, Workplace
Usage Purpose	Hidden, Navigation, Entertainment, Information Access, Assistive Technology, Communication, Capturing of Memories
Number of Bystanders	No Bystander, One Bystander, Two Bystanders, Many Bystanders
User-Bystander-Relationship	Unknown, Partner, Friend, Family, Colleague, Stranger

Fig. 1: Exemplary Scenario Created from its Components – A person ("the user") is interacting with his/her smart watch via a hand gesture. He/she does the interaction to get access to information. The scenario takes place at the user's workplace. There are also two bystanders present, who are colleagues of the user.

2.2 Selection of a Questionnaire

There is no established social acceptability questionnaire. However, some questions have been (re)used in prior work. These are, for example, the questionnaires proposed by Rico and Brewster [4, 16] and by Profita et al. [23]. The latter formulates thirteen statements about the user, the device and their interaction and asks for the participants' degree of agreement to them. The former asks the participant to select every location and audience from a list where they would be willing to perform a particular gesture. Some works exactly took over this questionnaire [7, 24], others modified the questionnaire for their purposes [6, 25–26]. However, at the SAGE website, location and audience are part of the scenario itself and the interaction modality is not necessarily restricted to gestures only. Thus, for SAGE we propose to adapt the questions to "Are you willing to perform the user's interaction?" or – if the Likert scale items proposed by [26] are adopted – "How willing are you to perform the user's interaction?". Based on prior work, we derived a unified questionnaire, where we aligned the phrasing and response options. This questionnaire, consisting of two items, is part of SAGE's on-site evaluation:

1. How much do you agree to the following statement: 'I would be willing to perform the users interaction in the given context.'?
2. How much do you agree to the following statement:' If I were the bystander,I would rate the user's interaction as acceptable in the given context.'?

As response options we chose a 5-point Likert scale adapted from Pearson et al. [27] ranging from "strongly agree" over "agree", "neither agree nor disagree" and "disagree" to "strongly disagree". Doing so, we deliberately give the participant the opportunity to take a neutral position.

3   Implementation

The implementation of the SAGE website functionalities was based on the programming language JavaScript due to its applicability as a browser-side as well as a server-side scripting language. To achieve a separation of concerns, we split SAGE into a Vue.js front-end and a Node.js back-end application. The website is currently reachable at the following URL: https://www.sage.uni-oldenburg.de Depending on the parameters of a scenario, SAGE constructs the scenario from a set of sub-images. The tool uses SVG images called by HTML code to

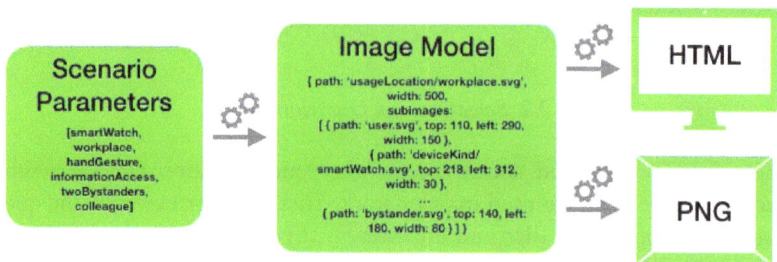

Fig. 2: Overview of SAGE's Image Generation Process.

display scenarios on the website, but provides downloadable scenario images as PNGs for an improved ease of use. In order to still ensure the same generated image for the same scenario, we established a so-called image model – a detailed description of the image structure for a specific scenario i.e. the necessary subimages with their sizes and positions. The format-independent image model will subsequently be processed into the final scenario image of the requested format. The image generation process is outlined in Figure 2.

4 Planned Evaluation

For SAGE to establish itself as a useful tool for research on social acceptability in HCI, it has to facilitate the creation of relevant scenarios for a broad range of research questions. In addition, the tool has to deliver appropriate data for statistical analysis. Based on those requirements, we plan a two-stage evaluation process. First, we aim to collect data directly on the SAGE website and compare the results to results obtained by prior work. For this purpose, we started a data collection in March 2019. In addition, we aim to present SAGE to researchers working on social acceptability aspects of HCI to collect feedback and evaluate its usefulness as a tool.

5 Conclusion

In this paper we introduced SAGE, a tool that generates scenarios from components – i.e., independent variables or constants – which facilitates evaluating social acceptability in user studies. Embedded in a website, it allows evaluation, automatic generation as well as export (download) of scenario illustrations for research purposes. Thus, in contrast to the *manual* creation of scenario illustrations, videos or photos, it increases efficiency, and enhances replicability as well as extendability of study designs. We hope – similar to the notion of "discount usability" [28] – that the fast and easy generation of study materials can promote social acceptability as a field of research by making it easier to get started and eventually prevent technology from failing due to a lack of social acceptance.

References

1. Goffmann, E.: The Presentation of Self in Everyday Life. In: Contemporary Sociological Theory, pp. 46–74. Wiley (2012)
2. Montero, C., Alexander, J., Marshall, M., Subramanian, S.: Would You Do That? Understanding Social Acceptance of Gestural Interfaces. In: Proceedings of the 12th International Conference on Human-Computer Interaction with Mobile Devices and Services, pp. 275–278. ACM New York, USA (2010)

3. Koelle, M., Kranz, M., M¨oller, A.: Dont look at me that way! Understanding User Attitudes Towards Data Glasses Usage. In: Proceedings of the 17th International Conference on Human-Computer Interaction with Mobile Devices and Services, pp. 362–372. ACM New York, USA (2015)
4. Rico, J., Brewster, S.: Usable Gestures for Mobile Interfaces: Evaluating Social Acceptability. In: Proceedings of the SIGCHI Conference on Human Factors in Computing Systems, pp. 887–896. ACM New York, USA (2010)
5. Schwind, V., Reinhardt, J., Rzayev, R., Henze, N., Wolf, K.: Virtual Reality on the Go? A Study on Social Acceptance of VR Glasses. In: Proceedings of the 20th International Conference on Human Computer Interaction with Mobile Devices and Services. ACM New York, USA (2018)
6. Serrano, M., Ens, B., Irani, P.: Exploring the Use of Hand-To-Face Input for Interacting with Head-Worn Displays. In: Proceedings of the SIGCHI Conference on Human Factors in Computing Systems, pp. 3181–3190. ACM New York, USA (2014)
7. Efthymiou, C., Halvey, M.: Evaluating the Social Acceptability of Voice Based Smartwatch Search. In: Ma, S. et al. (eds.) Information Retrieval Technology. AIRS 2016, LNCS, vol. 9994. Springer, Cham (2016).
8. Choe, E. K., Consolvo, S., Jung, J., Harrison, B., Patel, S., Kientz, J.: Investigating Receptiveness to Sensing and Inference in the Home Using Sensor Proxies. In: Proceedings of the 2012 ACM Conference on Ubiquitous Computing, pp. 61–70. ACM New York, USA (2012)
9. Denning, T., Dehlawi, Z., Kohno, T.: In Situ with Bystanders of Augmented Reality Glasses: Perspectives on Recording and Privacy-Mediating Technologies. In: Proceedings of the SIGCHI Conference on Human Factors in Computing Systems, pp. 2377–2386. ACM New York, USA (2014)
10. Miner, C. S., Chan, D. M., Campbell, C.: Digital Jewelry: Wearable Technology for Everyday Life. In: CHI'01 Extended Abstracts on Human Factors in Computing Systems, pp. 45–46. ACM New York, USA (2001)
11. Shinohara, K., Wobbrock, J. O.: In the Shadow of Misperception: Assistive Technology Use and Social Interactions. In: Proceedings of the SIGCHI Conference on Human Factors in Computing Systems, pp. 705–714. ACM New York, USA (2011)
12. Profita, H. P., Clawson, J., Gilliland, S., Zeagler, C., Starner, T., Budd, J., Do, E. Y.: Don't Mind Me Touching My Wrist: A Case Study of Interacting with On-Body Technology in Public. In: Proceedings of the 2013 International Symposium on Wearable Computers, pp. 89–96. ACM New York, USA (2013)
13. Williamson, J. R., Crossan, A., Brewster, S.: Multimodal Mobile Interactions: Usability Studies in Real World Settings. In: Proceedings of the 13th International Conference on Multimodal Interfaces, pp. 361–368. ACM New York, USA (2011)
14. Hoyle, R., Templeman, R., Armes, S., Anthony, D., Crandall, D., Kapadia, A.: Privacy Behaviors of Lifeloggers using Wearable Cameras.

In: Proceedings of the 2014 ACM International Joint Conference on Pervasive and Ubiquitous Computing, pp. 571–582. ACM New York, USA (2014)

15. Rico, J., Brewster, S.: Gestures all around us: user differences in social acceptability perceptions of gesture based interfaces. In: Proceedings of the 11th International Conference on Human-Computer Interaction with Mobile Devices and Services. ACM New York, USA (2009)

16. Rico, J., Brewster, S.: Gesture and Voice Prototyping for Early Evaluations of Social Acceptability in Multimodal Interfaces. In: International Conference on Multimodal Interfaces and the Workshop on Machine Learning for Multimodal Interaction. ACM New York, USA (2010)

17. Ronkainen, S., Häkkilä, J., Kaleva, S., Colley, A., Linjama, J.: Tap Input as an Embedded Interaction Method for Mobile Devices. In: Proceedings of the 1st International Conference on Tangible and Embedded Interaction, pp. 263–270. ACM New York, USA (2007)

18. Lum, H. C., Sims, V. K., Chin, M. G., Lagattuta, N. C.: Perceptions of Humans Wearing Technology. In: Proceedings of the Human Factors and Ergonomics Society Annual Meeting, pp. 864–868. SAGE Publishing Los Angeles, USA (2009)

19. Noothigattu, R., Gaikwad, S., Awad, E., Dsouza, S., Rahwan, I., Ravikumar, P., Procaccia, A. D.: A Voting-Based System for Ethical Decision Making. In: Proceedings of the thirty-second AAAI Conference on Artificial Intelligence. AAAI Press (2017)

20. Moral Machine Website, http://moralmachine.mit.edu. Last accessed 26 Apr 2019

21. Scholz, H., Haußmann, M.: bikablo 1: Das Trainerwörterbuch der Bildsprache. 9nd edn. Kommunikationslotsen Much, Germany (2017)

22. Scholz, H., Haußmann, M.: bikablo 2.0: Neue Bilder für Meeting, Training & Learning. 7nd edn. Kommunikationslotsen Much, Germany (2014)

23. Profita, H., Albaghli, R., Findlater, L., Jaeger, P., Kane, S. K.: The AT Effect: How Disability Affects the Perceived Social Acceptability of Head-Mounted Display Use. In: Proceedings of the 2016 CHI Conference on Human Factors in Computing Systems, pp. 4884–4895. ACM New York, USA (2016)

24. Lv, Z., Halawani, A., Feng, S., Ur Réhman, S., Li, H.: Touch-less Interactive Augmented Reality Game on Vision-Based Wearable Device. In: Personal and Ubiquitous Computing, vol. 19, pp. 551–567. Springer Nature (2015)

25. Hsieh, Y., Jylhä, A., Orso, V., Gamberini, L., Jacucci, G.: Designing a Willing-to-Use-in-Public Hand Gestural Interaction Technique for Smart Glasses. In: Proceedings of the 2016 CHI Conference on Human Factors in Computing Systems, pp. 4203–4215. ACM New York, USA (2016)

26. Bailly, G., Müller, J., Rohs, M., Wigdor, D., Kratz, S.: ShoeSense: A New Perspective on Hand Gestures and Wearable Applications. In: Proceedings

of the SIGCHI Conference on Human Factors in Computing Systems, pp. 1239–1248. ACM New York, USA (2012)

27. Pearson, J., Robinson, S., Jones, M.: Its About Time: Smartwatches as Public Displays. In: Proceedings of the 33rd Annual ACM Conference on Human Factors in Computing Systems, pp. 1257–1266. ACM New York, USA (2012)

28. Nielsen, J.: Usability Engineering at a Discount. In: Proceedings of the third International Conference on Human-Computer Interaction on Designing and Using Human-Computer Interfaces and Knowledge Based Systems (2nd ed.), pp. 394–401. Elsevier Science Inc. (1989)

Social Acceptability, Obstructions, Collaboration and Embarrassment

Robb Mitchell

University of Southern Denmark, Kolding, 6000, Denmark
robb@sdu.dk

Abstract

This position paper outlines my interest in socially acceptability and embarrassment as explored through low-tech interaction design undertaken in urban spaces, art galleries, industrial innovation events and games workshops.[1]

Keywords

Social interaction · facilitation · breaching experiments · interactive art

1 Introduction

In my experience, design experimentation that stretches the normal boundaries of social acceptability can actually lead to increasing, rather than diminishing the conviviality of a setting. Disrupting expectations of behaviours may spark novel exchanges, expressive play and lead to new ideas for people effected,

---

[1] This article is based upon a CHI2015 workshop position paper that was uploaded to the webpage of the Embarrassing Interactions workshop.

How to cite this book chapter:
Mitchell, R. 2020. Social Acceptability, Obstructions, Collaboration and Embarrassment. In: Loizides, F., Winckler, M., Chatterjee, U., Abdelnour-Nocera, J. and Parmaxi, A. (eds.) *Human Computer Interaction and Emerging Technologies: Adjunct Proceedings from the INTERACT 2019 Workshops.* Pp. 111–116. Cardiff: Cardiff University Press. DOI: https://doi.org/10.18573/book3.m. License: CC-BY 4.0.

whilst also offering a means for designers and researchers to better understand social situations.

My work is interaction design in the broader sense of the term. I do not view cutting edge technology as a prerequisite for exploring social issues in HCI. As the social media theorist Clay Shirky puts it: "Communications tools don't get socially interesting until they get technologically boring" [12].

Working across a variety of domains such as interactive arts, participatory design and event curating. I have devised artifacts, environments, processes, systems and events that aimed to help bring people closer together creatively, socially and professionally. In particular, addressing the barriers between: remote locations; different disciplines; experts and non-experts; and other co-located people who are not yet acquainted with each other.

2 Embarrassment as an interpersonal shield

The notion of barriers connects with the etymology of the word embarrassment, i.e. its origins in meaning obstruction. Although never an implicit aim, the powerful phenomenon of embarrassment has played a major role in many previous projects. Several themes concerning different connections between senses of embarrassment, obstruction and fostering positive co-located encounters are briefly discussed in the following.

2.1 Amplify awkwardness until it disappears

Embarrassment is relational – to be embarrassed normally involves a sense of negative imbalance of emotions such as dishonor or shame compared with other people. Having a witness to getting stuck in a typical revolving door would thus be an embarrassing experience for many people. However with a turnstile resembling social contraptions such as *Blender*, and *Heads Up of The Table* all participants found the artifact challenging to their movements. If disconcertment is universal within a context, then the potential for embarrassment is much reduced.

Both these contraptions are part of series of art installations that were designed to foster positive face-to-face interactions between strangers who may not otherwise interact [7]. Each contraption presented participants with a shared physical obstacle. This was intended to create a situation in which there are less predetermined "rules" concerning how to behave. Providing a novel constraint on "normal" behaviour was intended as a route to partially dissolve the everyday norms (both internal/individual and social/collective) that may inhibit social interactions between the unacquainted. This in turn, could provoke and encourage a fluidity of interaction between strangers.

2.2 Surfacing social design challenges

Human surrogates deployed to act as walking, talking avatars [9] may also offer insights relevant for understanding social (un) acceptability and embarrassment. These low-tech interventions can open up for discussion issues such as adaptation, control, visibly, accountability, sharing and differences in participant roles. Paradoxically, in comparison with digital social systems, the contraptions seem to move both towards making people's responses into a "material" that is visible and tangible. However, at the same time, in provoking a wide variety of unpredictable responses the contraptions make vivid how this is a tangibility that eludes a firm grip and is thus a visibility that both illuminates and obscures [10].

2.3 Breaching embarrassment to & from public collaboration

While physical constraints have long been exploited as a design tactic or inspiration in the overall quest for a more human-centered design and development process, another intuitive quality of interaction has been somewhat overlooked, namely that of social constraints and the instinctive social behavior of people [6].

Ordinary social order impedes attempts by technologists to provoke disparate individuals to collaborate or share experiences in urban public spaces. To address these barriers we analysed responses to a number of city center social interventions inspired by the sociological concept of breaching experiments.

In these cases, embarrassment was prominent in three ways. Firstly, and not surprisingly, it was detectable in the responses of passers by to the performed "breaches". Secondly, many of the students that devised and implemented these interventions reported great initial embarrassment before the public implementation of their experiments. And thirdly, the sense of embarrassment was profound when we as researchers sat down to watch video recordings of several of the interventions. For instance, watching documentation of students sit down at the café tables of strangers and making small talk prior to performing their "breach" of asking if they can taste the food on the strangers' plate [6] was particularly excruciating at times.

2.4 Unacceptable interactions to prompt more acceptable behaviours

I am proud to have been involved in supporting some recent student work with mechatronical furniture that also provokes and reveals issues of embarrassment. For instance a toilet brush that attempts to build a relationship with people sitting on the lavatory [1] and tables that respond to different speeds at which companions eat [10] or the speed at which people approach it [2]. Designs such as these offer potential both as research vehicles into social contexts and as a means of harnessing socially awkward experiences towards motivating behaviour change [2].

2.5 Clumsy mishaps breed insightful excuses

Based upon a survey of several years of innovation workshop activities focused upon fostering shared understanding of business challenges [5], we developed an argument for the value of "Oops! Moments" [8]. By which we mean the surprise and uncertainty evoked by the use of 'kinetic materials' (e.g. bouncing balls, springs, and seesaw like mechanisms) in business strategy discussions may facilitate fresh and spontaneous exchanges of perspectives.

To avoid potential embarrassment when being seen as unable to manipulate physical objects according to their intentions and expectations, workshop participants often improvise creative and humourous explanations that inadvertently serve to enliven and enrich shared sensemaking concerning innovation challenges [8].

2.6 Sensory deprivation prompts embarrassment

Blocking a perceptual channel of participants can contribute to increasing both bodily expressivity and vocalizations that might be considered prohibitively undignified under other circumstances.

Reindeer and The Wolves is a digital movement based game that features two blindfold participants in physical pursuit of three other players. Obstructing the perceptual channel of sight appeared to release players to perform expressive bodily actions and vocalizations that might be considered prohibitively undignified under most other circumstances [3]. However we could discern little sign of embarrassment amongst participants and audience.

For a person's action to be considered embarrassing, it is commonly understood that another person should either witness it, or come to know about it through some indirect means. This can help to explain how non-blindfold players felt free to act ignominiously towards their non-sighted competitors. However, it is interesting that blindfolded players themselves also performed very self-demeaning actions. It was as if the lack of two-way contact with witnesses to undignified actions serves to remove or reduce what would otherwise be their embarrassing qualities.

References

1. Boer, L., Hansen, N., Möller, R.L, Neto, A.I.C., Nielsen, A.H., and Mitchell, R. The Toilet Companion: A toilet brush that should be there for you and not for others. In: Proc. Augmented Human Conference, ACM (2015).

2. Boer, L., Mitchell, R., Caglio, A., and Lucero, A. Embodied Technology: Unravelling Bodily Interaction with Normative Types. In: CHI'15 Extended Abstracts, ACM (2015).

3. Finnegan, D., Velloso, E., Mitchell, R., Mueller, F.F., and Byrne, R. Reindeer & Wolves: Exploring Sensory Deprivation in Multiplayer Digital Bodily Play. In: Proc. CHI Play, pp. 411–412. ACM (2014).

4. Koelle, M., Boll, S., Olsson, T., et al. (2018) (Un) Acceptable!: Re-thinking the Social Acceptability of Emerging Technologies. In: Extended Abstracts of the 2018 CHI Conference on Human Factors in Computing Systems. ACM.

5. Heinemann, T., Boess, S., Landgrebe, J., Mitchell, R., & Nevile, M. (2011, October). Making sense of things: developing new practices and methods for using tangible materials in collaborative processes. In: Desire'11 Proceedings of the Second Conference on Creativity and Innovation in Design, pp. 221–225. ACM (2011).

6. Heinemann, T., and Mitchell, R. Breaching barriers to collaboration in public spaces. In: Proc. TEI '14, pp. 213–220. ACM (2014).

7. Mitchell, R. Physical contraptions as social interaction catalysts. 3rd International Workshop on Physicality, pp. 37–42. (2009).

8. Mitchell, R., Caglio, A., and Buur, J. Oops! Moments: Kinetic Material in Participatory Workshops. In Proc. NORDES – Nordic Design Research Conf., pp. 60–69, (2013).

9. Mitchell, R. An in your face interface: revisiting cyranoids as a revealing medium for interpersonal interaction. In: Proceedings of the 5th Student Interaction Design Research Conference (SIDeR): Flirting with the Future, pp. 56–59. Eindhoven, Eindhoven University of Technology (2009).

10. Mitchell, R., Gillespie, A., and O'Neill, B. Cyranic contraptions: using personality surrogates to explore ontologically and socially dynamic contexts. Desire'11, Proceedings of the Second Conference on Creativity and Innovation in Design pp. 199–210 ACM (2011).

11. Mitchell, R., Papadimitriou, A., You, Y., and Boer, L. Really Eating Together: A Kinetic Table To Synchronise Social Dining Experiences. In Proc. Augmented Human Conference, ACM (2015).

12. Shirky, C. Here Comes Everybody: The Power of Organizing Without Organizations. Penguin Press (2008).

Is Going Unnoticed More Socially Acceptable?: An Exploration of the Relationship Between Social Acceptability and Noticeability of Fitness Trackers

Yumiko Sakamoto*, Pourang Irani* and Khalad Hasan†

*University of Manitoba, Winnipeg, Manitoba, Canada
†University of Biritish Columbia, Okanagan, British Columbia, Canada
umsakamo@umanitoba.ca, pourang.irani@cs.umanitoba.ca,
khalad.hasan@ubc.ca

Abstract

While fitness trackers are becoming increasingly popular, the majority of such devices are relatively smaller and almost always worn around a user's wrist (e.g., smart watches). To expand the potential of novel design options for such devices, a study explored the link between social acceptability and device noticeability, in conjunction with two other factors; namely, the device size and the on-body location (i.e., on which body parts the user wears the tracker). The central question we investigated was: to develop a socially acceptable fitness tracker, should the device be less noticeable? For this exploration, an online questionnaire was distributed ($N = 32$), and results indicated that noticeability was correlated with social acceptability only in two situations: i) when the fitness tracker is large, or ii) when a female user wears it around their chest. That is, noticeability partially accounted for social acceptability only in these conditions. Jointly, the results point toward the great possibility for

---

How to cite this book chapter:
Sakamoto, Y., Irani, P. and Hasan, K. 2020. Is Going Unnoticed More Socially Acceptable?:
An Exploration of the Relationship Between Social Acceptability and Noticeability of
Fitness Trackers. In: Loizides, F., Winckler, M., Chatterjee, U., Abdelnour-Nocera, J.
and Parmaxi, A. (eds.) *Human Computer Interaction and Emerging Technologies:
Adjunct Proceedings from the INTERACT 2019 Workshops.* Pp. 117–124. Cardiff:
Cardiff University Press. DOI: https://doi.org/10.18573/book3.n. License: CC-BY 4.0.

novel design ideas of fitness trackers in other conditions (e.g., when the device is smaller or worn around the arm) without compromising social acceptability.

Keywords

Social Acceptability · Noticeability · Health and Fitness Tracker

1 Introduction

Over the last decade, technology has drastically changed the way we use personal health and fitness devices, and its associated software. Today, people use a wide range of fitness tracking devices to monitor their health condition, and/or maintain their motivation towards improving their health-related behaviors (e.g., eating nutritious food). These devices are commonly available in different form factors to nicely fit in various contexts. For instance, people often use small fitness bands on their wrist to continuously monitor their health status [4]. Similarly, many people attach their smartphones to their upper arm with armbands while they are exercising. Although it largely depends on the device size and the on body location (i.e., on which part of the body the device is worn), these devices are only slightly visually noticeable. Presumably, this is the case as one of the key factors for product success for such devices is social acceptability (i.e., How comfortable one feels about using a technology in a given social context) especially because fitness-tracking devices are often worn in public.

Understanding factors that affect user acceptance of new technology have received extensive attention recently. For instance, Rico et al. [9] investigated design dimensions that are related to smartphone gesture acceptance in various settings and revealed that user's location and the audience around the user are key factors for individual's preferred gestures. Likewise, Ahlström et al. [1] investigated mid-air gesture sizes that are socially acceptable in assorted locations and the types of audience. They found that small gestures are more acceptable than large ones, and people are more comfortable performing any of such gestures in a private space (e.g., home), and in front of familiar faces (e.g., friends). Thus, there are numerous works focusing on the acceptance of new technology, but, with only little known about the possible link between social acceptability and noticeability of devices.

In this paper, we investigate whether there is a relationship between noticeability and social acceptability in regards to health and fitness trackers. More specifically, we investigate whether the size of the device and the location of the device on the body could impact social acceptance. To do so, we conduct a study to collect participants' feedback on noticeability and social acceptability, asking them to imagine they are wearing different sized devices on different body parts. Our results indicate that social acceptability and noticeability of health and fitness tracking device are negatively correlated when i) the device is larger and ii) the device is worn around the chest specifically by female users. Based on these results, we generate design guidelines and recommendations for developing health and fitness trackers without compromising the levels of social acceptability.

2 Related Work

2.1 Social Acceptability

Social acceptability, or individuals' psychological comfort level towards technology use in social contexts, has been widely explored. Researchers often examine factors affecting the levels of social acceptability regarding the users' experiences of using new input devices. They have studied social acceptance and factors that influence users' willingness to use such input methods for interacting with devices. For instance, researchers investigated users' acceptance of device and body-centric gestures (e.g., tap on the nose) [9], around-device mid-air gestures [1–3] for interacting with smartphones [1] and smartglasses [2–3]. Their exploration primarily concentrated on gesture properties, such as gesture size and gesture location, that are socially acceptable in a wide range of usage contexts. Additionally, they explored how acceptability changes across user groups (e.g., family, friends, strangers), locations (e.g., private vs. public space) and users' perspective (performer vs. observer). Their results revealed that gesture properties, user groups, and location affect users' attitude towards using the input method/device. Our study is inspired by these research, and we investigated the relationship between users' social acceptability and the device noticeability.

2.2 Noticeability

As smart devices come in different shapes and sizes, a few recent studies examined noticeability of the devices themselves and the interaction methods with the devices. Researchers have often suggested that mobile devices and the interaction methods with the device should be unnoticeable. For instance, researchers suggested the devices [8], as well as the interaction methods [6, 10], need to be as natural, unobtrusive, and unnoticeable as possible to be used comfortably by users in diverse social contexts. Furthermore, users' preference for wearing devices on different on-body locations could influence the noticeability levels [9–10]. To further understand the social acceptability-noticeability relationship, in this paper, we aim to explore how varying the device size, and on-body locations affect this link.

3 Study

An online-based questionnaire was distributed to explore the relationship between social acceptability and device noticeability by manipulating participants' perceived device size and on-body location. The questionnaire was divided into three major sections. The first section asked for participants' demographic information. The second and third sections assessed the social acceptability and noticeability levels for different sized fitness devices and on body locations, respectively.

3.1 Participants

Participants were recruited from a local university ($N = 32$) with an equal male-to-female ratio. Their age ranged between 23 and 48 ($M = 30.69$; $SD = 6.94$). Approximately 44% of the participants had no prior experience in using fitness tracking devices, and about 31% of the participants used such devices for approximately one year.

3.2 Correlation between social acceptability & noticeability when the device size varies

Size-specific social acceptability of the fitness tracker was assessed with a question: "Now, please select an appropriate number to indicate 'How socially comfortable you would feel using a fitness tracking device that is in size'. That is, how comfortable do you feel about wearing these devices in public?" Three sizes were selected for our exploration (Small, Medium, and Large). To somewhat homogenize participants' perception on device size, three sample images were provided along with the scale (See Fig. 1a). Participants used a 7-point Likert scale where 1 was "Very Uncomfortable" and 7 was "Very Comfortable."

For the size-specific noticeability, the participants were asked to respond to a question; "Please imagine how noticeable the device would be if it was worn

Fig. 1: (a) The scale with sample images to standardize the participants' size perception and (b) On body location image provided to the participants.

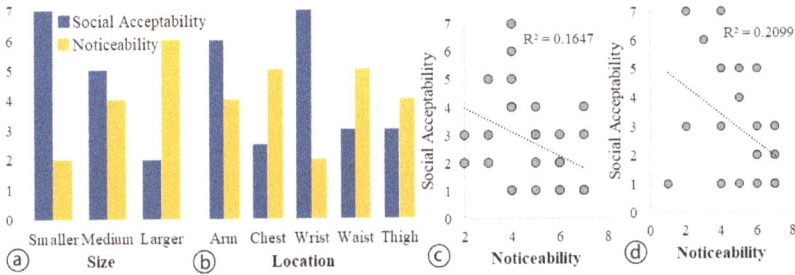

Fig. 2: Medians for social acceptability and noticeability for three device sizes (a), and five on body locations (b); Significant correlations found between social acceptability and noticeability when the device was larger (c) and the device was worn around the chest (d).

in a gym for each of the three sizes specified above. Participants used a 7-point Likert scale where 1 was "Very Unnoticeable" and 7 was "Very Noticeable." Since Kolmogorov Smirnov tests indicated the entire data were not normally distributed ($ps < .05$), nonparametric analyses were conducted throughout the study.

Spearman's rank-order correlations explored the relationship between social acceptability and noticeability. The level of social acceptability was negatively correlated with noticeability only when the device was larger ($rs = -.43$, $N = 32$, $p < .01$). Thus, only when the size of the device was larger, highly noticeable devices were perceived as not socially acceptable. In contrast, when the devices were smaller or medium-sized, highly noticeable device was not necessarily correlated with low social acceptability.

3.3 Link between on body location & social acceptability

Here, we explored the link between social acceptability and noticeability based on body locations. For this, participants read the following preamble prior to answering the questions in the next section: "Please imagine that these tracking devices are visible to the people around you in a gym while you are using them." Subsequently, participants were asked to "Select an appropriate number to indicate how socially comfortable you would feel using a fitness tracking device that is attached to your." Below this question, participants saw Fig. 1(b). They used a Likert scale where 1 was "*Very Uncomfortable*" and 7 was "*Very Comfortable*" based on the body parts they imagined to wear the device (i.e., Around the; Arm, Chest, Wrist, Waist, and Thigh).

Spearman's rank-order correlations were conducted. The level of social acceptability was negatively correlated with noticeability only for the chest location ($rs = -.65$, $N = 32$, $p < .01$). That is, only for the chest-worn devices, more noticeable devices are perceived as less socially acceptable. For other locations, noticeability and social acceptability were not linked ($ps > .05$).

Remarkably, this finding was consistent with some of the open-ended responses where participants responded to the following question: "Please tell us your ideas about: What makes certain wearable devices socially uncomfortable to wear, even when they function very well?" (E.g., "if they are closer to more sexualized body parts, especially for females" "around chest"). Accordingly, we re-ran a Spearman's rank-order correlation while splitting the data by gender. For female, social acceptability and noticeability were strongly correlated ($rs = -.65$; $n = 16$, $p = .007$) while there was no such correlation for male counterparts; ($rs = -.18$; $n = 16$, $p = .50$).

4   Discussion and Design Guidelines

This study explored the relationship between social acceptability and noticeability. Although, intuitively, noticeability might give the impression to be negatively correlated with social acceptability, our findings suggested that social acceptability and noticeability of fitness tracking devices are negatively correlated only when the devices are i) larger, or ii) worn around the chest specifically by female users.

When the devices are smaller to medium size, however, the expected correlation did not emerge. This potentially infers that when the devices are smaller to medium size, participants might not perceive the noticeable devices as socially unacceptable. Furthermore, the gender effect we discovered for the devices around the chest points toward a potential design solution: Chest worn fitness tracking devices could be designed differently for male and female users to improve the level of social acceptability. Specifically, for female users. Around the chest, devices should be particularly inconspicuous to be worn by them, while the device noticeability might not influence the male users' social comfort level as much.

In sum, our findings offer the following guidelines to designers and researchers of health and fitness tracking devices:

Device Size: use the smallest size as possible, since the acceptability decreases significantly with increased device size.

On Body Location: wearing fitness tracking devices on the upper arm or the wrist is more socially acceptable than other body parts such as the chest. Additionally, devices worn around the chest should be particularly less noticeable for female users.

Gender: researchers should pay closer attention to gender concerns while conducting social acceptability research as the acceptability ratings might vary across genders.

5   Limitation and Future Work

While the sample size ($N = 32$) used in our study was somewhat consistent with comparable HCI studies [5], we acknowledge that having a larger sample would further reinforce our claims, especially for non-significant results. Next, since all the participants were living within a Western culture, we would be wary of generalizing the study results across different cultural contexts. While exploring culturally motivated perceptual differences in acceptability and noticeability would be challenging, it would be a very fruitful path for future work. Finally, we acknowledge that this study was a computer-based questionnaire, and thus, a future laboratory experiment where participants actually experience using the fitness tracker is crucial to draw final conclusions.

6 Conclusions

Fitness tracking devices are evolving rapidly and becoming popular gradually, largely due to technological advances. However, such devices are almost always small and worn around the wrist. Oher potential on body locations remain mainly unexplored, presumably due to perceived lower social acceptability associated with other on body locations and device size. Indeed, it is intuitive to feel that highly noticeable devices are socially unacceptable. However, such negative correlations were not found for smaller to medium-sized devices, or around the arm, wrist, waist, and thigh devices. In sum, our results point toward great design potential for fitness tracking devices: even when the devices are noticeable, they may be perceived as socially acceptable, possibly because of other factors underlying the design of the device, when they are smaller or medium, and/or when they are worn on the arm, wrist, waist or thigh. Future studies need to explore the contributing factors for noticeability (e.g., color and shape).

Acknowledgment

We thank all the participants for their time and feedback. This research was partially funded by a Natural Sciences and Engineering Research Council (NSERC) grant.

References

1. Ahlström, D., Hasan, K., and Irani, P.: Are you comfortable doing that?: acceptance studies of around-device gestures in and for public settings. In *Proceedings of the 16th international conference on Human-computer interaction with mobile devices & services* (MobileHCI '14). pp. 193–202. ACM.
2. Alallah, F., Neshati, A., Sakamoto, Y., Hasan, K., Lank, E., Bunt, A., and Irani, P.: Performer vs. observer: whose comfort level should we consider when examining the social acceptability of input modalities for head-worn display?. In *Proceedings of the 24th ACM Symposium on Virtual Reality Software and Technology* (VRST '18), 9 pages. ACM.

3. Alallah, F., Neshati, A., Sheibani, N., Sakamoto, Y., Bunt, A., Irani, P. and Hasan, K.: Crowdsourcing vs Laboratory-Style Social Acceptability Studies?: Examining the Social Acceptability of Spatial User Interactions for Head-Worn Displays. In *Proceedings of the 2018 CHI Conference on Human Factors in Computing Systems* (CHI '18). Paper 310, 7 pages. ACM.

4. Amini, F., Hasan, K., Bunt, A., and Irani, P.: Data Representations for In-Situ Exploration of Health and Fitness Data. In *Proceedings of the 11th EAI International Conference on Pervasive Computing Technologies for Healthcare* (PervasiveHealth 2017). pp. 163–172 ACM.

5. Caine, K.: Local Standards for Sample Size. In *Proceedings of the SIGCHI Conference on Human Factors in Computing Systems* (CHI '16). pp. 981–992. ACM.

6. Costanza, E., Inverso, S., and Allen, R.: Toward subtle intimate interfaces for mobile devices using an EMG controller. In *Proceedings of the SIGCHI Conference on Human Factors in Computing Systems* (CHI '05). pp. 481–489. ACM.

7. Koelle, M., Heuten, W., and Boll, S.: Are you hiding it?: usage habits of lifelogging camera wearers. In *Proceedings of the 19th International Conference on Human-Computer Interaction with Mobile Devices and Services* (MobileHCI '17). Article 80, 8 pages. ACM.

8. Rekimoto, J.: GestureWrist and GesturePad: Unobtrusive Wearable Interaction Devices. In *Proceedings of the 5th IEEE International Symposium on Wearable Computers* (ISWC '01). IEEE.

9. Rico, J., and Brewster, S.: Usable gestures for mobile interfaces: evaluating social acceptability. In *Proceedings of the SIGCHI Conference on Human Factors in Computing Systems* (CHI '10). pp. 887–896. ACM.

10. Tung, Y., Hsu, C., Wang, H., Chyou, S., Lin, J., Wu, P., Valstar, A., and Chen, M.: UserDefined Game Input for Smart Glasses in Public Space. In *Proceedings of the 33rd Annual ACM Conference on Human Factors in Computing Systems* (CHI '15). pp. 3327–3336. ACM.

SECTION 4

User Experiences and Wellbeing at Work

User Experience at Work:
Four Perspectives on What It May Mean

Morten Hertzum

University of Copenhagen, Copenhagen, Denmark
hertzum@hum.ku.dk

Abstract

Most work involves the use of artifacts; thus, user experience (UX) is a factor in how most employees experience their work. This study revisits the tool, media, dialogue-partner, and system perspectives on artifact use to explore UX at work. It is found that artifacts foster positive UX when they lend the user expressive power (tool), are transparent (media) or perceptive (dialogue partner). They foster negative UX when they attract the user's attention or make the user a mere system component. The task focus inherent in the perspectives suggests that wellbeing at work is mostly promoted by factors other than UX.

Keywords

Perspectives on artifact use · User experience · Wellbeing · Work

1 Introduction

User experience (UX) is about the experiences associated with the use of artifacts [12]. Some definitions restrict UX to actual use [2], others include anticipated use [9], and still others also include aesthetics [5]. These differences appear, however, minor compared to the shared focus on the experiences associated

How to cite this book chapter:
Hertzum, M. 2020. User Experience at Work: Four Perspectives on What It May Mean.
In: Loizides, F., Winckler, M., Chatterjee, U., Abdelnour-Nocera, J. and Parmaxi, A.
(eds.) *Human Computer Interaction and Emerging Technologies: Adjunct
Proceedings from the INTERACT 2019 Workshops.* Pp. 127–132. Cardiff: Cardiff
University Press. DOI: https://doi.org/10.18573/book3.o. License: CC-BY 4.0.

with artifact use. Well-documented experiences with computer artifacts in work settings include burnout, deskilling, frustration, and helplessness [e.g., 4, 11]. Countering such negative experiences is central to employee wellbeing; replacing them with positive experiences would be an even nobler design goal.

Studies of technology acceptance find that perceived enjoyment, a concept similar to UX, predicts the intention to use an artifact as strongly as do perceived usefulness and perceived ease of use [8]. The relation between the artifact and the user's experience is, however, complex because UX is not determined by the artifact alone. Rather, UX results from the interrelations among the characteristics of the artifact, user, task, and context of use. While this observation is largely trivial, it raises the question of whether UX exerts much influence on wellbeing at work. It may well be that wellbeing at work is first and foremost facilitated by factors other than computer artifacts, that is, by experiences and conditions other than UX.

To explore what we might accomplish by designing for good UX at work this study revisits Kammersgaard's [10] four perspectives on human-computer interaction, ponders what constitutes positive and negative UX within each perspective, and discusses possible positive contributions of UX to wellbeing at work.

2 Four Perspectives on System Use and UX

Kammersgaard [10] outlines four perspectives on human-computer interaction by distinguishing between artifacts for individual and collaborative use and between artifacts for which agency rests with the user and artifacts that split agency between user and artifact. The four perspectives are the tool perspective, the system perspective, the dialogue-partner perspective, and the media perspective, see Table 1.

Table 1: Four perspectives on system use, adapted from Kammersgaard [10].

	Individual	*Collaborative*
User agency	**Tool perspective**	**Media perspective**
	• Artifact is an extension of the user's body	• Users communicate through the artifact
	• Ready to hand vs present at hand	• Media richness vs common ground
	• UX?: expressive power	• UX?: transparency, structure
Split agency	**Dialogue-partner perspective**	**System perspective**
	• Artifact displays human-like behavior	• User is similar to other system components
	• Intelligent vs annoying assistant	• Automation vs meaningful jobs
	• UX?: perceptive, adaptive	• UX?: deskilling, monotony

The *tool perspective* has its roots in craftwork and emphasizes that in the hands of a skilled user the tool is a seamless extension of the user, who attends to her task rather than to the tool: When hammering the skilled user's attention is on driving the nail, not on the hammer. Conceptually, the tool is said to be ready to hand [14]. It is only upon breakdowns that the tool becomes the focus of the user's attention – becomes present at hand. If the hammer is too light for the size of nail or otherwise inadequate for the task then the user's attention shifts from the task to the tool. These shifts are associated with frustration and other negative emotions because the breakdown thwarts progress on the task, at least temporarily. It appears that tools foster good experiences when they are out of mind – ready to hand – and poor experiences when they become present at hand. If we take the definition of UX to mean that the user must, in the moment, be conscious that she is using an artifact then the tool perspective rules out positive UX. The positive experiences do not qualify as UX because they are associated with an uninterrupted focus on the task. In contrast, the user is conscious of the artifact when it thwarts task progress; thus tools can foster negative UX. If we do not require that the user must, in the moment, be conscious that she is using an artifact – and this is probably the more sensible option – then positive UX is possible within the tool perspective and consists of designing for readiness to hand. The user may however not attribute the positive UX to the tool but, partly or wholly, to other aspects of the use situation.

The *system perspective* aligns with industrial perceptions of work and promotes a view in which a system consists of components that may be human or automated. Each component is characterized by the input it receives, the activities it performs on those inputs, and the outputs it delivers. The division of the system into components is made by management and defines a division of labor. To perform their work the users need only know the characteristics of the component they embody. Performance is measured by how cheaply, quickly, and consistently the components deliver their outputs. That is, the users' work is measured in the same way as that of the automated components. If the users perform poorer than an automated version of the same component then the users are at risk of being replaced by such a component. In this sense the users are measured by their ability to function as automated components. The automation inherent in the system perspective is often associated with deskilling of the users, who become operators of machines that perform more and more components of the work [1]. This negative UX results from a primary focus on automation, thereby leaving the users with the components that have not yet been automated. To create positive UX it is necessary to focus on creating meaningful and rewarding human components, for example by automating the parts of work that are monotonous or unhealthy. However, to create meaningful and rewarding human components it may also be necessary to reconsider the separation between a managerial level that defines the components and an operational level that merely performs according to these preset definitions. That is, it may be necessary to challenge the essence of the system perspective.

The dialogue-partner perspective sees the artifact as an intelligent assistant with which the users can interact in much the same way as they interact with humans. The intelligent assistant empowers the user by serving his or her needs and does so without requiring that the user learns special commands for interacting with the assistant. Unlike the system perspective, which tends to reduce humans to machines, the dialogue-partner perspective seeks to elevate machines to human-like performance. Unlike the tool perspective, which involves the user's moment-to-moment handling of the tool, the intelligent assistant acts autonomously in the user's service. The intelligent assistant may, for example, monitor an architect's work on a building and inform the architect when his current building design violates formal regulations or recognized principles for good design [3]. The intelligent assistant fosters positive and negative UX in much the same way as a human collaborator. Negative UX ensues if the assistant needs too many instructions, performs poor work, or delivers its work at inopportune moments. Positive UX ensues if the assistant is effective and efficient and, especially, if the assistant also picks up on the tacit conditions for good performance and reacts appropriately to dynamic changes in the environment. Often, intelligent assistants must be supervised by users who need to be ready to take over if the assistant encounters a situation it cannot handle. This creates poor conditions for positive UX because the user wants to offload the task to the assistant but must, instead, "stay in the loop" to be ready to step in whenever needed.

The *media perspective* positions the artifact as a medium through which the users interact with each other. That is, the medium is merely a channel; agency rests with the users. Rich media [13] provide for simultaneous interactions in multiple modalities and, thereby, for back-channeling (e.g., nods, raised eyebrows) to occur via some modalities at the same time as the main interaction occupies other modalities (e.g., speech). Thereby, rich media support users in establishing, sustaining, and repairing common ground, which is key to effective collaborative interactions. Conversely, lean media provide few or only a single modality and may be restricted to asynchronous interactions, thereby increasing the risk of breakdowns in common ground. Media provide positive UX when they are transparent – somewhat similar to when a tool is ready to hand. A transparent medium allows the interactions among the users to flow without distortions. Rich media are transparent with respect to more interaction modalities than lean media. In addition to transparency, some media aim to provide positive UX by structuring the interaction, for example by making explicit that an interactional turn is a request and therefore must be answered by accepting, declining or negotiating the request [14]. Media foster negative UX when they are insufficiently transparent or enforce a structure that is too rigid. In both cases the medium stands in the way of the interactions among the users.

3 Discussion

Most work involves the use of artifacts, such as products, systems or services. Thus, UX is a factor in how most employees experience their work. In the tool and media perspectives, an artifact fosters positive UX by not attracting the user's attention, which instead remains on the task. That is, it is by supporting the user in expressing her skills – as manifested in high-quality work task products – that tools and media foster positive UX. Positive UX is about *lending the user expressive power*. In the dialogue-partner perspective, positive UX is as much about how well the artifact engages in the process of its use as it is about the product that results from this process. That is, an artefact fosters positive UX if it is a *perceptive and adaptive dialogue partner*. In the system perspective, positive UX appears to be secondary to other concerns. That is, positive UX involves *abandoning the system perspective* or, at least, supplementing it with other perspectives. Abandoning the system perspective is a daunting undertaking because this perspective permeates much thinking about how to organize workplaces. For example, physicians are increasingly frustrated that they spend still more of their time documenting their work in electronic patient records and comparatively less time with patients, but the increasing documentation requirements are justified by pointing out that the physician is a component in a much larger system, which needs the documentation for hospital-level quality assurance, national performance indicators, and international healthcare research [4].

A less ambitious goal than fostering positive UX in the service of wellbeing at work would be to avoid negative UX. The tool and media perspectives agree that artifacts foster negative UX whenever they attract the user's attention. Thus, users become conscious of their artifact use when they experience problems with the artifacts. The distinction between, on the one hand, positive UX and a task focus and, on the other hand, negative UX and an artifact focus echoes a seminal study of wellbeing at work. In this study Herzberg et al. [7, p. 113] conclude:

When our respondents reported feeling happy with their jobs, they most frequently described factors related to their tasks, to events that indicated to them that they were successful in the performance of their work, and to the possibility of professional growth. Conversely, when feelings of unhappiness were reported, they were not associated with the job itself but with conditions that surround the doing of the job.

It may seem that factors other than the use of artifacts stand a better chance of creating wellbeing and that UX may mostly be about avoiding negative experiences. Finally, influence on the design of the artifacts used in performing the work may be a source of positive UX not covered by the four perspectives revisited in this study [6].

References

1. Braverman, H.: *Labor and monopoly capital: The degradation of work in the twentieth century*. Monthly Review Press, New York (1974).
2. Colbert, M.: User experience of communication before and during rendezvous: Interim results. *Personal and Ubiquitous Computing* 9(3), 134–141 (2005).
3. Fischer, G., Lemke, A.C., Mastaglio, T.: Critics: An emerging approach to knowledge-based human-computer interaction. *International Journal of Man-Machine Studies* 35(5), 695–721 (1991).
4. Gawande, A.: The upgrade: Why doctors hate their computers. *The New Yorker*, 62–73 (November 12, 2018).
5. Hekkert, P.: Design aesthetics: Principles of pleasure in product design. *Psychology Science* 48(2), 157–172 (2006).
6. Hertzum, M., Torkilsheyggi, A.: How do users perceive a design-in-use approach to implementation? A healthcare case. In: *Proceedings of the INTERACT2019 Conference on Human-Computer Interaction*. Springer, Cham (2019).
7. Herzberg, F., Mausner, B., Snyderman, B.B.: *The motivation to work*. Wiley, New York (1959).
8. Hornbæk, K., Hertzum, M.: Technology acceptance and user experience: A review of the experiential component in HCI. *ACM Transactions on Computer-Human Interaction* 24(5), Article 33 (2017).
9. ISO 9241: *Ergonomics of human-system interaction – Part 210: Human-centred design for interactive systems*. International Standard Organization, Geneva, CH (2010).
10. Kammersgaard, J.: Four different perspectives on human-computer interaction. *International Journal of Man-Machine Studies* 28(4), 343–362 (1988).
11. Lazar, J., Jones, A., Shneiderman, B.: Workplace user frustration with computers: An exploratory investigation of the causes and severity. *Behaviour & Information Technology* 25(3), 239–251 (2006).
12. Roto, V., Law, E., Vermeeren, A., Hoonhout, J.: *User experience white paper: Bringing clarity to the concept of user experience. Result from Dagstuhl Seminar* (2011). http://www.allaboutux.org/uxwhitepaper (accessed April 1, 2019).
13. Trevino, L.K., Lengel, R.H., Daft, R.L.: Media symbolism, media richness, and media choice in organizations: A symbolic interactionist perspective. *Communication Research* 14(5), 553–574 (1987).
14. Winograd, T., Flores, F.: *Understanding computers and cognition: A new foundation for design*. Ablex, Norwood, NJ (1986).

Prototype Design of Alert Device for Hearing Impaired Users

Priyank Kularia, Ganesh Bhutkar, Sumit Jadhav
and Dhiraj Jadhav

Center of Excellence in HCI, Vishwakarma Institute of Technology,
Pune, India
ganesh.bhutkar@vit.edu

Abstract

Sounds are essential pressure waves which keep humans informed about the events around them. Users with hearing impairment have difficulties in recognition of the sounds that are vital in their day-to-day life. This research paper discusses a paper prototype design of Alert Device for hearing impaired users within their work environment at home. This prototype of Alert Device is designed based on a detailed literature survey as well as peer Android application review. The device design focuses on recognition of sounds in the home environment such as detection of the doorbell, crying of a baby, fire alarm, motion detection alarm and phone ringing at home. It also includes features such as self-training of sound, Panic/SOS button and sound log. The proposed proto-type will reduce the dependency of hearing impaired users on other family members around them within the work environment at home and will improve their daily life activities through Information and Communication Technology (ICT).

How to cite this book chapter:
Kularia, P., Bhutkar, G., Jadhav, S. and Jadhav, D. 2020. Prototype Design of Alert Device for Hearing Impaired Users. In: Loizides, F., Winckler, M., Chatterjee, U., Abdelnour-Nocera, J. and Parmaxi, A. (eds.) *Human Computer Interaction and Emerging Technologies: Adjunct Proceedings from the INTERACT 2019 Workshops.* Pp. 133–138. Cardiff: Cardiff University Press. DOI: https://doi.org/10.18573/book3.p. License: CC-BY 4.0.

Keywords

Alert Device · Hearing Impairment Users · Deaf · Non-Speech Sounds · Hearing Disability · Hearing Loss

1 Introduction

The world human population has reached to about 7.7 billion by February 2019. According to WHO, around 466 million people worldwide have a hearing disability, of which 131 million are from South Asia [10]. It is estimated that over 900 million people all around the world will have a hearing disability by 2050, and South Asia will have a significant effect of this with an increment of about 2% making upto 267 million hearing disabled people [13].

A study by Gudyanga shows that the inability to detect any sounds in the surroundings leads to social, emotional and behavioural problems [4]. Also, hearing impaired user rely on sign language or lip-reading to understand speech sound. But, in the case of non-speech sounds, the users with hearing disability face numerous troubles in a home environment [3]. The major problems include **difficulty in communication with friends/family, lack of awareness about surrounding work environment, inability to handle dangers and emergencies, and behavioural issues like loneliness or depression**.

Hearing disability is based on the grade of impairment [12] which is summarized in Table 1. There are different kinds of devices available for hearing impaired users such as Assistive Devices, Augmentative Devices and Alert Devices [8]. The study of these devices reveals that there are only a few costly Alert Devices that are available as compared to Assistive and Augmentative devices. Due to this, the hearing impaired user always needs an interpreter to know about the events happing around him/her even in home environment. Thus, to make hearing impaired user self-sufficient regarding detection of Non-Speech Sound related events around; there is a need of a Universal Alert Device. This device should be portable and should detect all the desired Non-Speech Sounds for hearing impaired users.

Table 1: Grades of hearing impairment (dBHL: decibels Hearing Level)[12].

Grade of Impairment	Audiometric ISO value
No impairment	25 dBHL or less
Slight Impairment	26–40 dBHL
Moderate impairment	41–60 dBHL
Severe impairment	61–80 dBHL
Profound impairment	81 dBHL or greater

This research paper provides an overview of the investigation process and a related paper prototype design of the Alert Device for hearing impaired users within their work environment at home. The next section discusses an extensive literature review which tends to focus first on Alert Devices and then on Non-Speech Sounds.

2 Literature Review

A literature review on the Alert Devices and related Non-Speech Sounds has been comprehensive. This section discusses a few research articles which mainly focus on Alert Devices and related Non-Speech Sounds, which have helped in the initial process of prototype designing. These articles mainly include conference papers, journal papers and a patent published from 2004 till 2018. Most of these articles involve studies with a prototype design, real-world products, and mobile applications. The following sub-section discusses articles on Alert Devices first, and then about articles related to Non-Speech Sounds.

2.1 Articles on Alert Devices

Table 2 depicts details of different features and aspects present in the Alert Devices discussed in related research articles [1–2, 5–7]. The abbreviation NA in Table 2 stands for data Not Available. Major features are selected after the rigorous study of these research articles, which are -use of display unit (other than smartphone), use of vibrations, self-training of sound, Panic/SOS button and sound log. The important observations from data in Table 2 are provided as follows:

- **The smartphone is the most preferred device** for primary display.
- **Home and Work are the most preferred work environments** for deaf users.
- **100% (5 out 5) of the Alert Devices use vibrations** as an alert medium.
- **60% (3 out of 5) of the Alert Devices store sound log** and use display unit other than a smartphone.
- 40% (2 out of 5) of the Alert Devices have the ability of self-training of sound.
- **Only 20% (1 out of 5) of the Alert Devices provide Panic/SOS button.**
- The most common range of participant users is about 15 or fewer users.

2.2 Literature Review on Non-Speech Sounds

The different sounds which Alert Devices of different research studies are able to detect include **door knock, landline/phone, doorbell, loud noise, fire/smoke alarm, intruder alarm, motion detection alarm, baby cry and**

Table 2: Summary of features in Alert Devices of research studies.

Features and Aspects	Research Articles				
	Matthews et al. 2005	Ander et al. 2017	Obe et al. 2018	Mielke et al. 2016	Bragg et al. 2016
Primary Display	Smartphone	Smartphone, TV, Tablet	Smartphone	Smartwatch	Smartphone
Environment(s)	Office	Home, Office &Hotel	Home	Controlled room	Home, Office& Mobile
Display unit (other than smartphone)	No	Yes	Yes	Yes	No
Use of vibrations	Yes	Yes	Yes	Yes	Yes
Self-training of sound	No	Yes	No	NA	Yes
SOS/Panic button	No	Yes	No	No	No
Sound log	Yes	Yes	NA	NA	Yes
No. of participants in the user survey	12 Users (3 deaf, 3 mostly deaf & 6 hard of hearing)	NA	NA	6 Users (3 deaf, 2 mostly deaf & 1 hard of hearing)	87 Users (50 deaf & 37 hard of hearing)

opening/closing of the door [1–2, 5–7]. As per data researched, 80% (4 out of 5) of the Alert Devices are able to detect door knock. 60% (3 out of 5) of the Alert Devices are able to identify sound of landline/phone, doorbell, loud noise, fire/smoke alarm, intruder alarm and motion detection alarm, less than 50% of the Alert Devices are able to detect baby sound and door opening/ closing.

3 Android Application Review

A systematic review has been conducted for currently available leading Android apps related to alerts and sound detection used mainly by hearing impaired users. Applications reviewed include **Baby Monitor 3G, Flash Alert Call & SMS, Sentechtor, Sound Detector and Visualfy** [9, 11, 14–16].

Different features and details observed in these selected apps which are used mainly by hearing impaired users include a visual information, flash, alert from different mobile apps, vibration, sounds log, self-training of sound and Panic/SOS button. Important observations of these apps are provided below:

- **Most of the apps (4 out of 5) provide alert using mobile display and also store sounds log** which makes it is easy to understand the alert generated.
- **Most of the apps (3 out of 5) have provided a vibration feature** for better focus on alert **and Panic/SOS button** for making emergency contacts.
- **Only two apps give alert from different applications and also provide self-training of sound.**
- Flash feature is provided in only one app and it is an essential feature for deaf.

4 Paper Prototype Design for Alert Device

The prototype will be developed with the consideration of the home environment as a work environment for the hearing impaired users. These users can benefit from this device immensely by detecting everyday essential sounds as well as certain very important non-speech sounds like opening/closing of the door, fire alarm, intruder alarm and movement detection that are crucial for safety and security at home.

The proposed prototype of Alert Device consists of four main blocks which are **Sensors, Sound Detection Unit, Communication Unit and Output Unit**, designed to be utilized within work environment at home. The hardware components/design will be completed at later stage. Apart from the prototype design of Alert Device, design of Smartphone Application is also proposed which consists of **Alert Detection, Training of Sound and Sound Log**. In Alert Detection, user can have live detection of the sounds with options of doorbell, crying of baby, fire alarm, phone ringing, motion-detection alarm and sound log. User can also customize the pattern and intensity of vibration for individual sound.

5 Conclusion

A paper prototype for this Alert Device is designed based on allied literature review as well as Android app review. The prototype design includes a few functionalities which can support users from slightly to profound impairment within work environment at home. It has features such as detection of various sounds, self-training of sound, Panic/SOS button, and sound log. Thus, the proposed Alert Device is designed with the primary intention of helping hearing impaired users to detect sounds occurring at home environment. The development of the proposed Alert Device will reduce the dependency of hearing impaired users on other family members at home and will improve their work engagement through Information and Communication Technology (ICT). In the future, the proposed Alert Device will be developed with an initial focus to make a Universal Alert Device, which will be portable and able to recognize all the desired Non-Speech Sounds.

References

1. Ander, B., Ander, S., Kushar, A.: Alarm Monitoring System. United States Patent. (2017)
2. Bragg, D., Huynh, N., E. Lander, R.: A Personalizable Mobile Sound Detector App Design for Deaf and Hard-of-Hearing Users. 18th International ACM SIGACCESS Conference on Computers and Accessibility – ASSETS 2016, Reno, NV, USA, pp. 3–13. (2016)
3. Dobie, R., Hemel, S. (edts): Hearing Loss Determining Eligibility for Social Security Benefits, Chapter 6, National Academies Press, USA. (2005)
4. Gudyanga, E., Wadesango, N., Eliphanos, H., Gudyana, A.: Challenges Faced by Students with Hearing Impairment in Bulawayo Urban Regular Schools. Mediterranean Journal of Social Sciences, 5(9), pp. 445–451. (2014)
5. Matthews, T., Fong, J., Mankoff, J.: Visualizing Non-Speech Sounds for the Deaf. 7th International ACM SIGACCESS Conference on Computers and Accessibility – ASSETS 2005, Baltimore, Maryland, USA. (2005)
6. Mielke, M., Brück, R.: AUDIS Wear: A Smartwatch based Assistive Device for Ubiquitous Awareness of Environmental Sounds. Annual International Conference – IEEE Engineering in Medicine and Biology Society, Orlando, FL, USA, pp. 5343–5347. (2016)
7. Obe, O., Abe, S., Boyinbode, O.: Development of Wireless Home Automation System for The Disabled (Deaf, Dumb And Alzheimer) People. International Journal of Scientific & Engineering Research, 9(10), pp. 1–6. (2018)
8. Assistive Devices for People with Hearing, Voice, Speech, or Language Disorders, https://www.nidcd.nih.gov/health/assistive-devices-people-hearing-voice-speech-orlanguage-disorders, last accessed on 15th Jan 2019
9. Baby monitor 3G, https://play.google.com/store/apps/details?id=com.tappytaps.android.babymonitor3g.trial&hl=en_US, last accessed on 9th Feb 2019
10. Deafness and hearing loss, https://www.who.int/news-room/fact-sheets/detail/deafness-and-hearing-loss, last accessed on 7th Jan 2019
11. Flash Alert Call &amp SMS, https://play.google.com/store/apps/details?id=call.sms.flash.alert&hl=en, last accessed on 9th Feb 2019
12. Global burden of hearing loss in the year 2000, https://www.who.int/healthinfo/statistics/bod_hearingloss.pdf, last accessed on 10th Jan 2019
13. Global estimates on prevalence of hearing loss, https://www.who.int/deafness/Global-estimates-on-prevalence-of-hearing-loss-for-website.pptx?ua=1, last accessed on 10th Jan 2019
14. Sentechtor, https://apkpure.com/sentector/com.mobisys.android.sentector, last accessed on 9th Feb 2019
15. Sound detector, https://apkpure.com/sound-detector/dk.mvainformatics.android.sounddeector, last accessed on 9th Feb 2019
16. Visualfy, https://play.google.com/store/apps/details?id=com.fusiodarts.visalfy.lite&hl=en_IN, last accessed on 9th Feb 2019

The "aftermath" of Industry 4.0 in Small and Medium Enterprises

João Carlos Ferreira[*] and João Silva[†]

[*]Instituto Universitário de Lisboa (ISCTE-IUL), ISTAR-IUL, Portugal
[†]Instituto Universitário de Lisboa (ISCTE-IUL), Portugal
jcafa@iscte-iul.pt, silva.joao.pedro.goncalves@gmail.com

Abstract

With the development of new technologies and methodologies, multiple sectors start to experience the benefits and drawbacks. Currently, the industry is facing a new revolution known as Industry 4.0. This new path allowed all enterprises to further develop their methodologies and understand the disadvantages and advantages of it. With the sole purpose of retaining costs in production while maintaining the same degree of quality, companies desire to diminish their downtime due to malfunction or improper maintenance schedules that may not amount to the desired efficiency. Nevertheless, not all companies manage to enter this exclusive circle, since such technologies also deliver a high cost which some companies simply cannot support. Consequently, this generates a huge drawback to the outsiders of this revolution.

Keywords

Industry 4.0 · Cyber Physical Systems

How to cite this book chapter:
Ferreira, J.C. and Silva, J. 2020. The "aftermath" of Industry 4.0 in Small and Medium Enterprises. In: Loizides, F., Winckler, M., Chatterjee, U., Abdelnour-Nocera, J. and Parmaxi, A. (eds.) Human Computer Interaction and Emerging Technologies: Adjunct Proceedings from the INTERACT 2019 Workshops. Pp. 139–144. Cardiff: Cardiff University Press. DOI: https://doi.org/10.18573/book3.q. License: CC-BY 4.0.

1 Introduction

"Companies and their industrial processes need to adapt to this rapid change if they are not to be left behind by developments in their sector and by their competitors."[1]. Industries worldwide are becoming highly volatile, facing the same rhythms as their markets of choice. Taking in consideration the "big step" taken in industry regarding the systems being used, most companies face a problem regarding the data registered in their systems. Although it is collected, proper storage and analysis is not performed resulting in the incapability to extract viable knowledge crucial to decision making [2]. Consequently, this affects multiple areas of action such as maintenance, operations, etc. Therefore, companies must rapidly change their mindset to focus on the data generated to extract viable knowledge for decision making processes.

This article aims to analyze the main components that lie within Industry 4.0, advantages of its implementations and understand the main differences between SME's and MNE's. With this research the main goal is to and answer the research question: Is it possible that the main characteristics that define SME's justify the reason why they hold possible investments regarding the methodologies and practices inherent to this revolution?

2 Industry 4.0

Taking in consideration the developments led on during the past revolutions, a new development was needed to take full capabilities of the current infor-mation systems and produce a new output. As known, with the development of information systems in the previous revolution, data started being gener-ated by machines in industries across the world, providing the possibility to create an automated production flow. Nevertheless, data generated was not intended to provide overall view of the production systems, more specifically to the standard maintenance point of view. Since the automation was tackled in this revolution, all the major problems regarding industry were therefore resolved. Nevertheless, the "roads" to increase earnings and productivity were decreasing. Consequently, this led to the new path of Industry 4.0. A path where the main goal was to re-shape previous ideas and concepts, allowing to reproduce models with the current technology available for industry [3].

Throughout time this concept began to grow and became a "revolution" in 2015 propagated by Germany's government as an action to maintain its posi-tion as the global leader in the sector of manufacturing equipment. At its core, one cannot state or identify what triggers industry 4.0. "Instead it can be described more precisely by a conjunction of many technologies – both exist-ing and new which now – work together" [4]. Chesworth [5] considers that industry 4.0 is the joint effect of CPS's (Cyber Physical Sytems) and IoT (Inter-net of Things) therefore creating a decentralized control and advanced connec-

Table 1: Advantages of implementing Industry 4.0 [9–10].

Advantages of implementing Industry 4.0	Sector
Decrease production and logistic costs by 10–30%	Costs
Reduce Quality management costs by 10–20%	Costs
Shorter time-to-market products	Agility/Revenues
Improve customer responsiveness	Customer Experience
Mass production without increasing production costs	Efficiency
Reduce maintenance planning time (20–50%)	Efficiency
Increase equipment uptime (10–20%)	Efficiency
More confidence in data and information	Innovation
Material cost savings (5–10%)	Costs
Reduce inventory carrying costs	Costs
Reduced overall maintenance costs (5–10%)	Costs

tivity. Consequently, large quantities of data are generated justifying the final component of Big Data[5, 10–11]. This joint relation constitutes the key feature of this concept, the smart factory [8].

In terms of benefits to implement the methodologies and components associated with this methodology, follows the table below.

The advantages of implementing the practices and methodologies of industry 4.0 trigger interest in all the sectors of industry, yet some already face limitations prior to generating the first step towards this new world.

3 Industry 4.0 effect in SME

"Small and Medium-sized Enterprises (SME's) are the driving force of many manufacturing economies"[11]. Taking in consideration their position on each country's economy, the impacts of this latest industrial revolution are important to take in consideration. Even though these aren't the only type of enterprises in the world, they face more challenges and limitations than Multi-National Enterprises (MNE's). These two types of companies differ in multiple aspects as literature states. According to the European Commission [12], SME's consist of companies with a staff headcount of 250 or less and turnover that does not exceed 50 million Euros. Nevertheless, further differences arise regarding these two types of companies. Table 2 contains the main differences regarding SME's and MNE's in an overall perspective.

As stated above, SME's due to their small size, face a tremendous limitation due to their lack of resources, both physical and financial [11]. Nevertheless, exceptions rise in specific areas such aerospace and defense.

Table 2: Main differences between SME's and MNE's [11].

Feature	SME's	MNE's
(1) Financial Resources	Low	High
(2) Use of advanced Manufacturing	Low	High
(3) Research and Development	Low	High
(4) Human Resources Engagement	Multiple domains	Specific domains
(5) Knowledge and Experience	Focused in a specific area	Spread around different areas
(6) Important activities	Outsourced	Internal
(7) Alliances with Universities	Low	High
(8) Organization culture	Low	High

Regarding **financial sector (1)**, one of most vital sectors in these companies, a significant disparity lays between the two types of companies. For starters, SME's that want to obtain finance must face expensive process handlings. In other words, the cost of applying for a lone are nothing but immoderate. Legal fees, administrative costs and costs related regarding information related to the acquisition are fixed, regardless of the amount to be loaned. Further costs must be applied in the presence of outside financiers. All these points together with lack of information and proper financial facilities in developing countries leads to a more severe problem.

The low amount of financial resources leads to a chain of consequences, that can be described as a snowball effect for the SME's. In terms of **advanced manufacturing (2)**, the usage is considered low, since the investment in advanced manufacturing technologies is difficult to support. This lack of usage leads to incapability to invest in **research and development (3)**. This deeply affects the human resources sector. Instead, the **engagement of human resources (4)** is in multiple domains, "For example, the employees at SME's are more likely to be 'Jack of all Trades' and less likely to develop high levels of expertise" [11]. This leads to the fact that operators in SME's do not manage to gain a proper **specialization in a specific area (5)**, since the responsibilities inherited can range to multiple areas. This type of example does not present in MNE's due to their rich mass of employees. In these types of enterprises, the chances of an employee specialization in a certain area are higher due to sole focus performing related tasks [11].

The consequences of this methodology can easily be applied to production. A low skillset, and engagement lead to the **outsourcing of production (6)** to control costs and time. Due to inability to attain a proper specialization, SME's no longer sustain a proper platform to attract universities and institutes. Consequent to this lack of self-updating policy to maintain up-to-date and cutting-edge methodologies leads to SME's not being able to generate **alliances with universities and institutes (7)**.

With the financial, human resources and production sectors affected by this snowball link, the structure of the company is going to "feel" the consequences. With the outsourcing of production and low skill of collaborators, the **company culture (8)** become poor with low capability to dynamize [11].

These can be stated as the most relevant aspects in a theoretical stand point. Nevertheless, they do not differ from the main studies performed in conducted to SME's. According to the digital business readiness study, "Many enterprises are lacking financial and often human resource too, to promote digital change internally" [5]. This leads a low level of completely digitally up-to-date enterprises of 27%. The main reason behind this low percentage can be explained with the fact that "SME's are lacking confidence in information security and data protection. Without this confidence, the transformation of business and manufacturing processes threatens to stall" [13].

4 Conclusions

From the analysis conducted throughout this paper regarding Industry 4.0 and main features of SME's and MNE's it is possible to understand the main reasons that support the lack of investment in new technologies. Latest achievements regarding methodologies and practices require a solid foundation and finance, to provide a sustainable growth for SME's which justifies the holdback from SME's.

Due to their lack of positioning in current markets, which are more and more competitive, these companies desire fast solutions to their problems, therefore maintaining methodologies that MNE's tested and approved throughout the years. Due to their capability to shape-shift into their desired solution, these companies must face the output of the market in a short-term basis, therefore invalidating the main basis of thought regarding industry 4.0. This line of thought regards a long-term vision where hefty finance is a fixed variable in the equation of going a step towards new income. SME's behave in a solid perspective where they "Don't take a step bigger than their leg". Nonetheless, this strategy to maintain position may provide negative consequences, more considerably inadequate health in a long-term statement, due to their lack of capability to self-innovate and achieve new competitive advantages. Therefore, this confirms the simple line of survival, where the runt of the litter dies.

For SME's to enter this revolution without compromising their structure they must understand the possible implementations that allow to achieve the best results with a low initial investment. This step is vital to stop the snowball effect described in this paper. **One possible solution is the creation of a new framework**. In other words, by providing a "step-by-step" approach, vital information can be attained in a simplified way allowing SME's to understand prior to implementation phase which elements of Industry 4.0 can be implemented and how.

References

1. C. Finance, "Deloitte – Industry 4.0 Challenges and Solutions for Digital Transformation," 2015.
2. K. Efthymiou, N. Papakostas, D. Mourtzis, and G. Chryssolouris, "On a predictive maintenance platform for production systems," *Procedia CIRP*, vol. 3, no. 1, pp. 221–226, 2012.
3. N. Sakib and T. Wuest, "Challenges and Opportunities of Condition-based Predictive Maintenance: A Review," *Procedia CIRP*, vol. 78, pp. 267–272, 2018.
4. H. Meissner, R. Ilsen, and J. C. Aurich, "Analysis of Control Architectures in the Context of Industry 4.0," *Procedia CIRP*, vol. 62, pp. 165–169, 2017.
5. D. Chesworth, "Industry 4.0 Techniques as a Maintenance Strategy (A Review Paper)," *Researchgate.net/publication/322369285*, no. January, pp. 0–8, 2018.
6. A. T. Jones, D. Romero, and T. Wuest, "Modeling agents as joint cognitive systems in smart manufacturing systems," *Manuf. Lett.*, vol. 17, pp. 6–8, 2018.
7. S. Ferreiro, E. Konde, S. Fernández, and A. Prado, "INDUSTRY 4.0 : Predictive Intelligent Maintenance for Production Equipment," *Eur. Conf. Progn. Heal. Manag. Soc.*, pp. 1–8, 2016.
8. Shiyong Wang, Jiafu Wan, Di Li, and Chunhua Zhang, "Implementing Smart Factory of Industrie 4.0: An Outlook," *Int. J. Distrib. Sens. Networks*, vol. 2016, 2016.
9 C. Coleman, S. Damofaran, and E. Deuel, "Predictive maintenance and the smart factory," *Deloitte*, p. 8, 2017.
10. A. Rojko, "Industry 4.0 Concept: Background and Overview," *Int. J. Interact. Mob. Technol.*, vol. 11, no. 5, pp. 77–90, 2017.
11. S. Mittal, M. A. Khan, D. Romero, and T. Wuest, "A critical review of smart manufacturing & Industry 4.0 maturity models: Implications for small and medium-sized enterprises (SMEs)," *J. Manuf. Syst.*, vol. 49, no. November, pp. 194–214, 2018. EC, "What is an SME?".
12. L. Sommer, "Industrial revolution Industry 4.0: Are German manufacturing SMEs the first victims of this revolution?," *J. Ind. Eng. Manag.*, vol. 8, 2015.

Experience Design for Work Tools

Virpi Roto

Aalto University, School of Arts, Design and Architecture, Espoo, Finland
virpi.roto@aalto.fi

Abstract

This workshop paper approaches the topic of user experience at work from the perspective of designing work tools with a specific user experience (UX) as a goal. To demonstrate the different design approaches towards addressing the three time spans of user experience – momentary, episodic, and long-term – examples of related research areas are briefly introduced, as well as their deployment in work context. The concept of experience goal has been found useful in addressing the different time spans, but it is often hard for designer to define momentary experience goals due to the fleeting nature of momentary emotions.

Keywords

Experience Design · Work tools · User experience · Time spans

1 Introduction

Experience is a broad and multidisciplinary research topic. User experience research as one of the experience research fields has become highly popular during this millennium, even so that it dominates in volume the experience publications of all disciplines. There are several subfields that approach design for user experiences from different perspectives, such as affective computing, interaction aesthetics, gamification, positive design, etc. However, only a small

---

How to cite this book chapter:
Roto, V. 2020. Experience Design for Work Tools. In: Loizides, F., Winckler, M., Chatterjee, U., Abdelnour-Nocera, J. and Parmaxi, A. (eds.) *Human Computer Interaction and Emerging Technologies: Adjunct Proceedings from the INTERACT 2019 Workshops*. Pp. 145–150. Cardiff: Cardiff University Press. DOI: https://doi.org/10.18573/book3.r. License: CC-BY 4.0.

minority of this research is done in work contexts. This paper very briefly introduces and compares these design approaches, categorizing them into the user experience time spans – momentary, episodic, and long-term [12] – especially from the perspective of designing for experiences in the workplace through the interactive systems used at work.

2 Momentary user experience

Affective Computing refers to computing that relates to, arises from, or deliberately influences emotions [9]. The goal of affective computing is to build an affect model that enables an interactive system provide users intelligent, sensitive and friendly responses that match users' affective state. Affective computing research has been expanding with the boom of sensors and artificial intelligence, and new terms such as artificial emotional intelligence [14] are emerging. This line of research is based on emotion recognition and the goal is to make computers, such as social robots and other conversational agents, to express emotions in similar ways as humans. With its focus on affect and emotion, this research area contributes to user experience from a momentary perspective.

While affective computing has often been implemented into consumer systems such as chatbots on commercial web sites, there has been less research on its applications at workplaces. Conversational agents have arrived to workplaces, but it is not easy to find scientific publications on deploying affective conversational agents at work context.

3 Episodic user experience

Games are perhaps the best example of episodic user experiences. There is a plot in game design that aims to produce emotional episodes with excitement, disappointment, fun, reward, etc. After the game-over, the gamer evaluates her/his success as one episode. Naturally, there are various kinds of games, but it is hard to think about a game that would not consist of some kind of emotional episodes. While workplace is not a context targeted at having fun, gamification features have been adopted by many work related systems, as a recent literature review shows [15].

Most activities at work are episodic, i.e., tasks with a clear start and end point, and the interactive tools at work are often designed as stepwise user interfaces, e.g., wizards. With regards to work contexts, Zeiner have studied work experiences and identified 21 categories of positive experiences. From stories of pleasurable experiences at work, Zeiner et al. (2018) identified categories of meaningful episodes at work, such as Receiving feedback, Helping others, or Exchanging ideas.

4 Long-term user experience

Following the basic idea of Positive Psychology, a design approach called Positive Design does not target at fixing problems, but instead, it focuses on designs that make life worth living [1]. Thus, Positive Design aims to address a long time span. While a sum of pleasurable momentary experiences contributes to overall wellbeing, Pleasure is just one of the three elements of the Positive Design Framework (PDF). The other two are Personal Significance, which is about pursuing personal goals and aspirations, and Virtue about being a morally good person (ibid.).

Another insightful article about the universal grounding for experience design beyond momentary fun [3], who tested how the psychological needs [13] relate to experiences with technology. The psychological needs that were especially salient included stimulation, relatedness, competence, and popularity. We have found this list highly inspiring in designing for experiences. Experience designers can think what and how to design in order to fulfill these needs either through momentary, episodic, or long-term experiences. This means that the designers should define not only functional but also experience goals to design for.

5 Experience goals

Our own research has taken place in work contexts, in which we have aimed to provide tools for designers who want to improve employee experience via interactive systems used at work. We have focused on the means to set experience goals [8] and to utilize those goals during design process 6, 11. Experience goal is defined as the intended momentary emotion or the meaningful relationship/bond that a person has with the designed product or service [4]. Therefore, it can address all time spans of user experience discussed above. In the collection of 20 experience goals from student design cases on our Experience-Driven Design class [7, p. 70], there are separate goals to address the three time spans. For example, one student team defined Wow as a momentary experience goal, Proudness as episodic, and Trust as a long-term goal.

But what is the relationship between the time-span-specific design approaches and experience goals? In the Affective Computing approach, a designer might not define experience goals per se, but the affect model defines the appropriate emotional response to a certain recognized affect. The designer then designs a verbal, gestural, or other response that matches the emotion suggested by the affect model.

In case of episodic experiences, the main experience goal is defined based on the wanted emotional state after the episode. Based on this main goal, different experience goals can be defined for the different phases of the episode plot. The plots in games are not always designed with a specific emotion in mind in each phase, but I see potential in improving episodic user experience by constructing an emotional plot for, e.g., an hour reporting task.

The frameworks provided for long-term experience design provide an inspirational basis for setting experience goals. In our research, we have utilized the basic psychological needs and found that in work context, Competence experience is clearly the most frequent experience goal.

We also studied the Positive Design Framework [1] and developed it further to provide more specific guidance for designing meaningful experiences in the workplace [5]. This PDFwork framework is, according to our knowledge, the only framework that provides a relatively solid starting point for experience design in the domain of work tools. While the main focus of PDF is longterm experience, the three elements seem to match the momentary (Pleasure), episodic (Personal Significance) and long-term (Virtue) time spans.

6 Conclusion

Our research on experience design targets at employee wellbeing by designing meaningful interactions with technology at work. In this endeavor, we have studied momentary, episodic, and long-term user experience goals. It may be difficult for the designer to set experience goals for momentary experiences in isolation, but there is high potential in defining experience goals for an episodic experience. Our work has mostly focused on the long-term, meaningful user experiences at work, for example, the PDFWork framework [5].

This workshop paper briefly described some of the emotional design approaches for each UX time span, and discussed how they can be addressed in experience goals defined for design. I hope this paper opens up a useful, less addressed design perspective to the workshop discussions on user experiences at work.

References

1. Desmet, P. M., & Pohlmeyer, A. E. (2013). Positive design: An introduction to design for subjective well-being. *International journal of design*, *7*(3).
2. Egger, F. N. (2001, June). Affective design of e-commerce user interfaces: How to maximise perceived trustworthiness. In *Proc. Intl. Conf. Affective Human Factors Design* (pp. 317–324).
3. Hassenzahl, M., Diefenbach, S., & Göritz, A. (2010). Needs, affect, and interactive products–Facets of user experience. *Interacting with computers*, *22*(5), 353–362.
4. Lu, Y., & Roto, V. (2014, October). Towards meaning change: experience goals driving design space expansion. In *Proceedings of the 8th Nordic*

Conference on Human-Computer Interaction: Fun, Fast, Foundational (pp. 717–726). ACM.

5. Lu, Y., & Roto, V. (2015). Evoking meaningful experiences at work – a positive design framework for work tools. *Journal of Engineering Design, 26*(4–6), 99–120.

6. Lu, Y., & Roto, V. (2016). Design for pride in the workplace. *Psychology of Well-being, 6*(1), 6.

7. Lu, Y. (2018). Experience goals in designing professional tools: evoking meaningful experiences at work. Aalto University publication series DOCTORAL DISSERTATIONS, 131/2018.

8. Kaasinen, E., Roto, V., Hakulinen, J., Heimonen, T., Jokinen, J. P., Karvonen, H., ... & Tokkonen, H. (2015). Defining user experience goals to guide the design of industrial systems. *Behaviour & Information Technology, 34*(10), 976–991.

9. Picard. R. W. (1997). Affective Computing. Cambridge, MA: The MIT Press.

10. Roto, V., Clemmensen, T., Väätäjä, H., & Law, E. L. C. (2018). Designing interactive systems for work engagement. *Human Technology, 14*(2).

11. Roto, V., Kaasinen, E., Heimonen, T., Karvonen, H., Jokinen, J. P., Mannonen, P., ... & Kymäläinen, T. (2017, May). Utilizing experience goals in design of industrial systems. In *Proceedings of the 2017 CHI Conference on Human Factors in Computing Systems* (pp. 6993–7004). ACM.

12. Roto, V., Law, E., Vermeeren, A. P. O. S., & Hoonhout, J. (2011, September). User experience white paper: Bringing clarity to the concept of user experience. In *Dagstuhl Seminar on Demarcating User Experience*.

13. Sheldon, K. M., Elliot, A. J., Kim, Y., & Kasser, T. (2001). What is satisfying about satisfying events? Testing 10 candidate psychological needs. *Journal of personality and social psychology, 80*(2), 325.

14. Schuller, D., & Schuller, B. W. (2018). The age of artificial emotional intelligence. *Computer, 51*(9), 38–46.

15. Warmelink, H., Koivisto, J., Mayer, I., Vesa, M., & Hamari, J. (2018). Gamification of the work floor: A literature review of gamifying production and logistics operations.

User Persona of Mother of Preterm Neonate

Ganesh Bhutkar*, Aditya Dongre*, Shahaji Deshmukh†,
Lene Nielsen‡ and Jaydeep Joshi*

*Centre of Excellence in HCI, Vishwakarma Institute of Technology,
Pune, India
†Bharati Hospital, Bharati Vidyapeeth Deemed University, Pune, India
‡Business IT Department, IT University of Copenhagen, Denmark
ganesh.bhutkar@vit.edu

Abstract

This research paper presents a user persona of Indian mothers of preterm neonates. Many of these preterm neonates require hospitalization in Neonatal Intensive Care Units (NICUs), leading to mental stress for mothers and their families. The mother's persona is proposed based on hypothesis, user interviews and data analysis. The participant mothers of preterm neonates are graduates and homemakers from semiurban areas around Pune, India. These mothers prefer non-vegetarian diet, they visit a pediatrician more frequently and presently, they do not use any mobile healthcare app or YouTube videos for information about neonatal care. A mobile app will be developed for these mothers in future with due consideration to their user persona.

Keywords

User Persona · Mother · Preterm Neonate · Neonatal ICU · Mother's Persona

How to cite this book chapter:
Bhutkar, G., Dongre, A., Deshmukh, S., Nielsen, L. and Joshi, J. 2020. User Persona of Mother of Preterm Neonate. In: Loizides, F., Winckler, M., Chatterjee, U., Abdelnour-Nocera, J. and Parmaxi, A. (eds.) *Human Computer Interaction and Emerging Technologies: Adjunct Proceedings from the INTERACT 2019 Workshops*. Pp. 151–156. Cardiff: Cardiff University Press. DOI: https://doi.org/10.18573/book3.s. License: CC-BY 4.0.

1 Introduction

India is the second-most populated country in the world, with about 1365 million people [16], including about 653 million women [4]. Its population is growing, recently with a crude birth rate of 18.6 births per thousand population [2]. The effective population growth is about 1.1% per year, adding more than 15 million people to the Indian population [3]. Such high population growth results into national issues like unemployment, increased poverty level, unequal distribution of income, over-strained infrastructure, over-stretched health and educational services [12]. The challenging environment has led to deteriorating health conditions of women inflicting their pregnancies. It also results in too early, too late or too frequent pregnancies, creating complications at the time of childbirth. There is a need to use Information and Communication Technology (ICT) for advising and guiding these mothers on their health condition, along with growth tracking of their neonates, who are infants with an age of upto four weeks.

For usefulness of ICT to women in challenging healthcare conditions, the development process needs to take into account the work conditions of both the clinical staff and the mothers. The developers or researchers working with ICT do not have enough exposure to work environments such as Intensive Care Units (ICU). It generates a vital gap in the understanding of mothers of preterm neonates and their hospitalization in Neonatal Intensive Care Units (NICU). Lack of information may include understanding about mothers' requirements, preferences, day-to-day activities and the stress generated during hospitalization. This paper presents a case that aims at reducing the gap of knowledge through fieldwork in NICU and a proposed mother's persona.

2 Related Work

In this section, we present a few papers that are helpful in the understanding of the work environment in NICU, the psychology of parents of preterm neonates and the use of personas in health-related ICT. The papers have created a foundation for forming a hypothesis; especially related to the healthcare domain.

In an Italian study, Bouwstra et al. [1] examine the parent-to-neonate bonding experience in NICU. This research paper reveals that the parents of the hospitalized neonate are insecure about whether their neonate responds differently to them than to the medical staff. The mother is always eager to meet her neonate, especially for breastfeeding and may not be able to meet the neonate frequently throughout the day, which has been depicted in the hypothesis. The Indian research paper by Patil et al. reveals that mothers of a preterm neonate experience significant psychological distress, with elevated anxiety [12]. This study also points out the emotional problems of the mothers and their need for support. Thus, these mothers face an increased mental stress, which has been highlighted in the hypothesis.

A study from the USA, by Heidari et al. [6] states that due to a busy occupational schedule most of the fathers find it challenging to attend to the mothers all the time during hospitalization as well as follow-up hospital visits. Thus, most of the mothers are accompanied by their mothers or relatives. This is similar to our case and is reflected in the hypothesis. Finally, a study conducted in South Africa by Mburu et al. [7] aims to use technology to support mothers of a preterm infants. It shows that the mothers get to know the neonatal status information via text message, over the phone or through digital video. Similarly, Indian mothers get a lot of neonatal information over a phone call or via text message, which is reflected in the hypothesis.

Personas [11] is a popular UX method to understand the involved users. e.g. healthcare ICT products. As mentioned by van Velsen et al. [13], it has the potential to be a useful tool for designing usable eHealth services. Looking at the field, most personas are related to self-monitoring and tracking such as a public website with cancer related information [5], a handheld device to monitor chronic heart failure [15] or wellbeing [14].

3 Field Work

The research has been conducted in two local hospitals located in Pune, India. The larger hospital is housed in huge multi-story buildings with a capacity of more than 500 beds. Multispecialty departments have various units like Emergency, ICU, Burn centre and NICU. Preterm neonates who need intensive medical attention are often admitted into a special area of the hospital called the Neonatal Intensive Care Unit (NICU). This unit combines advanced technology and trained healthcare professionals to provide specialized care for the tiniest patients. It has continuing care areas for neonates who have health issues and need skilled nursing care. Such NICUs are categorized in different levels [8]. NICU at Level I looks after neonates who need more care than healthy neonates and require regular monitoring assistance. NICU at Level II provides special care where nurses are assigned to 3–4 neonates for constant attention and care. NICU at Level III take care of very sick neonates providing prolonged lung ventilation-support. **A neonatologist typically leads NICU and staffed with intensivists, nurses, therapists and dietitians**. Neonatologists are pediatricians with additional training in the care of sick and preterm neonates [8–9].

The research in NICU has started with the design of hypothesis about mothers of preterm neonates mainly focused on their personal traits, the medical context and mobile usage in practice. A questionnaire, designed on the basis of the hypothesis, has been used for interviews of selected mothers. To facilitate the active participation of mothers, the questions for the interviews are also provided in the local regional language Marathi along with English. The field work started with interviews of physicians and nurses working with NICUs while forming the hypothesis. The main participants of these interviews have been 19 mothers of preterm neonates in the next phase. In all these interviews, the aim has been to get the details about demographic information, sources of information for mothers, their preferences, related facts, challenges and issues in the work environment of NICUs. The participating mothers of preterm neonates has been in the age group of 18–32 years. Most of these mothers are graduates from semi-urban areas around Pune. They were married between the age of 18 to 25 years and are housewives/home-makers. Most neonates are their first child.

The interviews have been conducted three days over a fortnight. Each interview lasted for 15–20 minutes. The research team had limited medical knowledge despite putting sufficient effort into an understanding of the neo-natal context. **The all-male team in Pune has faced difficulties during the initial interviewing process of mothers due to gender incompatibility and therefore, a female intern from one of the hospitals is included as an inter-viewer of the mothers**. This intern has been there to help in sharing expecta-tions, priorities and experiences of these mothers.

4 Proposed User Persona

In this qualitative research, the user is the mother of a preterm neonate. A related user persona of a mother is proposed to analyze the maternal experience in NICUs. This study aims to understand a typical Indian mother, her experience and challenges in NICU. The process of creating the neonate mother personas started with formation of a hypothesis [10]. **The hypothesis is mainly focused on their personality, medical traits and active mobile usage**. The assumptions include demographic information such as age, education, marriage age, area and occupation. The health and medical science traits include personal Body Mass Index (BMI), diet, medication schedule, knowledge of medical terms/equipment, mental/physical stress and others. The mobile usage section includes factors such as internet access, use of messenger app, local language support, m-Health app usage, social media groups and so on.

After proposing hypothesis, a questionnaire has been prepared for conduction of interviews of selected mothers in hospitals. This questionnaire is prepared even in Marathithe local language to facilitate active participation of moth-ers in interviews. It has more than 30 objective questions with upto 4 options. More than one-third questions are of YES/NO type. Using this questionnaire, interviews of mothers of preterm neonates have been conducted in NICUs. The interviews of main participant mothers have been conducted to get the details about demographic information, sources of information for mothers, their preferences, related facts and challenges in work environment of NICUs. The collected interview data has been analyzed to get vital findings/insights, captur-ing mother's experience in NICU. The related detailed user persona and interest-ing observations made on the basis of hypothesis are presented in next section.

5 The Mother Persona

The results of interviews consist mainly of accepted and rejected statements in the proposed hypothesis as well as the user persona of a mother of preterm neonate.

The participant mothers of preterm neonates have been in the age group of 18–32 years. Most of these mothers are graduates from semi-urban areas around Pune, India. Most of them have been married when they were between 18 to 25 years and are housewives/homemakers. Most of the mothers prefer non-vegetarian diet and visit more frequently to pediatrician than a gynecologist. Most neonates are their first child and spontaneous preterm infants. These mothers are always eager to meet their neonates, especially for breastfeeding, but are not able to meet the neonates frequently; especially during nights. They do not use any mobile healthcare app. They do not join any user group related to neonate/pregnancy care on social media, but read related blogs. These mothers communicate with a physician in person and also, take appointments in person or over a phone. They do not use YouTube videos for information about neonate/pregnancy care. Thus, the proposed mother's persona presents the details about demographic information, sources of information for mothers, their preferences, related facts, challenges and issues in the work environment of NICUs.

6 Conclusion and Future Work

In this paper, a user persona for Mother of Preterm Neonate has been proposed. This user persona has provided interesting insights into demographic information, sources of information for mothers, their preferences, related facts, challenges and issues in the work environment of NICUs. It will help application developers and usability professionals in the design of related healthcare applications. In the future, an Android app will be developed for the mothers of preterm neonates with due consideration to their user persona derived during this research work. Furthermore, how the app fits into the work of the health-care staff in neonatal care, can also be addressed.

Acknowledgement

We thank **India Alliance and The African Academy of Sciences (AAS)** for providing **Africa-India Mobility Fund (AIMF) Grant** and supporting ICT research work related with Mothers of Preterm Infants.

References

1. Bouwstra, S., Chen, W., Feijs, L., Oetomo, S., Linden, W., Iisselsteijn, W.: Designing the Parents-to-Infant Bonding Experience in the NICU. First

International Conference on Global Health Challenges, Oct. 2012, Venice, Italy, pp. 7–13. (2012)

2. Crude Birth Rate Statistics by World Data Atlas. https://knoema.com /atlas/India/topics/Demographics/Population-forecast/Crude-birth-rate. Accessed on 10th April, 2019

3. Effective Population Growth. http://worldpopulationreview.com/countries /india-population/. Accessed on 23rd April, 2019

4. Female Population in India. http://www.indiaonlinepages.com/population /india-current-population.html. Accessed on 24th April, 2019

5. Goldberg, L., Lide, B., Lowry, S., Massett, H., O'Connell, T., Preece, J., Quesenbery, W., Shneiderman, B.: Usability and Accessibility in Consumer Health Informatics. American Journal of Preventive Medicine, 40(5), pp. S187–S197. (2011)

6. Heidari, H., Hasanpour, M., Fooladi, M.: The Iranian Parents of Premature Infants in NICU Experience Stigma of Shame. MED ARH, 66(1), pp. 35–40. (2012)

7. Mburu, W., Wardle, C., Joolay, Y., Densmore, M.: Co-designing with Mother and Neonatal Unit Staff: Use of Technology to Support Mothers of Preterm Infants. The 2nd African Conference for Human-Computer Interaction – AfriCHI'18, Windhoek, Namibia. (2018)

8. Neonatal Intensive Care Unit (Wikipedia). https://en.wikipedia.org/wiki /Neonatal_intensive_care_unit. Accessed on 26th April, 2019

9. Neonatal Intensive Care Unit. https://www.stanfordchildrens.org/en/topic /default?id=the-neonatal-intensive-care-unit-nicu-90-P02389. Accessed on 22nd April, 2019

10. Nielsen, L.: 10 Steps to Personas. http://personas.dk/?pageid=196. Accessed on 26th April, 2019.

11. Nielsen, L.: Personas. User Focused Design. Springer. (2019)

12. Patil, A., Bhutkar, G., Pendse, M., Tawade, A., Bodke, A., Shaha, S., Deshmukh, S.: Prototype Design of Android App for Mother of Preterm Infant. 5th IFIP WG 13.6 Working Conference, HWID 2018, Espoo, Finland. (2018)

13. van Velsen, L., van Gemert-Pijnen, L., Nijland, N., Beaujean, D., van Steenbergene J.: Personas: The Linking Pin in Holistic Design for eHealth. The Fourth International Conference on eHealth, Telemedicine, and Social Medicine – eTELEMED 2012, Valencia, Spain. (2012)

14. Vicini, S., Gariglio, A., Alberti, F., Oleari, E., Sanna, A.: Enhancing Personas for Well-Being e-Services and Product Service Systems. Design, User Experience, and Usability: Design Thinking and Methods – 5th International Conference, HCI International 2016, Springer Verlag, pp. 365–376. (2016)

15. Villalba, E., Peinado I., Arredondo, M.: User Interaction Design for a Wearable and IT-based Heart Failure System. 12th International Conference on Human-Computer Interaction, Beijing, China, pp. 1230–1239. (2007)

16. World Human Population. https://www.worldometers.info/world-population /india-population/. Accessed on 10th April, 2019

Opportunities for recommended mental health strategies to reduce stress at work

Robin De Croon, Francisco Gutiérrez
and Katrien Verbert

KU Leuven, Department of Computer Science, Celestijnenlaan
200A, BE-3001 Leuven, Belgium robin.decroon@kuleuven.be, francisco.
gutierrez@kuleuven.be, katrien.verbert@kuleuven.be

Abstract

Human resource management is undergoing a profound change in digital transformation: HR departments are expected to build a compelling employee experience and redesign entire talent practices. Achieving this requires tackling the mental health problems at both individual and workplace levels including proactively managing mental health of the employees. To meet such demanding transformations, interactive technologies to mitigate workplace related risk factors could offer a huge potential. However, they are currently underexplored. In this position paper, we explore four research themes that could be addressed in a research agenda in the area of user experiences and wellbeing at work: 1) personalized, in-time stress management therapies, 2) the application of health recommender systems to tailor interventions to employees, 3) the involvement of professional coaches to enable employees to explore recommendations outside therapy sessions, and 4) personalized gamification mechanics to increase employees' adherence to both recommended therapies and tracking data.

Keywords

Stress · mental well-being · mHealth · adherence · gamification

How to cite this book chapter:
De Croon, R., Gutiérrez, F. and Verbert, K. 2020. Opportunities for recommended mental health strategies to reduce stress at work. In: Loizides, F., Winckler, M., Chatterjee, U., Abdelnour-Nocera, J. and Parmaxi, A. (eds.) *Human Computer Interaction and Emerging Technologies: Adjunct Proceedings from the INTERACT 2019 Workshops.* Pp. 157–162. Cardiff: Cardiff University Press. DOI: https://doi.org/10.18573/book3.t. License: CC-BY 4.0.

1 Introduction

In 2015, 24.4% of EU employees were experiencing frequent or constant stress at work and 35.2% felt exhausted [18]. Besides the occupational burnout, long-term stress at work can cause multiple mental health disorders, such as anxiety, depression, chronic widespread pain, and concentration difficulties. Work-induced stress can be responsible for a large employee turnover/retirement and is often associated with an increased risk of depressive symptoms and clinical depression among employees [16]. Studies estimate that around 50% of all lost working days have some relation to work stress [4]. The cost to Europe of work-related depression was recently estimated to be 617 billion euros annually [17].

Although the abundance of sensors and tracking technologies allow development of tailored and personalized services to improve work satisfaction, productivity, and health of employees, research into assessing mental conditions is currently mainly conducted in theoretical studies. Real life uses in a professional context require additional researched methods, that are highly adaptive to differences in employee personalities and workplace settings. In this position paper, we explore opportunities for research into solutions tailored to the individual employee; into solutions that provide data-driven, actionable insights, but also into those solutions that are supervised and tailored by a professional coach. On the other hand, such remote solutions typically suffer from low adherence. It should, therefore, be researched how personalized gamification mechanics can be used in the context of well-being at work.

2 Personalized, in-time stress management therapies

Several studies have gathered positive impact on the use of mobile and/or online therapies for the treatment of health problems related to stress and anxiety [14, 22]. After all, mobile therapies are accessible 24/7 and can be customized depending on user needs and may reduce barriers to face-to-face help-seeking, such as the stigma or discomfort about discussing one's own mental health [13]. In the past few years, a large number of mobile applications were developed to help prevent and treat mental problems, e.g., to reduce stress and behavior disorders or to improve cognitive functions. However, they are mainly low-value apps, often lack scientific evidence [9, 11], and are largely knowledge-based in the way that they guide the user towards respected sources of information [19]. Despite a large number of apps available, the evidence base is still scarce and needs additional research.

A 2013 review of mobile mental health apps identified eight papers describing only five apps [9]. Four of the five apps demonstrated significant reductions in depression, stress, and substance use, although a number of issues with the quality of these studies suggest these conclusions need to be interpreted cautiously. A more recent systematic review [11] in 2017 included 24 publications, of which 15 described an app. They concluded that **there is currently insufficient research evidence to support the effectiveness of mental health apps**. *"Given the number and pace at which mHealth apps are being released on app stores, methodologically robust research studies evaluating their safety, efficacy, and effectiveness is promptly needed"* [11]. Furthermore, another high-quality systematic review [1] performed in 2016 concluded that mental health apps are not personalized towards the end-user, which provides an important research opportunity as Bakker et al. [1] stress that *"[t]ailored interventions are more efficacious than is rigid self-help."*

3 Health recommender systems to tailor interventions

In recent years, there has been an increasing interest to apply existing recommender techniques in a variety of health-related apps to provide actionable suggestions to end-users [20–21]. The overall objective is to empower people to monitor and **improve their health with technology-assisted coaching through personalized recommendations**. However, there is currently little research on health recommenders which provide stress related insights, especially in a professional context. For example, recommenders to alleviate stress include recommending books to read [23] or meditative audios [24]. The most relevant study is the RCT of Bidargaddi et al. [2] where actual patients (not regular employees, but people with a known health condition) were enrolled. A large group of patients (n = 192 + 195 control) were asked to use a web-based recommendation service for four weeks that recommended mental health and well being mobile applications. Their self-guided app recommendation service was able to halt a decline in mood, energy, and sleep.

4 Involvement of coaches

A third important topic for a research agenda is a stronger involvement of professional coaches. Similar to concordance, an *"alternative model proposed by the medical field that favours an equal and collaborative patient-doctor relationship in the negotiation of care"* [12], a professional coach and an employee should develop a relationship that involves a collaborative empiricism [5]; a collaboration to motivate employees effectively. This will enable employees to explore recommended strategies and beliefs outside their therapy session. This would ideally involve encouraging users to develop their own hypotheses about what may happen as a result of using the app or participating in certain activities. **An active collaboration can thus support autonomy and provide opportunities in a company for the development of competence in behavioral, emotional, or cognitive self-management.**

5 Gamification to increase adherence

The lack of adherence, "*the extent to which individuals experience the content to derive maximum benefit from the intervention, as defined or implied by its creators*" [15], to remote solutions is well documented [10]. However, little research can be found on how and what principles to implement in a workplace context. We, therefore, argue that researching how to increase employees' adherence to mental health therapies is crucial in a new research agenda. One potential approach to increase employees' experience is the use of gamification mechanics, i.e., "*the use of game design elements in non-game contexts*" [8]. After all, gamification harnesses the motivational affordances of gameful experiences to influence psychological outcomes and further behavioral outcomes and already has multiple applications in the healthcare domain [6].

Effective gamification is a combination of game design, behavioral economics, motivational psychology, and user experience and user interface design [3]. If implemented well, gamification can increase the motivation of user's trajectories [7]. However, gamification is not a panacea [6]. Different user groups and personality types necessitate different gamification mechanics. Hence, there is **a need for research with respect to which gamification mechanics are appropriate for specific personality types and user groups**. Careful consideration is needed to select a set of gamification mechanics for a specific user group. Finally, it is less known how gamification can be used within a sensitive setting such as the workplace where employees submit private health data.

6 Conclusion and future work

In this position paper, we proposed our position, that there is a demand and utility for a personalized and in-time stress management platform in a workplace context. By conducting a brief literature research, we came to the reasoned opinion, that the combination of health recommender systems, the involvement of professional coaches, and the use of gamification might have the potential to mitigate work-induced stress and thus increase the user experience and wellbeing of employees in a workplace context. However, this claim needs stronger research foundation and should be addressed in future research.

Acknowledgements

This work is part of the research project Personal Health Empowerment with project number HBC.2018.2012 and Panacea project with project number HBC.2016.0177, which are financed by Flanders Innovation & Entrepreneurship.

References

1. Bakker, D., Kazantzis, N., Rickwood, D., Rickard, N.: Mental health smartphoneapps: review and evidence-based recommendations for future developments. JMIR mental health 3(1), e7 (2016)
2. Bidargaddi, N., Musiat, P., Winsall, M., Vogl, G., Blake, V., Quinn, S., Orlowski, S., Antezana, G., Schrader, G.: Efficacy of a web-based guided recommendation service for a curated list of readily available mental health and well-being mobile apps for young people: Randomized controlled trial. J Med Internet Res 19(5), e141 (May 2017)
3. Chou, Y.k.: Actionable gamification: Beyond points, badges, and leaderboards. Octalysis Group (2015)
4. Cox T, Griffiths A, R.G.E..: Research on Work-related Stress. Tech. rep., Officefor Official Publications of the European Communities, Luxembourg (2000)
5. Dattilio, F.M., Hanna, M.A.: Collaboration in cognitive-behavioral therapy.Journal of Clinical Psychology 68(2), 146–158 (2012)
6. De Croon, R., Wildemeersch, D., Wille, J., Verbert, K., Vanden Abeele, V.: Gamification and serious games in a healthcare informatics context. In: IEEE International Conference on Healthcare Informatics. pp. 53–63. IEEE (2018)
7. De Schutter, B., Vanden Abeele, V.: Designing meaningful play within the psychosocial context of older adults. In: Proceedings of the 3rd International Conference on Fun and Games. pp. 84–93. ACM (2010)
8. Deterding, S., Dixon, D., Khaled, R., Nacke, L.: From game design elementsto gamefulness: defining gamification. In: Proceedings of the 15th International Academic MindTrek Conference: Envisioning Future Media Environments. pp. 9–15. ACM (2011)
9. Donker, T., Petrie, K., Proudfoot, J., Clarke, J., Birch, M.R., Christensen, H.: Smartphones for smarter delivery of mental health programs: A systematic review. J Med Internet Res 15(11), e247 (Nov 2013)
10. Eysenbach, G.: The law of attrition. Journal of medical Internet research 7(1), e11 (2005)
11. Grist, R., Porter, J., Stallard, P.: Mental health mobile apps for preadolescentsand adolescents: a systematic review. Journal of medical internet research 19(5), e176 (2017)
12. Grönvall, E., Verdezoto, N., Bagalkot, N., Sokoler, T.: Concordance: A criticalparticipatory alternative in healthcare it. Aarhus Series on Human Centered Computing 1(1), 4 (Oct 2015)
13. Gulliver, A., Griffiths, K.M., Christensen, H.: Perceived barriers and facilitators tomental health help-seeking in young people: a systematic review. BMC psychiatry 10(1), 113 (2010)
14. Heber, E., Ebert, D.D., Lehr, D., Cuijpers, P., Berking, M., Nobis, S., Riper, H.: The benefit of web-and computer-based interventions for stress: a

systematic review and meta-analysis. Journal of medical Internet research 19(2), e32 (2017)

15. Kelders, S.M., Kok, R.N., Ossebaard, H.C., Van Gemert-Pijnen, J.E.: Persuasivesystem design does matter: a systematic review of adherence to web-based interventions. Journal of medical Internet research 14(6), e152 (2012)

16. Madsen, I.E., Nyberg, S.T., Hanson, L.M., Ferrie, J.E., Ahola, K., Alfredsson,L., Batty, G.D., Bjorner, J.B., Borritz, M., Burr, H., et al.: Job strain as a risk factor for clinical depression: systematic review and meta-analysis with additional individual participant data. Psychological medicine 47(8), 1342–1356 (2017)

17. Matrix: Economic analysis of workplace mental health promotion and mental disorder prevention programmes and of their potential contribution to EU health, social and economic policy objectives. Tech. Rep. May (2013)

18. Parent-Thirion, A., Biletta, I., Cabrita, J., Vargas, O., Vermeylen, G., Wilczynska,A., Wilkens, M.: 6th European Working Conditions Survey: Overview Report. Eurofound (Europ. Foundation for the Improvement of Living and Working (2016)

19. Payne, H.E., Wilkinson, J., West, J.H., Bernhardt, J.M.: A content analysis of precede proceed constructs in stress management mobile apps. Mhealth 2 (2016)

20. Rabbi, M., Aung, M.H., Zhang, M., Choudhury, T.: MyBehavior: automatic personalized health feedback from user behaviors and preferences using smartphones. In Proceedings of the 2015 ACM International Joint Conference on Pervasive and Ubiquitous Computing (UbiComp '15) pp. 707–718 (2015)

21. Radha, M., Willemsen, M.C., Boerhof, M., IJsselsteijn, W.A.: Lifestyle recommendations for hypertension through rasch-based feasibility modeling. In: Proceedings of the 2016 Conference on User Modeling Adaptation and Personalization. pp. 239–247. UMAP '16, ACM, New York, NY, USA (2016)

22. Thórarinsdóttir, H., Kessing, L.V., Faurholt-Jepsen, M.: Smartphone-based selfassessment of stress in healthy adult individuals: a systematic review. Journal of medical Internet research 19(2), e41 (2017)

23. Xin, Y., Chen, Y., Jin, L., Cai, Y., Feng, L.: TeenRead: An Adolescents Reading Recommendation System Towards Online Bibliotherapy. Proceedings – 2017 IEEE 6th International Congress on Big Data, BigData Congress 2017 pp. 431–434 (2017)

24. Zaini, N., Latip, M.F.A., Omar, H., Mazalan, L., Norhazman, H.: Onlinepersonalized audio therapy recommender based on community ratings. ISCAIE 2012 – 2012 IEEE Symposium on Computer Applications and Industrial Electronics pp. 318–322 (2012)

Livability – Analysis of People's Living Comfort in Different Cities of India Using GIS: A Prototype

Shrikant Salve, Shubham Bombarde,
Ankit Agrawal, Smruti Paldiwal, Bishal Sharma Roy
and Bhagyashree Alhat

MIT Academy of Engineering, Pune, India
shrikantsalve@gmail.com

Abstract

The comfort of living for an average individual plays a crucial factor in urban development. It validates a city's ability to provide all the necessary comfort for modern livability standards. To analyze city livability, in this position paper we have proposed a system that provides a lifestyle overview through locality Indexing of a particular geographical area according to the ease of living for four particular age groups like a child, middle-aged, senior adult, and senior citizen. The system accounts for various indicators like health, transport, population, climate, pollution, crowd, etc. to yield a personalized result. The system consists of a web interface and a python backend which pulls desired data about the location from sources like Google Maps (Places API) and data.gov.in. (Indian Govt. website). This data is then mined and useful/relevant information is summarized to yield an end result. Parallel computations consisting of pattern discovery (by mining algorithms) and data aggregation are carried on a cloud service maintaining a local data store for processed queries. The generated end result is then presented to the user in the form of visualization charts.

How to cite this book chapter:
Salve, S., Bombarde, S., Agrawal, A., Paldiwal, S., Roy, B.S. and Alhat, B. 2020. Livability – Analysis of People's Living Comfort in Different Cities of India Using GIS: A Prototype. In: Loizides, F., Winckler, M., Chatterjee, U., Abdelnour-Nocera, J. and Parmaxi, A. (eds.) *Human Computer Interaction and Emerging Technologies: Adjunct Proceedings from the INTERACT 2019 Workshops.* Pp. 163–168. Cardiff: Cardiff University Press. DOI: https://doi.org/10.18573/book3.u. License: CC-BY 4.0.

Keywords

Livability · GIS · Locality Indexing and Analysis · Indicators

1 Introduction

Cities are emerging as the prime engines of the Indian economy. They are emerging as the generators of national wealth. India can be looked up to as one among the rapidly urbanizing nations in the world. According to the census report of 2017, India's urban population is 31.16% and there are 46 metropolitan cities [1]. It is necessary for the nation to invest in the social and economic functions of cities. As cities trace the path of Gross Domestic Product (GDP) growth rates by policies which adhere to the quality life, their comfort of living is highly challenged. Providing the person wanting to move to any city along with the complete knowledge of the surrounding of work place, with least efforts is the main motivation of our project. Therefore, adapting the suitable job location (work place) supports the person well-being [2].

The locality indexing or livability indexing is the sum of the factors that add up to a community's quality of life-including the built and natural environments, economic prosperity, social stability and equity, educational opportunity, cultural, entertainment and recreation possibilities [3]. There can be various types or categories of indexing like physical and natural amenities. It largely depends on the class of the user who is assessing the locality. For example, some people need things to feel safe and secure. The rest might need good schools, transportation, hospitals and so on. Keeping this in mind, livability can be classified into different age groups, to provide a reliable result. Our system provides a lookout into the quality of life in a particular area or region or city as it accounts all the social, economic, environmental and civic factors that determine the possibility of a citizen to live in a city [4]. To get an in-depth idea of this project we have gone through several existing works, that consists of all the possible survey knowledge using Structural Equation Modelling (SEM) and Geographic Information System (GIS) approach.

2 City Livability Index and GIS

Livability encompasses broad human needs ranging from food and basic security to beauty, cultural expression, and a sense of belonging to a community or a place [3]. Nowadays, 31.16 % of India lives in an urban area like towns and cities [5]. It is estimated that in the coming 20 years, nearly half of India would be shifting towards urbanized areas [5]. As a result, developing new cities for migration would be a major challenge. The City Livability Index 2010 [3] is a Government of India report which comments on the quality of life that our cities offer. It relies on entirely objective analysis, employing more than 300 indicators on a 10-year timeline series. For evaluating neighborhoods of Nigeria, a Structural Equation Modelling (SEM) approach has been introduced by Iyanda et.al [6]. This study employed a Delphi survey technique on fifteen livable human community experts in South Arica from which the conceptual variables for neighborhood features were developed for the study. A questionnaire survey was conducted among the residents of the selected low-income housing in South Africa. The data collected for the study were analyzed for factorial validity through SEM. The result obtained from the SEM analysis confirms only five indicators out of twenty-two indicators identified from the interview and literature review for the study. This study adopts structural equation modelling (a second order factor) to investigate the key factors of analyzing livability of planned residential neighborhoods in Minna, Nigeria. Using Geographic Information System (GIS) application tools, users can create interactive queries, information analysis, map data edition and display the results [7]. Therefore, we have used GIS to identify the livability index of a particular area.

3 Methodology

According to our survey, we have selected indicators that will fetch datasets corresponding to each of the indicators from sources like Google Places API [8], data.gov.in [9] and kaggle.com [10] into our environment and start standardizing it. Each of the datasets undergoes standardization and indexing in parallel until a raw figure that exhibits a particular indicator is obtained. These raw figures are then saved as variables which are reflected on the results page.

3.1 Identifying Indicators

During literature study from papers, government of India reports, we have identified several indicators are listed in Table–1 below. Livability is defined by a set of factors or in this paper we called it as 'indicators.' Some of these indicators may carry varying significance for different age groups, which could be ranked among to yield personalized result. Table–2 shows how indicators are grouped and mapped accordingly in specific livability classes, where each class may/may not have some importance over the other. These grouped indicators aim to perfectly imply and achieve all the quality standards essential for current day assessment. Indicators are prioritized among four classes-Child, Middle Aged, Senior Adult, and Senior Citizen depicted in Table–2 [3].

3.2 Fetching Datasets for Indicators

After identification of indicators, the Google Places API, data.gov.in and kaggle. com have used the fetch the dataset for a particular location.

Table 1: Livability Indicators.

Population	Planned Env./city	Literacy Rate
Migration	Communication	Purchasing Power
Education	Socio-cultural Env.	Tourism Attraction
Occupation	Labour Participation Rate	Business Env.
Political Env.	Open Space Index	Handicap Friendliness
Health Parameters (Pollution)	Energy Index	Economic Infrastructure
Safety (Police)	Pollution	Traffic
Crime	Climate	Income & Employment
Parks	Food Quality (Cafes)	Availability of Public Transport
Road Accidents	Food variability	Economic Env.
Housing Options	Food Availability	Parking Facility
Housing Cost & Availability	Water Availability	Infrastructure
Mobility Index	Waste Management	Night Life (Clubs)
Urban Household Crowding (Supermarkets, department store)	Transportation Infrastructure (Bus/Train Station)	Health & Medical Standards (Hospitals, pharmacy)

Table 2: Reference Table for Table 1.

Age Class	Range	Importance represented by colour
Child	0–15	
Middle Aged	15–30	
Senior Adult	30–50	
Senior Citizen	>50	

3.3 Indexing Technique

There are different indexing methods [11] explained below. Data is indexed by calculating the following interpretations confined in the spectrum of data points as defined by the dataset.

Dimensional Index Methodology. This method normalizes all the data points within a fixed range (0, 1). This enables to sort and compare any given data points.

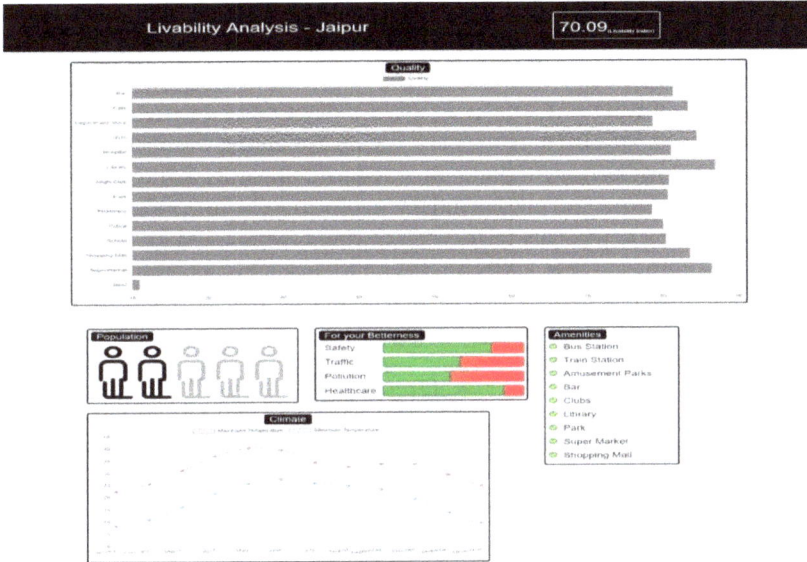

Fig. 1: The screenshot of tool's User Interface for Livability Analysis.

Z-Score or Standardization. This method classifies the data points across the median which helps in interpreting whether a given point has a positive/ negative impact.

Decile Scale Ranking. This method aggregately ranks all the data points using a calculated Decile Scale. We can calculate the ranking of each state based on the values of the decile scale. Similarly, we can compute the rankings for all the indicators taken into account and rank the cities accordingly [11].

The above methods are used to calculate the livability index for different cities, which are also incorporated in the tool that we have proposed for livability analysis. This tool accepts the name of the place from the user and livability class as input. It displays the livability index of that particular place and also demonstrates each indicator rating in bar-chart format. In Figure–1, upper right corner displays the livability index of *Jaipur* City and the bar-chart represents the indicators ratings. Below the bar-chart the relevant statistics like Population, Amenities, Climate etc. are displayed. The quick highlights of important factors of city livability.

4 Conclusion and Future Scope

The present work is inspired by a web portal 'AARP Livability Index' [12], aiming to incorporate analysis for Indian regions. We have developed a tool (prototype) for calculating the livability index of Indian cities. Livability index support to find out users well-being for particular workplace or city. We work with different data sources to provide a similar, and a bit more enhanced experience that the existing solution by customizing the results based on the user-intended age group. A combined system that can fetch geographical data from sources and process it accordingly for the end-user to deliver a content-rich visualization is henceforth developed. We plan to refine the feature selection and classification process by using machine learning techniques to reduce complexity and to improve the exactness. This project has the potential to evolve as a platform for city surveying and highlighting improvable sectors, which could stand useful for development planning at further stages. Lastly, we intend to make this application accessible to a broad group of end users by hosting it on a cloud service in the near future.

References

1. Urban population (% of data). data.worldbank.org. Retrieved 2019-04-20.
2. Tu, X., Huang, G., & Wu, J.: Review of the relationship between urban greenspace accessibility and human well-being. *Shengtai Xuebao/ Acta Ecologica Sinica*, 39(2), 421–431 (2019). https://doi.org/10.5846/stxb201802030294
3. Confederation of Indian Industry, Liveability index 2010: The best cities in India. A CII: Institute for Competitiveness Report, Northern Region, India (2010). http://indiaenvironmentportal.org.in/files/Liveability-Report.pdf
4. Yin, L., Yin, Y.: Research on Assessment of City Livability Based on Principle Component Analysis-Taking Shandong Province for Example. In: INTERNATIONAL CONFERENCE ON MANAGEMENT AND SERVICE SCIENCE 2009, (pp. 1–4). IEEE (2009).
5. India Population (2019), https://www.worldometers.info/world-population/india-population/, last accessed 2019/04/04.
6. Iyanda, Sule, A., Ojetunde, I., Foluke, O. F., Adekunle, S. A., Mohammad, A. M.: Evaluating Neighborhoods Livability in Nigeria: A Structural Equation Modelling (SEM) Approach. 5. 1, International Journal of Built Environment and Sustainability (2018).
7. Naik, G. M., M. Aditya, Naik, S. B.: GIS-based 4D model development for planning and scheduling of a construction project. International Journal of innovation, management and technology 2(6) 447 (2011).
8. Google Maps Places API. https://www.cloud.google.com/maps-platform/places, last accessed 2019/5/4.
9. Government of India data. https://data.gov.in, last accessed 2019/04/15.
10. https://www.kaggle.com, last accessed 2019/04/15.
11. Methodology for collection and computation of livability standards in cities, Ministry of Urban Development, Government of India. http://smartcities.gov.in/upload/uploadfiles/files/MethodologicalReportFinal.pdf.
12. AARP Livability Index Homepage, https://livabilityindex.aarp.org/, last accessed 2019/04/04.

Identification of Crop Disease using Augmented Reality-based Mobile App for Indian Farmers: A Prototype

Shrikant Salve

MIT Academy of Engineering, Pune, India

shrikantsalve@gmail.com

Abstract

In India agriculture provides employment for more than 50 percent of population and it also contributes about 18 percent of the total gross domestic product (GDP). The relevant and on time information is crucial for farmers to make effective decisions. Due to large failure rate in current agriculture in India many farmers are committing suicide. To empower the farmers it is imperative to incorporate right approach to provide agriculture information. So, it is important to increase the level of agriculture development making use of information communication technology (ICT). Several research have been done for development of mobile-based technologies for farmers like use of IoT for field monitoring and irrigation, Krishi Ville, AgroTIC and many more. Therefore, we have proposed a prototype of Augmented Reality-based mobile application to detect of crop diseases for farmers. This mobile-based application uses mobile camera to detect the crop disease and display name of crop on the mobile screen itself. The farmer will able to identify the crop disease immediately using his smart phone.

Keywords

Augmented Reality · Crop Disease · Farmer

How to cite this book chapter:
Salve, S. 2020. Identification of Crop Disease using Augmented Reality-based Mobile App for Indian Farmers: A Prototype. In: Loizides, F., Winckler, M., Chatterjee, U., Abdelnour-Nocera, J. and Parmaxi, A. (eds.) *Human Computer Interaction and Emerging Technologies: Adjunct Proceedings from the INTERACT 2019 Workshops.* Pp. 169–174. Cardiff: Cardiff University Press. DOI: https://doi.org/10.18573/book3.v. License: CC-BY 4.0.

1 Introduction

Agriculture is important sector of Indian economy and also it is the largest livelihood provider. The agriculture provides employment for more than 50 percent of population and it also contributes about 18 percent of the total gross domestic product (GDP) [1]. It is important to increase the level of agriculture development making use of information communication technology (ICT) like smartphones, cloud computing, big data, Augmented Reality, Internet of Things (IoT) to support the implementation of accuracy, improve crops and their management in agriculture sector.

Augmented Reality (AR) technology provides an interactive experience of a real world environment where the objects that reside in the real-world are 'augmented' by computer-generated perceptual information [2]. This technology can be used to support agriculture for Indian farmers those who uses smart phones. Currently there are various methods used by farmers to identify the crop disease like taking help from farmer friend, pesticide shop person, expert advice from agriculture officer or scientist or agronomist. But, neither all farmers have access to these experts nor these experts are always available. Also, it is inconvenient for farmers because most of the time these helps can take time to reach the farmers.

In this paper we have proposed a AR-based method to identify the diseases on crop. This technique uses mobile camera to view the crop disease. The crop leaf image capture through camera is matches with the online database of crop disease. Accordingly prediction of disease and preventive measure provided on the mobile screen itself. Now a days majority of farmers uses smart phone [3], this crop disease prediction mechanism through mobile app using AR technology would be convenient and easily available for the farmers.

2 Use of ICT in Agriculture

We have visited several villages near by Pune city, to investigate the problems related to farming. It has been observed that many farmers use smart phones to get help/information related to farming like through social networking (eg. WhatsApp, Facebook etc.), whether condition, market rates etc. We have also studied several literatures focusing on the use of ICT for farming which are stated below,

Rao and Sridhar [4] have proposed a smart agriculture project. They have developed Internet of Things (IoT)-based crop-field monitoring and automation irrigation system for farmers in India. This system generates reports on crop growth and irrigation decision support system. This kind of study would help farmers to make right decisions in farming. *GappaGoshti*^{TM} [5] is a mobile-based app developed by TCS Innovation Lab team for rural Indian farmers. It uses AR technology to recognize the insects on the crop. Some mobile-based applications available for agriculture but majority of them are proposed by Government of India and few are non-government like Kisansuvidha, Pusakrishi,

IFFCO kisan, Agrimarket, Crop insurance, Farm-o-pedia, Bhuvan Hailstorm [6], Agri App, Iffco Kisan App, Agri Media Video App, FarmBee-RML Farmer, Kisan Yojana [7] and many more. Krishi Ville [8] is one the Android-based application developed for Indian farmers. This mobile-based application provides agriculture related updates like different agriculture commodities, weather forecast and agriculture news. Another study proposed by Ganesan et. al. [9], they have developed multimedia agricultural advisory system (MAAS) tool which is easy to understand and user-friendly for Indian farmers so as to bridges information gaps in farmer's field. MAAS is call center like interface where farmers asked their queries to be resolved by experts providing personalized information on farmer's dashboard. In this system farmers can also upload images of disease attacked plant using their mobile phone. But this system does provide the immediate solution to the farmers query especially problem on crop/plant disease which needs immediate remedy. The same way to increase the productivity of Colombian farmers, Camacho and Arguello [10] proposed a social networking application for farmers called as AgroTIC. It consist of four modules like Communication for farmer to farmer, farmer to expert communication, Image processing and estimation of visible vegetation indices, production and marketing module. This is excellent study helped us to understand different aspects of problems occurred in agriculture. This paper also gives the idea of vegetation indices method which can be used to identify the crop disease using image processing.

3 Methodology

This project has been part of *Unnat Bharat Abhiya*n (UBA) [11] being carried out in Maharashtra Institute of Technology AOE Pune. UBA Scheme is proposed by Govt. of India for the betterment of India villages by providing engineering solutions to their problems. During our initial visit to several villages around *Pune* city and interaction with people especially farmers, we have observed several problems related to farming. We found that identification of crop disease is the major issue for the farmers. The literature study found that plenty of research has been done on agriculture sector. The study also shows that especially the mobile-based techniques have been implemented to support farmers. Therefore, we are developing mobile-based augmented reality application for prediction of crop disease. The below section explains the detailed methodology including participants, tools, procedure.

Participants. Twenty participants were voluntarily involved in this study from two villages like *Nirgudi, Dhanore* located nearby *Pune* city. The Figure–1 depicts the students conducting ethnographic study of farmers.

Tool and Procedure. The questionnaire has been prepared for conduction of interview with the farmers. This includes demographic information and questions related to how farmers deal with crop disease, use of technology for farming etc. The sample questionnaire is depicted in Figure 2.

We have developed a prototype of mobile-based application which uses augmented reality technology. This tool/app uses mobile camera to capture the image of infected crop leaf. The crop leaf image is matches with the online database of crop disease. Accordingly prediction of disease and preventive measure provided on the mobile screen itself. The following Figure 3 gives screen-shots of the developed application.

The drawback of this system is that mobile application needs to be tested by actual farmers. Also, the user interface of the applications is not in local language.

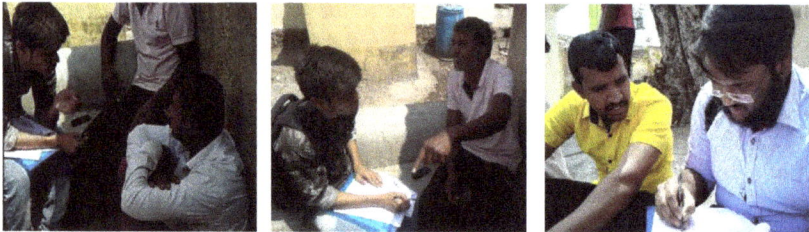

Fig. 1: Interaction with Farmers at *Nirgudi* and *Dhanore* Village.

आपण किती वर्षे शेती करत आहात? [How long you are doing farming?]
आपण शेती पूर्ण वेळ / अर्धवेळ करत आहात? [Are you doing farming full time/part time?]
आपण कोणत्या प्रकारचा फोन वापरत आहात? [What type of phone you are using?]   स्मार्ट फोन [Smart phone]   सामन्य फोन [Normal phone]
आपण इंटरनेटवर इंटरनेट वापरता का? [Do you use internet on mobile phone?]
आपण स्मार्टफोन वापरत असल्यास, आपण कोणत्याही सोशल नेटवर्किंग साइटचा वापर करता? [If you are using smart phone, Do you use any social networking site?]   व्हाट्सएप [WhatsApp]   फेसबुक [Facebook]   इतर कोणत्याही [any other]
शेतीविषयक क्रियाकलापांशी संबंधित माहिती / बातम्या तुम्हाला कसे मिळतील? [How would you get information/news related to farming activity?   टीव्ही.[TV]   न्यूज पेपर [News paper]   तज्ञ [Experts]   मोबाइल फोन (व्हाट्सएप/एफबी) [Mobile phone (WhatsApp/FB)]   इतर कोणतेही[Other]
आपण शेती संबंधित क्रियाकलापांकरिता कोणती माहिती शोधता? [What information would you search for farming related activity?]   उदाहरण- हवामानाची स्थिती [Example- Weather condition]

Fig. 2: Questionnaire used for data collection.

Fig. 3: The screen-shot of AR-based mobile app (a) Screen-shot of infected leaf (b) Screen-shot of non-infected or healthy leaf.

4   Conclusion

We have implemented the prototype of AR-based mobile application which successfully identifies the disease on the crop leaf. We have used image of the infected crop leaf as marker. The farmer will able to identify the crop disease immediately using his smart phone. In future we are planning to use the actual crop leaf as marker.

Acknowledgements

I am thankful to Mr. Omkar Pawar, Mr. Rahul Sahoo and Mr. Rupesh More, all are SY BTech students at MIT AOE, who helped in ethnographic study. I also appreciate the farmers who voluntarily participated in this research activity.

References

1. Madhusudhan, L.: Agriculture Role on Indian Economy. Bus Eco J 6(4), 176 (2015). doi: https://doi.org/10.4172/2151-6219.1000176
2. Azuma, R.T.: A Survey of Augmented Reality. Presence: Teleoperators and Virtual Environments 6(4), 355–385 (1997).
3. Mobile Usage In Agriculture & Healthcare Sector In India [Report], https://www.trak.in, last accessed 2019/05/15.
4. Rao, R. N., Sridhar, B.: IoT based smart crop-field monitoring and automation irrigation system. In: Proceedings of 2nd International Conference on Inventive Systems and Control (ICISC), pp. 478–483. Coimbatore (2018) doi: 10.1109/ICISC.2018.8399118

5. Nigam, A., Kabra, P., Doke, P.: Augmented Reality in agriculture. IEEE 7th International Conference on Wireless and Mobile Computing, Networking and Communications (WiMob), Wuhan, pp. 445–448 (2011).

6. Kailash: A study on use of mobile phone technology (smart phone) by the farmers of Nagapur district in Rajasthan. M.Sc. Thesis at Institute of Agricultural Sciences, Banaras Hindu University, Varanacy, India (2016).

7. Ahmed, Pasha, R., Prathap, V., Pasha, A., Kumari, D., Faraz: Survey on Precision Farming using Mobile Applications. Global Journal of Computer Science and Technology, (2019).

8. Singhal, M., Verma, K., Shukla A.: Krishi Ville Android based solution for Indian agriculture. Fifth IEEE International Conference on Advanced Telecommunication Systems and Networks (ANTS), Bangalore, pp. 1–5 (2011). doi: https://doi.org/10.1109/ANTS.2011.6163685

9. Ganesan, M., Karthikeyan, K., Prashant, S., Umadikar, J.: Use of mobile multimedia agricultural advisory systems by Indian farmers: Results of a survey. Journal of Agricultural Extension and Rural Development, 5(4), 89–99 (2013).

10. Camacho, A., Arguello, H.: Smartphone-based application for agricultural remote technical assistance and estimation of visible vegetation index to farmer in Colombia: AgroTIC. Proc. SPIE 10783, Remote Sensing for Agriculture, Ecosystems, and Hydrology XX, 107830K (2018).

11. Unnat Bharat Abhiyaan Homepage. http://unnatbharatabhiyan.gov.in.last accessed 2019/05/15.

'Digital Peer-Tutoring'. Early results from a field evaluation of a 'UX at work' enhancing learning format

Torkil Clemmensen and Jacob Nørbjerg

Copenhagen Business School
tc.digi@cbs.dk, jno.digi@cbs.dk

Abstract

This paper describes a learning format that enables workers to co-design their work with collaborative robots. The video-based digital peer tutoring format, enables shop floor workers to create their own peer-tutoring videos to share how-to knowledge with colleagues. Early field evaluation results indicate that workers benefit from the learning format and produced how-to videos for their colleagues. Furthermore, the learning format was also found useful by the company management and ownership as means of documentation and customer communication.

Keywords

Collaborative robots · assistive technologies · UX at work

1 Introduction

Peer tutoring has been put forward as a way to help students of all kinds deal with design problems [8]. Design, understood here as design thinking [3], is typically applied to solve non-routine, wicked problems. It is an iterative process that consists of generative and evaluative stages, which eventually converge on

How to cite this book chapter:
Clemmensen, T. and Nørbjerg, J. 2020. 'Digital Peer-Tutoring'. Early results from a field evaluation of a 'UX at work' enhancing learning format. In: Loizides, F., Winckler, M., Chatterjee, U., Abdelnour-Nocera, J. and Parmaxi, A. (eds.) *Human Computer Interaction and Emerging Technologies: Adjunct Proceedings from the INTERACT 2019 Workshops.* Pp. 175–180. Cardiff: Cardiff University Press. DOI: https://doi.org/10.18573/book3.w. License: CC-BY 4.0.

a solution to the design problem. Creating novel how-to knowledge requires hands-on experience, which is where peer tutoring becomes very helpful. We propose a new learning format, 'Digital Peer tutoring', that can help workers share their experience with collaborative robot interaction. We ask the questions: *How can a 'Digital Peer-Tutoring' learning format enable shop floor workers design positive UXs for themselves and their colleagues? What kind of* ethical stance does the use of 'Digital Peer-Tutoring' imply?

We report from the initial part of a research project aiming to develop Digital peer tutoring for shop floor workers. We aim to develop capabilities among shop floor workers to use short videos to design and document solutions to operational and collaboration issues related to assistive technologies (collaborative robots).

The research is situated within the KomDigital regional development project, which brings together 18 of the Copenhagen Capital Region's companies, unions, employer associations, and educational institutions. The partnership aims to improve digital competencies among employers and employees in SMEs (companies with fewer than 250 employees) thereby enabling them to adopt and implement digital technologies.

KomDigital achieves its goals through the development of digital learning formats, tailored to the working conditions and needs of companies and employees.

2 Related work

Peer tutoring [4, 8] overlaps somewhat with other notions of informal technical help giving between colleagues, such as over-the-shoulder-learning [11], over-the-shoulder guidance in tertiary education [2], and peer-assisted learning [5] and teaching [9] in the medical domain, and over-the-shoulder appropriation [1], and peer interaction [6] in software development.

We build primarily on the approach from Twidale [11] in that we aim to support informal technical help between colleagues, and follow Schleyer et al. [8] in that we acknowledge the role of peer tutors at various levels to the benefit of developing problem solving skills among colleagues. Specifically, we introduce a new role of digital competence facilitator, a 'Digital Coach', as we explain below.

What distingushes 'digital peer-tutoring' from traditional peer-tutoring is that the concept builds entirely on the use of video. The idea is that workers learn from creating and redesigning videos while sketching [7] as part of applying design thinking to design their own and their colleagues' work flow and interactions with collaborative robots. Ørngreen et al. [7] suggested to link various sketching techniques and creative reflection processes to video productions, and we extent this proposal to cover linking all parts of design thinking (problem definition and user needs finding, sketching, prototyping hypotheses, and evaluation) to workers' video production. Secondly, we propose that video-based reasoning, instead of simply paper or verbal exchange, empower workers to explore and take ownership of their work. Vistisen et al. [12] proposed to support ethical user stances during the design process of products and services, and proposes using animation-based sketching as a design method. We follow that line of thought, though we are less interested in professional designers, and more interested in workers' own production (and consumption) of videos-as-digital-peer-tutoring.

3 Case setting and method

The ABC company is a European SME specializing in glass processing. The company produces individual pieces and small batches with special specifications as well as entire series of several thousand units.

About a year prior to our visit, the ABC company purchased and installed a 100,000€ collaborative robot in order to explore if and how it could be used in their production. At the time of our visit, the robot was used only during the final polishing steps of one large scale order, and it was idle much of the time. Workers and management agreed, however, that the robot could be used for other purposes as well, and thus enable the company to accept more large batch orders, but no initiatives had been implemented for several months due to lack of time to experiment with the robot. Furthermore, the initial design decision had been a stationary installation, that is, the robot could not be moved to other positions on the floor where it could interact with other machines or workers.

The initial design decisions seemed to be related to a limited initial understanding of the robot's capability and a lack of strategic intent. In any case, it was clear that there was an unexplored potential (and risks) for enhancing the factory's capacity while empowering workers and help them design their own user experiences with the robot.

Our approach to building new digital competences is inspired by action design research (ADR). ADR argues that IT artifacts are 'ensembles' formed by the organizational context during development and use. Research in this tradition interweaves constructing the IT artifact, intervention in the organization, and evaluating outcomes [10].

We visited the company 6 times over a six-week period during the spring 2019. During first visit we gained insights into the company, the motivation for purchasing the robot, and challenges with its current as well as potential future uses. We observed the robot's current (very limited) use, interviewed and discussed with robot vendors, managers and shop-floor workers, and observed work and demonstrations of the robot.

The digital peer-tutoring learning format (see section 4) was implemented in four sessions over the next four visits, followed by a final evaluation on the sixth visit. We documented all observation, interviews, and learning sessions with video and audio recordings, and photos.

The learning format was evaluated after each session and at a final one-day meeting with participation from all key stakeholders.

4 The digital peer-tutoring learning format

The digital peer-tutoring learning format consisted of an ensemble of instruction-videos, quizzes, example solution-videos, and worker-created-how-to-videos. Together with the case company, we designed and implemented four training sessions with selected shop-floor workers. The themes of the sessions were:

1. Describe an interaction and a collaboration problem
2. Sketch solutions
3. Design a prototype
4. Test the prototype

Each session included short (3–5 minutes) instruction videos that explained the theme, introduced techniques that the participants could use to investigate problems and describe solutions, and an exercise where the participants should develop a short video (3–5 minutes). We also produced short example videos with our 'answers' to the assignment for each of the four session.

A 'digital competence facilitator' (student assistant) travelled to the factory for each session and discussed the material with the participants, and helped them produce their own 'employee-videos'. These were subsequently uploaded to a shared (secure) site for later download and knowledge sharing within the company.

5 Field evaluation results

The initial results from the final evaluation reveal both short and long-term benefits and challenges of Digital peer tutoring. Regarding short-term benefits, the workers liked the learning format: "...*worker-video on iPad [could be* useful]...", [Worker Br]. This confirms previous findings on the usefulness of video [7], and extends it to the shop floor workers.

However, the 'instruction videos' were too long and complicated. "*[They should be cut down on a list of four points*" [Worker Br]. Too long videos can be an expression of an 'apathetic ethical stance', a stance that reduces the worker-user to be a mean of input for the intended final design [12].

On the other hand, the workers expressed that they could use video to both think about the problem, sketch different solutions, and evaluate their use: "*Sketches .... I had read up on it, go and think about it....*" [Worker Br], and "the worker *should be able to pause the video ...*" [Worker Bi]. Thus, there were indications that the format helped workers explore new technologies from an emphatic ethical user perspective, that is, from their own perspective [12]. The Company manager K supported this: "*We, as a business must spend more time on* [workers' use of video to innovate]." The management perspective adds a new layer to understand short term benefits of video-sketching and ethical design, and thus center our focus on the multi-layered essence of user experiences at work.

The stakeholders also commented on the long-term benefits of the learning format:

- Help videos could be used to tackle issues in manufacturing, [Worker Bi], and retain knowledge even long after they were produced [Manager J].
- Introduce new employees to the job through [Manager J].
- Videos can replace manuals for dyslexic employees.
- Document supplier shop floor supplier courses [Consultant F] [Manager K]
- Introducing new production processes, for example "*recording the results from the company's informal and formal experiments on the shop floor*" [Manager J and K] and "*recording order-specific ideas for how-to, so next time this order comes in, the* video shows what to do" [Worker Bi], and retain good ideas [Teacher T].
- Producing videos for marketing purposes and quality documentation.

These benefits allude to a diversity of user experiences in work situations, and perhaps also tells us that the ethical stances taken by workers-as-designers-of-their-own-work may be confounded by management's strategic interest in how-to knowledge.

6 Discussion and conclusion

'Digital Peer-Tutoring' enabled shop floor workers design positive UXs for themselves and their colleagues, also beyond what we expected. The workers liked the Digital Peer tutoring how-to videos and found them useful. This is in line with [11] saying that it is possible to use peer tutoring to give informal technical help between colleagues, and with [7] that suggests to link various sketching techniques and creative reflection processes to video productions. The videos helped workers create ideas about robot use, identify problems not formulated before, sketch alternatives, test solutions, and demonstrate them to colleagues.

Company owners, management, and workers had unexpected ideas about how to use the peer-tutoring videos within and outside the company, in for example internal quality control and customer communication. Thus, similar to the point made about peer tutoring [8], we should acknowledge the role of Digital peer tutoring in developing problem solving skills at various organizational levels.

Finally we conclude, using the categories proposed in [12], that the ethical stance built into the 'Digital Peer-Tutoring' learning format could be characterized as 'apathetic' when too long and complex instructional videos lead the workers to give up. However, the learning format also showed to be 'empathetic' as workers produced their own videos and evaluated solutions together, effectively co-designing work procedures.

References

1. Sebastian Draxler, and Gunnar Stevens. 2011. Supporting the collaborative appropriation of an open software ecosystem. *Comput. Support. Coop. Work* 20, 4–5 (2011), 403–448.
2. Angela C Hague, and Ian D Benest. 1996. Towards over-the-shoulder-guidance following a traditional learning metaphor. *Comput. Educ.* 26, 1–3 (1996), 61–70.
3. Jon Kolko. 2010. Abductive Thinking and Sensemaking: The Drivers of Design Synthesis. *Des. Issues* 26, 1 (January 2010), 15–28. DOI: https://doi.org/10.1162/desi.2010.26.1.15
4. D J Magin, and A E Churches. 1995. Peer tutoring in engineering design: A case study. *Stud. High. Educ.* 20, 1 (1995), 73–85.
5. Johanna Martinez, Christina Harris, Cathy Jalali, Judy Tung, and Robert Meyer. 2015. Using peer-assisted learning to teach and evaluate residents' musculoskeletal skills. *Med. Educ. Online* 20, 1 (2015), 27255.
6. Emerson Murphy-Hill, Gail C Murphy, and Joanna McGrenere. 2015. How Do Users Discover New Tools in Software Development and Beyond? *Comput. Support. Coop. Work* 24, 5 (2015), 389–422.
7. Rikke Ørngreen, Birgitte Henningsen, Peter Gundersen, and Heidi Hautopp. 2017. The Learning Potential of Video Sketching. In *Proceedings of the 16th European Conference on elearning ISCAP Porto, Portugal 26–27 October 2017*, 422–430.
8. G K Schleyer, G S Langdon, and S James. 2005. Peer tutoring in conceptual design. *Eur. J. Eng. Educ.* 30, 2 (2005), 245–254.
9. Jacinta Secomb. 2008. A systematic review of peer teaching and learning in clinical education. *J. Clin. Nurs.* 17, 6 (2008), 703–716.
10. Sein, Henfridsson, Purao, Rossi, and Lindgren. 2011. Action Design Research. *MIS Q.* (2011). DOI: https://doi.org/10.2307/23043488
11. Michael B Twidale. 2005. Over the shoulder learning: supporting brief informal learning. *Comput. Support. Coop. Work* 14, 6 (2005), 505–547.
12. Peter Vistisen, Thessa Company manager Jen, and Søren Bolvig Poulsen. 2016. Animating the ethical demand: Exploring user dispositions in industry innovation cases through animation-based sketching. *ACM SIGCAS Comput. Soc.* 45, 3 (2016), 318–325.

Proposed System for a Socio-technical Design Framework for Improved User Collaborations with Automation Technologies

Parisa Saadati[*], José Abdelnour-Nocera[*]
and Torkil Clemmensen,[†]

[*]University of West London, UK
parisa.saadati@uwl.ac.uk
[†]University of West London and ITI/Larsys Portugal
abdejos@uwl.ac.uk
[‡]Copenhagen Business School
tc.digi@cbs.dk

Abstract

To improve human performance, interactive technologies are going towards more automated systems that involve computers, robots and cyber-physical systems into the decisionmaking process. While automation can lead to increased performance and reduced impact of human errors, interactive technologies without optimal design can have a negative impact on the experience of operators and end-users, leading to suboptimal performance of the automated systems. In this research, we aim to evaluate and refine Human Work Interaction Design (HWID) framework to be applicable in various highly-automated settings including Industry 4.0 environments. This will be performed via a thorough literature review as the first step. The list of identified

How to cite this book chapter:
Saadati, P., Abdelnour-Nocera, J. and Clemmensen, T. 2020. Proposed System for a
Socio-technical Design Framework for Improved User Collaborations with
Automation Technologies. In: Loizides, F., Winckler, M., Chatterjee, U.,
Abdelnour-Nocera, J. and Parmaxi, A. (eds.) *Human Computer Interaction and
Emerging Technologies: Adjunct Proceedings from the INTERACT 2019 Workshops.*
Pp. 181–188. Cardiff: Cardiff University Press. DOI: https://doi.org/10.18573/
book3.x. License: CC-BY 4.0.

factors playing a potential role in various interactive systems will then be evaluated and optimised in three case studies. We will try to understand how to maximise collaborations between the users and the machine in interactive systems. A practical approach for evaluating both employees' and end-users' perspectives in three scenarios with different levels of automation will be assessed. The ultimate output of the study will be a framework or model that will help in designing future research studies for semi-autonomous systems that involve high levels of interaction between users and the machine. We expect that the framework output of this research will provide a comprehensive guideline applicable to many Industry 4.0 technologies.

Keywords

Sociotechnical · human work interaction design · automation · augmentation · Industry 4.0

1 Introduction

During the life cycle of any organisation, a variety of environmental stimuli will influence its operations and decision-making processes [1]. Complex organisational systems inevitably rely now on large-scale software-intensive systems which should be in line with the organisational goals and strategies. In this paper, we hint at a possible sociotechnical HCI framework, with customized value propositions and a case presentation for a future investigation of three different scenarios with different levels of automation.

Socio-Technical System Design (STSD) developments have identified and addressed several problems in understanding and developing complex systems. Despite many positive outcomes, these methods have not materially changed industrial software engineering practices due to involving users only in the testing stage of any new system development instead of the design process [2].

Currently, 'automation' is one of the main means for supporting operators using systems that feature high complexity. Automation allows designers to transfer the burden from operators to machine by re-allocating the system tasks that were previously performed by human [3]. Several researchers have studied different aspects of implementation of advanced interactive technologies employing automation in different platforms [1, 3–7].

Organisations can now improve operations and decision making by implementing cyber-physical systems (CPS) and internet of things (IoT), and potentially linking them to blockchain technology in the future. Rising integration of Internet of Everything (IoE) into the industrial value chain is the foundation of "Industry 4.0" technologies [8]. These technologies can improve the end-users' experience but does not necessarily and automatically guarantee a positive response from workers and customers [9]. Hence, developments towards future 'smart workplaces' need to be carefully designed in order to achieve expected service quality goals for both end-users and employees. The main purpose of this study is to identify all humanistic/ social and technological elements in the design of newly automated systems applicable to Industry 4.0 that are affecting the human and machine collaborations. This paper is organised in two sections as follows; Section 2 introduces the findings of the literature review on different factors affecting the human and machine collaborations and categorising them into three main categories. Section 3 proposes the future research outcome by investigating into these factors from three case studies; university library, research platform and an airport.

2 Review

Replacing human habits with automated interactive systems requires consideration of potential changes on human activity and the new coordination demands on the human operators. These experiences highly depend on the type and level of automation [7] and to what extent the developer has allowed the machine to make decisions.

2.1 Technological elements of interactive systems

The fourth industrial revolution (Industry 4.0) which is now undergoing, will transform the design, manufacturing, and operation of various products and systems [7]. The increasing integration of the IoE into the industrial value chain has built the foundation for this revolution [8]. The increased connectivity and interaction among systems, humans and machines support the integration of various automated or semi-automated systems, and hence, increasing flexibility and productivity [10]. These automated systems will lead to interconnected manufacturing systems and supply chains with their own challenges.

To achieve sufficient autonomous awareness in a system, efficient integration of smart sensors and mobile devices is required alongside industrial communication protocols and standards. Economic impact of this industrial revolution is supposed to be huge and comes with changes in the existing business models [10–12].

Industry 4.0 advancements [7] are categorised into four main principles in general; technical assistance, interconnections, decentralised decisions, and information transparency. "Collaborations" is a sub-principle of the "Interconnections" principle (which includes Collaborations, Standards and Security). Three type of collaborations are considered in the context of Industry 4.0: human-human, human-machine and machine machine collaborations.

Main focus of this research is to improve the existing guidelines for human-machine collaborations.

2.2 Human Work Interaction Design

Human Work Interaction Design (HWID) is a comprehensive framework that aims to establish relationships between extensive empirical work-domain studies and HCI designs. It builds on the foundation of Cognitive Work Analysis (CWA) [5]. HWID is currently positioned as a modern lightweight version of CWA.

HWID studies how to understand, conceptualise, and design for the complex and emergent contexts in which information and communication technologies (ICT) and work are entangled [1]. HWID models are based on the characteristics of humans and work domain contents and the interactions during their tasks and decision making activities (Figure 1). HWID focuses on the integration of work analysis (i.e. CWA methods) and interaction design methods (e.g. goal-oriented design and HCI usability) for smart workplaces. The ultimate goal of HWID is to empower users by designing smarter workplaces in various work domains.

For applying HWID models to specific workplaces we need to consider several independent and entangled factors [5]. Considering numerous theories, concepts, techniques and methods developed for other work environments is the first step. Environmental contexts such as national, cultural, geographic, social and organisational factors will have an important role in designing optimal HWID models, as they impact interaction between users (i.e. both operators and employees) and smart systems in their work and life. There are more work-related factors including the users' knowledge/skills, application domain, work contents and goals, as well as the nature of tasks or newly introduced technologies to be considered in the interaction performance.

2.3 Humanistic elements of interactive systems

To address human element in designing complex interactive systems, design fiction and design ethnography should be linked [16]. This is in line with considering the impact of anthropology on the design's future-orientedness by understanding the cultural meanings and sensitivity to values and context [17]. Analysis of the allocation of functions is necessary to identify the optimal distribution of both functions and tasks between a partly-autonomous system and the user [3].

Physical support of human workers by robots or machines is an important aspect of new technologies. This is due to involvement of users in conducting a range of tasks that are unpleasant, too exhausting or unsafe [18–19]

For an effective, successful, and safe support of users in physical tasks, it is necessary that robots or machines interact smoothly and intuitively with their human counterparts [18], and that humans are properly trained for this kind of human-machine collaboration [8].

The value of information. In collaborations between human and machine, the value of information is now more recognised given high power of the machine in decision making in highly-automated systems. For instance, informing users about the sensor's reading power of Tesla's automated car can significantly increase their trust [6]. However, other studies show that the number of information items or tasks users receive in an automated process should be personalised and up to the point of their desire/tolerability. Not enough functions allocated to a user will lead to underload and boredom and thus decreased performance [20]. Too many allocated functions will lead to cognitive, perceptive or motoric overload and increase negative emotions (e.g. stress, anxiety) [21] and user's error [3, 20]. Meanwhile, users can cope with emotions after spending some time with the autonomous technology and developing some routines.

Providing an abundance of information and transparency is an important hypothesis in interactive technologies. Trust, transparency and acceptance of losing control (i.e. shared authority between the user and system [8]) can improve the interaction of the user by revealing the ambiguous feelings toward the automation. Other psychological factors under study include worries about practical challenges and security of the technology (e.g. hacking a system) and reliability of the process itself (e.g. flat mobile phone battery for systems that rely on applications). Users may lose their trust in decision-making of an automated system when other humans who won't follow the same process are involved and can impact on the outcome. Another important situation is when responsibilities are shared between users and the system. Ability to identify responsible party related to a bad outcome (i.e. user error versus system failure) can impact the performance of users [9]. Controllable designed interface and environment of work, as well as feeling safe while using new technologies, are among other factors that can increase the performance of the users.

Involving users in the design process. The design process should determine the content and format of information to be shared with users in order to create an experience of certainty and trust. The right amount and format of feedback from the users plays a major role for designing such systems. Motivating the users to engage with the new technologies is still a challenge due to lack of understanding of the end-users' individual experience and interaction with such technologies. Users can have different roles or backgrounds that can affect their discovery, collaboration and learning of the interactive system [11]. In some studies researchers have tried to recruit users for testing their interaction via use of flyers or instructions explaining the technology (a process known as augmentation) [22].

Furthermore, engaging users in designing the automated or augmented product will change their interaction time. It is recommended that the developing teams need to familiarise themselves with space and environment of practices, build trust with the employees and improve design ideas. Some of the studies suggested the relations between modes of discovery, design improvements, interaction and socio-spatial aspects. These relations can be developed more as an analytical and design tool to redefine the borders of opportunities for social interaction in daily automated spaces.

3 Proposed further research

For investigating independent and entangled factors related to human and machine collaborations in automated systems, we propose a practical approach for evaluating both end-users' and employees' (or operators') perspectives in an automatous environment.

First step (current stage) in this research is to produce a list of relevant factors from different sources including: review of the relevant literature, contact and interview with experts in this domain, and observation of some smart workplaces. This comprehensive list will then be evaluated and optimised in two scenarios (University of west London library and mKRISHI® research platform). These scenarios were selected carefully based on potentially important factors such as socio-behavioural (e.g. work pattern), psychological (e.g. trust in system), demographical (e.g. wealth and ethnicity), and geographical characteristics of their user populations.

We will analyse previously-available (via literature review and expert opinions) and newly-gathered data (via questionnaires and interviews) to produce a model to be validated on scenario 3 settings (i.e. London based airport). By several iterations in this highly-automated environment we will refine and provide the final output of the study, which will be a tool/guideline for designing HWID models for various interactive technologies. Given the variety of environments and different levels of automation, we will potentially achieve different lists of factors that affect the performance of users. In the final scenario, current shortcomings and future opportunities will be evaluated by using an HWID model for future smart workplaces using Industry 4.0 framework.

4 Conclusion

In summary, the overall objective of this paper was to present a review of the possible theoretical background for a to-be-developed sociotechnical HCI framework, including customized value propositions for the work domain of choice, and, finally, to present three scenarios to be considered in future research. One of the outcomes that the current stage is a comprehensive list categorises in main principle and number of sub-principles of the factors impact the machine and human counterpart collaboration from sociotechnical perspective. This is what we hoped to illustrate with this paper as start of a series of papers in different scenarios with various automation level.

References

1. Barricelli, B.R., Roto, V., Clemmensen, T., Campos, P., Lopes, A., Goncalves, F., Abdelnour-Nocera, J. (2018) Human Work Interaction Design 2018. Designing Engaging Automation. IFIP AICT 554, pp. 215–228. https://doi.org/10.1007/978-3-030-05297-3_15

2. Baxter, G. and Sommerville, I. (2011) 'Socio-technical systems: From design methods to systems engineering', Interacting with Computers, 23(1), pp. 4–17. https://doi.org/10.1016/j.intcom.2010.07.003

3. Barricelli, B.R., Roto, V., Clemmensen, T., Campos, P., Lopes, A., Goncalves, F., Abdelnour-Nocera, J. (2018) Human Work Interaction Design 2018. Designing Engaging Automation. IFIP AICT 554, pp. 36–56. https://doi.org/10.1007/978-3-030-05297-3_3

4. Abdelnour-Nocera J, Oussena S, Burns C (2015). Human Work Interaction Design of the Smart University. 4th IFIP 13.6 Working Conference on Human Work Interaction Design, AICT-468: pp. 127–140

5. Clemmensen T (2011) A Human Work Interaction Design (HWID) Case Study in E-Government and Public Information Systems. International Journal of Public Information Systems 3: pp. 105–113

6. Murat Dikmen and Catherine Burns. (2017) Trust in Autonomous Vehicles. 2017 IEEE International Conference on Systems, Man, and Cybernetics: pp. 1093–1098. https://doi.org/10.1109/SMC.2017.8122757

7. Parasuraman, R., Sheridan, T., Wickens, C. (2000) A model for types and level of human interaction with automation. IEEE Transactions on Systems, Man, and Cybernetics Part A:System and Humans, 30(3), pp. 286–297

8. Hermann, M., Pentek, T. and Otto, B. (2016) Design Principles for Industrie 4.0 Scenarios. IEEE, pp. 3928–3937. https://doi.org/10.1109/HICSS.2016.48

9. World Economic Forum. (2018) The fourth Industrial Revolution, https://www.weforum.org/pages/the-fourth-industrial-revolution-by-klaus-schwab, last accessed 22nd August, 2018

10. Davies, R. (2015) Industry 4.0: Digitalisation for productivity and growth. European Parliamentary Research Service

11. Eric Lesser and Larry Prusak. (1999) Communities of Practice, Social Capital and Organizational Knowledge. Information Systems Review 1, pp. 3–10. [Online] Available from: http://providersedge.com/docs/km_articles/Cop_-_Social_Capital_-_Org_K.pdf, last accessed 25th Feb, 2019

12. International Airport reviews, [Online] Available from: https://www .internationalair-portreview.com/article/25929/personalisation-smart -airport/, last accessed 18th Feb, 2019

13. Joseph Lindley, Dhruv Sharma, and Robert Potts. (2014) Anticipatory Ethnography: Design Fiction as an Input to Design Ethnography. Ethnographic Praxis in Industry Conference Proceedings 2014, pp. 237–253. https://doi.org/10.1111/1559-8918.01030

14. Ton Otto and Rachel Charlotte Smith. (2013) Design Anthropology: A Distinct Style of Knowing. In Design Anthropology: Theory and Practice, Wendy Gunn, Ton Otto and Rachel Charlotte Smith (eds.). Bloomsbury, London, New York, pp. 1–29. https://doi.org/10.1017/CBO9781107415324.004

15. M. awais, and D. Henrich. (2013) "Human Robot Interaction in an Unknown Human Intention Scenario", 11th International Conference on Frontiers of Information Technology, 2013, pp. 89–94

16. S. Kiesler, and P. Hinds. (2004) "Human-Robot Interaction", Human-Computer Interaction, Volume 19, 2004

17. Yerkes, RM., and Dodson, J.D. (1908) The relation of strength of stimulus to rapidly of habit formation. Journal of Comparative Neurology and psychology, 18(5), pp. 459–482.

18. Kirk, A, and Brown,D.F. (2003) Employee assistance programs: A review of the management of stress and wellbeing through workplace counselling and consulting, Australian Psychologist 38(2), pp. 138–143.

19. Wouters, N., Downs, J., Harrop, M., Cox, T., Oliveira, E., Webber, S., Vetere, F., Vande moere, A. (2016). Uncovering the Honeypot Effect: How Audiences Engage with Public Interactive Systems. Proceedings of the 2016 ACM Conference on Designing Interactive Systems (DIS '16), ACM, pp. 5–16. https://doi.org/10.1145/2901790.2901796

SECTION 5

Human(s) in the Loop
Bringing AI & HCI

Designing a Machine Learning-based System to Augment the Work Processes of Medical Secretaries

Patrick S. Johansen, Rune M. Jacobsen,
Lukas B. L. Bysted, Mikael B. Skov
and Eleftherios Papachristos

Department of Computer Science, Aalborg University, Denmark
pjohan15@student.aau.dk, rjacob15@student.aau.dk, lbyste15@student.aau.dk
dubois@student.aau.dk, papachristos@cs.aau.dk

Abstract

Advances in Machine Learning (ML) provide new opportunities for augmenting work practice. In this paper, we explored how an ML-based suggestion system can augment Danish medical secretaries in their daily tasks of handling patient referrals and allocating patients to a hospital ward. Through a user-centred design process, we studied the work context and processes of two medical secretaries. This generated a model of how a medical secretary would assess a visitation suggestion, and furthermore, it provided insights into how a system could fit into the medical secretaries' daily tasks. We present our system design and discuss how our contribution may be of value to HCI practitioners designing for work augmentation in similar contexts.

Keywords

Work Augmentation · Human-AI Interaction · Medical Domain

How to cite this book chapter:
Johansen, P.S., Jacobsen, R.M., Bysted, L.B.L., Skov, M.B. and Papachristos, E. 2020. Designing a Machine Learning-based System to Augment the Work Processes of Medical Secretaries. In: Loizides, F., Winckler, M., Chatterjee, U., Abdelnour-Nocera, J. and Parmaxi, A. (eds.) *Human Computer Interaction and Emerging Technologies: Adjunct Proceedings from the INTERACT 2019 Workshops.* Pp. 191–196. Cardiff: Cardiff University Press. DOI: https://doi.org/10.18573/book3.y. License: CC-BY 4.0.

1 Introduction

The promise of workforce augmentation through artificial intelligence (AI) or machine learning (ML) is the enabling of making professionals more efficient in their work practices. The goal is not to replace workers with fully automated systems but to utilize algorithms to carry out complex or repetitive tasks while high-level decision-making remains under human control. But designing AI-based systems pose significant challenges and is not a straight forward process. A successful system would require a deep understanding of the specific work context in order to be able to answer questions such as: which tasks of the workflow should be automated, and which require human intervention? How can we design in accordance with users' mental models [6]? What information, in what form, and at what time, has to be provided to aid the human decision making process? How can we establish confidence and trust in the systems [4–5]?

In this paper, we investigate and address some of these questions through the design of a system aimed to augment the workflow of medical secretaries (MS) in a hospital. Such systems could potentially make repetitive and administrative tasks more efficient and would free up time and resources that could be used to engage with patients. The system was designed in collaboration with a Danish company providing the system using ML algorithms trained on extensive Danish medical patient data and treatment history. We present our approach to understand and deconstruct the workflow of MS during the visitation process and the methods we used to design the user interface.

2 Method

In Denmark, the visitation process begins when a patient is referred from a general practitioner to a hospital. A hospital MS receives the referral and if necessary retrieves additional documentation (e.g. patient records) from various systems. The patient referrals are then preliminary sorted based on assessment and are handed over to the physicians. If no modifications are necessary, the physician appoints medical staff to treatment procedures and returns the documents to the MS, who schedules the treatments. In a booking system, the MS then assigns the appointed treatment to each referral on timeslot and selects the information letters that should be sent to the patient. Finally, the MS confirms the referral booking and checks status in a separate system. The visitation process is an intricate process involving multiple medical professionals and several work subtasks. The purpose of the ML-system is to automate the task of the hospital physicians and provide a suggestion for a visitation that the medical secretary is able to review and process. Each suggestion is based on a wide array of patient data. It is assumed that the augmentation of this process will shorten handling times considerably.

We conducted three user studies with staff at Aalborg University Hospital in order to deconstruct the workflow and understand the needs and work context of the MS. First, we did a semi-structured interview with one MS at in order to identify hospital staff responsibilities and tasks. Secondly, we conducted a contextual inquiry at the ward to gain insights into the context, environment, and technical details of the visitation process. Thirdly, we constructed a card sorting activity where the MS prioritized, sorted, and ranked visitation information in order for us to understand what cues they are looking for during the decision-making process. Afterwards, findings from the three studies were synthesized in a PACT analysis [3]. Before we present our design, we outline some design implications that emerged from the studies. The semi-structured interviews and contextual inquiry revealed the workflow of the MS and helped generate a list of additional visitation considerations that the medical secretary goes through and controls for when handling visitations (e.g. need to organize transportation or find a translator). It is important that the design is able to convey whether any of those additional considerations apply to a specific visitation suggestion. The bits of information needed to assess a referral were prioritized by the MS in the card sorting activity which proved to be very useful in guiding the design process of the visual user interface.

3 Design and Evaluation

A screenshot of the user interface that was developed can be seen in fig. 1. The system consists of two main parts, the visitation suggestion card, and the rest of the system which supports the general workflow of handling visitations. The system provides the MS with a summary of the diagnosis and the cause of referral, providing an overview of the patient in the specific case. This is currently the information that the MS looks for when she builds an understanding of a visitation case. The system also presents an initial suggestion of how the visitation could be handled. This suggestion includes a treatment type, date, time, as well as icons that communicate visitation considerations.

During our studies, we realized that the task of handling visitations is only one of many tasks carried out by the MS, and the process of handling multiple visitations may be interrupted by more urgent tasks. Therefore, we implemented an overview of visitation tasks in a sidebar, where suggestions are sorted in digital stacks according to recommended treatment. This corresponds to the current practice, in which the MS prints the received referrals, she reads them through, highlighting significant information, assigns a preliminary treatment, and sorts the referrals and from there work with the visitation as stacks. In addition, the system implements hourly notifications automatically informing the MS about any acute referrals that have been received during the last hour. This resembles a current work pattern, in which the MS manually checks for incoming referrals and handles them if perceived acute. Finally, if human intervention

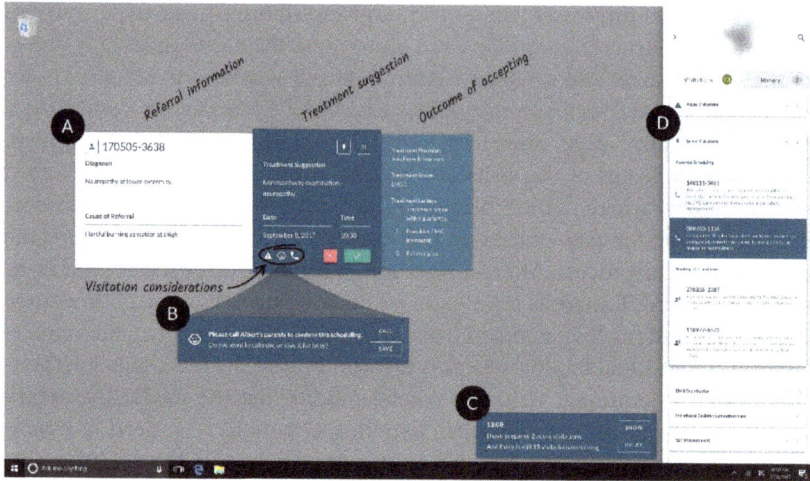

Fig. 1: The picture shows the user interface of our system. A) Visitation suggestion card, B) referral specific notification advising to book a translator for the patient, C) hourly updates about acute referrals, D) Sidebar/Overview. Two panes "Visitation" and "History". Below "Acute Visitations" followed by "Saved Visitations", and lastly categorized referrals by treatment.

is required for a visitation to be completed, the system notifies the MS via a message box (e.g. "This patient might need a translator..." and the phone number to the translators' office). The MS can also save the task for later to schedule the phone calls in bulk.

The design was evaluated by a MS assessing 20 visitation suggestions following the think-aloud protocol. The MS was encouraged to articulate the usefulness of the system as a tool for processing visitations, and furthermore express any concerns regarding use. We purposely created an incorrect visitation suggestion with an erroneous treatment for the patient to test if the MS could properly assess the information of the visitation suggestion, and the MS was able to detect and decline the wrongful suggestion. The result of the evaluation was a list of usability problems and insights on how the MS perceived working with the visitation suggestion system. In the preliminary findings, the MS expressed how the system worked very efficiently and that this, in particular, would free up more time for the MS to talk with patients and focus on patient treatment.

4 Discussion and Future Work

While our work is in an early stage, it provides insights from a specific example of how a system can be designed to fit into a complex work context and augment current work practices (e.g. checking for new visitations, notifying). We illustrate that it is important, for a system in this context, to be clear about its limitations, and communicating when and what human intervention is needed (e.g. booking translator and contacting under-age patients' parents). In this initial study, we only had access to a limited number of hospital staff but we will further develop our system and generate a stronger empirical foundation by engaging a broader group of medical professionals. Since different hospital departments may have unique challenges with their patient groups, we would expect that other considerations become evident as we change the setting of the system.

The design we propose only provides a static understanding of a suggestion and provides the user with a binary choice of accepting or reject. Abdul et al [1] note that most work on interfaces for intelligibility provides *static* explanations and that there might be possible to work on allowing users to explore a system interactively. While our system does not focus on explaining the actual AI system, we see the potential for allowing a user to explore elements of a suggestion in a flexible and interactive way (e.g. unfolding the information that a suggestion is based upon). But more importantly, we would like to study the implications of MS using the system over a longer period of time. We are concerned that users might start to rely on the suggestions of a system, introducing what is also known as *automation bias* [2]. We are especially interested in understanding the relationship between the user's ability to interact with and explore a suggestion, and the degree of complacency that may be introduced over time.

References

1. Ashraf Abdul, Jo Vermeulen, et al. 2018. Trends and Trajectories for Explainable, Accountable and Intelligible Systems: An HCI Research Agenda. *CHI 2018*: 1–18.
2. E. Alberdi, P. Ayton, A.A. et al. 2005. Automation bias and system design: a case study in a medical application. *IEE and MOD HFI DTC Symposium on People and Systems – Who are we Designing for?*, IEE, 53–60.
3. Benyon; David. 2013. PACT: a framework for designing interactive systems. In *Designing Interactive Systems*. Pearson, 25–48.
4. Monika Hengstler, Ellen Enkel, et al. 2016. Technological Forecasting & Social Change Applied artificial intelligence and trust—The case of autonomous vehicles and medical assistance devices. *Technological Forecasting & Social Change* 105: 105–120.
5. Andreas Holzinger, Markus Plass, et al. 2017. A glass-box interactive machine learning approach for solving NP-hard problems with the human-in-the-loop. 26.
6. Donald A Norman. 1994. How might people interact with agents. CACM 37, 7: 68–71

Interfacing AI with Social Sciences: the Call for a New Research Focus in HCI

Hamed S. Alavi and Denis Lalanne

Human-IST Institute, University of Fribourg, Switzerland

hamed.alavi@unifr.ch, denis.lalanne@unifr.ch

Abstract

We provide arguments for the necessity of broadening the engagement of HCI in translating knowledge created in social sciences to a major force that can drive AI and direct the ways in which it will impact various aspects of our world. We begin to sketch the outline of this engagement as a research agenda within HCI in reference to some of the definitional manifesto on the HCI's foundational role [4] as an action science [3]. Also, a part of our own research that scrutinizes some of the major AI projects [1–2] informs the presented arguments.

Keywords

Sociological Conception of Artificial Intelligence · Smart Agenda · Science and Technology Studies (STS)

1 Introduction

Similar to many other domains of research and design, the future of HCI is increasingly bound with the advances in Artificial Intelligence (AI). This is attributed to the opportunities it can create to enhance the processes

How to cite this book chapter:

Alavi, H.S. and Lalanne, D. 2020. Interfacing AI with Social Sciences: the Call for a New Research Focus in HCI. In: Loizides, F., Winckler, M., Chatterjee, U., Abdelnour-Nocera, J. and Parmaxi, A. (eds.) *Human Computer Interaction and Emerging Technologies: Adjunct Proceedings from the INTERACT 2019 Workshops.* Pp. 197–202. Cardiff: Cardiff University Press. DOI: https://doi.org/10.18573/book3.z. License: CC-BY 4.0.

and methods of research, but also to the challenging questions it raises such as "explainability", "agency", "trustworthiness", "ethics", and so forth.

However, the discussion that we would like to instigate in this paper takes a different standpoint and seeks to pronounce a new responsibility, a crucial and urgent one, that is embedded in the HCI's special scientific placement. Departing from a widely acknowledged observation that despite the substantial and multifaceted impact of AI on human life social sciences are far from being at a leading position, we argue that HCI can play a key role in rectifying this disconnect. The task, in a nutshell, is to bring the knowledge created in various areas of social science to the format and position that can effectively shape the development of non-human intelligent actors and inform the policies governing whether and how they should be adopted. The eventual objective is to ensure that AI as such will take us to a "better future" where human values and priorities are advanced, and prevent it from falling into the other paths that empirical findings and discourses already can forecast the ramifications. In the interest of clarity, we constrain the discussion of AI to what we refer to as "major AI projects", projects such as Smart City or Personalized Learning that are initially backed by certain technological possibilities and produced a wave of corporate investments and academic investigations. This is our primary interest in AI. Instead of discussing AI as a broad (and rather ambivalent) concept, the objective is to provide a platform in which major AI projects can be meticulously analyzed using the frameworks constructed in the relevant domains of social science.

We develop our argument is three steps: *1)* we start by highlighting a set of cross-domain concerns stemming from the current mechanisms through which major AI projects have been conceptualized and advancing. Then we describe *2)* why we think HCI holds the methodological capabilities to rectify those problems, and why it is only HCI that can do so. In the end, we *3)* try to extend this discussion beyond abstract reflections and begin to draft a research agenda that can reify some of the described objectives. Furthermore, we support our arguments throughout this text with one specific example of Autonomous Vehicles within the framework of Smart Cities as one major AI project.

2 The problem of tech-oriented market-led AI

Until social sciences produce a "sociological conception of AI" [6], the most conceivable forecast for the proliferation of AI relies on the existing unrivaled trend, in which it is the market-led tech sector that determines what AI is, how it should be invested in, and in what shape and function will reach the societies. In this model, our cities, our homes, our everyday social interactions, our education system and many fundamental aspects of our world will be subject of changes that are founded within the tech industry and, at its best, steered by the insights confined within the scope of computer and data sciences.

The problem of such a model is beyond the fact that data and computer sciences lack the necessary knowledge. One should, more importantly, see the principles embedded at the core of data science that are in contradiction with some of the human values. For example, the inherent desire for clustering or classification of data has shown that can engender division, discrimination, and segregation in social realms – the problem that has been already seen in the context of social media [12], but also the same has begun to manifest itself in the physical social environments [7, 11].

To our observation, across different domains, there is no shortage of critical scholarship that identifies the risks in the currently dominant formulation of AI projects. As an example, for the case of Smart City, beginning with technology and not with urban knowledge is rigorously criticized. Within the urbanism research community, Hollands describes his concerns for the obfuscation of the negative effects of IT on cities by it's business motivated promoters [9], Greenfield warns a return to the failed utopias of 20th century high modernism [15], Kitchen forecasts the rise of technocratic governance coming with the wave of smart city [10], Vanolo criticizes the current conceptions of smart city for the creation of discrimination against the "non-smart" citizens [13], Datta demonstrates, from the analysis of currently existing smart cities, the justification for regimes and processes of land dispossession [8], and Wiig criticizes the priorities given to the attraction of global business against local urgencies in dominant conception of smart cities [14].

The domain of urbanism and the case of Smart City is one example. To similar extents, one can observe critical discourses of the tech-oriented and market-led AI across many strands of social science.

3 The perennial mission of HCI

"HCI manages innovation to ensure that human values and human priorities are advanced, and not diminished through new technology. This is what created HCI; this is what led HCI onto and then off the desktop; it will continue to lead HCI to new regions of technology-mediated human possibility" [4]. It has been widely recognised, as exemplified in the above statement, that one of the perennial roles of our community is to search for, develop and apply various means of assessing technological innovations and their societal impacts. What we would like to highlight in this contribution is the necessity to found a special focus within HCI that investigates a specific type of projects, namely the highly invested and deeply impactful projects that capitalise on the advance in data and computer science to create non-human intelligent actors and integrate them into social contexts that they both utilise and modify. Projects such as self-driving vehicles, which are often rushed to performance test and production before understanding the changes they bring with themselves in terms of urban individual and collective experiences.

The distinguishing attributes of major AI projects – e.g. speed of proliferation and propagation – we believe, entail multidisciplinary analytical scholarship that is proactive in terms of guiding the trends and preventive of futures in which "human values and priorities" would be "compromised".

In order to understand whether or not HCI is capable of carrying out the task of interfacing social sciences with AI projects, one should consider the record of HCI research and design in embarking upon multidisciplinary endeavors. HCI has a successful history of intertwining with reflections and concepts in the various domain of social science, adopting and re-appropriating research methods from those domains, and creating situations of mutual learning. It also has shown that can speak the technical language of computer and data science and be visionary in the realm of technologies.

At the end, we would like to go one step further and claim that the onus falls uniquely on us, the HCI research and design practitioners. This is not only an interdisciplinary involvement; HCI should rather take the lead and commit itself with the responsibility of proactively checking AI agenda with social sciences and ensuring that AI takes us to a better world. This is justified by the intermediary placement of HCI between computing power and human values. The evolution of HCI methods, concepts, and reflections originally to interface computing systems with humans, has situated our domain in a unique position to interface computer science with humanities. This a unique position for HCI, which implies a unique responsibility. The other fields with similar placements, such as Digital Humanities (DL) and Science and Technology Studies (STS), define themselves within more confined scopes and consequently are limited in terms of methodological capacities needed for the described research focus. Loosely termed, DL applies digital tools to the study of humanity without concerning much with the impact of various technologies on humanity, and in STS the rise and adoption of technologies are examined as a social process, retaining the focus on the technology or science and rather than their effect on societies.

4 A new HCI research agenda

Without aspiring to a complete or a final picture, in this section, we would like to briefly mention some of the constituents of a research program that can be conducive to the mentioned objectives:

- Rigorous analytical discussions should be developed that scrutinise major AI projects. The analytical frameworks are borrowed from the relevant domain of social science corresponding to the project to be discussed, which provide the researchers with a list of agreed-upon subject matters in the specific context of the study. For example, a critical discussion of self-driving cars would be structured based on topics of interest when accounting for car mobility in urban design. Topics such as spatial justice, public health and well-being, sustainability, congestion, urban forms, and so forth. The immediate questions to be answered are whether the current formulation of the AI project would have a positive or negative impact on each of those topics. Moreover, the list of topics can be complemented by questions on the new interactive experiences that the AI project itself would impose to its users. For example, questions surrounding interaction between pedestrians and the self-driving vehicles and how to build up the sense of trust towards them.

- The outcome of such analysis may be in the form of proposals for modifications or amendments to the current formulation of the project or generate alternative narrations, new perspectives, and new schematisms for creativity and development. For example, in the context of smart mobility, one may see the value in redirecting the attention to how AI can enhance active mobility (walking and cycling). The same strand of multidisciplinary work in the first step continues here, this time in creating a new vision of what urban scientists see as enhancing human priorities and what HCI researchers may foresee as trustful intelligent mobile actors in the city and a realistic adoption scenario (that matches the constraints of the cities and avoids the mess and myth of technological pledges [5]).

- To be able to become an effective force that guides the evolution of AI projects, the resulting discourses should extend their reach beyond the borders of academic environments and interact with people and public policy-makers. Therefore, an essential part of the task is to translate the created visions and insights into the appropriate format that can offer the public opportunities for collecting alternative perceptions of, for example, what a smart city, smart mobility, and eventually smart mobile citizens can be.

These are some of the interrelated steps that together can support the engagement of different stockholder of AI projects to question technological innovations and to seriously contribute in shaping their future ideas that we believe should be scaffolded within the scope of HCI research and design related to the underpinning characteristics of our field as briefly sketched previously.

5 Concluding remarks

The discussion presented in this contribution is grounded in the fact that AI as such can lead our world to various futures. It can lead our cities to be even more car-dependent (through the promotion of autonomous vehicles); it can instead enhance active mobility (walking and cycling), make possible sustainable use of urban spaces and create human-scale public spaces. City is one example; such alternative futures extend to many aspects of life. The discourse that we initiate in this paper foregrounds the responsibility of HCI in studying such futures and providing directions for AI adoption policies.

References

1. Alavi, Hamed S., et al. "Is Driverless Car Another Weiserian Mistake?." Proceedings of the 2017 ACM Conference Companion Publication on Designing Interactive Systems. ACM, 2017.

2. Alavi, Hamed, and Farzaneh Bahrami. "Walking in smart cities." Interactions. 26(2) (2019): 66–68.

3. Argyris, Chris, Robert Putnam, and Diana McLain Smith. Action science. Vol. 13. Jossey-Bass Inc Pub, 1985.

4. Carroll, John M., and Mary Beth Rosson. "Wild at home: The neighborhood as a living laboratory for HCI." ACM Transactions on Computer-Human Interaction (TOCHI), 20(3) (2013): 16.

5. Dourish, Paul, and Genevieve Bell. Divining a digital future: Mess and mythology in ubiquitous computing. Mit Press, 2011.

6. Mlynar, Jakub, et al. "Towards a Sociological Conception of Artificial Intelligence." International Conference on Artificial General Intelligence. Springer, Cham, 2018.

7. Soderstrom, Ola, Till Paasche, and Francisco Klauser. "Smart cities as corporate storytelling." City, 18(3) (2014): 307–320.

8. Datta, A., 2015. New urban utopias of postcolonial India: Entrepreneurial urbanizationin Dholera smart city, Gujarat. Dialogues in Human Geography, 5(1), pp. 3–22.

9. Hollands, R.G., 2008. Will the real smart city please stand up? Intelligent, progressive or entrepreneurial?. City, 12(3), pp. 303–320.

10. Kitchin, R., 2014. The real-time city? Big data and smart urbanism. GeoJournal, 79(1), pp. 1–14.

11. McFarlane, C., and Sderstrm, O., 2017. On alternative smart cities: From a technology-intensive to a knowledge-intensive smart urbanism. City, 21(3–4), pp. 312–328.

12. Qian, X., Feng, H., Zhao, G., and Mei, T., 2013. Personalized recommendation combining user interest and social circle. IEEE transactions on knowledge and data engineering, 26(7), pp. 1763–1777.

13. Vanolo, A., 2014. Smartmentality: The smart city as disciplinary strategy. Urban studies, 51(5), pp. 883–898.

14. Wiig, A., 2015. IBM's smart city as techno-utopian policy mobility. City, 19(2–3), pp. 258–273.

15. Greenfield, A., 2013. Against the Smart City: A Pamphlet. This is Part I of "The City is Here to Use". Do projects.

Towards Diverse AI: Can an AI-Human Hybrid Council Prevent Future Apartheids?

Gabriel Diniz Junqueira Barbosa
and Simone Diniz Junqueira Barbosa

PUC-Rio, R. Marques de Sao Vicente, 225, Gavea, Rio de Janeiro, RJ, Brazil
gabrieldjb@gmail.com, simone@inf.puc-rio.br

Abstract

Artificial intelligence (AI) is becoming more prevalent in today's society. However, decisions are often made based on single AI models, which we call *single-minded AI*. The use of single-minded AI might bring great harm, while the use of AI-human collectives might help debias the decision-making process and thus promote better decisions. We illustrate through a speculative design fiction some of such potential risks and benefits. Our goal is to help frame the discussion on some of the necessary advances in managing AI to allow for better human-AI collaboration.

Keywords

AI-Human Collective Systems · Collective Intelligence · Decision making

---

How to cite this book chapter:
Junqueira Barbosa, G.D. and Junqueira Barbosa, S.D. 2020. Towards Diverse AI: Can an AI-Human Hybrid Council Prevent Future Apartheids? In: Loizides, F., Winckler, M., Chatterjee, U., Abdelnour-Nocera, J. and Parmaxi, A. (eds.) *Human Computer Interaction and Emerging Technologies: Adjunct Proceedings from the INTERACT 2019 Workshops*. Pp. 203–208. Cardiff: Cardiff University Press. DOI: https://doi.org/10.18573/book3.aa. License: CC-BY 4.0.

1 Introduction

During the years of 1948 to 1991 the South African government instituted oppressive policies, aimed at keeping control over a specific segment of their population. If, in that time, the Apartheid-instituting government had access to AI algorithms, perhaps history would have been different. That is the premise of our design fiction. In it, we create a narrative in which a major point in history is negatively impacted by single-minded AI technology, and explain how collective AI might help avoid such situations. By speculating through design fiction, we are able explore ethical and social issues of everyday life, asking what-if questions and opening the space for debate and discussion [5]. This work is meant to serve both as a warning on AI's potential for oppression and as a reframing of that potential for good.

Throughout our narrative, we reference tools that already exist today to illustrate how the narrative could come to pass. Some institutions use such tools to keep control over people [6, pp. 7–13], endangering freedoms that are essential to democracy. The following two-part story seeks to illustrate these potentials for abuse and a path to mitigate them.

2 Single-minded AI: The Menace

As Mandela walked away from prison, he knew he was not the same man he was 27 years earlier. The world had also changed. AI technology had made enormous strides during his prison sentence. Artificial intelligence tools were now widely available, with many governments using them in various ways.

The Apartheid-enforcing South African government was among the users of this technology. Various AI-based tools decided where you could go, what you could do, and who you could meet [6, pp. 7–13]. All of them were connected by a single artificial consciousness, called Orpheus. Orpheus made most of the governmental day-to-day decisions, with humans creating rules for it to follow but being kept out of the loop from the final decision making.

Mandela knew that Orpheus would be a great opponent in his fight for South African black liberation, as the AI strictly followed the racial separation rules implemented by the government. He decided to fight back by going into politics. However, when he tried to get approval to run for office, he was denied, as Orpheus had decided he was too dangerous, because of his criminal past [2]. He tried to appeal the ruling, but there were no processes in place for the people to challenge Orpheus [6, pp. 36–69].

Having seen the first push-back from this new AI-empowered government, Mandela decided to gather his supporters to protest against Orpheus. Every time his people gathered, they were dispersed by the police. The police had authority to do so because facial recognition software had, in these gatherings, recognized individuals whom Orpheus had labeled as dangerous. This system effectively prevented public gatherings, and protected the inequities supported by the Apartheid-enforcing government [7, 3].

Unable to argue with a machine, Mandela found no sign of hope. How could he and his allies defeat some algorithm that had singular control over many facets of day-to-day life? How could he argue against decisions whose reasoning was opaque? How could he prove that he and his allies had changed and become peaceful when the AI only followed past tendencies?

3 Diverse AI: A New Hope

As these forms of AI-boosted abuses started happening in authoritative regimes, the UN instituted councils where humans and AI could collaborate and discuss these issues. All representatives now have an ensemble of AI assistants who represent their interests and make them explicit, therefore creating a council with diversity of opinion [11]. Since all biases are explicit – and it can be checked that there are various interests being collectively represented in these councils – and humans have the last say, they would not easily succumb to authoritative decisions [1].

These collaborative human-AI councils started thinking about how they could avoid AI technology abuses, like those happening in South Africa. The AI counterparts would provide different rationales, explaining them to humans [10], and allowing for richer discussions [8, 11]. These improved discussions provided arguments for the international community to eventually convince the South African government to abandon Orpheus, allowing for Mandela and his allies to achieve South African liberation.

Single-minded AI, such as Orpheus, threatened freedom, but collective AI allowed humans to arrive at better decisions and prevent many humanitarian disasters. Humans work better together, and so might AI. By making biases and human interests explicit, they allowed for more transparent human-AI collaboration. By explaining the AI's rationale, humans were allowed to question them, and decide how much weight they should assign to their suggestions. By making AI work in a collective structure, people can ensure that no one AI can skew the collective, thus leading to more measured decisions [1].

AI offers humans great power. It is up to humans to decide how to use it, for good or for bad.

4 Discussion

AI will probably have increasing impact in the coming years. As illustrated in our Mandela story, oppressive regimes might seek to use these tools to perpetuate inequities and control their people [6, pp. 140–160]. AI is agnostic, and can serve for either good or bad. What will determine the outcome is the way in

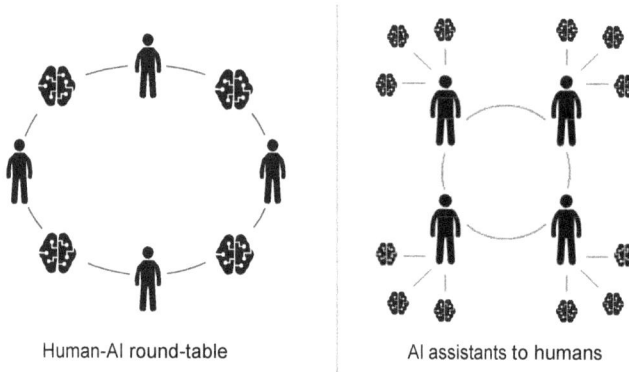

Human-AI round-table   AI assistants to humans

Fig. 1: A couple of structures for decision-making teams.

which humans will use these tools. There is much work to be done to ensure that humans use AI wisely, and that opportunities for abuse are mitigated. Explainability is still a major challenge for AI. For there to be proper humanAI collaboration, it ought to be possible for humans to understand how AI models arrive at their decisions [4, 10]. Moreover, humans also need to have some oversight or even control over them, to ensure that these AI models behave in the way that humans expect them to [1].

Human-AI collaboration offers great potential, but this form of interaction should be structured properly. By having AI models work together and having their biases explicit, it might be possible to avoid potential skews in collective decision-making [8]. We can organize these collectives in different ways, each with their own advantages and disadvantages. In Figure 1, we show a couple of such organizational structures. In addition to different structures, there can also be different ways to weigh each member's opinion, be they humans or AI. Selecting adequate structures and weights will then be essential for better collective decision-making.

Single minded AI, however, may be a source of concern. Individual models may not be transparent, and may generate extremely biased outcomes. If humans put these individual models in positions of power, and do not allow for transparency and appeal, negative consequences become quite likely [9].

References

1. Amershi, S., Weld, D., Vorvoreanu, M., Fourney, A., Nushi, B., Collisson, P., Suh, J., Iqbal, S., Bennett, P.N., Inkpen, K., Teevan, J., Kikin-Gil, R., Horvitz, E.: Guidelines for Human-AI Interaction. In: Proceedings of the 2019 CHI Conference on Human Factors in Computing Systems. pp. 3:1–3:13. CHI'19, ACM, New York, NY, USA (2019). https://doi.org/10.1145/3290605.3300233

2. Berk, R., Heidari, H., Jabbari, S., Kearns, M., Roth, A.: Fairness in Criminal Justice Risk Assessments: The State of the Art. Sociological Methods & Research p. 0049124118782533 (Jul 2018). https://doi.org/10.1177/0049124118782533
3. Bowyer, K.W.: Face recognition technology: security versus privacy. IEEE Technology and Society Magazine **23**(1), 9–19 (2004). https://doi.org/10.1109/MTAS.2004.1273467
4. Cheng, H.F., Wang, R., Zhang, Z., O'Connell, F., Gray, T., Harper, F.M., Zhu, H.: Explaining Decision-Making Algorithms Through UI: Strategies to Help Non Expert Stakeholders. In: Proceedings of the 2019 CHI Conference on Human Factors in Computing Systems. pp. 559:1–559:12. CHI '19, ACM, New York, NY, USA (2019). https://doi.org/10.1145/3290605.3300789
5. Dunne, A., Raby, F.: Speculative Everything: Design, Fiction, and Social Dreaming. The MIT Press (Dec 2013)
6. Eubanks, V.: Automating Inequality: How High-Tech Tools Profile, Police, and Punish the Poor. St. Martin's Press (Jan 2018)
7. Introna, L., Wood, D.: Picturing Algorithmic Surveillance: The Politics of Facial Recognition Systems. Surveillance & Society **2**(2/3) (Sep 2002). https://doi.org/10.24908/ss.v2i2/3.3373
8. Mohammed, S., Ringseis, E.: Cognitive Diversity and Consensus in Group Decision Making: The Role of Inputs, Processes, and Outcomes. Organizational Behavior and Human Decision Processes **85**(2), 310–335 (Jul 2001). https://doi.org/10.1006/obhd.2000.2943
9. O'Neil, C.: Weapons of Math Destruction: How Big Data Increases Inequality and Threatens Democracy. Crown, New York, 1 edition edn. (Sep 2016)
10. Wang, D., Yang, Q., Abdul, A., Lim, B.Y.: Designing Theory-Driven User-Centric Explainable AI. In: Proceedings of the 2019 CHI Conference on Human Factors in Computing Systems. pp. 601:1–601:15. CHI '19, ACM, New York, NY, USA (2019). https://doi.org/10.1145/3290605.3300831
11. Wang, X.H.F., Kim, T.Y., Lee, D.R.: Cognitive diversity and team creativity: Effects of team intrinsic motivation and transformational leadership. Journal of Business Research **69**(9), 3231–3239 (Sep 2016). https://doi.org/10.1016/j.jbusres.2016.02.026

Building a Trustworthy Explainable AI in Healthcare

Retno Larasati and Anna DeLiddo
Knowledge Media Institute, The Open University, UK
retno.larasati@open.ac.uk

Abstract

The lack of clarity on how the most advanced AI algorithms do what they do creates serious concerns as to the accountability, trust and social acceptability of AI technologies. These concerns become even bigger when people's well being is at stake, such as healthcare. This calls for systems enabling to make decisions transparent, understandable and explainable for users. This paper briefly discusses the trust in AI healthcare system, propose a framework relation between trust and characteristics of explanation, and possible future studies to build trustworthy Explainable AI.

Keywords

Trust · Explainable AI · AI Healthcare

1 Introduction

When it comes to human interaction, trust is one of the important factors influencing the adoption of AI systems. AI systems in healthcare are expected to help diagnose diseases and to gain better insights into treatments and

How to cite this book chapter:
Larasati, R. and DeLiddo, A. 2020. Building a Trustworthy Explainable AI in Healthcare. In: Loizides, F., Winckler, M., Chatterjee, U., Abdelnour-Nocera, J. and Parmaxi, A. (eds.) *Human Computer Interaction and Emerging Technologies: Adjunct Proceedings from the INTERACT 2019 Workshops.* Pp. 209–214. Cardiff: Cardiff University Press. DOI: https://doi.org/10.18573/book3.ab. License: CC-BY 4.0.

prevention that could benefit all of society. Developing trust is particularly crucial in healthcare because it involves an element of uncertainty and risk for the vulnerable patient [1]. How do we get to trust an AI system in such sensitive contexts in which people's health is at stake? What are the factors that affect people's trust in AI healthcare systems? And what does a good explanation looks like? In this paper we discuss the importance of trust in AI healthcare systems, describe some key factors that influencing user friendly explanations, and propose a framework to explore the relationships between trust and explicability. We conclude by indicating trajectories for future studies.

2 Background and Motivation

2.1 Trust in AI Healthcare System

The UK government issued a policy paper that declared its vision for AI to "transform the prevention, early diagnosis and treatment of chronic diseases by 2030."[1] However, many doctors are still skeptical about the AI healthcare system. Study found that among the 30% of clinicians respondent lack trust in AI.[2] Not only doctors, 61% general public correspondents in the UK are unwilling to engage with AI for their healthcare needs.[3] The lack of explainability, transparency, and human understanding of how AI works, are several reasons why people have little trust in AI healthcare system. Transparency [7] and understandability [10] would help to enhance trust in AI systems.

2.2 Trust and Interaction in Healthcare

Trust is the foundation of relationships and is important to build a better relationship between medical professional and patient. Some of the factors in trusting a medical professional are their care and concern for the patient as an individual, and the confidence in a patient's ability to manage their disease [4–16]. Being viewed as competent by a medical professional also increased patient trust [15]. Some other factors which encourage patient trust are the clinician's technical competence, information sharing, and their confidence in patient's ability to manage their illness [2].

---

[1] https://www.gov.uk/government/publications/the-future-of-healthcare-our
-vision-for-digital-data-and-technology-in-health-and-care/the-future-of
-healthcare-ourvision-for-digital-data-and-technology-in-health-and-care.

[2] https://newsroom.intel.com/news-releases/u-s-healthcare-leaders-expect
-widespread-adoption-artificial-intelligence-2023/.

[3] https://www.pwc.com/gx/en/industries/healthcare/publications/ai-robotics
-newhealth/survey-results.html.

2.3 Explainable AI and Trust

According to the Defense Advanced Research Projects Agency (DARPA), Explainable AI is essential to enable human users to understand and appropriately trust a machine learning system [3]. Some of the previous studies shows that explanations improves trust, however the characteristics of explanation have not been explored. This lead us to our research questions; what kind of explanation is needed for users to trust the healthcare intelligent system?

3 Framework for interpreting explicability and trust in healthcare

At our current state, we have 6 characteristics of meaningful explanations. First, explanations are **contranstive**. People usually ask for explanation as the cause of something relative to some other thing in contrast [9] [6]. Second, explanations are **domain or role dependent**. People usually select one or two causes from a variety of possible causes as the explanations [6]. People select the causes based on their domain knowledge and cognitive ability [12]. The process of explaining something in order to transfer knowledge is a social exchange [6] [5], therefore explanations are **social/interactive**. People expect explanations to be **truthful** and **thorough** explanation [8]. People usually prefer simpler and more **general** explanations[14].

This paper conceptualised a general framework for trustworthy Explainable AI in healthcare. It consist of two components: explanation characteristic and human-machine trust (see: Fig. 1). Human Machine trust here is divided by two

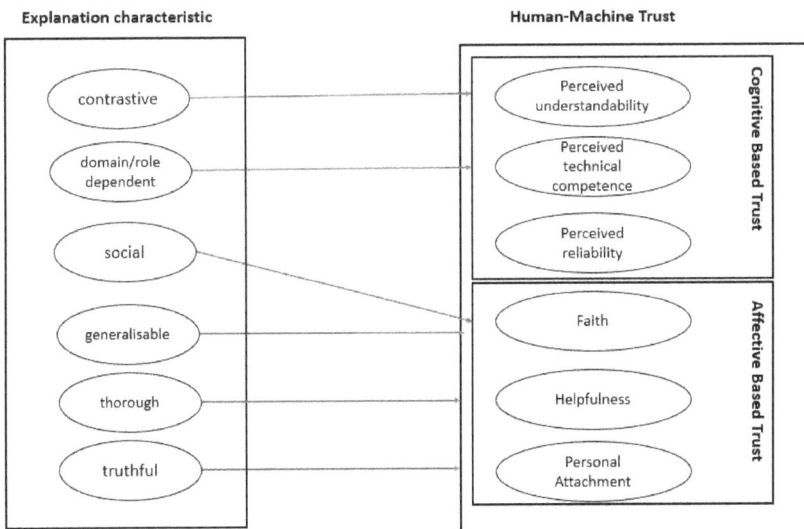

Fig. 1: Trustworthy explainable AI in healthcare framework.

types of trust, cognitive based trust and affect based trust. The human-machine trust items are based on several research studies about human-computer and human-machine trust [11, 13, 17]. However, the relation between the two is still a speculation and has yet been investigated.

4 Discussion and implication for future research

This paper proposed a framework of trustworthy explainable AI in healthcare. We derived characteristics of user-friendly explanations, and component of trust from previous studies. We are planning to undertake a qualitative and quantitative study to investigate the relation between explanation and trust in healthcare, validate the items inside the framework, and gain insights about the challenges and the opportunities on developing a trustworthy explainable AI in healthcare.

References

1. Alaszewski, A.: Risk, trust and health (2003)
2. Dibben*, M.R., Lean, M.: Achieving compliance in chronic illness management: illustrations of trust relationships between physicians and nutrition clinic patients. Health, Risk & Society **5**(3), 241–258 (2003)
3. Gunning, D.: Explainable artificial intelligence (xai) (2017)
4. Henman, M., Butow, P., Brown, R., Boyle, F., Tattersall, M.: Lay constructions of decision-making in cancer. Psycho-Oncology: Journal of the Psychological, Social and Behavioral Dimensions of Cancer **11**(4), 295–306 (2002)
5. Hilton, D.: Social attribution and explanation. In: The Oxford Handbook of Causal Reasoning (2017)
6. Hilton, D.J.: Conversational processes and causal explanation. Psychological Bulletin **107**(1), 65 (1990)
7. Holzinger, A., Biemann, C., Pattichis, C.S., Kell, D.B.: What do we need to build explainable ai systems for the medical domain? arXiv preprint arXiv:1712.09923 (2017)
8. Kulesza, T., Stumpf, S., Burnett, M., Yang, S., Kwan, I., Wong, W.K.: Too much, too little, or just right? ways explanations impact end users' mental models. In: 2013 IEEE Symposium on Visual Languages and Human Centric Computing. pp. 3–10. IEEE (2013)
9. Lipton, P.: Contrastive explanation. Royal Institute of Philosophy Supplements **27**, 247–266 (1990)
10. Lipton, Z.C.: The doctor just won't accept that! arXiv preprint arXiv:1711.08037 (2017)

11. Madsen, M., Gregor, S.: Measuring human-computer trust. In: 11th australasian conference on information systems. vol. 53, pp. 6–8. Citeseer (2000)
12. Malle, B.F.: How the mind explains behavior: Folk explanations, meaning, and social interaction. Mit Press (2006)
13. Mcknight, D.H., Carter, M., Thatcher, J.B., Clay, P.F.: Trust in a specific technology: An investigation of its components and measures. ACM Transactions on Management Information Systems (TMIS) **2**(2), 12 (2011)
14. Read, S.J., Marcus-Newhall, A.: Explanatory coherence in social explanations: A parallel distributed processing account. Journal of Personality and Social Psychology **65**(3), 429 (1993)
15. Rowe, R., Calnan, M.: Trust relations in health carethe new agenda. The European Journal of Public Health **16**(1), 4–6 (2006)
16. Thorne, S.E., Robinson, C.A.: Health care relationships: The chronic illness perspective. Research in Nursing & Health **11**(5), 293–300 (1988)
17. Yan, Z., Kantola, R., Zhang, P.: A research model for human-computer trust interaction. In: Trust, Security and Privacy in Computing and Communications (Trust-Com), 2011 IEEE 10th International Conference on. pp. 274–281. IEEE (2011)

A View from Outside the Loop

Anders Hedman

KTH The Royal Institute of Technology, Stockholm, Sweden

ahedman@kth.se

Abstract

There is a growing interest today in how to combine human intelligence with artificial intelligence in the best possible ways. One reason for this interest is that in this territory of combined intelligence it is, in many cases, unclear how the total system of human and machine will behave, and unless we know that, how could we know what the perils and opportunities might be? It is clear then that we need a body of research to investigate the nature of humans in the loop in order to design wisely. Such wise design would prima facie appear to be achievable through analysis of existing and possible human in the loop systems from a vantage point outside of such systems. But, is such a vantage point achievable today and if so, will such a vantage point be available in the future? This paper considers the possibility of humans as always being in the loop and what it might mean for our understanding of humans in the loop.

Keywords

human in the loop · AI · HCI

How to cite this book chapter:

Hedman, A. 2020. A View from Outside the Loop. In: Loizides, F., Winckler, M., Chatterjee, U., Abdelnour-Nocera, J. and Parmaxi, A. (eds.) *Human Computer Interaction and Emerging Technologies: Adjunct Proceedings from the INTERACT 2019 Workshops*. Pp. 215–220. Cardiff: Cardiff University Press. DOI: https://doi.org/10.18573/book3.ac. License: CC-BY 4.0.

1 A Perspicuous Loop

1.1 The Pervasive Loop

French renaissance enlightenment philosopher Denis Diderot [1] noticed a peculiarity about our human mental life, it is essentially recursive and not merely reflexive. In reflecting on mental life Diderot came to the conclusion that the brain is a book that reads itself. We have to use the mind to understand the mind and this situation is very different from using the eye to study the eye. This is because to some extent what we mean by the word mind is a construct. The term "mind" didn't come into widespread English usage until around the time when John Locke started to use it systematically in his 1690 *An Essay Concerning Human Understanding* [2]. We still lack direct cognates for the word mind in other languages and must as Locke had to, still improvise when translating the word "mind" to French, German and other languages.

As we try to understand how human intelligence might be combined with artificial intelligence in a loop of interaction do we run into an extended version of Diderot's book that reads itself? Has the book that reads itself become a hybrid of human and machine? Let us look at some examples. Whenever I type text, I get auto suggestions for words I can use. Let us suppose I am a novice and a poor writer; I pick words that I would not have chosen without this algorithmic help. I search for something online and search words are suggested to me there too and again, I might not have thought of them myself. My searches are automatically limited in accordance with my search history. If I ask myself what exactly I do online or with interactive technology that does not involve being inside a loop with AI I have to admit that I don't know. What I do know is that whatever I do could potentially be part of an AI loop and many of my actions are.

To have a point of view outside of the loop would mean that one would be certain that one was not affected cognitively by a persuasive or otherwise "helpful" AI system within the activity performed. Within our modern society such states are as we have seen through our mundane examples often not available. It seems rather that the normal state is to be in the loop. The question then of how to analyze and understand the human in the loop is therefore one that naturally is tackled from within the loop. What does this mean for our understanding of the human in the loop then? To better answer this question let us imagine a thought experiment.

Imagine that human-computer interaction advances to the point where suggestions for words that I type come not on my screen but are inserted into my visual field through some direct brain interface. I see the alternative word and can pick it automatically. Since the word appears so transparently, directly in my visual field, would I still be aware of it? What if the word instead simply entered my thought stream? Perhaps I could sense that the word came from outside of me or perhaps I couldn't. If I couldn't sense that the word came from outside of me then I would have no way of knowing if I was in a loop or not. The example here is a simple one of a very mundane task, but we can also imagine variations of it so that the thought insertions come in a broad variety of situations.

1.2 Lost in the Loop

We can imagine a future were we humans cannot step out of the loop because we no longer know where our thoughts come from. At this point, the philosopher who brought the word mind into common parlance would say that we have lost ourselves. For Locke the essential feature of a person was a unified consciousness that owned its mental contents throughout time.

In 2003 B. J. Fogg published his seminal work on persuasive technologies [3] on the basis of an idea that he had during a course on mind control with the mind control expert Philip Zimbardo. In that work [3] it appears that Fogg has a clear understanding of how persuasive technologies could be used for mind control, for he explicitly says that persuasive technologies are to be used for persuasion and not for coercion. Yet, it is unclear how AI driven persuasive technologies in, e.g., social media have been used for persuasion on any significant scale. It is clear instead that they are routinely used for coercion on a large scale and this has led some scholars to ask for a redefinition [4].

In a world of AI driven persuasive and other "helpful" technologies we may well ask how far we are from losing ourselves in the loop? We may also ask what the future may hold? Is one of the biggest threats to humanity really malevolent AI in the shape of a transcendent race of machine intelligence as the late Stephen Hawking suggested [5] or is it another, more subversive kind of AI, the kind which leaves us with no view outside of the loop?

Much of the discussions of today regarding the human in the loop appear to deal with ethical risks and challenges of using AI systems that are not part of the coercive artillery that quietly bombards us in our daily lives through technologies labeled as persuasive. This AI artillery poses ethical challenges that ought to be further discussed. But what exactly is the problem? It is not only that we may be coerced by AI and that we may with time develop cognitive problems. It goes deeper than that.

The philosopher Nick Nozick once designed a thought experiment called the *experience machine* [6]. Nozick images a future when we can choose to hook ourselves up to a machine that will give us all the experiences we would like to have. We can imagine that this machine gave us a perfect virtual reality world in which all of our dreams were fulfilled. If we would be bothered by the knowledge of being inside such a machine, then we can imagine that the memory of having hooked ourselves up to the machine was simply erased. We can also imagine other tweaks to our liking so that the machine becomes seemingly one without faults. Now the question is would you plug in to the experience machine? Intuitions differ. For those who don't want to plug in what matters most is that we live our lives authentically. In the light of Nozick's experience machine, the main problem with AI driven loops of persuasive technologies then is not necessarily that they will not help us get what we want, but that they pose an existential threat of losing control over our lives as authentically lived.

1.3 Making the Loop Perspicuous

What can we do then to retain a view from outside the loop or at least one that makes it perspicuous to us? It seems to me that a first step is to stop calling AI driven technologies for coercion, persuasive. It ought to be clear by now that if indeed Fogg believed his work would lead to a world of persuasion that dream failed. We live more in a world of coercion and not surprisingly perhaps, the project of persuasive technologies that came out of a course on mind control, has led, in the mains, to mind control and that is how we ought to refer to persuasive technologies that coerce: as technologies of mind control. We ought to reserve the term persuasive technologies for those technologies that, like humans offer us arguments that we can consciously entertain and may or may not be persuaded by. It is part of the notion of persuasion that we are offered such arguments. If we continue on the path of today, we may well find ourselves one day interacting in coercive loops that we cannot detect and loose touch of who we are in the Lockean sense of being conscious continual owners of our mental contents.

A second step would be to realize that any discussion of AI and the human in the loop depends in turn on how we define ourselves and our mind. In Diderot's time it made sense to refer to the brain as a book that reads itself (Diderot didn't use the term mind as it was unavailable to him in French). Today, we have since the inception of cognitive science a perspective on the human mind with roots in cybernetics and information processing. If we say that our best construction of the human mind is as an information process-ing machine as in cognitive science or in more general terms, a functional-ist machine, as in the philosophy of mind, that is nevertheless a construction undergoing a cultural evolution. In a cognitive science and philosophy where no one knows what a thought is or what consciousness is, we are continually reinventing the mind as at least partly constructed. If we see ourselves as essen-tially different from AI systems along the lines of the critics of AI such as, e.g., John Searle and the late Hubert Dreyfus then this will naturally color the debate over the human in the loop with humanist and existentialist overtones. If on the other hand, we construct AI as part and parcel of an accepted cognitive sci-ence and as being near a point of transcending human intelligence then we will naturally color the debate very differently. If we believe, for example, that there is in principle no difference between human intelligence and machine intel-ligence then our world becomes much simpler than if we acknowledge with the critics of AI that human intelligence is essentially different. This debate is not solely over the question of intelligence but also about existential questions about how we wish to live our lives.

References

1. Garrett, A. (2017). The Routledge companion to eighteenth century philosophy, p. 104. London: Routledge Taylor & Francis Group.
2. Locke, J. (1970). An essay concerning human understanding: 1690. Menston: Scolar Press.
3. Fogg, B. J. (2003). Persuasive computing: Technologies designed to change attitudes and behaviors. San Francisco, Calif: Morgan Kaufmann.
4. Kampik, T., Nieves, J. C., Lindgren, H., & 20th International Trust Workshop, TRUST 2018. (January 01, 2018). Coercion and deception in persuasive technologies. Ceur Workshop Proceedings, 2154, 38–49.
5. Hawking, S., & Whishaw, B. (2018). Brief answers to the big questions.
6. Nozick, R., & Nagel, T. (2013). Anarchy, state, and utopia. New York: Basic Books.

Nonverbal Communication in Human-AI Interaction: Opportunities and Challenges

Joshua Newn, Ronal Singh, Fraser Allison,
Prashan Madumal, Eduardo Velloso and Frank Vetere
School of Computing and Information Systems, The University of Melbourne,
Melbourne, Australia
newnj@unimelb.edu.au, rr.singh@unimelb.edu.au,
f.allison@unimelb.edu.au, madumalp@unimelb.edu.au,
evelloso@unimelb.edu.au, f.vetere@unimelb.edu.au

Abstract

In recent years, we have explored the use of *gaze*—an important nonverbal communication signal and cue in everyday human-human interaction—for use with AI systems. Specifically, our work investigated whether an artificial agent, given the ability to observe human gaze, can make inferences on intentions, and how aspects of these inferences can be communicated to a human collaborator. We leveraged a range of humancomputer interaction techniques to inform the design of a gaze-enabled artificial agent that can predict and communicate predictions. In this paper, we include a snapshot of how AI and HCI can be brought together to inform the design of an explainable interface for an artificial agent. To conclude, we outline the challenges we faced when designing AI systems that incorporate nonverbal communication stemming from our work.

How to cite this book chapter:
Newn, J., Singh, R., Allison, F., Madumal, P., Velloso, E. and Vetere, F. 2020. Nonverbal Communication in Human-AI Interaction: Opportunities and Challenges. In: Loizides, F., Winckler, M., Chatterjee, U., Abdelnour-Nocera, J. and Parmaxi, A. (eds.) *Human Computer Interaction and Emerging Technologies: Adjunct Proceedings from the INTERACT 2019 Workshops.* Pp. 221–226. Cardiff: Cardiff University Press. DOI: https://doi.org/10.18573/book3.ad. License: CC-BY 4.0.

Keywords

Human-AI Interaction · Explainable Interfaces · Nonverbal Communication · Multimodal Input · Intention Recognition · Gaze Input

1 Overview

Imagine walking up to a group of peers playing a competitive board game around a table (as shown in Scenario 1 below). You start to observe the situation, the actions and the behaviours of individual players; curious to see which player has the upper hand by inferring their potential plans. The player closest to you asks your opinion as to what might happen in the next rounds. Based on your observations, you will be able to provide inferences to some degree of accuracy and subsequent reasons to why you think they might occur. Now imagine a scenario where humans and AI systems (or robots as depicted in Scenario 2) are playing the same board game together. If the AI systems are able to make the same observations as you (a human spectator) in the previous scenario, would the AI systems make similar inferences? Would these inferences be accurate and timely? Would they be able to explain how they have arrived at their deductions? What information and how much information should such intelligent systems include? Our published and ongoing body of work explores such questions from the perspective of 'gaze awareness'—if intelligent systems can observe where humans are looking and understand the gaze behaviours within the context, would they be able to improve their interactions with their human counterparts better?

The availability of affordable and improved sensor technologies such as eye-trackers used in our work, combined with our collective experience in designing and conducting HCI and AI studies has presented us opportunities to investigate the incorporation of natural human inputs for Human-AI collaboration. Our initial work focused on understanding gaze in human-human interaction [10, 12], especially for gaze-based intention recognition. We conducted these studies within the context of strategic games and collected rich data using a variety of HCI methods. We found that gaze-based intention recognition is especially beneficial in strategic planning scenarios, allowing players to adapt their strategies preemptively. To elaborate, if a player is able to make accurate and early

SCENARIO 1   SCENARIO 2

inferences on the opponent's plans afforded by observing the opponent's gaze, the player can adjust their own strategy according to the predictions if necessary.

Through the findings and data from our human-centred studies, we developed an artificial agent that combines gaze and planning for human intention recognition [13]. Our gaze-aware agent uses a 'white-box' approach that allows us to understand the underlying algorithms and data structures, which makes it simpler to interrogate the model and its predictions. Our latest paper, forthcoming at INTERACT 2019 [11], evaluates the intention-aware agent in a dynamic collaboration setting. Our findings contribute to the understanding of how researchers can support Human-AI teams through a number of considerations when designing collaborative agents with intention-aware capabilities, including information presentation, context-awareness and explainable agency. The paper highlights the importance of nonverbal communication in Human-AI interaction and provides a general approach for applications where knowing the intentions of others are important for effective interaction (e.g. air traffic control, wargaming). In essence, our research so far serves as the first step towards addressing prerequisites for *man-computer symbiosis* outlined by Licklider in 1960 [7].

2 Case Study

As part of our forthcoming paper [11], we designed a study to determine *how* humans formulate predictions and subsequently explain their reasoning process when shown a visual representation of gaze of an opponent in a strategic game.[1] We recruited 20 participants (M = 25, SD = 3.7) with high proficiency in English.

In this study, we employed an 'inverted' Wizard-of-Oz protocol. In a typical Wizard-of-Oz study, a researcher secretly plays the role of the computer system while a participant interacts with it. In our variation, we asked the participant to play the role of the computer system, and the secret is that there is no enduser. The benefit of this is that it allows us to directly collect a large number of different messages that reflect how the participants think the computer 'should' communicate in an assistive fashion. We posed no restrictions on the language format participants could use for communication, allowing them to freely formulate their messages as long as each message contained a *prediction* of their opponent's intentions followed by an *explanation*. At the end of the study, the participant was given a short questionnaire on their experience, followed by a brief interview based on their responses and communication strategies employed.

We elicited a variety of messages through a well-defined protocol that reinforced the participants' belief in the deception and familiarised them with the task, where they were asked to use a chat application. In our analysis, we found that the ability to successfully formulate messages depended on several factors, including individual ability, experience with the game, the communication strategy adopted and the details of the game recording that was shown.

---

[1] Ticket to Ride—http://www.daysofwonder.com/tickettoride/en/.

Participants provided a wide range of explanations for their predictions. We found that complex explanations contain *spatial*, *temporal* and *quantitative* properties, in line with findings using expert explainers [4]. Simplistic explanations, on the other hand, typically described observed behaviours and often only with one property (e.g. *"The opponent was looking at those routes."*). In order to build a general model, we turn to Malle and Knobe [9]'s explanation model for labelling the properties for more complex explanations elicited with the assumption that the model can be generalised to explain human nonverbal or combined inputs.

Our results show that participants formed explanations from different sources of information available to the agent, such as gaze and actions. Explanations can also include information about past and potential future actions derived following Malle and Knobe [9]'s model. This involves *Causal History of Reasons*, defined as O^a, and *Intentional Action*, defined as I^a. Participants showed a strong reliance on gaze to explain their predictions. We believe that gaze being 'always on' [6] became more prominent throughout the game for enabling predictions as compared to observable game actions. For this reason, we shall include gaze (O^g) as part of every explanation generated using our piece-wise function below.

$$Explanation = \begin{cases} O^g, O^a & \text{if ontic actions observed} \\ O^g, I^a & \text{if intentional action likely} \\ O^g, I^a, O^a & \text{otherwise} \end{cases} \quad (1)$$

Below is an example that combines all three sources of information using our function, forming a prediction with an explanation that is highly detailed:

> *"The opponent is building a route from Washington to New Orleans through Nashville in the South East [Prediction (i)]. The opponent has claimed part of this route [O^A], has been looking at the routes between Raleigh and Little Rock repeatedly [O^g] and is likely to claim Nashville to Raleigh next [I^A]."*

In summary, this study presents a simple case of how human-centred approaches from HCI can be used to inform the design of explainable interfaces. The results from this study form the basis for a computational model of explanation, in which we can use gaze and ontic actions to form explanations, and we can vary the level of detail as needed. Beyond answering the *how* and *what* questions to meet our design goals, we learn it is crucial to know *when* (or how often) to provide an explanation in the context of predictions, and this requires the agent to be contextually-aware of the what the assisted-player already knows and whether the information to be communicated is helpful to them. Lastly, we also learn that it is possible and essential to consider the portrayal of uncertainty when communicating predictions as used in natural language, providing an alternative to using confidence levels as used in traditional AI systems.

3 Opportunities & Challenges

The case study presented in this paper is just one example of how we have utilised a human-centred approach to inform the design of AI systems, which has subsequently led us to better augment the agent's ability to detect human intention from gaze. Hence, we posit that for AI to work with their human collaborators effectively, AI systems first need to harness nonverbal cues commonly present in human-human interaction. Since, we have expanded our work to explore other nonverbal inputs (e.g. gestures, facial expression) for Multimodal Human-Agent Collaboration.[2] Simultaneously, we have continued to use the combination of AI and HCI in our work, such as to develop and further evaluate a general dialogue model for explanations by putting AI-assisted humans in the loop [8]. At present, our work focuses on the adoption of nonverbal communication in Human-AI interaction and is situated at the crossroads of addressing the design aspects (e.g. [2, 5]), overcoming the technical challenges (e.g. [3]), and the existing work on nonverbal communication in human-robot interaction (e.g. [1]).

However, many challenges remain until we can understand how to utilise nonverbal inputs fully. In the first place, it is often difficult to find a suitable use case to investigate that fully demonstrates benefits from Human-AI integration. In our work we were challenged to think differently due to the nature of gaze as a subtle and often unnoticed signal; it required the use of HCI to build an understanding of how humans utilise gaze before we could design a system that performs similarly or better. In the context of building explainable AI interfaces, we aim to tackle some immediate challenges, such as by determining the proper explanation interface and medium (e.g. visual, verbal, textual explanations). Perhaps the most prominent challenge faced is to ensure that the models that integrate multimodal input can be generalised to other contexts. Nevertheless, our work presents the first step towards our goal of building explainable agents that can assist, mediate or negotiate with knowledge of multiple users' intentions.

References

1. Admoni, H., Scassellati, B.: Robot nonverbal communication as an ai problem (and solution) (2015)
2. Amershi, S., Weld, D., Vorvoreanu, M., Fourney, A., Nushi, B., Collisson, P., Suh, J., Iqbal, S., Bennett, P.N., Inkpen, K., Teevan, J., Kikin-Gil, R., Horvitz, E.: Guidelines for human-ai interaction. In: Proceedings of the 2019 CHI Conference on Human Factors in Computing Systems. pp. 3:1–3:13. CHI '19, ACM, New York, NY, USA (2019). https://doi.org/10.1145/3290605.3300233
3. Bednarik, R., Eivazi, S., Vrzakova, H.: A Computational Approach for Prediction of Problem-Solving Behavior Using Support Vector Machines and Eye-Tracking Data, pp. 111–134. Springer London, London (2013)

---

[2] https://cis.unimelb.edu.au/agentlab/human-agent-collaboration/.

4. Dodge, J., Penney, S., Hilderbrand, C., Anderson, A., Burnett, M.: How the experts do it: Assessing and explaining agent behaviors in real-time strategy games. In: Proceedings of the 2018 CHI Conference on Human Factors in Computing Systems. pp. 562:1–562:12. CHI '18, ACM, New York, NY, USA (2018)

5. Eiband, M., Schneider, H., Bilandzic, M., Fazekas-Con, J., Haug, M., Hussmann, H.: Bringing transparency design into practice. In: 23rd International Conference on Intelligent User Interfaces. pp. 211–223. IUI '18, ACM (2018)

6. Jacob, R.J.K.: What you look at is what you get: Eye movement-based interaction techniques. In: Proceedings of the SIGCHI Conference on Human Factors in Computing Systems. pp. 11–18. CHI '90, ACM, New York, NY, USA (1990)

7. Licklider, J.C.R.: Man-computer symbiosis. IRE Transactions on Human Factors in Electronics **HFE-1**(1), 4–11 (March 1960)

8. Madumal, P., Miller, T., Sonenberg, L., Vetere, F.: A grounded interaction protocol for explainable artificial intelligence. In: Proceedings of the 18th International Conference on Autonomous Agents and MultiAgent Systems. pp. 1033–1041. AAMAS '19, International Foundation for Autonomous Agents and Multiagent Systems, Richland, SC (2019), http://dl.acm.org/citation.cfm?id=3306127.3331801

9. Malle, B.F., Knobe, J.: Which behaviors do people explain? a basic actor–observer asymmetry. Journal of Personality and Social Psychology **72**(2), 288 (1997)

10. Newn, J., Allison, F., Velloso, E., Vetere, F.: Looks can be deceiving: Using gaze visualisation to predict and mislead opponents in strategic gameplay. In: Proceedings of the 2018 CHI Conference on Human Factors in Computing Systems. pp. 261:1–261:12. CHI '18, ACM, New York, NY, USA (2018). https://doi.org/10.1145/3173574.3173835

11. Newn, J., Singh, R., Madumal, P., Velloso, E., Vetere, F.: Designing interactions with intention-aware gaze-enabled artificial agents. In: Human-Computer Interaction – INTERACT 2019. pp. 255–281. Springer International Publishing, Cham (2019). https://doi.org/10.1007/978-3-030-29384-0 17

12. Newn, J., Velloso, E., Allison, F., Abdelrahman, Y., Vetere, F.: Evaluating realtime gaze representations to infer intentions in competitive turn-based strategy games. In: Proceedings of the Annual Symposium on Computer-Human Interaction in Play. pp. 541–552. CHI PLAY '17, ACM, New York, NY, USA (2017). https://doi.org/10.1145/3116595.3116624

13. Singh, R., Miller, T., Newn, J., Sonenberg, L., Velloso, E., Vetere, F.: Combining planning with gaze for online human intention recognition. In: Proceedings of the 17th International Conference on Autonomous Agents and MultiAgent Systems. pp. 488–496. AAMAS '18, International Foundation for Autonomous Agents and Multiagent Systems, Richland, SC (2018), http://dl.acm.org/citation.cfm?id=3237383.3237457

MARVIN: Identifying Design Requirements for an AI powered Conversational User Interface for Extraterrestrial Space Habitats

Youssef Nahas[*], Christiane Heinicke[*,†]
and Johannes Schöning[*]

[*]University of Bremen, Germany
[†]Center of Applied Space Technology and Microgravity (ZARM), Germany
schoening@uni-bremen.de, christiane.heinicke@uni-bremen.de

Abstract

In this workshop paper we report on our early work to design a conversational interface for astronaut scientists in an extraterrestrial habitat (e.g. a habitat on Moon or Mars). At the workshop we will report on our initial design and first evaluations of our conversational user interface called MARVIN. Our goal with MARVIN is to support scientists on their missions and during their daily (scientific) routines within and outside the habitat. We are installing our interface in MaMBA. The MaMBA project aims to build a first functional extraterrestrial habitat prototype.

Keywords

Conversational Interfaces · Design Requirements · Extraterrestrial Space Habitats · Mars · Moon · ZARM · NASA · MARVIN

How to cite this book chapter:
Nahas, Y., Heinicke, C. and Schöning, J. 2020. MARVIN: Identifying Design Requirements for an AI powered Conversational User Interface for Extraterrestrial Space Habitats. In: Loizides, F., Winckler, M., Chatterjee, U., Abdelnour-Nocera, J. and Parmaxi, A. (eds.) *Human Computer Interaction and Emerging Technologies: Adjunct Proceedings from the INTERACT 2019 Workshops.* Pp. 227–230. Cardiff: Cardiff University Press. DOI: https://doi.org/10.18573/book3.ae. License: CC-BY 4.0.

1 Motivation & Related Work

Today, conversational interfaces such as Google Assistant, Amazon Alexa or Siri are one of the most ubiquitous artificial intelligent (AI) systems that have been incorporated into our everyday lives. While having a long history [5–6], conversational user interfaces (CUI) just recently became more and more ubiquitous with the advent of devices like Google Home, Amazon Echo or the HomePod in our living rooms [2]. It was also shown in the past, that interaction with these devices is not trivial [8] and general design guidelines for human-AI interaction are needed [1].

While there is first work on understanding the ways people interact with conversational interfaces in everyday scenarios [2, 6, 7–9], there is little research on how this class of AI powered interfaces can support humans in other (more professional) contexts.

Extraterrestrial habitats are an extreme example for such a professional context. It is very likely that conversational interfaces will support astronauts on their often very long and challenging missions and assist them performing research tasks during space flight or planetary exploration missions. For example, a first prototype of a CUI called CIMON[1] was recently tested on the International Space Station (ISS). CIMON is a CUI that runs IBM's Watson technology to mainly help astronauts with their daily tasks (many of them not mission critical by design). Besides that, there are also many examples in Sci-Fi literature and movies. Most prominently are HAL 9000 in the movie Space Odyssey and the "Computer" in the Star Trek franchise. Nevertheless, the requirements of a CUI in a habitat on a planetary body other than Earth will be different from one in a space station orbiting Earth.

Fig. 1: Rendering of six MaMBA modules and an airlock on the Moon covered artificial cave.

---

[1] https://www.space.com/42574-ai-robot-cimon-space-station-experiment .html.

2 MARVIN

We have the unique opportunity to study requirements of a CUI for a space habitat within MaMBA (Moon and Mars Base Analog). MaMBA [4] aims to build a first functional extraterrestrial habitat prototype. The habitat is developed at the ZARM in Bremen, Germany, and comprises five to six connected, but independent modules. In its final state, the habitat is intended to serve for testing technologies such as life support, power systems, and remotely operated set-ups communication [4]. A mock-up of the first module, the laboratory module, has recently been completed and first preliminary tests were run in late June 2019.

The first test consisted of a crew of 4 scientists performing biological and geological experiments in the module. During the test, we had a microphone and speaker within a 3D printed case in the module that acted as our *Wizard of Oz* [3] prototype of MARVIN. The analog astronauts were instructed that there would be a CUI installed in the module, but they were not aware that MARVIN was a *Wizard of Oz* prototype during the evaluation. The astronauts could trigger MARVIN and subsequently received responses from the operator. In the workshop we will report first insights on the needs and requirements of MARVIN and discuss potential challenges.

References

1. Saleema Amershi, Dan Weld, Mihaela Vorvoreanu, Adam Fourney, Besmira Nushi, Penny Collisson, Jina Suh, Shamsi Iqbal, Paul N. Bennett, Kori Inkpen, Jaime Teevan, Ruth Kikin-Gil, and Eric Horvitz. 2019. Guidelines for Human-AI Interaction. In Proceedings of the 2019 CHI Conference on Human Factors in Computing Systems (CHI '19). ACM, New York, NY, USA, Paper 3, 13 pages. DOI: https://doi.org/10.1145/3290605.3300233
2. Beirl, D., & Rogers, Y. Using Voice Assistant Skills In Family Life. In Proceedings of Proceedings of CSCL'19, May 2019.
3. Dahlbäck, N., Jönsson, A., & Ahrenberg, L. (1993). Wizard of Oz studies—why and how. Knowledge-based systems, 6(4), 258–266.
4. Heinicke, C., Orzechowski, L., Abdullah, R., von Einem, M., & Arnhof, M. (2018, September). Updated Design Concepts of the Moon and Mars Base Analog (MaMBA). In European Planetary Science Congress (Vol. 12).
5. Horvitz, E. (1999, May). Principles of mixed-initiative user interfaces. In Proceedings of the SIGCHI conference on Human Factors in Computing Systems (pp. 159–166). ACM.
6. Klopfenstein, L. C., Delpriori, S., Malatini, S., & Bogliolo, A. (2017). The rise of bots: A survey of conversational interfaces, patterns, and paradigms. In Proceedings of the 2017 Conference on Designing Interactive Systems (pp. 555–565). ACM.

7. Porcheron, M., Fischer, J. E., Reeves, S., & Sharples, S. (2018, April). Voice interfaces in everyday life. In proceedings of the 2018 CHI conference on human factors in computing systems (p. 640). ACM.

8. Dounia Lahoual and Myriam Frejus. 2019. When Users Assist the Voice Assistants: From Supervision to Failure Resolution. In Extended Abstracts of the 2019 CHI Conference on Human Factors in Computing Systems (CHI EA '19). ACM, New York, NY, USA, Paper CS08, 8 pages. DOI: https://doi.org/10.1145/3290607.3299053

9. Sciuto, A., Saini, A., Forlizzi, J., & Hong, J. I. (2018, June). Hey Alexa, What's Up?: A Mixed-Methods Studies of In-Home Conversational Agent Usage. In Proceedings of the 2018 on Designing Interactive Systems Conference 2018 (pp. 857–868). ACM.

You should not control what you do not understand: the risks of controllability in AI

Gabriel Diniz Junqueira Barbosa
and Simone Diniz Junqueira Barbosa

PUC-Rio, Rua Marques de Sao Vicente, 225, Gavea, Rio de Janeiro, RJ, Brazil
gabrieldjb@gmail.com, simone@inf.puc-rio.br

Abstract

In this paper, we posit that giving users control over an artificial intelligence (AI) model may be dangerous without their proper understanding of how the model works. Traditionally, AI research has been more concerned with improving accuracy rates than putting humans in the loop, *i.e.*, with user interactivity. However, as AI tools become more widespread, high-quality user interfaces and interaction design become essential to the consumer's adoption of such tools. As developers seek to give users more influence over AI models, we argue this urge should be tempered by improving users' understanding of the models' behavior.

Keywords

Controllable AI · Explainable AI · Risks of Controllability · Human-AI Interaction

---

How to cite this book chapter:
Junqueira Barbosa, G.D. and Junqueira Barbosa, S.D. 2020. You should not control what you do not understand: the risks of controllability in AI. In: Loizides, F., Winckler, M., Chatterjee, U., Abdelnour-Nocera, J. and Parmaxi, A. (eds.) *Human Computer Interaction and Emerging Technologies: Adjunct Proceedings from the INTERACT 2019 Workshops*. Pp. 231–236. Cardiff: Cardiff University Press. DOI: https://doi.org/10.18573/book3.af. License: CC-BY 4.0.

1 Introduction

Human-Computer Interaction (HCI) is becoming increasingly concerned with how users interact with artificial intelligence (AI) models [2]. Usual considerations of HCI apply: How does a user interact with AI models? Can they understand how these models' decision-making processes work? Do they trust AI-based tools? Should they trust them? These are just a few concerns within the HCI community about how humans and AI may interact.

As AI tools become more widespread in commercial settings, industry is starting to notice how poor user experience – in regard to human-AI interaction – can act as a barrier. Users may have trust issues with tools that exclude them from the decision-making process, as well as very high expectations regarding their performance [3]. It might be tempting for industry to yield some control over these models to appease users, but this urge may lead to graver consequences.

Control without understanding is dangerous. Users that engage with systems they do not understand are more prone to errors [5, 9]. Depending on the AI model's responsibilities, the negative consequences of these errors may end up being more severe [6].

2 Transparency & Understanding

Users often do not understand how artificial intelligence works. This results in a mostly exploratory use of AI-based systems. In certain contexts of use, this is not a problem. However, as tasks executed by users and AI become more important, exploratory use starts to become a greater problem. An individual testing out controls becomes more prone to errors, with potentially harmful results [9].

Learnability is an essential aspect of human-computer interaction [9]. Learning often takes place in controlled environments, *e.g.*, through tutorials or reversible actions. This process allows the user to try different commands without fear of negative consequences. However, AI's behavior is either unpredictable or too complex for humans to predict. This makes it more difficult for users to understand model behavior through trial and error [7].

The behavior of machine-learning models also depends on the data being input to the model. In real usage scenarios, users of a model do not have prior knowledge about the data used to generate it, nor do they know what kinds of input data the model can process effectively. If their learning process is limited to trial and error, it becomes more difficult for the users to anticipate the possible outcomes in these novel scenarios.

Some systems are too complex for trial and error. A user may have to spend an enormous amount of time testing possibilities until he/she understands how the AI model works [7]. These models need to be more explainable, so as to make it easier for users to grasp the basics of model behavior. These explanations usually involve some degree of simplification. It is important not to simplify too much, however, otherwise the explanation may not be precise enough to explain specific model behaviors [11].

Explainable models must also be transparent, so as to allow the user to evaluate how they are operating and thus assess which outcomes are more trustworthy. In this context, transparency may also help in user learning [1].

Explaining models to users is also context dependent. Different models and contexts of use may require different explanations. So do different users. A mathematician does not require the same level of simplification as a child. It then becomes paramount for interaction designers to conduct user research, and understand how stakeholders use these tools, so as to create explainable models more adjusted to the users' profiles and circumstances [11].

Users ought to have some understanding of the model's behavior prior to being given control over it. Exploratory behavior may end up being harmful [6], and controlled learning environments can be inefficient in helping users understand model behavior [7]. Proper explanation requires designers who understand stakeholders' needs and can create different ways to explain model behavior [11].

As the users start to understand the model, they become less likely to err when given control over it. Understanding possible outcomes allows the user to avoid making risky changes, therefore promoting a conservative ("safe") approach to their interactions with the model [1].

3 Controllability

As defined by Roy et al. [8], controllability is the amount of control a user has over an AI model. Traditionally, users would not have much control over model behavior. Once models have been configured or trained, they would make decisions autonomously. However, as users increasingly engage with AI-based technology, this autonomous behavior has been met with suspicion [3, 12].

Users do not appreciate being left out of decisions. Even if they do not want to affect the outcomes, they want to be afforded the opportunity to do so. Shneiderman, in his 1997 discussion with Mae, argues that users seek a feeling of mastery and responsibility, and not the sense that they were not helpful to the process [10].

To ensure higher user satisfaction, developers may be tempted to allow users to control some aspects of AI models. As mentioned above, doing so before the user has proper understanding of model behavior may be dangerous.

There are different ways to give the user control. Developers may give them control over the outcomes, or control over the models themselves [8]. The latter is more complex, as it requires better explanations and understanding of model behavior.

In machine-learning models, users configure the model training by tuning its hyperparameters. This allows them to input their own preferences and create a model that is compatible to their preferences and experience [4]. However, once these models are trained, changing them would require retraining. Moreover, the users of a trained model may not have access to information about how the model was trained, and therefore would be unaware of limitations and biases.

All of these control scenarios may result in errors if the user does not sufficiently understand the model behavior. Through different explanations, it is possible to increase users' understanding of the model, therefore allowing them to exert some control over it [11].

4 Discussion

In this paper, we argued that, although controllability in AI is generally considered desirable, giving users control over AI models without ensuring they have a proper understanding of the models' behavior may lead to dire outcomes. Depending on the situation in which these AI models are implemented, these outcomes may be catastrophic [6]. It is therefore important to develop ways to make models transparent and explain their behavior to users.

Once users understand better how these models work, they will be less prone to making mistakes. They may then be given control, resulting in less undesirable outcomes. Different models may allow for different control methods, with some being more permissive than others [8].

In the end, no one solution will fit all situations. AI models are quite different from one another, and each requires specific methods of explanation and control. Users are also very diverse, so it is important to understand for whom these models and explanations are being designed.

Users want more control over AI models and outcomes in their tools. However, if the models are not properly explained and users do not understand how they work, this control may end up being catastrophic.

References

1. Amershi, S., Weld, D., Vorvoreanu, M., Fourney, A., Nushi, B., Collisson, P., Suh, J., Iqbal, S., Bennett, P.N., Inkpen, K., Teevan, J., Kikin-Gil, R., Horvitz, E.: Guidelines for Human-AI Interaction. In: Proceedings of the 2019 CHI Conference on Human Factors in Computing Systems. pp. 3:1–3:13. CHI '19, ACM, New York, NY, USA (2019). https://doi.org/10.1145/3290605.3300233
2. Inkpen, K., Chancellor, S., De Choudhury, M., Veale, M., Baumer, E.P.S.: Where is the Human?: Bridging the Gap Between AI and HCI. In:

Extended Abstracts of the 2019 CHI Conference on Human Factors in Computing Systems. pp. W09:1–W09:9. CHI EA '19, ACM, New York, NY, USA (2019). https://doi.org/10.1145/3290607.3299002

3. Kocielnik, R., Amershi, S., Bennett, P.N.: Will You Accept an Imperfect AI?: Exploring Designs for Adjusting End-user Expectations of AI Systems. In: Proceedings of the 2019 CHI Conference on Human Factors in Computing Systems. pp. 411:1–411:14. CHI '19, ACM, New York, NY, USA (2019). https://doi.org/10.1145/3290605.3300641

4. Linden, G., Hanks, S., Lesh, N.: Interactive Assessment of User Preference Models: The Automated Travel Assistant. In: Jameson, A., Paris, C., Tasso, C. (eds.) User Modeling. pp. 67–78. International Centre for Mechanical Sciences, Springer Vienna (1997)

5. Norman, D.: The Design of Everyday Things: Revised and Expanded Edition. Basic Books (Nov 2013)

6. O'Neil, C.: Weapons of Math Destruction: How Big Data Increases Inequality and Threatens Democracy. Crown, New York, 1 edition edn. (Sep 2016)

7. Phelan, C., Hullman, J., Kay, M., Resnick, P.: Some Prior(s) Experience Necessary: Templates for Getting Started With Bayesian Analysis. In: Proceedings of the 2019 CHI Conference on Human Factors in Computing Systems. pp. 479:1–479:12. CHI '19, ACM, New York, NY, USA (2019). https://doi.org/10.1145/3290605.3300709

8. Roy, Q., Zhang, F., Vogel, D.: Automation Accuracy Is Good, but High Controllability May Be Better. In: Proceedings of the 2019 CHI Conference on Human Factors in Computing Systems. pp. 520:1–520:8. CHI '19, ACM, New York, NY, USA (2019). https://doi.org/10.1145/3290605.3300750

9. Sharp, H., Preece, J., Rogers, Y.: Interaction Design: Beyond Human Computer Interaction. John Wiley & Sons, Indianapolis, IN, edio: 5th edn. (2019)

10. Shneiderman, B., Maes, P.: Direct manipulation vs. interface agents. interactions 4(6), 42–61 (Nov 1997). https://doi.org/10.1145/267505.267514

11. Wang, D., Yang, Q., Abdul, A., Lim, B.Y.: Designing Theory-Driven User-Centric Explainable AI. In: Proceedings of the 2019 CHI Conference on Human Factors in Computing Systems. pp. 601:1–601:15. CHI '19, ACM, New York, NY, USA (2019). https://doi.org/10.1145/3290605.3300831

12. Zhou, J., Li, Z., Hu, H., Yu, K., Chen, F., Li, Z., Wang, Y.: Effects of Influence on User Trust in Predictive Decision Making. In: Extended Abstracts of the 2019 CHI Conference on Human Factors in Computing Systems. pp. LBW2812:1–LBW2812:6. CHI EA '19, ACM, New York, NY, USA (2019). https://doi.org/10.1145/3290607.3312962

Using AI to Improve Product Teams' Customer Empathy

Valentina Grigoreanu, Monty Hammontree
and Travis Lowdermilk

Microsoft Corporation, Redmond, WA 98053, USA
valeng@microsoft.com

Abstract

During customer conversations, it is important to know both *what* questions to ask at any point during the development cycle, and *how* to ask them. Asking the right questions to capture rich, accurate, and relevant customer feedback is not easy, and professionally-trained researchers cannot be a part of every customer conversation. To scale out researchers' knowledge, we built an artificial intelligence system, the VIVID whisper-bot, trained on three theories: the Hypothesis Progression Framework (contextual research questions for each product development phase), the VIVID grammar framework (asking who, what, why, how, where, how much, and when type questions to recreate rich stories), and the syntactical structure of biased and leading questions. The whisper-bot listens in on a customer conversation, highlights customers' key verbalization (e.g., pain points using the product), and suggests follow-up interview questions (e.g., removing bias or enriching a story). It thereby encourages good interview practices for everyone, which we believe will increase empathy on product development teams, and lead to improvements in the products' user experience.

How to cite this book chapter:

Grigoreanu, V., Hammontree, M. and Lowdermilk, L. 2020. Using AI to Improve Product Teams' Customer Empathy. In: Loizides, F., Winckler, M., Chatterjee, U., Abdelnour-Nocera, J. and Parmaxi, A. (eds.) *Human Computer Interaction and Emerging Technologies: Adjunct Proceedings from the INTERACT 2019 Workshops.* Pp. 237–242. Cardiff: Cardiff University Press. DOI: https://doi.org/10.18573/book3.ag. License: CC-BY 4.0.

Keywords

AI/ML · HCI · Cognitive Services · Design/Customer Research · User Experience · Empathy · Product Development · Software Development

1 Introduction and Background

One area at the intersection between AI and HCI is how artificial intelligence systems can help improve HCI research (or user research, customer experience research, usability engineering, design research, etc.). We will refer to this space as "AI for UX Research. It aims to explore: *How can the research skills of anyone doing customer, product, or business development be augmented through artificial intelligence systems?*

There are few publications on "AI for UX Research" to-date (e.g., [1, 3]). These examples applied AI to help analyze customer research data. However, at the time of this paper, we found no previous research on how AI can be used at the *data collection* stage, particularly for qualitative data. Our VIVID whisper-bot solution scales out research interview skills to *anyone* wanting to conduct customer interviews, no matter their level of UX research training. This is of interest to our Research team in the Developer Division at Microsoft, where customer conversations are happening on a larger scale than ever before. Our corporate vice-president credits our data-driven and customer-obsessed culture for a major increase from 2 million to 14 million active users in a handful of years [2]. With an estimate of more than 10,000 customer interviews conducted every year by our product teams, researchers split their time between conducting research and training product team members to have better customer conversations (e.g., through a distribution list, workshops, bootcamps, and a book).

We also took an AI approach to scale out UX research knowledge, by teaching a bot to "whisper" suggestions to product team members about what questions to ask during an interview and how to best ask them.

2 Results: Reasons for the Empathy Gap

Based on data collected during a survey and two focus groups, four themes emerged for improving our product teams' interviews:

1. Taking notes during customer conversations is challenging.
2. Patterns of leading, biased, and closed questioning during interviews are common.
3. It is hard to identify opportunities to probe for deeper insights.
4. It is difficult to share empathy post-interview, to get the organizations' attention.

We wondered whether we could design an artificial intelligence system that would achieve the goals above when a Researcher cannot be present during a customer conversation. The idea of the VIVID whisper-bot was born.

3 Working Prototype: The VIVID Whisper-bot

We hypothesized that we could teach an AI system the rules of asking rich, relevant, and unbiased questions – and that this would solve many of the gaps mentioned in the previous section.

1. Real-time speech-to-text transcription: Our first step was to build a component that transcribes speech-to-text, as accurately as possible. This provides the interviewer conversation notes and is also the venue for showing the agent's feedback real-time within the context of the conversation being held.
2. Trained LUIS (natural language processing) models to identify biased and closed questions: Training the models so that we could accurately identify closed and leading interview questions was mostly based on sentence structure. Most closed questions started with commonly used auxiliary verbs (such as, "do", "can", "would"). For leading questions, the adjectives and adverbs mattered, and emotions were more prevalent in the questions. Another tool for feedback about the quality of the interview was the *Conversation Mix*: an indicator that tracks how much the interviewer was talking in relation to the customer. Depending on the goal of the interview, this could be a useful reminder to the interviewer to leave adequate time for the customer to express their thoughts.
3. Trained models to identify opportunities to probe deeper: Two frameworks were core to our ability to train our VIVID whisper-bot *when* to probe deeper, and *how* to do so. (1) The first is the Hypothesis Progression Framework (HPF) [4], which we used to teach the model five product development stages: Customer, Product, Concept, Feature, and Business. Based on a combination of common sentence structures in each stage and key words that might be used within each, we taught the model to identify when a customer is talking about one of their responsibilities, or a problem they are encountering. (2) The second framework was the VIVID grammar [5]. We found that having vivid stories helps move an organization to inspired action, but that having such stories requires having vivid conversations to begin with. This framework ensured teams capture crucial elements of a vivid customer story: the who/what, how many, where, when, how, and why? We combined the HPF with VIVID grammar, so that the model was trained on sets of rich vivid questions at each phase of the HPF. The end-result was that the whisper-bot could now identify a job responsibility or a problem in the customer's verbalizations and suggest follow-up questions to probe deeper with VIVID questions to get a rich meaningful story.

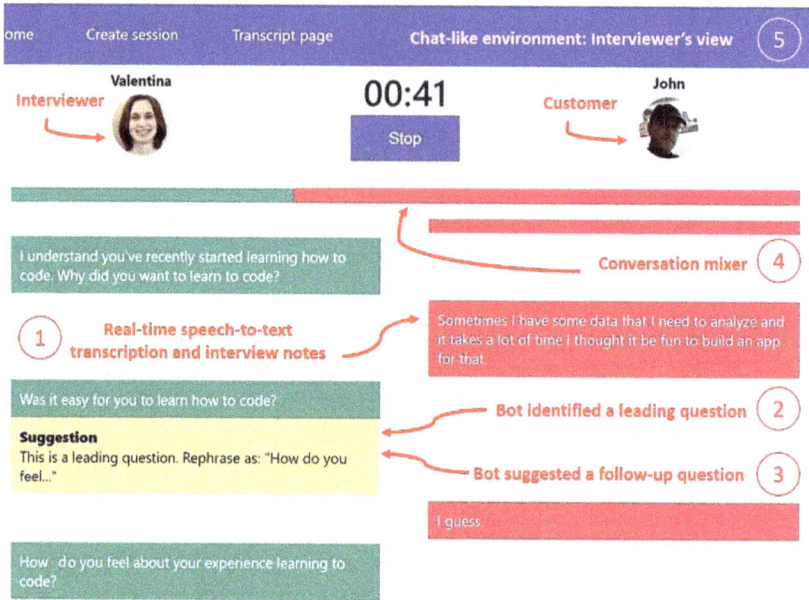

Fig. 1: Working proof-of-concept prototype of the 'VIVID whisper-bot.'

4. The whisper-bot interface: For our proof-of-concept, we created a webservice that mimicked an IM environment, showing a real-time transcript of the conversation to the interviewer (see Fig. 1) and its real-time feedback (based on the analysis of the interviewer's and the customer's verbalizations), to gently guide the interviewer to a richer conversation.

4 Conclusions and Future Work

We have introduced a framework for training an AI system to augment anyone's skills for conducting better interviews. Our whisper-bot prototype helps product team members ask the right questions, at the right time, and in the right way.

For the whisper-bot to move from proof-of-concept to a minimum viable solution, it would need to reach customers through their existing conversational tools (e.g., Microsoft Teams), and be updated with the latest advances in speech-to-text transcription (including some innovative methods, such as creating a training dictionary from the interview's discussion guide, to help identify domain-specific words and phrases).

How to surface the AI system's information to the user such a way that it is helpful and not disruptive is an important part of the future work. This will require improvements to the dialog management service, which manages what response to suggest next. This service has all the information to make the conversation as natural and productive as possible (e.g., how to respond for each category of feedback, how often, when to interject and when not to, as well as the specifics of the response). It is important that the whisper-bot is not leading to cognitive overload for the interviewer, but rather making his/ her job easier.

Finally, this same concept can be extended for everything from planning conversations (e.g., using the whisper-bot framework to build the interview questions), all the way through to analyzing the data (e.g., easy filtering or highlights where "problems" are stated), and sharing insights (e.g., video clips of the vivid stories the bot helped the interviewer unearth).

Acknowledgements

We would like to thank Kelly Zhao, Maxim Lobanov, Steven Clarke, Jessica Rich, JP Carrascal, Mike Hall, and Wil Voss, and Jason Shaver for their contributions in building and designing the VIVID whisper-bot.

References

1. Fern, X., et al.: Mining problem-solving strategies from HCI data. ACM Transactions on Computer-Human Interactions 17(1), 22 pages (2010).
2. Greenwood, M.: Five years to the top: Microsoft's software boss Julia Liuson, https://techvibes.com/2019/04/09/five-years-to-the-top-microsofts -software-boss-julia-liuson, last accessed 2019/05/06.
3. Grigoreanu, V., et al.: "Gender Differences in End-User Debugging, Revisited: What the Miners Found." In: VISUAL LANGUAGES AND HUMAN-CEN-TRIC COMPUTING (VL/HCC'06), pp. 19–26, Brighton (2006).
4. Lowdermilk, T., Rich, J.: The customer-driven playbook: Converting customer feedback into successful products. O'Reilly Media (2017).
5. Roam, D.: Blah, blah, blah: What to do when words don't work. Portfolio/ Penguin, New York (2011).

Supporting the Experience of Stakeholders of Multimedia Art – Towards an Ontology

Danzhu Li[*,†] and Gerrit C. van der Veer[†,‡]

[*]Human Media Interaction, University Twente, Enschede, the Netherlands
[†]Multimedia and Animation, Luxun Academy of Fine Arts, Liaoning, China
[‡]Multimedia and Culture, Computer Science, Vrije Universiteit, Amsterdam, the Netherlands
lidanzhu@me.com, gerrit@acm.org

Abstract

We introduce the rapid change of the visual art ecosystem, triggered by current science and technology development. ICT enables new multimedia based an interactive art forms, with an increasing variety of stakeholders. We provide examples of audience involvement, of immersion, and of braincomputer interaction as a new paradigm for participation. We point to the use of new material dimensions, as well as to expanding shared creation and cognition. We also point to opportunities to apply this development to accommodate special needs. In order to support the dissemination of these possibilities, we advocate the development of a task-modeling based ontology to describe, analyse, and support the evolving art ecosystem.

Keywords

Contemporary Visual Art Ecosystem · Stakeholders · Ontology

How to cite this book chapter:
Li, D. and van der Veer, G.C. 2020. Supporting the Experience of Stakeholders of Multimedia Art – Towards an Ontology. In: Loizides, F., Winckler, M., Chatterjee, U., Abdelnour-Nocera, J. and Parmaxi, A. (eds.) *Human Computer Interaction and Emerging Technologies: Adjunct Proceedings from the INTERACT 2019 Workshops.* Pp. 243–252. Cardiff: Cardiff University Press. DOI: https://doi.org/10.18573/book3.ah. License: CC-BY 4.0.

1 Visual Art on the Move

Our profession includes to support modern art, i.e., to teach, and to publish, relevant knowledge and skills to participate in the current and future art ecosystem. For the various stakeholders, the relevant view will be different, but stakeholders need to collaborate and communicate so a common language is needed that supports an intuitive cultural base. We are aiming on that and we intend to discuss this with the workshop/panel.

From ancient times, innovation of tools and techniques did push art to a new level. But today, with ICT, dramatic changes occur everywhere, including in the world of visual arts. Rich media, as well as information visualization, became a common way of modern visual communication, and these interact with each other. We have been exploring how contemporary artists are modifying the relationship between human beings and new realities. This will lead to an expansion of the multidimensional concept of experience, including the notion of values of visual art for its different stakeholders.

This paper analyses the current situation and developing trends of contemporary visual art from the perspective of enriching all stakeholders' experience, which suggests that contemporary visual artists should be aware. Through observation, practice, interviews and other research methods, we analyze and study the development and changes of the work and survival of stakeholders in contemporary visual (mainly interactive) art. Contemporary visual arts move to a cross disciplinary or interdisciplinary context, related to the development of science and technology and the change of human aesthetic ability. A new type of cross-border artists is coming out, and the evolution of society will make the space of art broader, evolving to a new visual art ecology.

2 Different Experiences Brought by Science and Technology

Under the influence of science and technology, new forms of art have emerged. These new terms may be controversial, but their names do reflect a future trend of contemporary art: digital art; interactive art; technique art; generative art; bio art; and singularity art [1]. We observed that visual art in due time approaches motion art. In relation to this, the operations of the artists and performers changed, including a gradual transfer from mainly perceptual motor skill activities to cognitive activities, gradually including application of ICT. It urges us to predict the short-term future of art, based on our collection and collation of long-term historic technology-related information. Contemporary dynamic visual art is oriented towards integrated media, the involvement of science and technology, and interactive, cross-border, multi-disciplinary cooperation. We predict that in the short term, art will go through a period where the practical value is greater than the aesthetic value. We analyze the impact and reflect on the changes and demands of experience and on the different levels of values from a cognitive perspective.

3 Interactive Media are Multi-dimensional

Modern visual art has developed to the interactive stage, resembling the development of HCI (human-computer interaction) technology. Artists explore the possibilities of interaction between human beings and machines, as well as between machines. Due to the rapid development of mobiles and wearable devices, interactive art features in a multi-dimensional context, serving a multi-sensory experience. The change of experience elicits artists and audiences to co-create. The continuous improvement of technology has a direct relationship with the impact of artistic creation. Consequently, artists need to understand and learn to use new technologies.

Interactive media art based on virtual reality and augmented reality is becoming to a major form of contemporary visual art innovation. From the commercialization of tools, to the development of models, to the sharing of various open-source information platforms, artists are becoming more familiar with this performance form and are as devoted as their audience. Mixed Reality technology enables participants (artists and spectators) to extend their experience in the dimension of time and space, breaking the old way of appreciation. We will provide some examples:

3.1 Chinese Artists Play with their Audiences

XuanPin, "The Field", is a comprehensive media art work. The work is intended to celebrate the tenth anniversary of the birth of a game DNF, created by LAFA [2] teachers and students, the Tencent Company, and Chinese folk artists. Based on the ancient shadow play, this work combines shadow play with animation and laser printing, MR immersion interaction, and other comprehensive media. It triggers people to think about tradition and modern art and technology. In order to let young people know about traditional culture, the team applied the latest Halo lens hybrid reality technology to interpret the scenes and images in DNF games and show them in the form of shadow play. In this arena, audiences can watch the performances of nonhereditary artists, and experience the performances made with new materials by players of cos-play roles, and, in addition, take HoloLens glasses to watch and try the performance of the shadows in virtual scenes. This multi-dimensional interaction is an innovation and exploration of traditional visual art. Figure 1 shows the character designed in the game DNF, created with shadow play techniques. Figure 2 shows Cos-play actor performance in the game by using shadow play, where the audience

Fig. 1: Character design in the game DNF created with shadow play techniques (2018). Picture by the authors, Dalian, China.

Fig. 2: Cosplay actors' performance of the DNF game by using shadow play and the audience manipulating the shadow puppet in the virtual scene through HoloLens. Picture provided by Media and Animation college, LAFA.

manipulates the shadow puppet in the virtual scene through HoloLens. One of the authors participated in the creation.

3.2 Lie down and enjoy artsImmersion experience

Both authors participated in the Art exhibition of SIGCHI2018, lying down on the floor to experience the art and enjoying it. The figure 3 shows one of the works. In the exhibition hall, artists built a dome theatre with dozens of cushions on the floor. Under the half dome, audiences had to lie down to see the dynamic visual art projected on the inside of the dome. In figure 3 we can see a Korean artist playing with instruments and electric fans moving under the dome. At the same time, they were "projected" into the dome. This combination became a rich comprehensive performance. Obviously, artists have broken the traditional form of experience, like under the domes of ancient churches or palaces in Europe. The artists challenge the audience's experience to complete their co-creation and to become part of this dynamic artistic performance.

Fig. 3: Art exhibition, SIGCHI 2018, Montreal. Picture by the authors.

Fig. 4: Exquisite Corpse – Visual Arts, http://uhbmi.ee.uh.edu/portfolio/ec-m-2/.

3.3 Life Information Visualization Brain-Computer Interface Art

The history of BCI as an artistic means is still short. Current BCI for artistic creation is mainly the application of non-invasive systems (EEG) to ensure a safe and noninvasive experience for artists and viewers. The brain signals picked up by electrodes are sent to the computer, which uses sophisticated software to translate them into computer commands. Portability and relatively low prices make the technology easy to promote. In this way, the audience can participate in the dynamics of the art without physical actions on the piece of art, and can even co-create, either individually or (when appropriately designed by the artist) as a group of spectators. This is the embodiment and the charm of BCI in an aesthetic application, which changes the form of traditional art and of the appreciation (no longer restricted to an objective perspective).

Obviously, contemporary artists need to understand the changing perspective on the role of the audience, as well as the technical aspects of designing the interaction, to apply this in their creation. Fig. 4 shows scientists using Mobile Brain-body Imaging (MoBI) technology to study the human improvisational creative process in the spirit of the "Exquisite Corpse" (an improvisational creative game created by surrealists in the 1920s, where three artists create a three-part art piece). The performance study seeks to uncover clues to what happens in the brain as people create and contemplate art [3].

4 A Plea for the Role of Material Science Development

An increasing number of artists focus on interaction mechanisms with wearable and implantable devices as well as integrating Internet-of-Things technology with new interactive art paradigms. In fact, both artists and scientists are aiming at a substance between visible and invisible. With the development of material science, new artistic forms such as nano-art, bio-art and integrated material art have brought challenges to those avant-garde artists in exploring future art. Though many mainstream artists and stakeholders turn a blind eye, or lack foresight, to the rapid development of contemporary science and technology, some artists are exploring the humanization of technology. New materials like nanomaterials are expected to be widely used in future artistic creation. Today we may already witness contemporary artistic practices in this direction. For example, nano-printing art, nano-sculpture, and nano-animation.

Jonty Hurwitz's work "The FRAGILE GIANT" (Fig. 5) on animal protection is the smallest nano-sculpture in history. In this microcosmic world, the artist explores the relationship between man and nature. This elephant sculpture is just over on tenth of a millimeter high. It is walking along the stark and perilous landscape of a human fingerprint. It can be destroyed by a human breath. According to Hurwitz the sculptures are so tiny that they are invisible to the human eye, and able to be placed on the forehead of an ant. Details of the works are at 300-nanometer scale, similar to the wavelengths of visible light and are therefore nearly impossible, according to the laws of physics, to see in the visible spectrum. The only way to observe these works is through a non-optical method of magnification like a scanning electron microscope[4].

IBM Research claimed to make the "World's Smallest Movie Using Atoms" (Fig. 6). IBM took the challenge of moving 5,000 atoms around in order to create a short stop motion video, capturing the images using a scanning tunneling microscope. "A Boy and His Atom" depicts a character named Atom who befriends a single atom and goes on a playful journey that includes dancing, playing catch and bouncing on a trampoline. Set to a playful musical track, the movie represents a unique way to convey science outside the research community [5].

Technology turns inspiration and creativity into reality, challenging traditional thinking and bringing about an art revolution, and even triggering to build a new world view. This innovation requires collaboration between many different interdisciplinary experts. The cooperation and co-creation will generate a new cognitive system (a symbiotic relationship between human beings' wearables, and the context). Wearable devices may have powerful effect on our experience of the context, of interactive art, and of life. Smart fabric in wearable devices is a representative case. Sensors are becoming smaller (to nanoscale units), and smart fabric applications become more flexible and comfortable [6]. Artists' exploration of science and art has stimulated people's re-recognition of the reality of contemporary art.

Fig. 5: Jonty Hurwitz: "*THE FRAGILE GIANT*". The smallest man-made object ever to be filmed. (2015) https://jontyhurwitz.com/fragile-giant.

Fig. 6: IBM: "*A Boy and His Atom*". The world's smallest movie (2013). https://www-03.ibm.com/press/us/en/pressrelease/40970.wss.

5 Exploration of Cognition

For all stakeholders of visual art, the improvement of knowledge is accompanied by the development of technology, by interdisciplinary cooperation, lifelong learning, and the application advanced technology and machine learning to assist artistic creation. Candy and Edmonds [7–8] mention three categories of activities in the creative person's thinking and working practice were identified: knowledge, visualization, and collaboration. The quality of the type of collaboration can be assessed in terms of its durability and stimulus to creative thinking as well as the outcomes achieved.

From brush to electronic pen; from clay and stone to 3D printing: artists need to master the accessibility of technology; need to learn to use new technology for creation. Tools should meet artists' needs, and be easy to learn and use, as well as be timely updated and upgraded to meet new needs. With the development of personal computing and the coming of the era of Internet of Everything, we foresee that customized tools will serve more and more artists and stakeholders of art.

We call for the exploration and development of cognitive ergonomics in a broader scope and the application of cooperation in the field of art [9]. This includes the special community of artists with special needs. In our practice, one graduate student from the art school (LAFA) in China is a hearing-impaired artist. He is very distressed by his limitation. He worries that if he always makes silent films, he will lose audiences and his works will be excluded from the art market. At present, he can only rely on the production of silent films to solve the problem of production. This case is representative of a considerable group of artists. In combination with our participation in the Artistic BCI workshop at CHI in Montreal in 2018, we analyzed the possibility of future support for hearing-impaired artists to edit music through EEG or other bioinformatics technologies [10]. Similarly, visually impaired artists and artists with language barriers can be assisted in their creation. We currently consider Ear Touch, a one-handed interaction technique that allows visually impaired people to interact with a smartphone using the ear to tap or draw gestures on the touchscreen, facilitating one-handed use as an alternative to headphones and addressing privacy and social concerns [11]. A smart glove can already work out what the wearer is manipulating from its weight and shape [12].

6 An Ontology of Modern Visual Art

When applying ICT, artists revise the way they work. We observe that contemporary interactive art is an artistic act co-created by artists and participants. We briefly review its production process: from the manufacturing stage, artists need to cooperate with participants in many disciplines (using brainstorming, sketching, technology and tools, exhibition forms, interactive models, etc.). After completion of the artwork, it is expected to be co-creative with audience, e.g., through recording the behavior of the experiencer, visualizing the emotional information and the interactive behaviors needed. The stronger the participation, the higher the experiential value. This is precisely the purpose of some artists 'creation: the value of such works of art. We envision an ontology to analyse, describe, and support the future art ecosystem: with new roles, new objects, and new activities. Our conceptual framework is based on GTA [13], and we mainly consider to focus on development of the concepts Roles (with mandating and delegation), Objects (including tangible and intangible artifacts, and the context as an object), Tasks (as goal-triggered activities of (co-)creation, performance, and experiencing); and the multidisciplinary concept of values and forces that trigger action.

- **Objects** of art, both intangible (scripts, programs, video and sound streams) and tangible. Each may well have an electronic identity, with possible tags regarding ownership, location, history of use and movement.
- Stakeholders are the various **Agents** in the art ecosystem: artist; supporters of techniques and tools; stage keepers, museums and gallery owners; brokers and auction houses; performers and actors; and the audience.
- Roles. In the art ecosystem, collaboration between people (and other agents) changes: new roles develop (co-creating members of the audience) and roles get exchanged more easily between actors, activities get more easily delegated to systems, and mandating of roles and delegation of activities occurs at a more detailed level than before.
- Each agent will have one or more different **roles** (defined by **goals**, and related sets of **activities** regarding art objects), and each role will relate to different types of experience (including: understanding; emotions; tendencies to act; values toward the piece of art).
- **Activities** with their **goals** will be related to creation; reproduction; performance; exhibition; ownership and maintenance; documentation and communication about; etc.

Our analysis will allow us to set design goals for supporting technology. A new addition contribution to GTA is exploration and research of experience and values. We decide to add values aspect for the case of art, based on observing the impact of values in the current art ecosystem on artists, art markets, audiences, buyers, and other stakeholders. With the rise and development of industry, art is gradually industrialized, which is representative of film and television animation. The film industry is a complete industrial chain. The embodiment of aesthetic value is only one of the links, though it is the most basic. After the production and distribution of films, value is still fermenting. If the cultural value and aesthetic value of a film have a broad and lasting influence, then its collection value, commercial value and other values will change with time. This phenomenon is not only controlled by the art market. Artists and agents should think about how to create valuable art, and our expanding task analysis ontology is intended to provide a scientific theory and practical tool that can help artist and stakeholders.

References

1. Qin Tan, L.: Singularity Art – How Technology Singularity Will Impact Art. China Machine Press (2018).

2. LuXun academy of fine arts (LAFA), China http://www.lumei.edu.cn
3. Exquisite Corpse – Visual Arts. http://uhbmi.ee.uh.edu/portfolio/ec-m-2/
4. Hurwitz, J.: THE FRAGILE GIANT – The smallest man-made object ever to be filmed. (2015) https://jontyhurwitz.com/fragile-giant
5. IBM: A Boy and His Atom – The world's smallest movie. (2013) https://www-03.ibm.com/press/us/en/pressrelease/40970.wss
6. Li, D., van der Veer, G. (2017). From Painter to Interaction Designer: The Evolution of Visual Art Things. In: Anirudha Joshi, Devanuj Balkrishan, Girish Dalvi, Marco Winckler (Eds.): Adjunct Proceedings INTERACT 2017 Mumbai. Springer: pp. 139–149
7. Candy, L. (1997) Computers and Creativity Support: Knowledge, Visualization and Collaboration. Knowledge-Based Systems, 10, (1), pp. 3–13.
8. Candy, L., Edmonds, E.A.: Modeling Co-Creativity in Art and Technology. Conference: Proceedings 4th Conference on Creativity & Cognition, Loughborough, United Kingdom, 2002. https://dblp.uni-trier.de/db/conf/candc/candc2002.html
9. Li, D., van der Veer G.C.: Cognitive ergonomics on the move. ECCE 2019 workshop. UK. (2019)
10. Nijholt, A. (Ed) (2019) Brain Art: Brain-computer Interfaces for Artistic Expression. Springer, Switzerland.
11. Wang, U., Yu, C., Yang, X.D., He, W., Shi, Y.: EarTouch: Facilitating Smartphone Use for Visually Impaired People in Mobile and Public Scenarios. (2019). CHI 2019, ACM Digital Library
12. Smart glove works out what you are holding from its weight and shape. Nature, DOI: https://doi.org/10.1038/s41586–019–1234-z. published 8 June 2019. https://www.newscientist.com/article/2204736-smart-glove-works-out-what-youreholding-from-its-weight-and-shape/
13. Van der Veer G.C., Kulyk O., Vyas D., Kubbe O., Ebert A. (2011) Task Modeling for Collaborative Authoring. In: Anke Dittmar & Peter Forbrig (Eds) Designing Collaborative Activities Proceedings of ECCE 2011. ACM Digital Library, pp. 171–178

SECTION 6

Handling Security, Usability, User Experience and Reliability in User-Centered Development Processes

Characterizing Sets of Systems: Across-Systems Properties and their Representation

Elodie Bouzekri[*], Alexandre Canny[*], Célia Martinie[*]
and Philippe Palanque[*,†]

[*]ICS-IRIT, Toulouse University, Toulouse, France
[†]Department of Industrial Design, Eindhoven University of Technology,
Eindhoven, The Netherlands
elodie.bouzekri@irit.fr, alexandre.canny@irit.fr, martinie@irit.fr,
palanque@irit.fr

Abstract

System quality is assessed with respect to the value of relevant properties of that system. The level of abstraction of these properties can be very high (e.g. usability) or very low (e.g. all the "Ok" buttons in the application have the same size). These properties can be generic and thus applicable to a large group of systems (e.g. all the interactive systems should be usable) or very specific to a system (e.g. the "Quit" button in my application should always be visible). While properties identification and verification is at the core of interactive systems engineering, much less attention is paid to properties that aims at characterizing a pair (or more) of systems. In this paper, we propose to study such properties (defined as across-systems properties) and propose a notation for representing them. We also present several examples of across-systems properties and demonstrate their importance and use on a simple example of aircraft cockpits buttons.

How to cite this book chapter:
Bouzekri, E., Canny, A., Martinie, C. and Palanque, P. 2020. Characterizing Sets of
Systems: Across-Systems Properties and their Representation. In: Loizides, F.,
Winckler, M., Chatterjee, U., Abdelnour-Nocera, J. and Parmaxi, A. (eds.) *Human
Computer Interaction and Emerging Technologies: Adjunct Proceedings from the
INTERACT 2019 Workshops.* Pp. 253–266. Cardiff: Cardiff University Press. DOI:
https://doi.org/10.18573/book3.ai. License: CC-BY 4.0.

Keywords

Properties · Within-system properties · Across-systems properties · Interactive Systems · Notation · Aircraft cockpits

1 Introduction

The term property conveys multiple meanings in different domains. However, in computing systems domain [18], they are used to describe characteristics that the system should exhibit but their assessment (on a given system) is usually a complex and cumbersome activity. Formal description techniques are aimed at describing both the system and their expected properties and to demonstrate (or not) that the system really exhibits these properties.

Fig. 1 presents the process advocated by DO178-C standard [22] for the design of computing systems in the aeronautics domain. That process highlights the need for explicit representation of expected properties for a given aircraft system (bottom of the Figure) and the formal methods supplement to this standard [17] even recommend the use of CTL (Computational Tree Logic) from [21] to represent them. The right-hand side of the Figure highlights the activity of formal verification that checks whether properties hold on the behavioral description of the system produced in the LLR phase (upper part of the Figure). Such approach follows the work done by Sistla and Pnueli [19] on the safety and liveness properties of reactive systems. Their focus, and the one of DO 330 standard, is on the representation of multiple properties for a single system under design or evaluation.

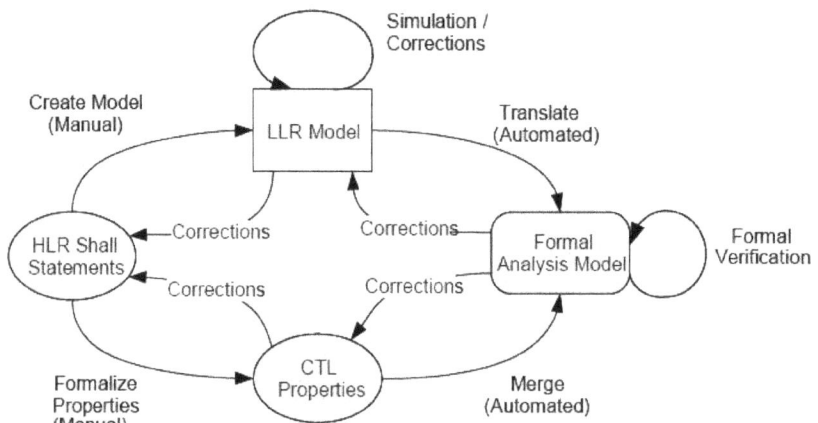

Fig. 1: Formal Approach to System Design as in DO178C – Supplement 330 on Formal Methods [17].

The HCI community usually focusses on properties that characterize a single system in relation to the user and his/her environment. For instance, the well-studied usability property determines the effectiveness, the efficiency and the satisfaction according to standard ISO 9241 [7] of the system for a given user (or set of users). Other usability definitions add learnability [12] or accessibility [14] to the standard definition. Usability evaluation can be performed on one single system. In other words, the usability evaluation function needs one parameter (a system) and returns a set of value. This means that for usability evaluation would blend a value for the effectiveness of the system, a value for the efficiency of the system and one for the satisfaction of the user using the system. One important aspect of this is that the type of the values depends on the property. It can be Boolean (the property is true or false) but also enumerated type or a number (e.g. error rate). We call *within-system* property this kind of property for which the evaluation function needs one single system as parameter. User Experience [15], privacy [5], dependability and security [2] are other examples of *within-system* properties that can be evaluated on a single system. In contrast, other systems properties can be evaluated only with, at least, two systems as parameter. For instance, similarity property determines the distance between several interfaces in terms of orientation, order and density of their items (according to the definition in [6]). The evaluation function of similarity needs at least two parameters (two user interfaces) and returns a set of three values: one for the orientation, one for the order and one for the density. We call this kind of properties *across-systems* properties. Proximity [16] and congruence [3] are other examples of *across-systems* properties, as their evaluation function needs at least two parameters too. Less attention is paid to *across-systems* properties even though these properties can be extremely useful to characterize sets of systems as, for instance, in the prototyping phases of interactive systems development where multiple alternatives are designed and assessed. We propose to investigate and define different *across-systems* properties and a mean to describe explicitly these properties in interactive systems design process.

In the next section, we detail different examples of *across-systems* properties. In the third section, we propose a specific notation supported by the DREAMER tool to represent *across-systems* properties. The fourth section illustrates how this notation helps in describing the *across-systems* properties of aircraft cockpit elements. Section 5 concludes the paper and highlights directions for future work.

2 Examples of existing across-systems properties

Across-systems properties are meant to characterize the quality of a set of systems. As mentioned in the introduction, Similarity is an *across-systems* property that aims at assessing the distance between the visual layouts of several systems interfaces in terms of orientation, order and density as introduced in [6], refined in [11] and more recently used for experience gathering [23]. This Similarity property can be included as a dimension of the Proximity property. The term Proximity is used by Wickens and Carswell [16] as compatibility principle between sets of displays for interface design. We propose to use the term Proximity as defined in [16] to be an *across-systems* property. The Proximity *across-systems* property is composed of Perceptual Proximity and Processing Proximity [16]. Perceptual proximity includes:

— the spatial proximity of displayed items,
— the visual connection between displayed items,
— the similarity (e.g. color, orientation) between displayed items,
— the homogeneous information display (i.e. all digital, all analogous, both),
— the object integration (i.e. contiguity, contour and spatial integration) of displayed items.

Processing proximity includes:

— the cognitive processing proximity of the tasks,
— the similarity between units of the displayed parameters,
— the temporal proximity of the task (i.e. the time to perform the task).

Another example of *across-systems* property is Congruence. Dekker and Hollnagel [3] define Congruence as the ability of the system to take into account the variation of user capabilities and needs depending on the current situation. Extending this proposal, we propose to consider congruence across a set of systems. In other words, Congruence property aims at characterizing the ability of a set of systems to maintain their input/output compatible with user capabilities and needs whatever the situation.

Finally, we propose a list of *across-systems* properties that are initially within-system properties but that can also be applied as *across-systems* properties:

— Equivalency: One or several systems exhibit the same properties as another system or several systems.
— Dependency: One or several systems depend on the outputs of other systems. For instance, a set of radio receptors are dependent from a radio transmitter, as receptors need the radio waves of the transmitter.
— Complementarity: Each system belonging to a set of systems performs a share of the overall activity. The complete work is the union of each part. For instance, a set of factory robots of production line highly support complementary property, as each robot completes the work produced by the previous one.
— Diversity: Each system of the set of systems is implemented in a different language or technology. A set composed of a C++ application, a JAVA application and a Python application highly supports diversity property [24].

— Redundancy: Each system of the set of systems offers the same functions. For instance, a set composed of a computer extinguisher application and an extinguisher physical button of the computer highly support redundancy property for the shutdown function [26].
— Equality: The control authority is equally distributed between the systems of the set. For instance, a set of systems under the so-called "master-slave" protocol have a very low equality property.
— Uniformity: Each system of the set contributes with the same amount of work to the overall activity.
— Concurrency: Each system of the set of systems work at the same time [25].

Defining properties of set of systems is useful to analyze how to integrate several systems for a particular function or to replace a system by another one inside an integrated set of systems. For example, in aircrafts, to integrate a system as a backup in case of a failure of another system, redundancy and diversity are important properties (that are related to the implementation of fault tolerance mechanisms [2, 4]). Another example is the replacement of a system by a newest one in a factory. In order to minimize the learning time for the operators, the proximity property has to be assessed (to ensure that the required number of new cognitive tasks to learn is low). In the same way that *within-system* properties may be used to define requirements for the systems and then drive the design of these systems, *across-systems* properties also may be targeted during the design of an integrated set of systems. In order to provide support for the comparison of design options with respect to a set of *across-systems* properties, we propose to extend TEAM design rationale notation (which is based on QOC [9]).

3 Extensions to the QOC and TEAM notations

MacLean et al. [9] introduced the QOC (Question Option Criteria) notation for system design rational. QOC allows to document design choices with their explanations during the design process. This notation is also a tool for reasoning and communicating with various stakeholders as it uses very simple concepts. The TEAM (Traceability, Exploration and Analysis Method) [10] notation extends the QOC notation with the description of properties and factors associated to the criteria, as well as with the identification of design artefacts associated to the design options.

We propose to extend the TEAM notation to enable the representation of *across-systems* properties, in order to take into account across-systems properties when designing a set of systems. For that purpose, we propose to slightly adapt the TEAM notation:

• Question: Design question about the system under design (Square in Fig. 2).
• System: possible option for the system to answer the design question (Disc in Fig. 2) replaces design option of the TEAM notation.

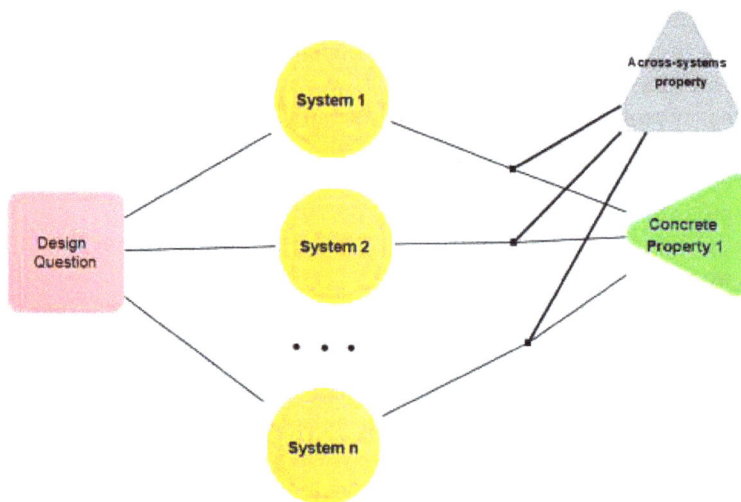

Fig. 2: Main elements of the extensions to the notation TEAM edited with the DREAMER tool.

- Concrete property: Desired property met (or not) by the related set of systems (Lower right triangle in Fig. 2) replaces the desired property met by one or several design options of TEAM notation.
- *Across-systems* property (Upper right triangle in Fig. 2) encompassing the concrete property of several systems. If a system option highly supports an across-systems property, a plain line is drawn between this *across-systems* property and the line that connect a system option and the concrete property associated to this across-systems property. If a system option gives few support to an across-systems property, a dashed line is drawn between this *across-systems* property and the line that connect a system option and the concrete property associated to this across-systems property. *Across-systems* property replaces the notation element *Argument* of the TEAM notation. The notation element *Argument* stands for the reason behind the choice of one design option in the TEAM notation.

The DREAMER (Design Rationale Environment for Argumentation and Modeling and Engineering Requirements) tool supports recording, edition and analysis of TEAM models [10]. For the illustrative example of this paper, we use the DREAMER tool [10] to represent across-systems properties of different system designs for the FIRE push button in an aircraft cockpit.

4   Representing across-systems properties: illustrative example

In the A350 aircraft cockpit, there are guarded FIRE push-buttons on the overhead panel, one for each engine of the aircraft. These buttons are composed of a backlighting system, a guard and a toggle button (see Fig. 3). When a fire is

Fig. 3: Engine 1 FIRE push-button on the overhead panel.

Fig. 4: Interactions sequence for pushing overhead panel-like FIRE push button.

detected in an engine, the backlighting system turns on and the pilot must raise the guard and press the toggle button [1] to acknowledge the alarm. When the button is pressed, all the systems that are connected to the engine are isolated and the fire extinguisher bottles are armed for a possible discharge [1].

In this example, we study the digitalization of such FIRE push-button (FIRE pb). Two different designs of the digital FIRE pb are proposed.

The first design option mimics all the graphical aspects and interactions of the physical FIRE pb. The difference is that the button is no more physical and user interactions must be performed with a mouse. The sequence of interaction is visible in Fig. 4. Like the physical FIRE pb, the user sees the backlighting system on, raises the guard and presses the button to isolate the engine and to prepare the bottles to discharge. We call this design option "overhead panel-like FIRE pb".

The second design option supports a different interaction sequence that still enables the guard of the button. This interaction sequence is similar to the GoPro[1] unlock interaction and is called GoPro-like FIRE pb. This sequence of interactions is presented in Fig. 5 and is composed of the following steps: the user sees the backlighting system on, drags the button on the bolt area, maintains the button in this area until the animation finishes, releases and presses the button to isolate engine and prepare the bottles to discharge. For this proposed interaction design, the attention has been paid to respect the same interaction time to remove the guard and press the button as with the physical FIRE pb.

---

[1] https://gopro.com.

Fig. 5: Interactions sequence for pushing GoPro-like FIRE push-button.

We propose to analyze these different designs with the physical FIRE pb with respect to a subset of the *across-systems* properties presented in section 2.

The Fig. 6 presents *across-systems* properties relevant for the FIRE pb, the overhead panel-like FIRE pb and the GoPro-like FIRE pb. The actual FIRE pb and overhead panel-like FIRE pb have the same graphical rendering. Then, they support the Similarity *across-systems* property (first multi-systems property from the bottom of Fig. 6). All the systems have the same functions: fire alert, isolate engine and prepare the fire extinguisher bottles to discharge. Then, these systems support the Redundancy *across-systems* property (second multi-systems property from the bottom of Fig. 6). All the systems are designed so that it takes the same time to perform the button push. Then, they support the temporal proximity *across-systems* property. The physical FIRE pb is physical whereas overhead panel-like and GoPro-like FIRE pb are digital. Then, they provide low support to the homogeneous information display *across-systems* property. Finally, all systems require the same logical processing user task: the button can be pushed to prepare fire extinguishing when the backlighting system is on and guard raised. Then, all the systems support the processing proximity *across-systems* property.

Across-systems properties can inform the design option decision if a single digital option must be chosen. In order to not modify the pilot training procedure as applied with the current physical FIRE pb, the preferred option should be the overhead panellike FIRE pb one. Indeed, all of the design options are graphically alike and user cognitive tasks are close (similarity and processing proximity). Otherwise, despite the use of different input devices and interactions techniques used for the three design options, their *across-systems* properties indicate that they are alike. In this case, usability evaluation can be performed to discriminate the most suitable option according to the users.

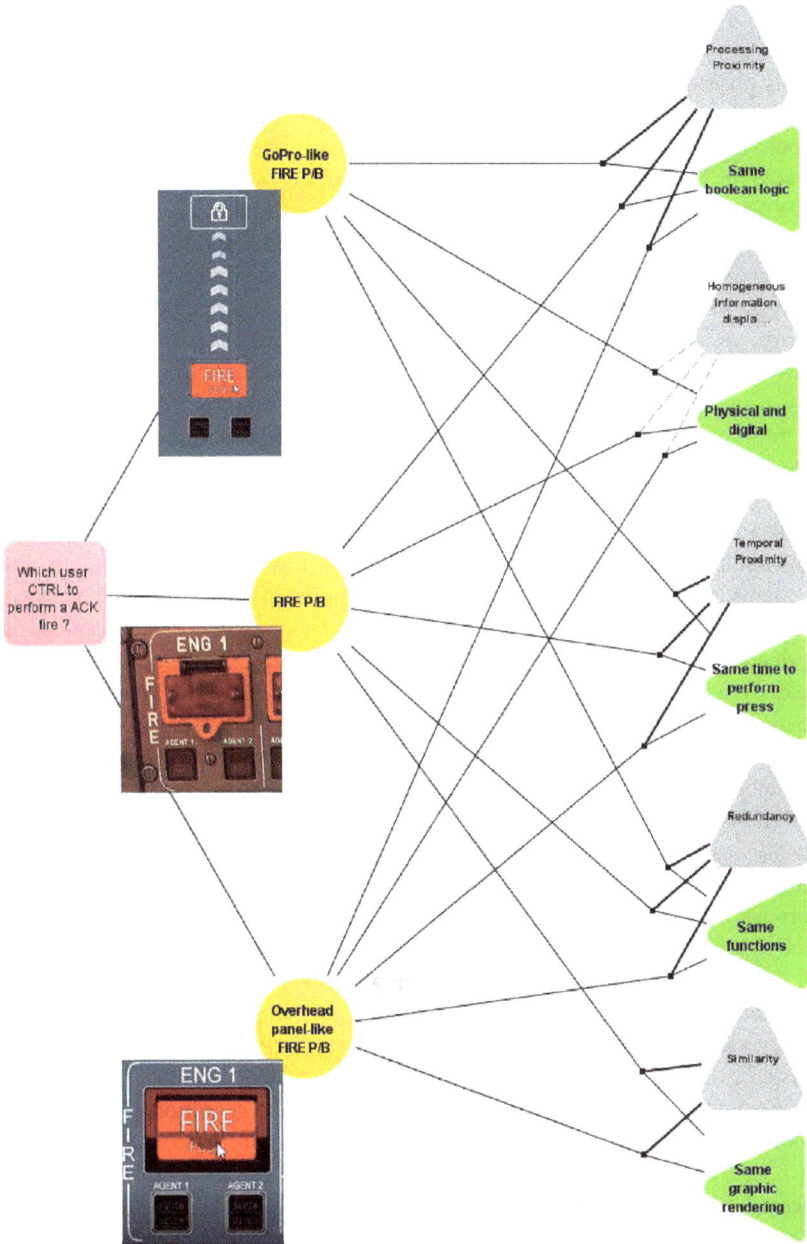

Fig. 6: Representation of across-systems properties of FIRE pb, GoPro-like FIRE pb and overhead panel-like FIRE pb using extended QOC & TEAM notations to answer the design question "Which user control to perform acknowledge fire action?".

5 Conclusion

This position paper introduces the concept of *across-systems* properties and highlights the lack of support for their description in existing notations and tools. It proposes a mean to represent *across-systems* properties using a notation based on TEAM and illustrates (on an example) how one can use it. This example is based on the physical FIRE push-button found in an aircraft cockpit and on its digital design alternatives (if we consider that future cockpits would replace such physical buttons with touch screen interactions). Even though, the physical FIRE push-button and digital alternatives seem to be very different, *across-systems* properties highlights their common characteristics and suitability to pilot tasks. In addition, if designers want to replace the current system by a digital one or want to integrate a redundant one, the representation of *across-systems* properties can guide design choices depending on the properties designers want to preserve and the ones they are ready to abandon.

In the same way as the pilot does not only use the FIRE push-button to deal with an engine fire (they could do testing for instance), it is common for users to manipulate several systems to reach a goal. In other words, users can use complex systems composed of several sub-systems to perform their work. For instance, an office employee use several systems such as a computer, a telephone and a printer to perform his/her work. All these systems compose a workstation complex system. For this reason, it might be interesting to investigate possible links between *within-system* properties of systems and *across-system* properties of the entire work environment. For instance, redundancy *across-system* property is also a fault tolerant technique to contribute to the *within-system* dependability [2] of a given system. Looking at each redundant component, we might want to identify *within-system* properties (e.g. performance). The variants used for redundancy must exhibit similar behaviors and thus similarity is, for them, an across-system property. If similarity is guaranteed then the fault-tolerant system embedding all the redundant ones will exhibit dependability as a *within-system* property.

One perspective to this work lays in the analysis of how *within-system* properties can help designers when they have to integrate several systems. For example, if several systems of the cockpit have a high proximity, the integration of these systems to support a user goal may enhance the usability of the whole cockpit, as pointed out by Huchins in the work on distributed cognition [27]. In other words, the description of the relationship between *within-system* properties and across-system properties can enable to understand how the first influences the second and to design systems with a more global integrated perspective.

References

1. Airbus A350 Flight Crew Operating Manual, 5T1 A350 FLEET FCOM. Technical Report. Airbus.

2. Avizienis, A., Laprie, J.C., Randell, B., Landwehr, C.: Basic concepts and taxonomy of dependable and secure computing. IEEE Transactions on Dependable and Secure Computing. 1, 11–33 (2004). https://doi.org/10.1109/TDSC.2004.2.

3. Dekker, S., Hollnagel, E.: Coping with Computers in the Cockpit. Routledge (2018).

4. Fayollas, C., Martinie, C., Navarre, D., Palanque, P., Fahssi, R.: Fault-Tolerant User Interfaces for Critical Systems: Duplication, Redundancy and Diversity As New Dimensions of Distributed User Interfaces. In: Proceedings of the 2014 Workshop on Distributed User Interfaces and Multi-modal Interaction. pp. 27–30. ACM, New York, NY, USA (2014). https://doi.org/10.1145/2677356.2677662.

5. Gerber, P., Volkamer, M., Renaud, K.: Usability Versus Privacy Instead of Usable Privacy: Google's Balancing Act Between Usability and Privacy. SIGCAS Comput. Soc. 45, 16–21 (2015). https://doi.org/10.1145/2738210.2738214.

6. Heil, S., Bakaev, M., Gaedke, M.: Measuring and Ensuring Similarity of User Interfaces: The Impact of Web Layout. In: Cellary, W., Mokbel, M.F., Wang, J., Wang, H., Zhou, R., and Zhang, Y. (eds.) Web Information Systems Engineering – WISE 2016. pp. 252–260. Springer International Publishing (2016).

7. International Standard Organization: "ISO 9241-11" Ergonomic requirements for office work with visual display terminals (VDT) – Part 11 Guidance on Usability (1996)

8. Lazar, J., Feng, J.H., Hochheiser, H.: Research Methods in Human-Computer Interaction. Morgan Kaufmann (2017).

9. MacLean, A., Young, R.M., Bellotti, V.M.E., Moran, T.P.: Questions, Options, and Criteria: Elements of Design Space Analysis. Human–Computer Interaction. 6, 201–250 (1991). https://doi.org/10.1080/07370024.1991.9667168.

10. Martinie, C., Palanque, P., Winckler, M., Conversy, S.: DREAMER: A Design Rationale Environment for Argumentation, Modeling and Engineering Requirements. In: Proceedings of the 28th ACM International Conference on Design of Communication. pp. 73–80. ACM, New York, NY, USA (2010). https://doi.org/10.1145/1878450.1878463.

11. Navarre, D., Palanque, P., Hamon, A., Della Pasqua, S.: Similarity as a Design Driver for User Interfaces of Dependable Critical Systems. In: Clemmensen, T., Rajamanickam, V., Dannenmann, P., Petrie, H., and Winckler, M. (eds.) Global Thoughts, Local Designs. pp. 114–122. Springer International Publishing (2018).

12. Nielsen, J.: Usability Engineering. Elsevier (1994).

13. Oxford Dictionary https://en.oxforddictionaries.com/definition/property

14. Petrie, H., Kheir, O.: The Relationship Between Accessibility and Usability of Websites. In: Proceedings of the SIGCHI Conference on Human Factors in Computing Systems. pp. 397–406. ACM, New York, NY, USA (2007).

15. Pirker, M.M., Bernhaupt, R.: Measuring User Experience in the Living Room: Results from an Ethnographically Oriented Field Study Indicating

Major Evaluation Factors. In: Proceedings of the 9th European Conference on Interactive TV and Video. pp. 79–82. ACM, New York, NY, USA (2011).

16. Wickens, C.D., Carswell, C.M.: The Proximity Compatibility Principle: Its Psychological Foundation and Relevance to Display Design. Human Factors: The Journal of the Human Factors and Ergonomics Society. 37, 473–494 (1995).

17. DO-333 Formal Methods Supplement to DO-178C and DO-278A, published by RTCA and EUROCAE December 13, 2011.

18. Manna, Z., Pnueli, A.: A Hierarchy of Temporal Properties. ACM Symposium on Principles of Distributed Computing1990: 377–410 (1990).

19. Sistla, A. P.: On characterization of safety and liveness properties in temporal logic. In: Proceedings of the fourth annual ACM symposium on Principles of distributed computing, pp. 39–48, ACM (1985).

20. Pnueli A.: Applications of Temporal Logic to the Specification and Verification of Reactive Systems: A Survey of Current Trends. LNCS n° 224 p. 510–584. Springer Verlag (1986).

21. Clarke E. and E. A. Emerson. Design andsynthesis of synchronization skeletons using branchingtime temporal logic. InLogic of Programs: Workshop,Yorktown Heights, NY, May 1981, volume 131, 1981.

22. DO-178C/ED-12C, Software Considerations in Airborne Systems and Equipment Certification, published by RTCA and EUROCAE, 2012.

23. Zhao, X., Littlewood, B., Povyakalo, A. A., Strigini, L. and Wright, D. (2018). Conservative Claims for the Probability of Perfection of a Software-based System Using Operational Experience of Previous Similar Systems. Reliability Engineering and System Safety, 175, pp. 265–282

24. Gashi I., Andrey Povyakalo, Lorenzo Strigini: Diversity, Safety and Security in Embedded Systems: Modelling Adversary Effort and Supply Chain Risks. EDCC 2016: 13–24

25. Best E. Semantics of sequential and parallel programs. Prentice Hall International series in computer science, Prentice Hall 1996, ISBN 978-0-13-460643-9, pp. I–XI, 1–351

26. Avizienis A., "The Methodology of N-version Programming", Software Fault Tolerance, edited by M. Lyu, John Wiley & Sons, 1995.

27. Hollan J., Hutchins E., Kirsh D. Distributed cognition: toward a new foundation for humancomputer interaction research. ACM Trans. Comput.-Hum. Interact. 7(2): 174–196 (2000)

Aligning Security, Usability, User Experience: A Pattern Approach

Bilal Naqvi, Jari Porras, Shola Oyedeji and Mehar Ullah

Software Engineering, LENS, LUT University, Finland

syed.naqvi@student.lut.fi

Abstract

Security and usability have evolved independently, therefore, expertise in both of these domains are hard to find in one person. This research aims to assist security and usability designers and developers by influencing their decision-making abilities when it comes to the conflicts between security and usability. It does so by proposing the use of usable security patterns for assisting the developers and designers in making accurate choices when handling the conflicts. A novel methodology is presented for identifying usable security patterns from existing implementations, which are effectively managing the security and usability trade-offs. The aim is to identify such implementations while documenting the suitable trade-offs in the format of patterns for use by other developers and designers. To instantiate the methodology, a case study was conducted whose results are also presented in the paper.

Keywords

Security · usability · usable security · patterns

How to cite this book chapter:

Naqvi, B., Porras, J., Oyedeji, S. and Ullah, M. 2020. Aligning Security, Usability, User Experience: A Pattern Approach. In: Loizides, F., Winckler, M., Chatterjee, U., Abdelnour-Nocera, J. and Parmaxi, A. (eds.) *Human Computer Interaction and Emerging Technologies: Adjunct Proceedings from the INTERACT 2019 Workshops.* Pp. 267–278. Cardiff: Cardiff University Press. DOI: https://doi.org/10.18573/book3.aj. License: CC-BY 4.0.

1 Introduction

Security and usability are considered as conflicting goals [1]. The trade-offs between the two are discussed at different forums not limited to cyber-security and Human Computer Interaction (HCI). Typical examples of the security and usability conflict include, (1) complex password guidelines having an impact on memorability, (2) implementation of password masking to protect against 'shoulder surfing attacks' but at the cost of feedback (usability element), among others. Traditionally security and usability have evolved independently as different domains, therefore, expertise in both security and usability are hard to find in one person [2]. Despite this, the developers are ones who face most of the criticism when the security solutions are unusable, or when usability features pose a threat to system security. The domain considering the integration of principles of security and dimensions of usability is known as *usable security*.

The early efforts in the field of usable security date back to 1998 when different properties of usability problems for security systems were identified [3]. Despite that recognition, state of the art concerning usable security still has some catching up to do. Practices and trends followed in the large organizations reveal a lack of motivation in considering usable security as a quality dimension [4]. One possible reason for this state are the costs associated with usable security [19]. The implementation of security due to the constantly evolving threat environment, and usability due to rapid technological advancements has been so demanding that it leaves less time and costs to manage the trade-offs between the two. Among the other reasons for the current state of the art, it is imperative to discuss the following.

— *Different perceptions concerning security and usability*: The community has a different opinion concerning the existence of trade-offs between security and usability. Most of the research argues the existence of trade-offs between security and usability [5–6]. However, in parallel with the research establishing the existence of the trade-offs, there is some research classifying security and usability trade-offs as mere myths [7–8]. When the opinion on the existence of the problem is divided, then it is difficult to effectively contribute towards solving it.

— *Studying the conflicts by different communities in silos*: Various communities and interest groups have been studying usable security in silos, independently from each other. Some of these include, (1) SOUPS (Symposium on Usable Security and Privacy), small community studying trends, avenues and advancements in usable security. Much of the content is tactical, rather than being strategic, (2) The cybersecurity community dealing with the wider scope of security services; usability is a minor concern for this community, (3) The software engineering community where security and usability are considered as quality characteristics. Some of the standards provide contradictory perceptions and models for the same software quality characteristics, e.g. definition of usability in ISO 9126 and ISO 9241-11, (4) The HCI community, where the researchers try to explain from a cognitive perspective how users make poor security decisions leading to system compromises. There is no medium for collaboration that enables views from different communities and perspectives to be incorporated.

— *In effective joint working groups*: Because of independent activities, there is a lack of joint efforts concerning usable security. However, there exist multiple working groups specifically on usable security, but combining their findings in order to come up with a strategic vision for usable security, still remains a challenge.

— *Lack of strategic approach*: Much of the work related to usable security suffers from a cosmetic approach that is the solutions are limited to specific problems, rather than contributing towards management of the conflicts in general [2]. For example, there was a perception that CAPTCHA (*Completely Automated Public Turing Test to Tell Computers and Humans Apart*) poses readability problems for the users, therefore, new CAPTCHAS were developed that allow the user to select relevant images in response to the challenge. The question that remains valid for the community to address is, '*do we really need CAPTCHAS?*'. The prime purpose of CAPTCHA is to protect against denial of service (DoS) attacks, which is the responsibility of the service provider, and then why the user should bear the burden to deal with the CAPTCHA especially they cause deviation from the users' primary task. Likewise, majority of the work on usable security has been on the operational and tactical level and therefore, have a cosmetic effect on the usable security problem. However, what is required in this regard are the long term and strategic solutions, for example, a requirement-engineering framework for aligning security and usability during the phases of the software development lifecycle (SDLC).

Moreover, one aspect on which there is a consensus among different groups working on usable security is to focus on learning and assisting the developers in handling the security and usability conflicts. This forms the primary research question addressed in this paper, which is '*how to assist security and usability developers in handling the conflicts and identifying suitable trade-offs while enabling learning in a specific context of use?* This research advocates the concept of '*usable security by design*', which is aimed at assisting the developers in handling the conflicts and identifying suitable trade-offs by using design patterns. Each design patterns solves a recurring design problem in a particular context of use. Using the patterns' approach can be advantageous not only for the developers but for the organizations as well. Software development organizations can also contribute to the catalog of patterns, based on previous experiences from the projects. Furthermore, using the patterns while ensuring effective management of the trade-offs does not affect the timely completion and costs associated with the project.

There are some existing usable security design patterns, but there is a need to collect those patterns, add them to a catalog and disseminate the catalog among the developers and designers. Furthermore, it is imperative to identify more patterns to be added in the catalog. For identifying more usable security patterns, the proposal for a three-staged methodology is presented in this paper. The remainder of the paper is organized as follows. Section 2 presents the background and literature review. Section 3 presents the proposed methodology for the identification of usable security patterns from existing implementations. Section 4 presents the case study to instantiate the proposed methodology, and Section 5 concludes the paper.

2 Background and literature review

In line with the research question addressed in this paper, the literature review was conducted considering the following objectives.

1. To rationalize the use of patterns as a way of assisting developers in handling inter-disciplinary conflicts e.g. security and usability conflicts.
2. To identify existing usable security patterns (if any) and methodologies for identification for such patterns.

The authors [9] state, "insufficient communication with users produces a lack of user-centered design in security mechanisms". The approach advocated in this research is the use of patterns. Both usability and security professionals recognize the importance of incorporating their concerns throughout the design cycle and acknowledge the need for an iterative rather than a linear design process. Patterns' ability to be improved over the time and incorporate multiple viewpoints make them suitable for inter-disciplinary fields like usable security [1].

Patterns provide benefits like means of common vocabulary, shared documentation, improved communication. In addition, the pattern can be incorporated during the early stages of system development in contrast to considering usability and security later in the development lifecycle; handling the usable security problem earlier in the development lifecycle helps in saving significant costs and delays associated with rework.

An architect Christopher Alexander in the book 'A Pattern Language' originally introduced the concept of patterns [10]. Deriving inspiration from this, the same concept was implemented in computer science particularly in software engineering to assist the designers of the system, while providing guidelines and high-level principles. The similar concept was introduced in HCI to assist the development of user interface design (e.g. [11–12]).

Each pattern expresses a relation between three things, *context*, *problem* and *solution*. Patterns provide real solutions, not abstract principles, by explicitly mentioning the context and problem and summarizing the rationale for their effectiveness. Since the patterns provide a generic "core" solution, its use can vary from one implementation to other.

Furthermore, the patterns have three dimensions: descriptive, normative, and communicative [17]. From the perspective of usable security, the communicative dimensions of the patterns enable different communities to discuss design issues and solutions. Patterns also prove effective in the domains, which lack an existing body of knowledge; in such cases the patterns assist in identifying effective practices as they emerge and capture them as objects for discussion, scrutiny and modification [17].

In line with the second objective of the literature review, it was identified that the authors [13], while listing 20 usable security patterns also presented the results after analysis of commonly used software browsers like Internet Explorer, Mozilla Firefox and email clients like Microsoft Outlook. It was revealed that the identified patterns had 61.67% application in the analyzed software implementations. The authors state "patterns make sense and can be useful guide for software developers". However, the work was limited to listing the patterns and justifying their usage.

The authors [14] presented a list of patterns to align security and usability. They classified the patterns in two categories: data sanitization patterns and secure messaging patterns. Different patterns listed include, 'explicit user audit', 'complete delete', 'create keys when needed', among others.

The authors [15] proposed a set of user interface design patterns for designing information security feedback based on elements of user interface design. In addition, the authors created prototypes incorporating the user interface patterns in the security feedback to conduct a laboratory study. The results of the study showed that incorporating the elements of usability interface design patterns could help in making security feedbacks more meaningful and effective.

The authors [1] presented a methodology for deriving usable security patterns during the requirements engineering stage of system development. The methodology relies on handling the conflicts during the early stages of system development, and documenting the suitable trade-offs in the form of design patterns for reuse. What distinguishes the methodology presented in this paper from the work [1] is that, the methodology discussed in this paper focuses on identifying and documenting instances of good implementations by experienced developers in the form of design patterns. This is more of a bottom-up approach involving identification of the patterns from existing implementations. However, the work [1] focuses on the creation of new patterns based on system requirements where possible trade-offs are identified and managed. The managed trade-offs are documented as patterns for implementation in the specific project and re-use by other developers.

3 Methodology for identification of usable security patterns

In this section, the proposed three-staged methodology for identification of usable security patterns is presented. As stated earlier, the methodology relies on extracting or identifying new patterns from existing implementations, which are setting good practices in the industry (see Fig.1). This methodology provides uniform means to identify new patterns, and an opportunity for various stakeholders to contribute towards identification of the patterns and building the usable security patterns catalog. Particularly, from the industrial perspective, it can enable documenting new patterns from the implementations by experienced developers, thereby facilitating learning and training of new developers.

- *Stage-1*: The first stage involves the selection of a common usable security problem. The next step is to identify existing implementations addressing the problem. Since the implementations can have different ways of approaching the problem, therefore, to document the pattern it is imperative to fulfill the '*Rule of Three*'. The rule of three requires at least three instances of similar implementations before a pattern could be identified

Fig. 1: The Proposed Methodology for Identification of Usable Security Patterns.

and documented [17]. Once three instances of similar implementations for a particular problem are identified, the pattern is documented on a standard template. The details of usable security patterns' template are presented elsewhere [16].

- *Stage 2*: The second stage involves a review of the newly documented pattern by one or more experts in the field. This stage involves activities like selection of expert(s), gathering the reviews. Based on reviews the pattern is either accepted, which means it is ready to be finalized (*Stage 3*), or require modification, which means it goes back for modification to the experts who identified it during Stage 1, and in other cases it may be rejected, which means it is discarded. The review by experts besides validation of the pattern has two advantages, (1) ensuring compliance with the underlying standards and best practices concerning security and usability, and (2) ensuring that the solution proposed in the pattern manages the trade-off effectively. The expert(s) review concerning each pattern is recorded on a checklist (see Table 1).
- *Stage 3*: This stage comprises the following activities subject to the decision by the expert(s):
- — *Accept*: The accepted patterns are added to the catalog. The patterns in the catalog can be disseminated among the community of developers and designers. The ways of disseminating the patterns include online pages, pocketbook for developers, and whitepapers.

Table 1: Usable Security Pattern Review Checklist.

Usable Security Pattern Review Checklist									
Description: For the pattern under consideration fill in the columns below. Accessing ISO standards on security and usability is highly recommended to ensure compliance									
Name of the pattern	Relevant to Usable Security		Effectively Manages the trade-off			Compliance with the standards and best practices			Deci-sion	Additional Recommen-dations
/*Unique name of the pattern */	Y	N	Y	N	Y/N	Y	N	Y/N	Accept Modify Reject	Include recommenda-tions for improvement of pattern, proposal for modification, compliance to the standard, reasons for rejection etc.

— *Modify*: The documented pattern is referred back to the security and usability experts who identified it. The proposal for modification is considered and after necessary amendments, the pattern is subjected to review for the second time.

— *Reject*: The rejected patterns are discarded, however, the recommendations are considered for compliance in the other identified patterns with similar as well as the varying context of use.

4 Instantiating the methodology: A case study

To instantiate the methodology and identify a usable security pattern, a case study was conducted. The participants in the case study were the members of the software engineering laboratory at LUT University. Participation in the case study was voluntary. The objective behind the case study was to identify instances of good implementations by experienced developers, which set best practices in the field concerning the problem described below.

Case Description:
Mobile devices, particularly smartphones and tablets have become an inseparable companion for human users, as they have a wide range of features not just limited to communication. With such increased usage, we have seen an increase in cases of loss/theft of mobile devices, which ultimately leads to data breaches.

Consider a scenario when someone's smartphone is lost. Even if the lost smartphone it was locked, the victim would still be worried about ways in which an adversary could bypass the authentication mechanism and get access to the device. Access to the device could mean a breach of privacy and identity (if payment options were linked to the lost device). The authors [18] report a user study revealing that 50% of the respondents did not feel protected in case of loss/ theft of their smartphone. Based on the scenario, the following problem statement was formulated.

Problem Statement:
In case of loss/theft of the users' device, the data on the device increases the impact of loss in the form of breach of privacy. The user needs to have trust and protection feeling in order to use the device for personal/work purposes.

Stages of Case Study:

• **Stage 1**: This first stage involved the selection of the aforementioned usable security problem. The next step involved the application of the 'rule of three'. Once three similar implementations addressing the problem were identified, the pattern (see Fig. 2) was documented on the standardized template.

The usable security solution offered by the pattern for the problem identified above is to "Offer the user with remote deletion functionality hosted by the mobile vendor or mobile service provider". A secure service available online will work in this regard. It should offer the remote deletion by invoking the restore factory settings procedure, which would erase all the information from the device in case of loss/theft. This procedure not only ensures the security of data but also incorporates the human aspect of security, achieving human satisfaction and trust (elements of the global usability), to the security procedure.

Implementations of this pattern are available in the form of a "remote data deletion" functionality made available by smartphone manufacturers like Samsung and Apple for their users. Now the question arises who will use this pattern when this feature is already implemented? One scenario for application of this

- **Title**: Data Deletion Pattern
- **Classification**: Data Protection, Device protection
- **Prologue**: To reduce the impact of loss in case of loss/theft of a device carrying sensitive personal/business information.
- **Problem statement**: In case of loss/theft of the users' device, the data on the device increases the impact of loss in the form of breach of privacy. The user needs to have trust and protection feeling in order to use the device for personal/work purposes.
- **Context of Use**: Whenever there is loss/theft of device carrying user's data,
- which can lead to a breach of data.
- **Affected Sub Characteristics**: The subcharacteristics of usability and security being affected/involved when this pattern is applied.
  - Usability: satisfaction, trust, *efficiency in use*
  - Security: privacy, confidentiality, integrity
- **Solution**: Offer the User with remote deletion functionality hosted by the mobile vendor or mobile service provider via usable secure interface.
- **Discussion**: Even if the lost smartphone was locked, the human user can still be bothered by breach of their privacy and device's security. However, when the data has been removed from the device, the impact of loss can be minimized to an exclusively monetary loss.
- **Type of service**: Mobile devices or similar used in the same context.
- **Target Users**: *developers, designers*
- **Epilogue**: Improved data protection and reduced impact of loss.
- **Related Patterns**: Can be added later from the catalogue

Fig. 2: Data Deletion Pattern.

Usable Security Pattern Review Checklist					
Description: For the pattern under consideration fill in the columns below. Accessing ISO standards on security and usability is highly recommended to ensure none of the patterns violates the standards.					
Name of the pattern	Relevant to Usable Security	Effectively Manages the trade-off	Compliance with the standards and best practices	Decision	Additional Recommendations
Data Deletion Pattern	Y N — Y	Y N Y/N — Y	Y N Y/N — Y	□ Accept	1. An addition of Target users to the Pattern will be good such as developers, interface designers, or even end users. 2. The affected sub characteristics can also include *efficiency in use*

Fig. 3: Data Deletion Pattern Review Checklist.

pattern is in the case of other mobile devices including PDAs for inventory records, GPS, etc. Phone vendors who do not provide the remote deletion functionality can also apply this pattern.

- **Stage 2**: This stage involved the validation of the patterns by the experts. It is pertinent to state that the pattern presented in Fig. 2 is a validated version of the pattern after reviewing by the experts. The items in *italic* were added based on experts' recommendations. The pattern review checklist from one of the experts is presented in Fig. 3.
- **Stage 3**: Involved addition of this pattern to the catalog we are maintaining for dissemination and re-use by other developers.

5 Conclusion

Inter-dependencies and trade-offs between security and usability need to be accessed in a strategic manner. Efforts need to be put in to develop a framework within the scope of the software development life cycle (SDLC) for eliciting the conflicts between security and usability while identifying suitable trade-offs between the two. Use of patterns can be influential in regards to documenting the outcomes of employing such frameworks. Patterns can assist also assist in improved communication between various segments working on the project more precisely the security and usability teams.

Additionally, the use of patterns does not only assist the developers within the organizational setting but also free-lancers in assessing the usability of their security options and vice versa. Furthermore, one pattern only solves one problem in a particular context of usage; therefore, an entire catalog of usable security patterns is required just like user interface patterns catalog. Development of such catalog is a timeconsuming process and requires community-level efforts, therefore, we intend to present our proposal of using patterns and the methodology for identifying patterns to participants of the Human-Centered Software Engineering and HCI community for their feedback and participation in the development of the usable security patterns catalog.

Acknowledgment

The first author wishes to thank Professor Ahmed Seffah for his feedback during the initial phases of this research.

References

1. Naqvi, B., Seffah, A.: A Methodology for Aligning Usability and Security in Systems and Services. In: 2018 third International Conference on Information Systems Engineering, pp. 61–66 (2018).
2. Garfinkel, S., Lipford, H.R.: Usable Security History, Themes and Challenges. Morgan and Claypool, USA (2014).
3. Whitten, A., Tygar, J.D.: Usability of security: A case study. School of Computing Science, Carnegie Mellon University. Rep. Technical Report CMU-CS-98-155 (1998).
4. Caputo, D.D. et al.: Barriers to Usable Security? Three Organizational Case Studies. IEEE Security and Privacy, pp. 22–32. (2016).
5. Garg, H., Choudhury, T., Kumar, P., Sabitha, S.: Comparison between significance of usability and security in HCI. In: 2017 3rd International Conference on Computational Intelligence Communication Technology (CICT). pp. 1–4 (2017).
6. Kulyk, O., Neumann, S., Budurushi, J., Volkamer, M.: Nothing Comes for Free: How Much Usability Can You Sacrifice for Security? IEEE Secur. Priv. 15, 24–29 (2017).
7. Sasse, M.A., Smith, M., Herley, C., Lipford, H., Vaniea, K.: Debunking Security–Usability Tradeoff Myths, pp. 33–39 (2016).
8. Cranor, L.F., Buchler, N.: Better Together: Usability and Security Go Hand in Hand. IEEE Secur. Priv. 12, 89–93 (2014).
9. Cranor, L., Garfinkel, S.: Security and Usability. O'Reilly Media, Inc (2005).
10. Alexander, C., Ishikawa, S., and Silverstein, M.,: A pattern Language. Oxford University Press (1977).

11. Tidwell, J.: Designing Interfaces. O'Reilly Media, Inc. (2005).
12. Welie: Patterns in Interaction Design. Available at http://www.welie.com/patterns/
13. Ferreira,A., Rusu, C., Roncagliolo, S.: Usability and Security Patterns, In: Second International Conference on Advances in Computer-Human Interaction, pp. 301–305, (2009).
14. Cranor, L., Garfinkel, S.: Patterns for Aligning Security and Usability, Symposium on Usable Privacy and Security (SOUPS), Poster Presentation (2005).
15. Munoz-Arega, J. et al.: A methodology for designing information security feedback based on user interact patterns. Advances in Engineering Software 40(2009), 1231–1241 (2009).
16. Naqvi, B., Seffah, A.: Interdependencies, Conflicts and Trade-offs between Security and Usability: Why and how should we Engineer Them?. ACCEPTED for Publication In: 21st International Conference on Human-Computer Interaction (HCII), (2019).
17. Mor, Y., Winters, N., Warburton, S.: Participatory Patterns Workshops Resource Kit. Version 2.1. Available at: https://hal.archives-ouvertes.fr/hal-00593108/document. (2010)
18. Sophos: Security Threat Report. Available at: http://www.sophos.com/sophos/docs/eng/papers/sophos-security-threat-report-jan-2010-wpna.pdf. (2010)
19. Kirlappos I., Sasse M.A.: What Usable Security Really Means: Trusting and Engaging Users. In: Tryfonas T., Askoxylakis I. (eds) Human Aspects of Information Security, Privacy, and Trust. HAS, pp. 69–78 (2014).

Towards Intelligent User Interfaces to Prevent Phishing Attacks

Joseph Aneke, Carmelo Ardito and Giuseppe Desolda

Università degli Studi di Bari Aldo Moro Via Orabona,
4 – 70125 – Bari, Italy
joseph.aneke@uniba.it, carmelo.ardito@uniba.it, giuseppe.desolda@uniba.it

Abstract

Phishing is a type of fraud designed to steal important sensitive information such as credit card numbers, passwords and bank account data. The fraudulent website is graphically very similar to the original one and invites the users to enter some personal information then used to steal the identity of the person who takes the scam. Other times, the website injects malicious code in the user's computer. Despite the notable advances made in the last years by the active warning messages for phishing, this attack remains one of the most effective. In this paper we propose an intelligent warning message mechanism, that might limit the effectiveness of phishing attacks and that might increase the user awareness about related risks. It implements an intelligent behavior that, besides warning the users that a phishing attack is occurring, explains why the specific suspect site can be fraudulent.

Keywords

Usable Security · Intelligent User Interfaces · Cybersecurity.

How to cite this book chapter:
Aneke, J., Ardito, C. and Desolda, G. 2020. Towards Intelligent User Interfaces to Prevent Phishing Attacks. In: Loizides, F., Winckler, M., Chatterjee, U., Abdelnour-Nocera, J. and Parmaxi, A. (eds.) *Human Computer Interaction and Emerging Technologies: Adjunct Proceedings from the INTERACT 2019 Workshops.* Pp. 279–288. Cardiff: Cardiff University Press. DOI: https://doi.org/10.18573/book3.ak. License: CC-BY 4.0.

1 Introduction

Phishing is a fraudulent practice that includes an attempt by an attacker to acquire sensitive information such as usernames, passwords and credit card details by masquerading as a dependable entity in an electronic communication. A common phishing attack is (for a phisher) to obtain a victim's authentication information corresponding to one website that is mimicked by the attacker and then use this at another site. This is a successful attack given that many users reuse passwords – whether in verbatim or with only slight changes. This attack is typically carried out by e-mail or instant messaging, and often directs users to enter details at a fake website [1]. A common example is "we need you to confirm your account details or we must shut your account down". The reason why an individual falls prey to this type of trap is that the message, which appears as the victim expects, and therefore legitimate, directs the user to visit fake webpages whose look and feel is similar or identical to the legitimate one. This phishing modality is also known as context-aware attack and is becoming increasingly common. Fig. 1 shows an example of a phishing attack sent to a user by email. The email appears genuine from a trusted sender, i.e. "uniba.it" which is the email service provider of the user. However, visualizing the details of the sender's identity reveals that it was masquerading to get the user to fill a form.

The effectiveness of phishing techniques, and more in general of cyberattacks, is not only related to the obsolescence of software and hardware. Federal Computer Week reports that almost 59% of security incidents that involve human errors are the result of simple mistakes as opposed to intentional malicious actions [2]. Hosteler found that human error is one of the first cause of cyberattacks (37%) [3]. Furthermore, the simplest and fastest way to start an attack is by means of phishing and social engineering attacks, where 91% of all cyberattacks starts with some kind of phishing email that manipulates users to provide sensitive information via various methods of social engineering [4].

Because of the risks associated with cyberattacks, it is crucial for Internet users to be aware of when they are being attacked and to be successfully

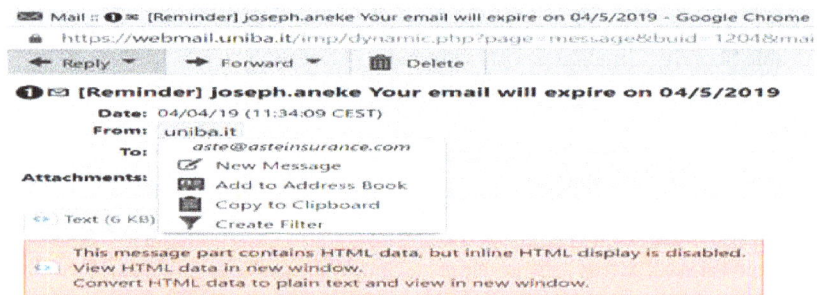

Fig. 1: Example of phishing attack sent by email.

informed on how to combat them. The recent demography results by Anti-Phishing Working Group 4th quarter report shows that around 45,794 phishing reports have been chronicled [1]. There is no single way that can prevent all types of phishing. But different methods applied at different stages of a phishing attack can abort the attempt and properly applied technology can significantly reduce the risk of identity theft [5]. Different approaches are already proposed to automatically detect phishing websites [6–8]. These methods and algorithms determine the likelihood that a website can be suspect but without absolute certainty. When the resulting likelihood exceeds a critical threshold, typically the users are informed about the potential risk of phishing attacks. This is done through a visual warning message that should help users in deciding to access or not the suspect website. Despite the significant advances of current warning messages, this attack still remain very effective since the users often is not able to take the right decision.

There is a direct need for us to design such a remedy which can address the above problem and stand out from the traditional warning messages available. In this paper, we report on an ongoing work about an intelligent warning message that might limit the effectiveness of phishing attacks and that might increase the user awareness about the related risks. The proposed solution implements an intelligent behavior that explains why the specific suspect site can be fraudulent. It is well-known that explaining the reasons about a fact helps the user being aware of the danger and taking more conscious and adequate decisions [9].

2 Literature Review

Successful security depends on systems, technology and people (including users) collaborating to identify threats, weaknesses, and solutions. However, many initiatives today focus on systems and technology, without addressing well-known user-related issues. In fact, users have been identified as one of the major security weaknesses in today's technologies, as they may be unaware that their behavior while interacting with a system may have security consequences. The user interface is where the human users interact with the computer systems. It is where the user's intention transforms into the system operation. It is where the semantic gap arises [10]. And this is the aspect that needs more attention to further limit the effectiveness of cyberattacks.

One typical anti-phishing approach is to use visual indicators, for example an informative toolbar, to differentiate legitimate messages from phishing messages [11]. This approach tries to bridge the semantic gap by unveiling to human users the system model and expects them to make a wise decision under phishing attacks. User studies in [12] show that the tested anti-phishing toolbars fail to effectively prevent high quality phishing attacks. Many subjects failed to constantly pay attention to the toolbar's messages; others disregarded the warnings shown in the toolbar if the web page content looked legitimate. The studies also found that many subjects did not understand phishing attacks or realize how sophisticated such attacks can be.

In [13], the authors sought to determine if user's education was a possible solution to prevent phishing attacks. They explored the impact of both specific users' characteristics (age, gender, education, knowledge about phishing) and of their Internet usage habits on their ability to correctly identify e-mail messages. Quantitative data was collected by showing to participants e-mail messages and quizzing their ability to correctly categorize them. The results show the variables listed above did influence the participant's ability to correctly identify email messages.

A study to determine the impact that communicating to users different security policies has on mitigating phishing attacks is discussed in [8]. The research results reveal that a security policy that contains an explanation of the impact of an attack or a statement indicating an evaluation for non-compliance or a statement from a direct authority provides no significant impact on mitigating phishing attacks [14]. The use of online games to teach users good habits to help them avoid phishing attacks is investigated in [15]. The authors explore the relationship between demographics and phishing susceptibilities, and the effectiveness of several anti-phishing educational materials. Results suggest that women are more susceptible to phishing than men and participants between the ages of 18 and 25 are more likely to be a victim of a phishing attack than other age groups.

A new anti-phishing approach which uses training intervention for phishing web sites detection is discussed in [16]. The results of this work show that technical ability has minimal effect whereas phishing knowledge has a positive effect on phishing web site detection. A system called PhishGuru incorporating an embedded training methodology and learning science principles is proposed in [17]. Author evaluates the proposed methodology through laboratory and field studies. Results show that people trained with the proposed system retain knowledge even after 28 days. A major drawback is that the system will need to be trained and updated regularly. Robert W et al [18] found that web browser warnings should help protect people from malware, phishing, and network attacks. Adhering to these warnings keeps people safer online. They further demonstrated that recent improvements in warning designs have raised adherence rates, but they could still be higher. And prior work suggests many people still do not understand them. Thus, two challenges remain: increasing both comprehension and adherence rates. The authors in [18] suggested that further improvements to warnings will require solving a range of smaller contextual misunderstandings.

Most phishing sites are simply copies of real sites with the above mentioned feature slightly distorted or in some cases masqueraded [19]. This property of phishing sites has made them difficult for humans to detect, but fortunately, easier for computers. However, the attacker community has proved itself able to quickly adapt to anti-phishing measures mainly warning messages. Different warning messages have been already evaluated during controlled experiments [18, 20]. Besides evaluating the efficacy of different solutions, these experiments provided useful indications on how to design and evaluate phishing warning messages. Despite the notable advances made in the last years by the active warning messages for phishing [18, 20], this attack remains one the most effective. Indeed, algorithms for detecting phishing attacks are only able to determine the likelihood with which a website can be suspect but without absolute certainty. When the likelihood exceeds a critical threshold the warning messages alert the users about a possible risk and the users have to decide to access or not the website. However, current warning messages have large room for improvement, as shown by the high success rate of phishing attacks reported in [21]. One of the first problems is the clickthrough effect [22]: the users tend to skip these alerts because they appear always in the same way, thus pushing most users in neglecting these messages. The second problem is the wrong design of the warning messages in term of colors, words, interaction, as underlined by [18, 20]. Lastly, the users are not experts in cybersecurity, they do not know what a phishing attack is and what are the risks they are exposed to [18].

In order to overcome these limitations, in the following section we propose an intelligent warning message mechanism that might limit the effectiveness of phishing attacks and that might increase the user awareness about related risks. It implements an intelligent behavior that, besides warning the users that a phishing attack is occurring, explains why the specific suspect site can be fraudulent.

3 A Polymorphic User Interface to Warn Users about Phishing Attacks

An example of polymorphic user interface to warn users about phishing attacks is reported in Fig. 2. In addition to addressing the design guidelines and lesson learned proposed in [18, 20], this prototype shows three panels that explain the reasons why the target website can be a fake. In this example, the first panel specifies that the URL of the target website (www.paypaI.com) looks similar to the original one but the l has been replaced by capital I, thus confusing the users. The second panel reports that the suspect website was created three weeks ago, an age typical of phishing websites. The last box reports information about the HTTPS certificate of the suspect website, explaining that even if the users see safe navigation in the browser toolbar, with a self-signed certificate they are not guaranteed that the site behavior is legitimate.

It is worth remarking that the three panels show different information according to the suspect website, thus different reasons would be reported with different phishing websites. Thank to this intelligent warning message, we address three important goals, i.e.:

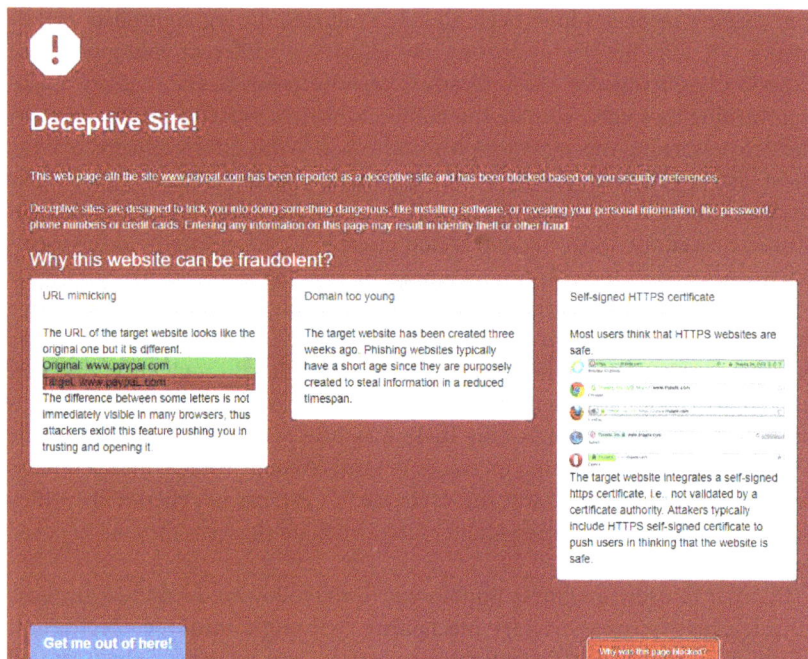

Fig. 2: A prototype of intelligent warning message for phishing attacks.

1. *Prevent user habituation*: a polymorphic message decreases the click-through effect caused by the user habituation [22];
2. *Provide explanation about the attack*: useful information about the causes of the phishing attacks support the users in deciding if the website is (or not) a phishing attack;
3. *Train the users on cyberattacks and related risks*: a long-term training of the users on phishing attacks is performed since they understand the reasons for this attack.

In our work we are not interested to classify phishing websites [6–8]. We start from the assumption that the browser can detect the phishing website through its internal algorithm, or that we use an API to detect malicious sites.[1] Regardless of which of the two solutions we adopt, when a phishing website is detected, instead of displaying the traditional warning messages implemented in the browser, we show the intelligent UI proposed in this paper (see Fig. 2).

To provide users with information that explain the reasons of the phishing attacks, our approach consists of two main steps, i.e., 1) the computation of a set of indicators that can reveal phishing websites and 2) the use of machine learning approaches to select the most important indicators. The three most

---

[1] https://safebrowsing.google.com.

important indicators will be shown and explained to the user, as shown in the example above.

According to our goal and a literature review [6–8], we are considering indicators for the suspect web sites like:

- *URL*: phishing sites typically have URLs containing more than 2/3 number of digits or "-". In addition, they often try to mimic the original URL changing character that looks similar, for example, "l" with "I";
- *Server location*: phishing websites are often hosted by a web server located in countries where there are not strict laws against cyberattacks;
- *Alexa or search engine rank*: phishing website typically appear after the first 1 million Alexa top results, or in the last positions of search engines like Google Search;
- *Timelife*: this cyber-attack is usually concentrated in a limited time span, thus the suspect website is typically created few days/weeks before the attack;
- *Top level domain*: attackers typically use free domains to host phishing web sites; one of the most popular is freenom.com, thus domains like ".cf", ".gq", ".ml", ".tk" and ".ga" are common among phishing web sites;
- *Name length*: Attackers may create domains using a specific template, such as random strings of a given length;
- *Archived domain*: a domain archived on the "Wayback Machine" is more likely to be legitimately owned, and vice versa;
- *Self-signed https certificate*: the suspect websites often integrate a self-signed https certificate, i.e., not validated by a certification authority. Including this certificate, attackers confuse users who see safe navigation in the browser toolbar, but without any guarantee about the web site behaviour.

We defined different metrics to calculate each indicator for the suspect website. For example, Alexa rank can be obtained through its API; the Wayback Machine APIs are used to get information about website archiving; SSL certificate is inspected to see if a trustable certification authority signed it. Those indicators, resulting in a numeric value, are normalized in a 0–1 interval using a min-max function, with min and max values obtained calculating each indicator on all the phishing websites available in the *PhishTank* database and selecting for each indicator the min and max value.

After the computation of the indicators, we use a decision tree model to select the most important indicators. In particular, we adopted the C4.5 algorithm to generate our decision tree. This algorithm was developed by Ross Quinlan [23] and it is an extension of Quinlan's earlier ID3 algorithm. The decision trees generated by C4.5 can be used for classification, and in our case to classify the suspect website. However, we are not interested to understand if it is a phishing site, since we already know it. We only exploit this tree to select those three nodes that positively contribute in determining it as phishing. In other words, we use it to filter the indicators that are more influential in the classification process.

After the selection of the three most important indicators, we dynamically create three panels that are visualized in the warning message and properly adapted if necessary. For example, if a panel has to report the information on the URL, it is customized with the URL of the suspect website and the URL of the Website that is mimicked.

4 Conclusion

In this paper, we discussed the current trend of phishing attack from an HCI perspective. We aimed at revealing to the user some schema phishers use. We agree with [18] that users need to understand and use systems warnings correctly in order to guarantee the efficacy of any security strategy that has been implemented. An intelligent user interface is presented aimed at training users, improving the effectiveness of warning messages and prevent habitation.

Acknowledgments

This work is partially supported by the Italian Ministry of University and Research (MIUR) under grant PRIN 2017 "EMPATHY: EMpowering People in deAling with internet of THings ecosYstems".

References

1. APWG Anti Phishing Working Group: Phishing Attack Trends Report – 4Q 2018 (2018). Available at: http://docs.apwg.org/reports/apwg_trends _report_q4_2018.pdf
2. Thales: Insider Threat Report. Available at: https://go.thalessecurity.com /ESG-Insider-Threat-WP.html
3. BakerHostetler: Is Your Organization Compromise Ready? 2016 Data Security Incident Response Report (2016). Available at: https://www .bakerlaw.com/files/uploads/Documents/Privacy/2016-Data-Security -Incident-Response-Report.pdf
4. Gupta, B.B., Tewari, A., Jain, A.K., Agrawal, D.P.: Fighting against phishing attacks: state of the art and future challenges. Neural Computing and Applications 28(12), pp. 3629–3654 (2017)
5. Emigh, A.: Online identity theft: Phishing technology, chokepoints and countermeasures. ITTC Report on Online Identity Theft Technology and Counter measures (2014). Available at: http://www.anti-phishing.org /Phishingdhs-report.pdf
6. Varshney, G., Misra, M., Atrey, P.K.: A survey and classification of web phishing detection schemes. Security and Communication Networks 9(18), pp. 6266–6284 (2016)

7. Abu-Nimeh, S., Nappa, D., Wang, X., Nair, S.: A comparison of machine learning techniques for phishing detection. In: Anti-phishing working groups 2nd annual eCrime researchers summit (eCrime '07). pp. 60–69. ACM, New York, NY, USA (2007)

8. Almomani, A., Gupta, B.B., Atawneh, S., Meulenberg, A., Almomani, E.: A Survey of Phishing Email Filtering Techniques. IEEE Communications Surveys & Tutorials 15(4), pp. 2070–2090 (2013)

9. Biran, O., Cotton, C.: Explanation and justification in machine learning: A survey. In: IJCAI-17 workshop on explainable AI (XAI '17), (2017)

10. Wu, M.: Fighting phishing at the user interface. Massachusetts Institute of Technology (2006)

11. Department of Justice Federal Bureau of Investigation: FBI Says Web Spoofing Scams Are a Growing Problem (2003). Available at: http://www .fbi.gov/pressrel/pressrel03/spoofing072103.htm

12. Wu, M., Miller, R.C., Garfinkel, S.L.: Do security toolbars actually prevent phishing attacks? In: ACM SIGCHI Conference on Human Factors in Computing Systems (CHI '06). pp. 601–610. ACM, New York, NY, USA (2006)

13. Martin, T.D.: Phishing for Answers: Exploring the Factors that Influence a Participant's Ability to Correctly Identify Email. Capella University, Minneapolis, MN (2008)

14. McNealy, J.E.: Angling for Phishers: Legislative Responses to Deceptive E-Mail. Communication Law & Policy 13(2), pp. 275–300 (2008)

15. Sheng, S., Holbrook, M., Kumaraguru, P., Cranor, L.F., Downs, J.: Who falls for phish?: a demographic analysis of phishing susceptibility and effectiveness of interventions. In: ACM SIGCHI Conference on Human Factors in Computing Systems (CHI '19). pp. 373–382. ACM, New York, NY, USA (2010)

16. Kumaraguru, P., Cranshaw, J., Acquisti, A., Cranor, L., Hong, J., Blair, M.A., Pham, T.: School of phish: a real-world evaluation of anti-phishing training. In: Symposium on Usable Privacy and Security (SOUPS '09). pp. 1–12. ACM, New York, NY, USA (2009)

17. Kumaraguru, P., Sheng, S., Acquisti, A., Cranor, L.F., Hong, J.: Teaching Johnny not to fall for phish. ACM Trans. Internet Technol. 10(2), pp. 1–31 (2010)

18. Reeder, R.W., Felt, A.P., Consolvo, S., Malkin, N., Thompson, C., Egelman, S.: An Experience Sampling Study of User Reactions to Browser Warnings in the Field. In: ACM SIGCHI Conference on Human Factors in Computing Systems (CHI '18). pp. 1–13. ACM, New York, NY, USA (2018)

19. Afroz, S., Greenstadt, R.: PhishZoo: Detecting Phishing Websites by Looking at Them. In: IEEE International Conference on Semantic Computing (ICSC '11). pp. 368–375, (2011)

20. Egelman, S., Cranor, L.F., Hong, J.: You've been warned: an empirical study of the effectiveness of web browser phishing warnings. In: ACM

SIGCHI Conference on Human Factors in Computing Systems (CHI '08), Florence, Italy. pp. 1065–1074. ACM, New York, NY, USA (2008)

21. IBM: IBM X-Force Threat Intelligence Index 2018. Available at: https:// microstrat.com/sites/default/files/security-ibm-security-solutions-wg -research-report-77014377usen-20180329.pdf

22. Felt, A.P., Ainslie, A., Reeder, R.W., Consolvo, S., Thyagaraja, S., Bettes, A., Harris, H., Grimes, J.: Improving SSL Warnings: Comprehension and Adherence. In: ACM Conference on Human Factors in Computing Systems (CHI '15). pp. 2893–2902. ACM, New York, NY, USA (2015)

23. Quinlan, J.R.: C4.5: programs for machine learning. Morgan Kaufmann Publishers Inc. (1993)

Selecting the Best Agile Team for Developing a Web Service

Marta Kristin Larusdottir and Marcel Kyas

Reykjavik University, Menntavegur 1, 102 Reykjavik, Iceland

marta@ru.is; marcel@ru.is

Abstract

Selecting a good agile software development team to develop a particular software is a complex issue for public authorities. This selection is often based on the estimated total cost of the project in an official request for proposals. In this paper we describe an alternative approach where three performance factors and the estimated cost were evaluated and weighted to find the best agile team for the project. The performance factors included: team collaboration, user experience focus, user stories delivery and the quality of the code. Teams that fulfilled predefined technical requirements were invited to take part in workshops. We describe the process of evaluating the three performance factors during and after the workshops and the results of the evaluations. The team that focused on one user story during the workshop and emphasised user experience, accessibility and security issues got the highest rating and were selected for the project.

Keywords

User experience · Accessibility · Security · Agile development · Team collaboration

How to cite this book chapter:

Larusdottir, M.K. and Kyas, M. 2020. Selecting the Best Agile Team for Developing a Web Service. In: Loizides, F., Winckler, M., Chatterjee, U., Abdelnour-Nocera, J. and Parmaxi, A. (eds.) *Human Computer Interaction and Emerging Technologies: Adjunct Proceedings from the INTERACT 2019 Workshops*. Pp. 289–302. Cardiff: Cardiff University Press. DOI: https://doi.org/10.18573/book3.al. License: CC-BY 4.0.

1 Introduction

When public authorities want to make new software systems to be used by citizens and employees for solving various tasks they often negotiate with software companies for developing the software. The selection of the software company for making the software needs to be free and open for competition according to European Union legistration, so the public authorities must issue a public request for proposal (RTF). Typically the RTF contains two sections: (1) the requirements and needs for the system to be developed, and (2) the selection criteria [12]. Often the selection criteria is based on the cost solely, so the software companies estimate the hours needed to be able to develop the software fulfilling the requirements and needs stated. The company with the lowest prize gets the job [12]. In a case study of four software companies in Denmark developing for public authorities, the software companies focused on what the public authorities are willing to pay for and what they wanted to citizens to be able to do [2]. So the software companies did not include quality factors like user experience (UX) or security issues, in their proposal, if it was not requested in the RFT.

In some cases the selection criteria is based on both the prize and quality factors, so the price could weight 60% and the quality criteria 40% for example [12]. Requirements for quality factors, like user experience (UX) and security, can be included in the requirement section of the RTF defining the level of the UX and security in the developed system. The requirements can also be included in the selection criteria, defining how much weight in the selection process the UX and security factors have [22]. Typically, the usage of particular methods like user testing and the frequency of using those methods would be stated in the selection criteria. Another option would be that the public authority may state performance criterias for the users, for example that the users will be able to accomplish a particular task within a particular time limit [22]. One possibility is to base the selection criteria on the competences of the software team getting the job, but that is not frequently done. The selection criteria should state the wanted knowledge, skills and competences of the team, in that case. Possibly, the criteria could also include the focus on quality aspects that the team should have. In any case, the objective of the process is to find the best team for the job according the predefined criteria and thereby get the best outcome for the money spent.

There are many aspects that affect an project outcome. A study of four similar software teams developing software to fit the same needs, described 1 to 6 variation in the prizes of the outcome [21]. The teams were similar in technical competences. The quality of the outcome was also evaluated and the team with the next lowest price scored best on the three quality aspects in the study, usability, maintainability and reliability. That team had one project manager, one developer and one interaction designer in the team, but the other teams had two developers and one project manager. The best team used intermediate process models for the development, with analysis and design in the first four weeks, then implementation from week 4 to 10 and testing in the last six weeks of the project [21].

In this paper we describe an approach, where the performance of five software teams was evaluated as a part of the selection criteria for selecting the best agile team for making a web service. The performance factors included: team collaboration, user experience, user stories delivered and quality of code including accessability and security. The performance factors were evaluated during and after a one day workshop with the team, where the teams were observed and their deliverables reviewed. The performance factors weighted 70% and the cost 30% in the selection criteria for the best agile team.

2 Related Work on the Performance Factors

In this section we briefly describe the related literature on the performance factors evaluated in this study. First we give a brief overview of agile development and team collaboration, we explain the format and usage of user stories and then we briefly describe the concept of user experience and code quality.

2.1 Agile Development and Team Collaboration

The agile process Scrum [20] has gained popularity in the software industry in recent years. According to an international survey, Scrum was the most popular process of the agile processes with more than 50% of the IT professionals surveyed were using it [23].

A similar trend is seen in the software industry in Iceland, but the lean process Kanban [17] has also been gaining popularity lately [15].

A characteristic of Scrum is the observation that small, cross-functional teams historically produce the best results. Scrum is based on a rugby metaphor in which the team's contribution is more important than each individual contribution. Scrum teams typically consists of people with three major roles: 1) a Scrum Master that acts as project manager/buffer to the outside world; 2) a Product Owner that represents stakeholders, and 3) a team of developers (less than 10). One of the twelve principles behind the agile manifesto is: "The most efficient and effective method of conveying information to and within a development team is face-to-face conversation" [16]. In agile development the teams should collaborate openly and all the team is responsible for delivering a potentially shippable product after each sprint.

Some of the more important artifacts and ceremonies with-in Scrum is the Sprint, which defines 15–30 days ite-ra-ti-on, the Product backlog of requirements described by user stories and managed by the Product Owner and the Daily Scrum meeting, which is the daily meeting for the team and the Scrum Master to plan the work of the day and report what was done the day before [20].

2.2 User Stories

In Scrum, the user requirements are usually described by user stories. The most common format for describing a user story is: "As a [user role], I want to [do some task] to [achieve a goal]" [4]. The user stories are used to describe the requirements for the whole system being developed kept in the Product Backlog. During the Sprint planning meeting, the team, the Scrum Master and the Product Owner select the user stories that the team will work on during the next sprint in accordance to how many user stories it is possible to implement during the time of a sprint. The Product Owner describes the priorities of the user stories, so the most important user stories will be selected for the particular sprint according to the Product Owners criterias. During the daily Scrum meeting, the team members report what user stories and tasks they will be working on during the day and what the finished they day before.

2.3 User Experience

UX has gained momentum in computer science and is defined in the ISO 9241-210 in the following way [10]: "Person's perceptions and responses resulting from the use and/ or anticipated use of a product, system or service". Researchers agree that UX is a complex concept, including aspects like fun, pleasure, beauty and personal growth. An experience is subjective, holistic, situated, dynamic, and worthwhile [8]. A recent survey on what practitioner's think is included in the term UX shows that respondents agreed that user-related factors, contextual factors and temporal dynamics of UX are all important factors for defining the term UX [14]. The temporal dynamic of UX also reached consensus amongst the respondents.

Many methods have been suggested for active participation of users in the software development process with the aim of developing software with good user experience. Some of the methods for focusing on either the expected UX or the UX after users have used a particular system, including interviews with users, surveys, observations and user testing [19]. IT professionals rated formal user testing as the most useful method for active participation of users in their software development for understanding the UX of the developed system [11].

2.4 Quality of Code Including Security and Accessibility

Code quality is generally hard to define objectively. Desirable characteristics include reliability, performance efficiency, security, and maintainability [5]. Metrics to assess code quality usually include volume of code, redundancy, unit size, complexity, unit interface size, and coupling [1, 9]. The process of measuring properties like complexity and the decision on what unit size is acceptable depend on the context and is often subjective.

Accessibility of web application is typically realised by conforming to the WCAG 2.0 recommendation [3]. Following these recommendations allows a web page to be interpreted and processed by accessibility software. For example, by a.o. preferring relative font sizes over absolute ones allows the web page to be rendered in any font size and making it accessible to users with visual impairments. The WCAG is seen as an important part of making web pages accessible [13].

Indeed, for any web application and any mobile application used by the public sector in the European Economic Area must conform to the WCAG [6].

3 The Case – The Financial Support RTF

Reykjavik city has decided to make the digital services easy to use for all the citizens of Reykjavik. The motivation came from two new employees, that wanted to change the web services to being more user centred. One of the first projects for this attempt had the objective to make the application for financial support more usable to citizens, but to focus also on security and reliability of the code. An official request for proposals was made to select "the best" team for taking part in developing a web service in collaboration with IT professionals at Reykjavik city. One of the constraints was that the team had to follow an agile development process similar to Scrum, by using user stories, conducting daily Scrum meetings and focus on the values of agile team work and collaboration.

The teams that submitted a proposal were evaluated according minimal technical requirements and their performance and delivery after a one day workshop. There were five steps in the selection process: a) First the team submitted a proposal, b) The applying teams were evaluated according to the minimum technical requirements, c) the teams fulfilling the technical requirements were evaluated according to performance criteria, d) the hourly prices of each team member were evaluated and e) the final selection of a team was decided. In this section we describe the minimal technical requirements for the teams and the three performance factors evaluated during and after the one day workshops.

3.1 The Minimal Technical Requirements

The minimal technical requirements were described in the request for proposals document. The teams had to provide at least 5 team members, whereof at least:

a) 2 members had to be skilled backend programmers, which had experience in writing code that was tested for security. For confirming these skills, the team members were asked to deliver a list of projects were they had worked on security issues for the system. They also had to list at least 5 software projects that they had been involved in. They had to be experienced in automated testing and have knowledge of.NET programming.

b) 1 member had to be a user interface programmer. This persons had to have the experience of making apps or web services that fulfilled the accessibility standard, European Norm EN 301 549 V1.1.2 [7] that includes the WCAG 2.0 Level A and Level AA and are scalable for all major smart equipment and computers. This person had to describe his/her involvement in five software development projects.

c) 1 member had to be interaction designer or a UX specialist. This member had to have taken part in developing at least 5 software systems, (apps or web services), with at least 100 users each. They should describe their experience of user centred design with direct contact with users and what methods they had used to integrate user in the development.

d) 1 member should had to be an agile coach or a Scrum Master. To fulfill this, the person had to have led at least one team with at least three members with at least 10 two week sprints. This member should describe his experience regarding coaching team members.

3.2 The Workshop Organisation

Five teams fulfilled the above minimum technical requirements. Each of them were invited for a one day performance workshop. The workshops took place at an office at the IT department of Reykjavik city in October and November 2018.

The teams got four user stories to as possible tasks to work on during the workshop. The user stories were the following:

1. As a citizen of Reykjavik that has impaired intellectual ability I want to be able to apply for financial assistance via web/mobile so that I can apply in an simple and easy-to-understand manner.

2. As a employee of Reykjavik city with little tech know-how I want to be able to see all applications in a "employee interface" so that I have a good overview of all applications that have been sent.

3. As a Reykjavík city employee which is colorblind I want to be able to send the result of the application process to the applicant so that the applicant can know as soon as possible if the applicant is eligible for financial assistance.

4. As a audit authority for financial assistance I want to be able to see who has viewed applications so that I can perform my audit responsibility.

The workshops were organised by a project manager at Reykjavik city. The schedule was the following:

1. The team got an one hour introduction to the schedule of the day and to the work environment at Reykjavik city, the services and systems, the organisation and work practices. Also the user stories were introduced briefly.

2. The teams were asked to do a daily Scrum meeting for 15 minutes for selecting the tasks for the day and to organise the day for 15 minutes. The experts focusing on team collaboration and UX focus observed this part of the workshops.
3. The teams worked on developing their deliverables during the day.
4. The last 45 minutes of the day, the teams were asked to present to all the involved experts and the organising team, their work practices and their deliverables. The teams could plan these 45 minutes as they preferred. They had been introduced to the performance factors that were being evaluated, so some of the teams deliberately organised the presentation according to these factors.

3.3 The Performance Factors Evaluated During and After the Workshops

The workshops had the goal of evaluating the following three performance factors:

1. The teams collaboration and user experience (UX) focus
2. Their delivery of user stories
3. The quality of the code delivered

An evaluation scheme was conducted for each of the three factors. Four external experts were asked to conduct the evaluation. The team collaboration and UX focus contained four subfactors and in total these gave the maximum of 25 points. These were evaluated by two external experts by observing the teams twice during the one day workshop. The delivery of user stories and the quality of the code delivered were evaluated after the workshop. Two external experts in security issues and performance were asked to review the code delivered. The user stories delivered gave maximum 10 points and the quality of the code 35 points. In total these three performance factors added up to 70 points. The hourly price for the team members could give a maximum of 30 points. Experts at Reykjavik city reviewed the hourly prizes. The agile team could get 100 points in total, if they got the maximum points for all the three performance factors and the hourly prizing. We will describe the process of the data gathering for evaluating the three performance factors resulting from the workshops in the next section.

4 Data Gathering for Evaluating the Performance Factors

In the following we will describe the process of gathering data to be able to evaluate the team collaboration, the user stories delivered and the quality of the code.

4.1 Data Gathering for Evaluating the Team Collaboration and UX Focus

Two experts in team collaboration and UX focus were asked to evaluated this performance factor. Four subfactors were defined:

1. How well did the team perform at the daily meeting (max 4 points) ?
2. How problem solving oriented was the team (max 8 points)?
3. How much did the team emphases UX (user experience) (max 8 points)?
4. How well did the team present their work at the end of the workshop (max 5 points)?

The two experts observed the teams during an half an hour session in the morning, when the teams had a daily Scrum meeting and when selecting tasks for the day. The experts took notes and evaluated the first subfactor. They tried to keep silent and not ask questions so the five workshops would be as similar as possible.

Forty five minutes were used as the last part of the workshop for presenting the work practices that the team used during the day and the deliverables. The two experts observed the presentation and took notes. The experts only asked, if there were issues, which the experts were about to evaluate, that were not mentioned during the presentation, to have better information on all the performance factors.

There was a short evaluation meeting with all the experts involved and the organising team at Reykjavik city right after each workshop. The goal was to discuss the first impression of the workshop of that day. Each of the experts rated the teams within 48 hours on the four subfactors and noted an argument for each of the ratings. The two experts met shortly after that evaluation and discussed their individual ratings and made a consolidated rating for the team that was sent to the project manager of the workshops. When all the teams had been evaluated the two experts met again to make the final comparison of all the rating and made the final version of the ratings that was sent to the project manager of the workshops as the final rating from the experts.

4.2 Data Gathering for Evaluating the User Stories Delivered

A second team of two experts was assigned the task of evaluating whether the user stories had been successfully implemented. The second team had to rely on the documentation of the submission to identify the code that was supposed to implement the feature described by the user story and the test cases for that story.

Each agile team submitted their project as a dump of a git repository. Some teams also submitted sketches, mock-ups and photographs of all documentation written down during the workshop day. In addition, some teams kept a test instance of their system running for the two experts to test.

The evaluation criteria were:

1. Did the submitting team make a claim that a user story was implemented? Lacking such a claim the experts would assume that the story was not implemented.
2. Did the submitting team document what functions were used to implement the user story? The experts would look at the code only for names that related to concepts in the user story.
3. Did the submitting team provide test cases to test the user story?

The verdict for each user story was pass or fail. The score was with respect to the maximum achieved by all teams. One team managed to implement 3 stories, which gave the maximum number of 10 points. All other teams scored a fraction of three, according to the number of stories they achieved. A finer distinction than pass and fail was rejected, because the experts could not agree on how that should be done objectively, and they felt that it was not worth the effort.

4.3 Data Gathering for Evaluating the Quality of the Code

As mentioned above, each team submitted their code as a clone of a git repository. This enabled the experts to evaluate the way the teams were documenting their software development process. The properties that the two experts evaluated were:

1. Quality of the documentation in the code
2. Quality of the log messages in version control
3. Quality of web accessibility
4. Error handling in the interface
5. Error handling in code
6. Functionality of the database scripts
7. Correct use of the model-view-controller pattern
8. Error free functionality

Points 3 and 4 were most relevant to the interaction with the user. The experts used the WAVE web accessibility evaluation tool to assess the quality of web accessibility and to check compliance with WCAG 2.0 at levels A and AA [7]. The experts investigated the choice of colors by hand and by using filters to simulate how color vision deficient users would see the web site. Overall, all submissions had some issues with web accessibility, like laying out information in the wrong order, missing alt tags for images, and so forth.

The two experts referred to the way erroneous behaviour is conveyed by the user for evaluating the error handling in the interface. The experts checked whether the error messages were displayed in a meaningful manner, how an encountered error would be addressed, and whether a pointer to assistance was provided.

No formal audit was defined concerning security. The evaluation of secure coding standards was guided by the documents of the Open Web Application Security Project [18]. The two experts audited the submitted projects for possible injection attacks and sufficient logging and monitoring, as well as security configuration. However, ensuring security of the system and verifying that security goals have been met was outside of the scope of the evaluation.

5 Results and Discussion

The results from the evaluations of the performance factors are shown in table 1.

Team A got the highest number of points in total for the three performance factors. This team had an interesting approach. They only focused on one user story, which was user story 1, during the workshop, but all the other teams selected more than one user story to focus on. This is why Team A got the lowest number of points for the user stories delivered.

The user story that Team A selected was the only story that included the citizens of Reykjavik, the other three user stories included employees of Reykjavik city. Team A got the highest number possible for team collaboration and UX focus. This was the only team that contacted a domain expert to understand the needs of the this particular group of citizens. They called a person at the service center to interview her/him to enhance their understanding of the needs of the user group. One of the team members also went to the service center, which was in the same building, and tried out how the application process was during the day of the workshop. The other teams did not contact any people outside the team for gathering information on the users and only imaged how the users would behave.

The team collaboration factors were more similar for the teams, but still there were some differences. For some teams we did not see much communication during the daily Scrum meeting and the organizing meeting, so the team

Table 1: The total points that each team received for the three performance factors evaluated.

Performance factor	Team A	Team B	Team C	Team D	Team E
Team collaboration and UX focus max 25 points	25,0	12,4	9,4	7,6	19,4
Delivery of user stories max 10 points	3,3	6,7	6,7	10,0	6,7
Quality of code max 35 points	22,0	16,2	18,0	22,4	22,4
Total max 70 points	50,3	35,3	34,1	40,0	48,5

members did sit by their computers and work individually. This is against the fundamental rules of agile, where team communication and collaboration is vital [16].

The aggregate score for the quality of the code had much less variation between the teams. Teams A, D, and E received almost the same score on code quality. Each of these teams were very competent. The experts observed some differences in each of the 8 categories among these teams but the differences averaged out.

Team B did not document their code and did not trace decisions to requirements and stories. Exceptional behaviour was not handled, and no tests were provided. Team C did not document parts of their code well, had many non-descriptive messages like "log in stuff" as commit messages to their version control systems, and did not take care of exceptional code paths. One error message displayed to the user was: "An unexpected error happened" and some errors were silently ignored. They aimed to implement three of the four stories, but only managed to finish two of them. Team D worked on a technical level, planning to implement all the user stories with a high standard of quality. At the same time, they chose the simplest stories. Team D and E received the same scores on code quality but aspects of code quality differed, e.g., team E had worse documentation of their process and the code, but handled web accessibility, error handling, and software architecture better than Team D.

To summarize, it was surprising for all the experts how much variation there was in how the teams worked and what they delivered. All the teams included IT professionals with the technical requirements fulfilled. Team A got the job since they got the highest score of the summary of all the performance factors and their prize estimations were in line with the other teams, so they got the highest total score and the job. They were the only team that reached out to understand the users of the service, while focusing on the code quality in parallel.

References

1. Baggem, R., Correia, J. P., Schill, K., and Visser J.: Standardized code quality benchmarking for improving software maintainability. Software Quality Journal, 20(2), 287–307 (2012). doi: https://doi.org/10.1007/s11219-011-9144-9
2. Billestrup, J., Stage, J., & Larusdottir, M.: A Case Study of Four IT Companies Developing Usable Public Digital Self-Service Solutions. In The Ninth International Conference on Advances in Computer-Human Interactions, (2016).
3. Caldwell, B., Cooper, M., Guarino Reid, L., and Vanderheiden, G.: Web Content Accessibility Guidelines (WCAG) 2.0. W3C, (2008).
4. Cohn, M.: User Stories Applied. O'Reilly Media (2004).

5. Curtis, B., Dickenson, B., and Kinsey, C. CISQ Recommendation Guide (2015) https://www.it-cisq.org/adm-sla/CISQ-Rec-Guide-Effective-Software-Quality-Metrics-for-ADM-Service-Level-Agreements.pdf (last accessed June 27, 2019).
6. Directive (EU) 2016/2102 of the European Parliament: Directive (EU) 2016/2102 of the European Parliament and of the Council of 26 October 2016 on the accessibility of the websites and mobile applications of public sector bodies (Text with EEA relevance). Homepage: http://data.europa.eu/eli/dir/2016/2102/oj, last accessed 27th June 2019.
7. European Telecommunications Standards Institute: Accessibility requirements suitable for public procurement of ICT products and services in Europe, EN 301 549 V1.1.2 (2015). Retrievable: https://www.etsi.org/deliver/etsi_en/301500_301599/301549/01.01.02_60/en_301549v010 102p.pdf
8. Hassenzahl, M. (2013). User experience and experience design. In: Soegaard, Mads and Dam, Rikke Friis (Eds.). The encyclopedia of human–computer interaction, 2nd Ed. Århus, Denmark: The Interaction Design Foundation.
9. Heitlager, I., Kuipers, T., & Visser, J.: A practical model for measuring maintainability. In 6th international conference on the quality of information and communications technology (QUATIC2007), pp. 30–39. IEEE Computer Society. (2007).
10. International organisation for standardisation: ISO 9241-210:2010. Ergonomics of human-system interaction Part 210: Human-centred design process for interactive systems, (2010).
11. Jia, Y., Larusdottir, M. K., & Cajander, Å.: The usage of usability techniques in Scrum projects. In Human-Centered Software Engineering (pp. 331–341). Springer Berlin Heidelberg, (2012).
12. Jokela, T., Laine, J., & Nieminen, M.: Usability in RFP's: The current practice and outline for the future. In International Conference on Human-Computer Interaction (pp. 101–106). Springer, Berlin, Heidelberg, (2013).
13. Kelly, B., Sloan, D., Phipps, L., Petrie, H., & Hamilton, F.: Forcing standardization or accommodating diversity?: A framework for applying the WCAG in the real world. In Proceedings of the 2005 International Cross-Disciplinary Workshop on Web Accessibility (W4A) (pp. 46–54). ACM., (2005), https://doi.org/10.1007/s11219-011-9144-9
14. Lallemand, C., Guillaume G., Vincent, K.: User experience: A concept without consensus? Exploring practitioners' perspectives through an international survey. Computers in Human Behavior 43: 35–48, (2015).
15. Law, E. L., Lárusdóttir, M. K.: Whose experience do we care about? Analysis of the fitness of Scrum and Kanban to User Experience, International Journal of Human-Computer Interaction, Vol. 31 (9), pg. 584–602, (2015).

16. Manifesto for Agile Software Development homepage, https:// agilemanifesto.org/, last accessed 27th June, 2019.

17. Ohno. T.: The Toyota Production System: Beyond Large-Scale Production. Productivity Press, (1988).

18. OWASP Homepage, https://www.owasp.org, last accessed 27th June, 2019.

19. Preece, J., Rogers, Y., Sharp, H.: Interaction design: beyond human-computer interaction, 5th edition, John Wiley and sons, Inc., (2019).

20. Sjøberg, D. I.: The relationship between software process, context and outcome. Proceedings of International Conference on Product-Focused Software Process Improvement (pp. 3–11). Springer, Cham (2016).

21. Schwaber, K.: Scrum development process. In: SIGPLAN Notices, 30(10), (1995)

22. Tarkkanen, K., Harkke, V.: Evaluation for Evaluation: Usability Work during Tendering Process. In Proceedings of the 33rd Annual ACM Conference Extended Abstracts on Human Factors in Computing Systems (CHI EA '15). ACM, New York, NY, USA, 2289–2294, (2015). DOI: https://doi.org/10.1145/2702613.2732851

23. Version One (2019): 13th Annual State of Agile survey. Online at: https:// www.stateofagile.com/#ufh-i-521251909-13th-annual-state-of-agile -report/473508, (last retrieved 27th of June, 2019)

A Model-based Framework
for Context-aware Augmented
Reality Applications

Enes Yigitbas, Ivan Jovanovikj, Stefan Sauer
and Gregor Engels

Paderborn University,Fürstenallee 11,
33102 Paderborn, Germany
Enes.Yigitbas@upb.de, Ivan.Jovanovikj@upb.de, Stefan.Sauer@upb.de,
Gregor.Engels@upb.de

Abstract

Augmented Reality (AR) is a technique that enables users to interact with their physical environment through the overlay of digital information. With the spread of AR applications in various domains (e.g. product design, manufacturing or maintenance) and the introduction of concepts such as Pervasive Augmented Reality (PAR), the aspect *context-awareness* started to play an important role. By sensing the user's current context and adapting the AR application accordingly, an adequate user experience can be achieved. Due to the complex structure and composition of AR applications, their development is a challenging task. Although, context-awareness for AR systems was addressed to some extent, a systematic method for development of context-aware AR applications is not fully covered yet. Therefore, in this paper, we identify the main challenges for development of context-aware AR applications and sketch our solution idea for a model-based development framework.

How to cite this book chapter:
Yigitbas, E., Jovanovikj, I., Sauer, S. and Engels, G. 2020. A Model-based Framework for Context-aware Augmented Reality Applications. In: Loizides, F., Winckler, M., Chatterjee, U., Abdelnour-Nocera, J. and Parmaxi, A. (eds.) *Human Computer Interaction and Emerging Technologies: Adjunct Proceedings from the INTERACT 2019 Workshops.* Pp. 303–312. Cardiff: Cardiff University Press. DOI: https://doi.org/10.18573/book3.am. License: CC-BY 4.0.

Keywords

Augmented reality · context-awareness

1 Introduction

Augmented Reality (AR) is a user interface metaphor, which allows for interweaving digital data with physical spaces. AR relies on the concept of overlaying digital data onto the physical world, typically in form of graphical augmentations in real-time [1].

Augmented reality has been researched for a considerable amount of time, with first implementations as early as Sutherlands head-mounted three dimensional display "The sword of Damocles" [5] from 1966. The expression *Augmented Reality* was first coined by Tom Caudell in 1992 in his work on the "Application of Heads-Up Display Technology to Manual Manufacturing Processes" [3].

In more recent years, AR technology is strongly on the rise, with many different devices available. One main technology are Head-Mounted-Displays (HMDs) like Microsoft's HoloLens[1] or the Magic Leap One:[2] Headsets with integrated display and optics. Some of them also have built in hardware to process the programs that run on the HMD, while other headsets need to be connected to a computer and only serve as a special kind of display which also includes control functions. An alternative way in AR-technology is to use a smartphone as the main hardware. The smartphone can be worn in a headgear (Head-mounted Smartphone), which is not very common for AR applications yet, as many of the headgears only support VR, for example because the phone-camera's lens is simply covered by the gear. More often smartphones are used in their original purpose, as handheld AR devices.

With the spread and increasing usage of Augmented Reality (AR) techniques in different domains, the need for context-awareness in AR was underlined in previous work [4]. Supporting context-awareness, can greatly enhance user experience in AR applications, for example by adjusting to the individual needs of each user. It also makes the usage more intuitive and effective: The more the application can adjust to the user and his situation, the more natural the AR is experienced and the more ergonomic it is to work with.

However, due to the complex structure (tasks, scenes) and composition (inter-relations between real and virtual information objects) of AR applications [6], the development of context-aware AR applications is a challenging task. While context-aware AR applications were introduced for specific application domains, e.g. maintenance [8], a systematic method for supporting the efficient development of context-aware AR applications is not fully covered yet. Therefore,

---

[1] https://www.microsoft.com/en-CY/hololens.

[2] https://www.magicleap.com/magic-leap-one.

in this paper, we discuss the main challenges in developing context-aware AR applications and sketch a first solution idea for a model-based development framework for context-aware augmented reality applications.

The rest of the paper is structured as follows: In Section 2, we discuss main challenges in developing context-aware AR applications. In Section 3, we present architectural patterns as basic solution concepts for addressing these challenges. Section 4 provides an overview of our integrated model-based framework supporting the development of context-aware AR applications. Finally, Section 5 concludes our work with an outlook on future work.

2 Challenges

The challenges in developing context-aware AR applications can be divided up in to three main categories: multi-platform capability, adaptation capability, and round-tripping capability. In the following, we describe each category in more detail.

2.1 Multi-Platform

An augmented reality application can be used across heterogeneous computing platforms spanning over head-mounted display devices to mobile hand held devices. Each computing platform can have different properties regarding hardware and sensor, operating system, used AR SDKs etc. To support multi-platform AR experience across heterogeneous computing platforms, an efficient way of developing various AR applications is needed.

2.2 Adaptation

For supporting context-aware and adaptive AR applications various aspects have to be taken into account.

First of all, context monitoring is an important prerequisite for enabling context-aware applications in general. An important challenge in this regard is to continuously observe the context-of-use of an AR application through various sensors. The context-of-use can be described through different characteristics regarding user (physical, emotional, preferences etc.), platform (Hololens, Handheld, etc.), and environment (real vs. virtual environmental information). Due to the rich context dimension which is spanning over the real world and virtual objects, it is a complex task to track and relate the relevant context information to each other. The mixture of real (position, posture, emotion, etc.) and virtual (coordinates, view angle, walk-through, etc.) context information additionally increases the aspect of context management compared to classical context-aware applications like in the web or mobile context.

Based on the collected context information, a decision making process is required to analyze and decide whether conditions and constraints are fulfilled to trigger specific adaptation operations on the AR application. In general, an important challenge is to cope with conflicting adaptation rules which aim at different adaptation goals. This problem is even more emphasized in the case of AR applications as we need to ensure a consistent display between the real world entities and virtual overlay information. For the decision making step it is also important to decide about a reasoning technique like rule-based or learning-based to provide a performant and scalable solution.

As AR applications consist of a complex structure and composition, an extremely high number of various adaptations is possible. The adaptations should cover text, symbols, 2D images and videos, as well as 3D models and animations. In this regard, many adaptation combinations and modality changes increase the complexity of the adaptation process.

2.3 Round-trip

Beside the before mentioned challenges, it is important for a context-aware AR application to support the flexible usage of various information objects. On the one hand information objects can be text, symbols, 2D and 3D objects which are predefined and available in an existing object repository. On the other hand, it should be also possible to digitize existing real world physical objects, e.g. through a 3D scan, so that further objects can be stored in the object repository and reused at runtime. We call this flexible way of transferring real world physical objects in to a repository and making them reusable again as round-trip.

3 Solution Idea

In order to support the development of context-aware augmented reality applications, we have identified basic architectural patterns to address the identified challenges: Multi-platform, Adaptation and Round-trip capabilities.

3.1 Multi-platform capability

For increasing the efficiency of multi-platform user interface development in the context of AR, we envision to establish a model-based development process. Based on the *CAMELEON Reference Framework* [2], as described in Figure 1, we propose a stepwise model-based development process.

The top layer Task & Concepts includes a task model that is used for the hierarchical description of the activities and actions of individual users of the AR user interface. The abstract user interface (AUI) is described in the form of a dialogue model that specifies the user's interaction with the user interface

Fig. 1: Multi-platform support.

independent of specific technology. The platform specific representation of the user interface is described by the concrete user interface (CUI), which is specified by a presentation model. The lowest layer of the framework is the final user interface (FUI) for the target platform. The vertical dimension describes the path from abstract to concrete models. Here, a top-down approach is followed, in which the abstract description of relevant information about the user interface (AUI) is enriched to more sophisticated models (CUI) through modelto-model transformations (M2M). Subsequently, the refined models are transformed (model-to-code transformation, M2C) to produce the final augmented reality user interface (AR FUI). Based on this architectural pattern, it is possible to enable multi-platform capability for the different UIs that are generated during the development process.

3.2 Adaptation capability

Based on our previous work in the area of UI adaptation for web and mobile apps [7], we propose an extended version of IBM's MAPE-K architecture (shown in Figure 2) to support context-aware AR applications.

AS depicted in Figure 2, the MAPE-K architecture consists of two main parts *Adaptation Manager* and *Managed Element*. In our case, the *Managed Element* is an AR application consisting of *Tasks*, *Scenes* and *Interrelations* between

Fig. 2. Adaptation support.

them. The *Adaptation Manager* is responsible for monitoring and adapting the AR application through sensors and effectors in order to provide a highly usable AR experience. In the following, the functionality of each subcomponent of the *Adaptation Manager* is briefly described.

The monitor component is responsible for observing the context information. Context information changes are then evaluated by the analyze component to decide whether adaptation is needed. If so, the planning of an adaptation schedule is done by the plan component. Finally, the adaptation operations are performed by the execute component, so that an adapted UI can be presented. The knowledge management base is responsible for storing data that is logged over time and can be used for inferring future adaptation operations.

3.3 Round-trip capability

For supporting roundtrip functionality in a context-aware AR application, we envision to establish a client-server architecture that enables digitization, storage and reuse of physical objects in an object repository. For this purpose, as depicted in Figure 3, we propose a *AR/VR Server* consisting of an *AR/VR Object Repository*. This repository can contain already predefined virtual objects. On the other hand it is possible to use the *AR Client*, e.g. a handheld AR device, to scan and digitize phiscal real worl objects. These objects can be refined and add to the local AR/VR repository which is synchronized with the central *AR/ VR Object Repository*. This enables the user to transfer physical objects into the repository, in order to build an object basis as well as projects the repository objects back into reality via augmentation.

Fig. 3. Round-trip support.

4 Model-based Framework for Context-aware AR Application

In the previous section, we have presented different architectural patterns for supporting the development of context-aware AR applications. While these patterns address basic solution concepts for tackling the different challenges, it is important to design an integrated framework which combines the several aspects of multi-platform capability, adaptation capability and roundtrip capability. For this reason, we propose an integrated model-based framework for context-aware AR applications. Our framework is depicted in Figure 4 and consists of the previously described solution patterns. At design time, the described model-based development process supports to generate the final AR user interfaces for various target platforms. The generated final UI is deployed to a specific AR client which enables the described roundtrip functionality at runtime. Also, the generated final UI of the AR application is monitored and adapted through the *Adaptation Manager* at runtime as described in the previous section.

In addition to the provided framework, we elaborate on the adaptation process as it is a crucial prerequisite for enabling context-aware AR applications.

To address the adaptation process at different development stages, we combine our previous work on model-driven development of adaptive UIs for web and mobile apps [7] with an existing method for structured design of AR UIs [6]. As shown in Figure 5, our solution concept addresses three different aspects: *AR UI, Context,* and *Adaptation*. Regarding the *AR UI* aspect, shown in the leftmost column in Figure 5, we rely on the approach and the *SSIML/AR* language of Vitzhum [6]. *SSIML/AR (Scene Structure and Integration Modeling/ Augmented Reality)* is a visual modeling language which provides model elements for modeling virtual objects and groups in a virtual scene. Additionally, the relations between application classes and the 3D scene can also be specified. Using *SSIML/AR*, an abstract specification of the user interface of the AR application is created. This *Abstract AR UI Model* is the input for the *AR UI*

Fig. 4. Model-based Development Framework for Context-aware AR Apps.

Generator, which generates the *Final AR UI*. In order to support the creation of contextaware AR apps, we complement the development method with two additional aspects, namely the *Context* and *Adaptation*, originally presented in [7]. The *Context* aspect serves to characterize the dynamically changing context-of-use parameters by providing an abstract specification in terms of a *Context Model*. Based on the *Context Model*, the *Context Service Generator* generates the *Context Service* which monitors context information like brightness, acceleration or noise level. The *Adaptation* aspect addresses the specification of the adaptation logic in terms of abstract AR UI adaptation rules represented as the *Adaptation Model*. The specified AR UI adaptation rules reference the *Context Model* to define the context constraints for triggering adaptation rules and they also reference the *Abstract AR UI Model* to define which AR UI elements are scope of a UI adaptation change. The *Adaptation Model* is the input for the *Adaptation Service Generator* which generates an *Adaptation Service*. At runtime, the *Adaptation Service* monitors the context information provided by the *Context Service* and adapts the *Final AR UI*.

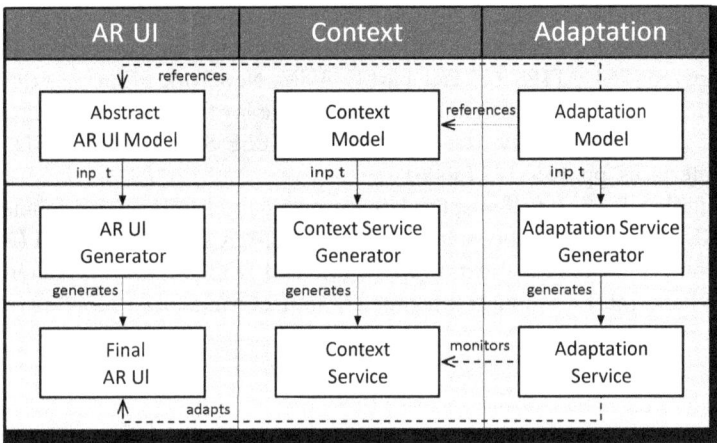

Fig. 5. Model-based Solution Architecture for Adaptive AR Apps.

5 Conclusion and Outlook

This paper discusses main challenges in developing context-aware augmented reality applications and presents architectural solution patterns to address them. Based on the identified architectural solution patterns, we propose an integrated model-based development framework for context-aware AR applications. Furthermore, we elaborate on the adaptation process and propose a model-based solution architecture for adaptive AR applications.

In future work, we plan to implement tool-support for model-based development of context-aware AR applications. Our goal is to support the efficient development of context-aware AR applications for different application scenarios from various domains.

References

1. Azuma, R.: A survey of augmented reality. Presence **6**(4), 355–385 (1997)
2. Calvary, G., Coutaz, J., Thevenin, D., Limbourg, Q., Bouillon, L., Vanderdonckt, J.: A unifying reference framework for multi-target user interfaces. Interacting with Computers **15**(3), 289–308 (2003)
3. Caudell, T.P., Mizell, D.W.: Augmented reality: an application of heads-up display technology to manual manufacturing processes. In: Proceedings of the Twenty-Fifth Hawaii International Conference on System Sciences. vol. ii, pp. 659–669 vol.2 (Jan 1992)
4. Grubert, J., et al.: Towards pervasive augmented reality: Context-awareness in augmented reality. IEEE Trans. Vis. Comput. Graph. **23**(6), 1706–1724 (2017). https://doi.org/10.1109/TVCG.2016.2543720, https://doi.org/10.1109/TVCG.2016.2543720

5. Sutherland, I.E.: A head-mounted three dimensional display. In: Proceedings of the December 9–11, 1968, Fall Joint Computer Conference, Part I. pp. 757–764. AFIPS '68 (Fall, part I), ACM, New York, NY, USA (1968)
6. Vitzthum, A.: SSIML/AR: A visual language for the abstract specification of augmented reality user interfaces. In: IEEE Symposium on 3D User Interfaces. pp. 135–142 (2006)
7. Yigitbas, E., et al.: Self-adaptive UIs: Integrated model-driven development of UIs and their adaptations. In: Proc. of the ECMFA 2017. pp. 126–141 (2017)
8. Zhu, J., et al.: A context-aware augmented reality assisted maintenance system. Int. J. Computer Integrated Manufacturing **28**(2), 213–225 (2015)

SECTION 7

Pushing the Boundaries of Participatory Design

Adapting UCD for Designing Learning Experiences for Romanian Preschoolers. A case study

Adriana-Mihaela Guran[*], Grigoreta-Sofia Cojocar[*] and Anamaria Moldovan[†]

[*]Babeş-Bolyai University, Cluj-Napoca, Romania
adriana@cs.ubbcluj.ro, grigo@cs.ubbcluj.ro
http://www.cs.ubbcluj.ro
[†]Albinuţa Kindergarten, Cluj-Napoca, Romania
anabeekindergarten@gmail.com

Abstract

Living in a world where almost every aspect of our life becomes digital requires attention on digital skills development of young generations of citizens. Education is the driving force that can support equality of chances in digital skills acquirement. In this paper we describe our experience in developing educational software for Romanian preschoolers (3–5/6 years) attending the public formal educational system. To be successful, the educational software should be both accepted by preschoolers and their teachers. We propose a two steps User (Child) Centered Design (UCD) approach focusing both on preschoolers and their teachers. The results obtained by applying the proposed method on a real case study are presented.

How to cite this book chapter:
Guran, A-H., Cojocar, G-S. and Moldovan, A. 2020. Adapting UCD for Designing Learning Experiences for Romanian Preschoolers. A case study. In: Loizides, F., Winckler, M., Chatterjee, U., Abdelnour-Nocera, J. and Parmaxi, A. (eds.) *Human Computer Interaction and Emerging Technologies: Adjunct Proceedings from the INTERACT 2019 Workshops*. Pp. 315–320. Cardiff: Cardiff University Press. DOI: https://doi.org/10.18573/book3.an. License: CC-BY 4.0.

Keywords

UCD · preschoolers · education · digital

1 Context

The world surrounding us becomes more and more digital, and the new children generations are considered *digital natives* [8]. This falsely suggest that the children posses the digital skills required by the future European Digital Market [3]. Studies on teenagers digital skills show that while their confidence in their digital skills is high, the results of the assessments are under expectations. Romania, as part of the European Union, ranks on the last position (28th of 28 countries) of digital skills assessment [4]. Interventions need to be done for the future generations, and the public formal educational system should be the leading part of the process. ICT classes are thought starting from primary classes until the end of the mandatory studies program. In the public formal preschool educational system, no measures for fundamental digital skills development are considered. Although every class room from kindergartens has a computer connected to the Internet, it is used solely to play multimedia content (most of the time youtube videos). This approach is not appropriate, as the before mentioned studies also show that Romanian citizens posses only the so-called *lifestyle digital skills*, but lack a vision of using technology to support work-related tasks. We consider that by appropriate interventions we can help the young generations embrace the technology as support in their knowledge gathering process and provide support on fundamental digital skills development. The form of intervention envisioned by us is the development of educational interactive products to support the classical teaching activities.

2 Method

Designing and developing educational applications for preschoolers brings two major challenges: designing for preschoolers and ensuring the educational nature of the products. The first challenge is determined by the lack of design guidelines for this particular age range. Although there is a large body of literature regarding designing for children, it focuses only on children aged 8 years or more [2, 5–7]. Romanian preschoolers are 3 to 5/6 years old. The differences between preschool children and school children are the following: preschoolers can not read or write, they cannot complete adult stated tasks without being rewarded and their main activity is playing. The second challenge, referring to the educational characteristic of the interactive applications, needs focus on the content presented, on the engagement it determines, and on the fundamental digital skills that are required to interact with. In order to achieve the educational goal, we knew from the beginning that the participation of an expert in children education is mandatory. We have required the support of a kindergarten teacher to guide and support us through the design stages. Gaining childrens' acceptance of the products was equally important as providing the right content and interaction. We decided to involve children also in the design process. Our intention was to apply UCD, although our final users lack some cognitive and physical skills that would empower them to actively participate through all the steps in the design process. We considered that they can still be represented by the kindergarten teacher which will replace them (being a *surrogate*) in all the phases of the design. We have involved in the design process Computer Science students from the Faculty of Mathematics and Computer Science, Babeş-Bolyai University, attending the Human-Computer Interaction (HCI) optional course. The students have worked in 3–5 members teams. The final goal of the HCI classes is to make the students aware of the importance of user focus during the design of products. We considered that our project suits the goal of the HCI classes. The only doubt we had was if the final products will be accepted by the children and by other kindergarten teachers, their acceptance being the measure of our products success or failure. Thus, we have imagined a two steps process of creating successful products: the first one we have called *product design* and the second one we have called *product validation*.

The *product design* was organized as an adapted UCD, in the sense that in some design steps we have replaced our users (preschool children) by a kindergarten teacher with the role of representing their interests. Thus, in the requirements phase only the kindergarten teacher has participated by stating the curricula domains that will be targeted by the educational applications, the age range they address, the content (information) that should be presented and the tasks children should perform to gather the intended knowledge. Still, the children have been included in this step, as informants. The design teams have participated to observation sessions in the kindergarten to gather information about children knowledge about their project subject and their digital skills (verify if fundamental interaction skills are present: using the mouse, performing a click, drag and drop, key pressing: blank, enter). The kindergarten teacher required that all the phases in the teaching process (focus capturing, new knowledge presentation and fixation game) be covered by the applications. Also, she specified that the applications should be conceived as games or at least they should expose games-related characteristics in order to be suitable. Game based interactive applications improve children engagement, their comprehension and retention, and make the content more relevant to them. After generating alternative design ideas, the kindergarten teacher has provided feedback on the designs and guided the design teams further in the process. Based on her feedback, the teams have built executable prototypes. The prototypes have been evaluated twice: once by the surrogate user that gave feedback on the presented content, task order, task formulation and second by the preschoolers. Individual play-testing sessions have been organized, followed by post-test interviews with the children. The kindergarten teacher has been present during all user testing sessions to provide comfort and support to the little users. Peer tutoring has been used to replace think aloud protocols in order to assess how children have understood the applications. Satisfaction was also assessed by the use of smileyometers.

The *product validation* step was intended to check the opinion of other kindergarten teachers. We have considered that a positive evaluation would be a good predictor for the future intention of use. We considered that heuristic evaluation is the most cost and time-effective method. We have encountered the same problem as in the design phase: the lack of evaluation tools targeting preschool children educational applications. After researching the literature we have decided to adapt an existing heuristics set, namely Heuristic Evaluation of Child E-Learning (HECE) [1]. We considered it appropriate because it consists of three heuristics subsets referring to navigability, children skills and learnability. It was developed for children aged 10 or above. Twelve kindergarten teachers have participated in the evaluation of the developed applications. Each application has been assessed by two kindergarten teachers.

3   Results

During the play testing sessions the most frequent problem was that the children did not understand what is the goal of the application, because the applications lack an introductory part. This problem has been addressed by introducing characters that would welcome the children in the application's world, shortly presents the available functionality and how it is accessible, and guide them through the learning/interacting process. Another problem was related to task formulation. Initially, the tasks were stated using sentences like *select/find the object(s)* .... The children used to answer to these kind of tasks by pointing with their fingers on the screen. The solution was to explicitly state how the task is expected to be accomplished by saying *select with a click the object* .... Children were very engaged during the user testing sessions and they repeatedly played the proposed games. Because the applications haven't been designed for multiple levels of difficulty, the children gave up using them only they became bored. Every child participating to the evaluation session has marked the happiest face on his/her smileyometer. The results of heuristic evaluation with the kindergarten teachers showed a large consensus on the children and learnability components of the heuristics set. All the participating evaluators agreed on these aspects, considering that the heuristics are successfully implemented. Regarding the navigation subset of heuristics, evaluators have identified problems about objects position consistency on the screens, lack of hints that would help children understand where he is in the application's space, interaction related terms that were considered too abstract.

4 Discussion

After having the experience of applying UCD for building educational software for preschoolers we can draw the conclusion that UCD is feasible even for such small age users. They can participate in every step of the design process, but the presence and support of an adult representing their interests is necessary in the requirements and alternative design evaluation steps. Although we did not involve the children in the alternative design evaluation phase, we consider that they could provide as new design ideas. Our decision was determined by the lack of time (the wireframes and sketches were too abstract to be understood by the children and too much time should have been spent to make the children understand and generate new ideas). The results of user testing show that children are eager to embrace technology during their learning activities as long as the learning experience takes the form of games or contain games-specific characteristics. The results of heuristic evaluation confirm the strength of participatory design: the kindergarten teacher participation during the entire design process has ensured a large agreement on the educational and children related aspects of the products. One drawback of our heuristic evaluation is that it was performed by colleagues of the kindergarten teacher participating in the design and a common organizational culture probably influenced the results.

The presence of navigational difficulties may be explained by the fact that inexperienced developers have applied their first interaction design project to a category of special users (with supplementary interaction constraints). We must specify that during their studies, the Computer Science students have experience in building command-line systems or Graphical User Interfaces used only by (expert) adults. This project has challenged the students in multiple aspects: focusing on the user, understanding the cognitive (inability to read or write, short periods of time when they can focus) and physical constraints (the mouse is too big for some of the little users hands) and identifying proper solutions, evaluating the final product based on criteria they have never considered before (usability, acceptability). At the end of the semester, many students have mentioned that the participation on this project was the best experience during their studies. It make them feel like having a contribution in the development of younger generations. Moreover, one of the kindergarten teacher participating in the evaluation step has expressed her availability and intention to be part of the design process in the future.

5 Conclusions and further work

In this paper we have presented our initiative of building educational software for public formal preschool educational system from Romania. We have proposed a two steps approach: an adapted UCD approach in the design phase and an adapted heuristics set in the validation stage. The results of the first iteration show us that our approach worth the effort, based on children and kindergarten teachers feedback. In the future we need to evaluate the learning outcomes of using the interactive products in the educational settings in terms of domain knowledge and fundamental computer skills acquisition/improvement.

References

1. Asmaa, A., and Asma, Al-O. *Usability heuristics evaluation for child e-learning applications.* In Proceedings of the 11th International Conference on Information Integration and Web-based Applications & Services (iiWAS '09). ACM, New York, NY, USA, 425–430.
2. Crescenzi, L., and Gran, M. An Analysis of the Interaction Design of the Best Educational Apps for Children Aged Zero to Eight. Comunicar, 46, 77–85. doi: https://doi.org/10.3916/C46-2016-08
3. European Commission, Digital Single Market, 2017, retrieved from https://ec.europa.eu/digital-single-market/
4. Europe's Digital Progress Report (EDPR) 2018, *How digital is your country? Europe needs Digital Single Market to boost its digital performance,* retrieved from https://ec.europa.eu/digital-single-market/en/news/how-digital-yourcountry-europe-needs-digital-single-market-boost-its-digital-performance
5. Fails, A., Guha, M. L., and Druin A., *Methods and Techniques for Involving Children in the Design of New Technology for Children.* Hanover, MA, USA: Now Publishers Inc., 2013.
6. Hourcade, J. P. Interaction Design and Children Found. *Trends Hum.-Comput. Interact. 1,* 4 (April 2008), 277–392.
7. Bekker, T., and Markopoulos, P. *Interaction design and children.* In:Interacting with Computers 15 (2003)
8. Prensky, M. *Digital Natives, Digital Immigrants,* On the Horizon 9(5): 1–6, doi: https://doi.org/10.1108/10748120110424816 2001.
9. Sefton-Green, J., et al. *Establishing a Research Agenda for the Digital Literacy Practices of Young Children: a White Paper for COST Action IS1410.* 2016.

Applying Participatory Design with Users with Intellectual Disabilities

Julio Abascal, Myriam Arrue and Juan Eduardo Pérez

University of the Basque Country/Euskal Herriko Unibertsitatea,
Egokituz Laboratry of HCI for Special Needs,
Manuel lardizabal 1, 20018 Donostia-san Sebastián, Spain
julio.abascal@ehu.eus, Myriam.Arrue@ehu.eus

Abstract

This paper presents an experience of participatory design with people with intellectual disabilities. The main goal was to create a Sheltered Social Network intended to train people with cognitive disabilities in the use of social networks and to allow the early detection of any type of danger they could face when they use a regular social network. In the first phase, we designed a strategy to allow the users to participate in the discussions without restrictions or barriers. In the second phase, we successfully applied this strategy in order to develop the *Guremintza* social network.

Keywords

Participatory Design · Intellectual Disabilities

How to cite this book chapter:
Abascal, J., Arrue, M. and Pérez, J.E. 2020. Applying Participatory Design with Users with Intellectual Disabilities. In: Loizides, F., Winckler, M., Chatterjee, U., Abdelnour-Nocera, J. and Parmaxi, A. (eds.) *Human Computer Interaction and Emerging Technologies: Adjunct Proceedings from the INTERACT 2019 Workshops.* Pp. 321–326. Cardiff: Cardiff University Press. DOI: https://doi.org/10.18573/book3.ao. License: CC-BY 4.0.

1 Introduction

The *Egokituz*[1] Laboratory of Human-Computer Interaction for Special Needs was created in 1985. Through this time, *Egokituz* obtained experience in participatory design working with people with sensory and physical disabilities. These experiences were principally focused to the development of computer mediated communication and navigation systems. In these cases, the most difficult challenge was the communication with the users. Once overcome this barrier, the participatory design was developed following common procedures for this methodology.

When we were contacted to create a social network for people with intellectual disabilities we had no previous experience in these types of disabilities and we found scarce references to help us. Therefore, we adapted our procedures on the progress with the assistance of their educators and care staff.

As a result we designed the *Guremintza*[2] sheltered social network following participatory design principles with the close participation of the users in order to collect their objectives, interest, likes, and restrictions. After a five months period of testing, the social network is currently fully operational and deployed in the industrial group *Gureak*[3] created to assist the full social integration of people with intellectual disabilities through employment. In this paper, we describe the methods we adopted to make possible participatory design with people with intellectual disabilities.

2 Development of *Guremintza*

Gureak approached the *Egokituz* Laboratory of HCI for Special Needs to discuss the possibility of creating a social network intended to train people with cognitive disabilities in the use of social networks and to allow the early detection of any type of danger they could face when they use a regular social network. We agreed to create a work team composed of *Gureak*, *Lotura* (a small company specialized in accessible Web Design), and two laboratories of the University of the Basque Country: *Egokituz* (specialized in accessible HCI design) and

---

[1] *Egokituz* is the Basque word for "Adapting".
[2] *Guremintza* means "Our Expression" in Basque Language.
[3] Gureak (meaning in Basque Language "Our People") is a Basque group of companies, which generate and manage steady work opportunities, suitably adapted, for persons with disabilities, with priority on people with intellectual disability. It provides jobs for more than 4000 people with diverse types of disabilities (39% cognitive, 16% mental illness, 6% physical, 22% sensory, 17% no disabilities) [1].

Aldapa (specialized in Data Mining and Machine Learning). We also agreed to apply a participative design methodology.

2.1 Requirements for the design of the Guremintza social network

In the firsts meetings, the following main requirements for the design of the Guremintza Social Network were stablished:

- **Features:** a) Accessible for people with cognitive, physical and sensory disabilities. b) Multilingual structure with access in Basque, Spanish and English languages. c) Personalized support to each user. d) Fully privacy protection (by means of codification techniques that made the users remain anonymous).
- **Functionality**: a) Periodical collection of activity data (only available to the supervisor) to follow the activity in the network. b) Early detection of possible misuses or dangers, triggered to a selected supervisor when unusual usage occurs. c) Testbed for research: data-mining techniques used to build dynamic user models in order to allow adaptive interaction.
- **Design methodology**: User centered design based on participatory design.

3 Participatory design with users with intellectual disabilities

We started having meetings with a group of seven selected users with diverse intellectual disabilities (four with Down syndrome and three with mental disabilities) who had previous experience in the use of computers. In these first meetings, we detected that the participant users tended to remain silent, deviate their interventions to other topics and provide positive answer to all the questions. *Gureak* care personnel, who had long experience in participatory decision taking meetings with people with disabilities, soon detected that the users were intimidated by the technicians and therefore they were not behaving as they did usually. Initially they supposed that after a number of meetings the users would become more familiar with the technicians and would freely participate, but it did not happen. Therefore, a new strategy was studied.

In addition, participatory Design [Schuler, 93] with users with cognitive disabilities requires special procedures that allow the eliciting of requirements while trying to avoid asking direct questions that could be impossible for some people with cognitive restrictions to answer [Dave, 2013]. Therefore, each consultation was reworded in such a way that was easy to answer for the users. In this way, we found an intelligible way for each question. For instance, initially we used paper mock-up versions to identify the requirements and difficulties that users had using them.

3.1 Design of an ad hoc participatory design methodology

We conceived some special procedures for participatory design with people with cognitive disabilities:

Two boards were formed for the design process: the Users Board and the Designers Board.

The **Users Board** was composed of six workers of Gureak, four with Down syndrome and two with mental diseases. All of them had some basic experience in using computers. There were assisted by two educators of Gitek (the R&D team of Gureak). This board participated in all the design and development phases (functionality, interface, look & feel, etc.) and validated each prototype. They were regularly informed about the progress of the project.

The **Designers Board** was composed of four people from the University of the Basque Country (in charge of conception, accessibility, usability, usage data management, coordination, and dissemination); one person from Lotura (devoted to development, implementation, and maintenance); 2 people from Gitek (for the assessment on user needs and coordination with the Users Board). This board converted the design decisions made by the Users Board into design specifications, and developed them.

With respect to the procedure, the technical staff avoided any type of manipulation of the decisions made by the Users Board to be fair to them. Members of the Users Board were punctually informed about the results of the Design Board meetings. Only when proposals from the Users Board could not be implemented they were asked to select an alternative. This procedure very much enhanced the interest and participation of the users.

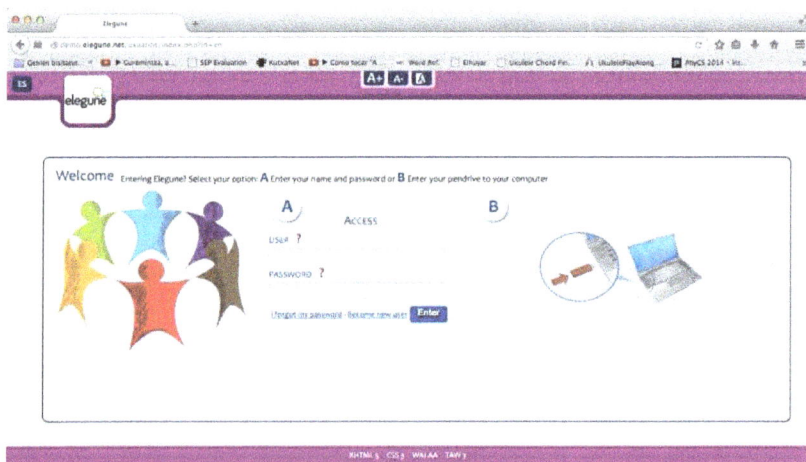

Fig. 1: Registering and entering: write name/password or Insert pen drive.

Both boards meet separately, but coordinated by Gitek. They had fortnightly meetings for seven months. A paper mock-up version of the social network was initially used to identify the best procedures and the difficulties that users have in using them. After this period, a first fully functional prototype was tested by the users for five months. After fixing the problems detected by them, the final version of the social network was designed, tested and deployed. Currently, *Guremintza* is fully operational in the *Gureak* industrial group. In addition to training/supervising people in the use of social networks, it is actually an effective way for internal communication to encourage personal relationships among the workers.

4 Conclusions

A number of conclusions can be drawn from this experience:

- Participatory design with people with cognitive disabilities is possible, provided that adequate procedures are designed to collect their opinions.
- Participation of the users in the design allows a progressive development based on users' needs and capabilities, always ensuring their understanding of the application.
- This method minimizes the possibility of including barriers that are rooted in the basic design and, therefore, cannot be removed.
- Participatory design increases the users' affinity to the resulting application and increases its usage.

References

1. Gureak. https://www.gureak.com/en/ (last accessed May 2, 2019)
2. Schuler D., Namioka A. (eds) (1993) Participatory Design: Principles and Practices. Lawrence Erlbaum Associates, Hillsdale, NJ.
3. Dawe M. Design Methods to Engage Individuals with Cognitive Disabilities and their Families. https://pdfs.semanticscholar.org/e391/b31f8e3c7fd0fac7f594fdc08fed6f4c5d2f.pdf (Last accessed: May 7, 2019)
4. Sahib N.G., Stockman T., Tombros A., Metatla O. (2013) Participatory Design with Blind Users: A Scenario-Based Approach. In: Kotzé P. et al. (eds) INTERACT 2013. LNCS 8117. Springer, Berlin, Heidelberg
5. Satterfield D., Marc F. (2017) User Participatory Methods for Inclusive Design and Research in Autism: A Case Study in Teaching UX Design. In: Design, User Experience, and Usability: Theory, Methodology, and Management, 186–197.
6. Sitbon L., Farhin S. (2017) Co-Designing interactive applications with adults with intellectual disability: a case study. OzCHI '17, Brisbane
7. Guremintza in YouTube: https://www.youtube.com/watch?v=aZjIbrPj7OE

Participatory Design in Māori Cultural Contexts

Judy Bowen and Annika Hinze

University of Waikato, Hamilton, New Zealand
jbowen@waikato.ac.nz, hinze@waikato.ac.nz

Abstract

The Hakituri project aims to develop practical and ethical wearable monitoring solutions for workers in hazardous industries. We identified specific challenges pertinent to our participatory design process for this project which relate to the indigenous participants, cultural expectations and data sovereignty. As we developed the ideas for our design process, further challenges became evident. In this paper we explore the challenges that unfolded and describe how we began to mitigate them and develop ideas for similar future challenges.

Keywords

Minority culture · Indigenous data sovereignty

1 Introduction

Forestry is one of New Zealand's most dangerous industries. Māori workers are over-represented in such higher risk occupations. The Hakituri project aims to develop practical and ethical wearable monitoring solutions for hazardous work industries, and is currently working with the New Zealand forestry industry. The particular challenges we face with our participatory design process are

How to cite this book chapter:
Bowen, J. and Hinze, A. 2020. Participatory Design in Māori Cultural Contexts. In: Loizides, F., Winckler, M., Chatterjee, U., Abdelnour-Nocera, J. and Parmaxi, A. (eds.) *Human Computer Interaction and Emerging Technologies: Adjunct Proceedings from the INTERACT 2019 Workshops.* Pp. 327–332. Cardiff: Cardiff University Press. DOI: https://doi.org/10.18573/book3.ap. License: CC-BY 4.0.

based on both the nature of the participant group and their relationship with the researchers (Māori/non Māori; non technical/technical; domain experts/ domain novices) and the context of incorporating data sovereignty (DS) and indigenous data sovereignty (IDS) into both the technical solution and the design process.

Extensive research into designing for, and with, minority groups does not typically address the power balance that occurs when the minority group are the indigenous people of a post-colonial country. Most of the research that does consider this is in the domain of social sciences (e.g., [1, 12]) rather than in computing design. Similarly, while it is understood that mixed participant groups which contain a power imbalance (workers/managers) can lead to particular problems in participatory design (workers may not feel empowered to express their real needs) we also introduce whānau (extended family) and community elders into the design process. Their voice is important, but their presence may also influence the response of others. Finally, our requirements include that the participatory design process itself follows IDS principles.

We thus find ourselves in what Linda Smith called the "Tricky Ground" of indigenous research methodologies [14]. Hotere-Barnes acknowledges *Pākehā paralysis* [6]: non-Māori (Pākehā) researchers concerned about perpetuating Māori cultural tokenism, and their engagement in Māori-focussed research while power imbalances are in favour of Pākehā. While these issues have been discussed extensively for educational and social science research [1, 12], they are rarely acknowledged in technical fields. Western research practices traditionally disadvantage and distance Māori from "real participation and voice" [2]. Revitalised traditional indigenous practices, known as Kaupapa Māori, resists traditional Western research methodologies and seek to balance unequal power relations [13]. Pertinent Māori-relevant research methodologies are an ethics framework [9], Appreciative Inquiry [4], and Whānau Tuatahi [8]. While most focus on collaboration and communication, none of these consider an ICT context. Similarly, research on the adoption of values of Indigenous people in workplace situations is sparse, both in Aotearoa New Zealand and internationally [5, 11].

Our design process requires understanding and adoption of the relevant principles from the work discussed above. This led us in the first instance to engage an external Māori research facilitator for the design workshops and to work with her to reframe our design questions and process. We initially describe the design process we set up, with a structure envisaged to address the challenges outlined above (see Section 2). We then highlight the specifics that unfolded as we finalised the process and began to run the design process.

2 Participatory Design Process and Challenges

The concepts of indigenous data sovereignty [10] and indigenous intellectual property [3] are about the data rights and interests of indigenous peoples,

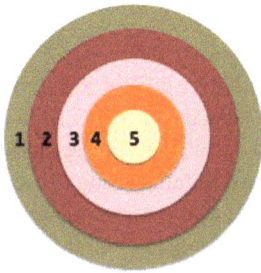

1. Power imbalances of working with a cultural minority where researchers are from different ethnic and cultural backgrounds
2. Data sovereignty management requirements to be addressed both in the technical solution and in participatory design process
3. Lack of participatory design literacy and also general literacy of participants
4. Inclusion of whānau and other workplace representatives (supervisors, management companies, external agencies) with conflicting requirements
5. Fear of technical solutions as something which will lead to job loss personally and in the future for whānau

Fig. 1: The Increasing Challenges at Each Level.

addressing questions of collection, ownership, access, use, and dissemination of data pertaining to indigenous people. As the Hakituri project aims to develop a wearable monitoring solution, the gathering of large amounts of personal data from indigenous people means that IDS is a relevant consideration. However, we are also gathering data during the design process itself, and all information gathered needs to treated in keeping with IDS concepts. Te Mana Rauranga have developed a framework that can be used to consider attributes of data under a Māori lens to understand the interconnectedness of key concepts [7]. It can be used in part to help determine whether or not a particular dataset can/ should be considered as taonga (treasure). Using these resources, the participatory design process was structured around three workshops:

1. Introductory discussions to explore the concepts of personal data gathering in the workplace.
2. Based on the information gathered above we provide storyboards and scenarios for exploration and reflection.
3. A participatory evaluation session to explore refined storyboards and scenarios (from information gained from 1 and 2 above).

These workshops were planned to be carried out at one-week intervals. The process was designed to address both (1) the challenges around minorities with different cultural and ethnic backgrounds, as well as (2) IDS. Throughout the workshops, a number of further challenges emerged (see Fig. 1):

3. Literacy: The range of technical and written literacy of the participants was hugely varied.
4. Inclusion of secondary users: There were conflicting requirements from workers and whānau about who should have access to which data. There was also a wide divergence across age groups.
5. Focus on job security: Workers worried more about their workplace security than about any data misuse.

3 Outcomes and Lessons

We addressed these five challenges as follows.

A representative of the minority culture was included as part of the design team to facilitate the process. Our workshops were structured by non-Māori computer scientists and then tailored by the Māori facilitator. This included specific cultural aspects such as starting with whakawhanaungatanga (introductions based around recitation of genealogies), using Māori terminology for key concepts, ensuring that groups were structured to respect the hierarchies of elders present without influencing the inputs of the participants.

Data sovereignty in the participatory design process is addressed by reporting back any conclusions and by transferring all collected data to the participants.

In general the younger (16–30) participants were familiar with smart-phone use, the internet and (in some cases) computer gaming. We were able to use this to frame our descriptions of IoT technology, monitoring and data gathering around these concepts to make them more understandable. During the workshop activities participants were split into groups and given large sheets of paper and marker pens to write down answers to 3 questions. For each group we ensured there was a participant who was comfortable with writing down everyone's answers, and the question was both written on a whiteboard as well as read out and repeated verbally as required.

It was made clear that workers are in charge and have the final say in all aspects of data management and sharing. While the whānau may have a desire to get all of the information all of the time, this does not necessarily meet the requirements of the workers. We will need a higher level of personalisation for our tools than we had first envisaged to make sure this is easily satisfied for all groups. Understanding how such personalisation may be controlled by the primary users was incorporated into the activities of the third workshop.

Regular reminders of what we are/are not doing were incorporated into the activities. Agreement regarding the importance of jobs for now and the future, and how health and safety supports this (less pressure to remove workers from the equation if accident rates are lower) were used as motivations for the work.

In summary, barely any consideration has been given to the situation of minorities in participatory design in post-colonial settings, let alone the consideration of indigenous data sovereignty. Our work aims to address these issues by developing a suitably methodology for participatory design. This paper contributes by identifying issues relating to cultural expectations and data sovereignty that were observed during participatory design activities with Māori forestry workers.

References

1. Barnes, A.: What can pākehā learn from engaging in kaupapa māori educational research. Tech. rep., New Zealand Council for Educational Research (2013)

2. Berryman, M.: Kaupapa maori: The research experiences of a research-whanau-of-interest. Culturally responsive methodologies, pp. 263–286 (2013)
3. Commission on Human Rights: Mataatua declaration on cultural and intellectual property rights of indigenous peoples (1993), First Int. Conf. on the Cultural & Intellectual Property Rights of Indigenous Peoples, Whakatane, New Zealand
4. Cram, F.: Appreciative inquiry. Mai Review **3**(1), 3: 1–13 (2010)
5. Harris, F., Macfarlane, S., Macfarlane, A., Jolly, M., Cram, F.: Māori values in the workplace: Investing in diversity. MAI Journal **5**(1), 4: 1–15 (2016)
6. Hotere-Barnes, A.: Generating 'Non-stupid optimism': Addressing Pākehā paralysis in Māori educational research. NZ J. of Educ. Studies **50**(1), 39–53 (2015)
7. Hudson, M., et al.: He Matapihi ki te Mana Raraunga - Conceptualising Big Data through a Māori lens, pp. 64–73. University of Waikato, New Zealand (2017)
8. Jones, B., Ingham, T., etc.: Whānau Tuatahi: Māori community partnership research using a Kaupapa Māori methodology. MAI Review Journal **3**(1), 1–14 (2010)
9. Kennedy, V., Cram, F.: Ethics of researching with whānau collectives. MAI Review Journal **3**, 2: 1–8 (2010)
10. Kukutai, T., Taylor, J. (eds.): Indigenous data sovereignty: Toward an agenda, vol. 38. Anu Press (2016)
11. Kuntz, J.R., N¨aswall, K., Beckingsale, A., Macfarlane, A.H.: Capitalising on diversity: espousal of maori values in the workplace. The Journal of Corporate Citizenship **2014**(55), 102 (2014)
12. Kaupapa maori and rangahau website, http://www.rangahau.co.nz/
13. Smith, G.H.: Reform and Maori educational crisis: A grand illusion. Research Unit for Maori Education, University of Auckland Auckland (1991)
14. Smith, L.T.: On tricky ground: Researching the native in the age of uncertainty. The landscape of qualitative research **1**, 85–113 (2007)

Adapting Participatory Design for Romanian Preschoolers Educational Software Development

Adriana-Mihaela Guran and Grigoreta-Sofia Cojocar

Babeş-Bolyai University, Cluj-Napoca, Romania
adriana@cs.ubbcluj.ro, grigo@cs.ubbcluj.ro

Abstract

The Participatory Design (PD) approach cannot be applied to developing software applications for small children (3–5/6 years) without considering the main constraint brought by their age: they cannot be involved in every step of the design. This paper presents our approach in adapting PD for preschoolers in the context of developing educational software that can be used as support for the teaching activities in Romanian kindergartens. We describe and discuss the results of evaluating the obtained software products with preschoolers and their teachers.

Keywords

Participatory Design · preschool children · educational software

1 Context

We live in a world that is more and more digital, and the children born nowadays are considered *digital natives*. This label can lead to the conclusion that the today generations possess the digital skills required by the European Union

How to cite this book chapter:
Guran, A-H. and Cojocar, G-S. 2020. Adapting Participatory Design for Romanian Preschoolers Educational Software Development. In: Loizides, F., Winckler, M., Chatterjee, U., Abdelnour-Nocera, J. and Parmaxi, A. (eds.) *Human Computer Interaction and Emerging Technologies: Adjunct Proceedings from the INTERACT 2019 Workshops*. Pp. 333–338. Cardiff: Cardiff University Press. DOI: https://doi. org/10.18573/book3.aq. License: CC-BY 4.0.

labor market of the future, when 90% of jobs will require digital skills. The European Union statistics on digital skills rank Romania on the last position, from 28 countries, in the last 2 years [5]. An effective intervention would necessarily target education. In Romania, ICT is studied from the primary school until the end of the mandatory education. We propose a shift in the classical approach of introducing computer skills, by using technology to learn, rather than teaching children how to use technology. Our approach tries to go even further, by providing support in developing the digital skills of preschoolers (3 to 5/6 years) in the form of tools (interactive applications) that can be used in the public formal preschool education system during the teaching activities. Our initiative needs to achieve two goals: being educative (such that kindergarten teachers want to use it) and being entertaining (such that the children want to interact with). Such goals cannot be achieved without focusing our design on children and kindergarten teachers. Thus, we have considered that we need to involve both categories in the design process. Although we have experience in PD with adults, the challenge is to keep the focus on the final users (the children) while respecting the constraints imposed by the client (the kindergarten teachers).

2 Procedure & Results

Although a large number of design guidelines for children have been proposed [2, 6–7], little attention is given to designing for preschoolers. Recent studies [3, 8] show that most of the applications consider the children aged 0 to 8 being a homogeneous group. They also suggest that the interaction techniques and content are not adapted to children development. The main differences between preschool and school children are that preschool children cannot read or write, they cannot complete adults stated tasks without being rewarded, and their main activity is playing. All these differences add new constraints on the design of interactive applications for preschool children: the applications should be conceived as games or at least they should expose games-related characteristics in order to be suitable, they should not use written output and they should not require written input. The interaction of the children with the applications should require basic (fundamental) computer skills: pressing a key on the keyboard (space, enter, arrows), moving the cursor on the screen or clicking. The content provided by the applications should also align with the Curriculum for preschool children from Romania. In order to keep our focus on the final users, we have decided to apply PD and to involve the final users during the design and development as much as possible. We knew from the beginning that children can not be involved in every stage of the design process because of the cognitive constraints imposed by their age. Still, we have tried to keep them present in our approach by means of the kindergarten teacher which played the role of a *surrogate* (proxy) of our real users. We considered it a good strategy as the kindergarten teacher has in-depth knowledge about children development, their cognitive and physical capabilities and limitations, and the appropriate learning goals for their age. In order to design and develop the intended educational applications, we have benefited the participation of Computer Science students from our faculty attending the HCI elective course. One of the main goals of this class is to make the students understand the importance and benefits of PD. They worked in teams of 3 to 5 members. The teams have started the PD process with an initial meeting with the client (the kindergarten teacher) who briefly described her need for interactive applications as support in her classic teaching activities, the environment where she works and how the teaching activities take place at that moment. She also specified initial requirements for each team containing the age range of the users, the general theme, the integrated curricula domains and some task examples (e.g. theme: The fall (children aged 3–4); integrated domains: Language and Communication and Physical Education; tasks: Poems, rhymes, a story about leaves; Verbal tasks: such as *We turn around, we kneel at once, a yellow leaf we hope to find*). She specified that the applications should consider all the stages in the teaching process: focus capturing, content presentation, and fixation game. Afterwards, students have participated to observation sessions in the kindergarten with the goals of meeting the final users and finding information about children knowledge of the domain and their digital skills. This way, students realized that most of their initial ideas about preschoolers were wrong. They thought children are capable of reading, they supposed children can perform click, double-click, or drag and drop operations. But the reality was, that, in some cases, children could not even hold a mouse on their hands (the mouses were physically too big for their small hands). As such, during the requirements, we have involved the kindergarten teacher as client and the preschoolers as informants. In the second step, students have created design alternatives and the kindergarten teacher has provided feedback regarding the presented content, interaction, and proposed tasks. It was the only step where children haven't been directly involved, but they have been represented by their *surrogate*. She played the role of the children in terms of answering to the proposed tasks and commented on the presented content simulating the children reaction to them. In the third step the high fidelity executable prototypes have been developed taking into consideration the feedback from the kindergarten teacher. The teams have visited again the children in the kindergarten to gather feedback on the prototypes. Children have participated as users and testers of the applications. Comments of the children regarding the characters and objects on the application have been then transposed into design decisions. The evaluation sessions were organized as play-testing sessions with individual users. The kindergarten teacher and the students observed the children freely exploring the application. After that, short post-interviews to reveal the subjective opinion of children have been organized. They consisted in simple questions, such as: *Would you like to play/show this game with/to your friends?*. Some teams have decided to use peer tutoring to simulate think aloud protocols, and others have used smileyometers [10] to help children express their attitude toward the applications. This step has brought more unexpected information regarding the way preschool children understand the interaction. The most frequent problem was related to how the tasks were stated. For example, if the children were required to choose the objects on the screen having a certain property, they were always using their finger to indicate them. Afterwards, the indications were explicitly reformulated by *select with a click* statements. Also, the children had frequent questions about the tasks they should perform, how do they go back to a previous screen or how they can exit. The solution for this type of problems was to introduce characters that greet the children in the beginning, and guide them through the interaction (providing interaction support). The results of the usability testing sessions were encouraging, as the children were willing to use again and again the assessed application. We have validated the results of the usability testing by applying a preschooler adapted HECE (Heuristic Evaluation of Child E-Learning) [1] with 12 expert users (other kindergarten teachers) for ten applications. Each application was assessed by two evaluators. Seven out of ten applications were considered successful related to the HECE heuristics. The other three applications presented problems on the NUH component from HECE (navigation related heuristics). Two applications had problems on the CUH component (children skills) that were related to the use of abstract concepts, that are too difficult to understand by the children. The learning component (LUH) has been evaluated with the highest scores, due tot the active participation of an expert in the design process.

3 Discussion

In this paper we have presented an approach of using participatory design with Romanian preschool children. We have involved the preschoolers in almost all design phases: during requirements as informants, during prototyping as users and informants, and during evaluation as users and testers. The only step where they haven't been involved was the initial design, where the design sketches were too abstract to be evaluated by children, but their surrogate has successfully replaced them. The results of usability testing and validation testing show us that preschoolers can be used as informants, users and testers during the design process. Potentially, they could play a more significant role as design partners, but only if they are accompanied by an expert in the educational field.

References

1. Asmaa A. and Asma Al-O. *Usability heuristics evaluation for child e-learning applications.* In Proceedings of the 11th International Conference on Information Integration and Web-based Applications & Services (iiWAS '09). ACM, New York, NY, USA, 425–430.

2. Bekker, T., and Markopoulos P. Interaction design and children. In:*Interacting with Computers* 15 (2003)
3. Crescenzi, L., and Gran, M. An Analysis of the Interaction Design of the Best Educational Apps for Children Aged Zero to Eight. *Comunicar*, 46, 77–85. doi: https://doi.org/10.3916/C46-2016-08
4. European Commission, *Digital Single Market*, 2017, retrieved from https://ec .europa.eu/digital-single-market/
5. Europe's Digital Progress Report (EDPR) 2018, *How digital is your country? Europe needs Digital Single Market to boost its digital performance*, retrieved from https://ec.europa.eu/digital-single-market/en/news/how -digital-yourcountry-europe-needs-digital-single-market-boost-its-digital -performance
6. Fails, A., Guha, M. L., and Druin, A. *Methods and Techniques for Involving Children in the Design of New Technology for Children*. Hanover, MA, USA: Now Publishers Inc., 2013.
7. Hourcade, J. P. Interaction Design and Children Found. *Trends Hum.- Comput. Interact. 1*, 4 (April 2008), 277–392.
8. Kazakoff, E. Technology-based literacies for young children: Digital literacy through learning to code. In K.L. Heider & M.R. Jalongo (Eds), Children and Families in the Information Age: Applications of Technology in Early Childhood (pp. 43–60). New York: Springer, (2015)
9. Prensky, M. *Digital Natives, Digital Immigrants*, On the Horizon 9(5): 1–6, doi: https://doi.org/10.1108/10748120110424816 2001.
10. Read, J. C., and MacFarlane, S. *Using the fun toolkit and other survey methods to gather opinions in child computer interaction*. In Proceedings of the 2006 conference on Interaction design and children (IDC '06). ACM, New York, NY, USA, 81–88.(2006)
11. Sefton-Green, J., et al. *Establishing a Research Agenda for the Digital Literacy Practices of Young Children: a White Paper for COST Action IS1410*. 2016.

SECTION 8

HCI Challenges in Human Movement Analysis

Human Movement Tracking as Fine Grained Position Input for Wide Area Virtual Reality

Bill Rogers, Robert Caunter, Xiangyan Gao
and Bryny Patchet

Computer Science Dept., University of Waikato, Hamilton, New Zealand
coms0108@cs.waikato.ac.nz

Abstract

The paper describes current progress towards providing untethered relative location tracking in a wide area setting for virtual reality applications. The goal is to allow a user to walk and turn in a virtual space by walking in the real world. Our implementation uses accelerometer and gyroscope sensors on to the user's ankles to detect and track leg motion. Tracking is detailed, picking up not just steps, but also the size and timing of those step. Estimated location change information is communicated wirelessly to a stand-alone virtual reality headset where it is used to drive player movement in a game setting. Small scale testing has established that the system provides a comfortable movement experience in which users can confidently get from point to point. It has also identified issues concerning: maintenance of stability in direction estimation; detection of sideways steps; and lag from detection to observed movement.

Keywords

Human movement · Location tracking · Virtual reality

How to cite this book chapter:

Rogers, B., Caunter, R., Gao, X. and Patchet, B. 2020. Human Movement Tracking as Fine Grained Position Input for Wide Area Virtual Reality. In: Loizides, F., Winckler, M., Chatterjee, U., Abdelnour-Nocera, J. and Parmaxi, A. (eds.) *Human Computer Interaction and Emerging Technologies: Adjunct Proceedings from the INTERACT 2019 Workshops.* Pp. 341–348. Cardiff: Cardiff University Press. DOI: https://doi.org/10.18573/book3.ar. License: CC-BY 4.0.

1 Introduction

The ultimate goal of virtual reality technology is to allow a person or group of people to experience being in a new environment in such a way that it seems as though they are really there. The sensation of presence in such an environment would involve vision, sound, feeling, and smell. The ability to act in an environment would include being able to look around, to move one's body, to grasp and interact with objects, to climb on objects, etc. Current VR applications can provide good experiences with some of the capabilities.

Being able to stand in one place and look around requires the vision component, coupled to orientation tracking of the user's head. Such a system provides a powerful experience for users, allowing them to clearly appreciate size and relationships of items in the environment. Adding positional sound can further enhance the experience. In recent years great progress has been made in the performance and accessibility of virtual reality vision and sound systems. Headsets are now readily available which allow a wide visual field to be presented, and in which the view can be made to respond to head movement with minimal lag. Popular current systems include the Occulus Rift and HTC Vive. Google Cardboard and Daydream systems; and Occulus Go are examples of vision systems built using mobile technology.

Adding the ability to move in an environment is a natural next step. Loosely gathering terminology from [1] and [2] we can classify movement systems in VR systems as:

- Teleportation: The user issues a command, usually by pointing a hand held controller and clicking. They are then instantly placed at the destination location. A visual fade-in/fade-out transition may help, but disorientation and motion sickness is likely.
- Artificial Locomotion. The user moves continuously in the virtual space using a controller to set direction and speed, without movement in real space. The metaphor of controlling a vehicle is often used – e.g. flying a spaceship. The inconsistency between real and visual motion can also induce motion sickness.
- Perambulation or Natural Locomotion: Picking up the actual movement of the user in real space. This is the system which is the least disorienting and least likely to cause motion sickness. Redirected motion [3] can be used to give the impression of moving in a larger area than that actually used. There are many existing approaches to the implementation of perambulation movement.

The Occulus Rift and HTC Vive systems use cameras to track the user's headset and hand controllers. A typical setup involves two cameras, mounted on opposite corners of an area of up to 4m by 4m. The user can move freely in this space, with the proviso that their headset is tethered by a cable feeding video and other data, their movement being directly reflected in the virtual experience. The fidelity is good, but the space is very limited. In particular it is not large enough for motion redirection.

Other systems allow for larger spaces. Motion capture studios have users wear special suits (marked or augmented with reflectors) and track movement with a number of cameras ranged about the capture space. Capture spaces can be quite large, even 10's of metres on a side. Such a system is used for game playing commercially by Zero Latency [4] where cameras track user's headsets and weapons in a warehouse sized space. The space is large enough for motion redirection.

Systems which provide arbitrarily large virtual spaces include the omnidirectional treadmill [5] and human sized hamster ball [6]. There are also a number of commercial treadmill style movement systems. Typical is the Virtuix Omni [7] in which the user's feet slip on a basin shaped surface to allow stepping motion in any direction, with the feet slipping back to a centre position after each step. These systems allow large virtual spaces, but have unnatural motion.

In summary, current VR motion systems can offer accurate motion detection in limited spaces or they can offer unnatural or limited accuracy detection in large spaces. Our project uses Human Movement tracking to allow accurate motion detection in a large (outdoor) space.

2 The System

The system we are developing consists of a portable (untethered) head mounted display. At present we are using a Google Pixel phone in a Daydream headset [8]. The Google Daydream system is used to host a virtual reality game environment developed using Unreal Engine 4. The user wears gyroscope and accelerometer sensors on each ankle. Rather than building a system around the sensor electronics ourselves, we are using cell phones in simple holders (sold as arm-bands for joggers). The ankle phones transmit movement data to the display phone which updates the player position in the virtual world accordingly. The result is a system in which a user can walk in the real world, over a large area, and have that movement, or a modified version of it, reflected in a virtual space.

The advantage of the system is the detail with which movement can be captured. It combines the fidelity of small scale systems with a wide area for motion. Our system allows:

- Movement in any direction. The user can step forward or backward, left or right. They can turn and walk in any direction.
- Movement direction is independent of view direction. The user can look around freely as they move.

- Movement is captured in fine detail. The user may lift a foot into the air, then pull back. They may move quickly or slowly. The view in the headset reflects these motions. Note that we cannot track sustained motion of this kind. The system expects the foot to be put back on the ground frequently.
- The scale of movement is great enough to implement redirection, including redirection of user orientation. We have done some experiments, including having a user walk around the inside of a cylinder. (In that virtual world, it was assumed that gravity acted radially.)

3 Implementation

Software running in each of the ankle phones receives inputs from Gyroscope and Accelerometer sensors at approximately 300Hz. Motion is reconstructed from these values as follows.

When the user is stationary, with feet flat on the ground, an averaged accelerometer reading is taken, to be used as an estimate of gravity (approx. 9.81 m/sec/sec upward). The phones are each mounted on the outside of the leg, just above the ankle. They are flat against the leg and oriented roughly upright in portrait mode. The axis system of the phone sensors therefore has x pointing mostly forward, y mostly upward and z mostly outward. It cannot be assumed that the phones are exactly upright, or that they do not move a little against the legs as the user walks. The gravity estimate gives part of the initial orientation of the phone. It will be re-estimated frequently as explained later. The initial orientation from gravity is just a measure of how upright the phone is. We take the initial horizontal direction to be towards 'North' – or any chosen direction in the virtual world.

Motion estimation begins by subtracting the gravity estimate from measured acceleration values to provide acceleration due to movement. In human leg movement there is considerable rotation (most about the z axis) from the knee. This is accounted for in our software by integrating information from the gyroscope to track changes in the phone orientation and using this to continually convert acceleration readings to the coordinate system in which the gravity estimate was taken.

The next step is to integrate the acceleration values to give velocity and velocity to give position change. As is well known, the double integration is not reliable, typically giving rise to large velocity and consequentially position errors. In our case however, we can take advantage that each foot rests on the ground while the other is moving. We need only integrate for the duration of a step. When the foot returns to the ground, integration stops. Advantage is taken of periods on the ground to repeat the gravity estimation. New gravity estimates allow us to correct some drift in the orientation. In particular, if a phone has slipped in its holder, or the holder has slipped against the user's leg, changes to vertical orientation can be corrected, making sure that gravity can be reliably subtracted from observed acceleration. Correction is performed as a rotation making minimal change to the dimensions of orientation related to horizontal direction. The result preserves a horizontal direction that is the result of continuous gyroscope integration. In early experiments we have found the accuracy to be moderate. In one experiment a walk around a circle of radius 35m ended with total drift of 20 degrees. The direction drift is such that orientation does not maintain a precisely fixed relationship with the real world, but does change slowly enough for the change to be imperceptible – rather like the effect of deliberate orientation redirection.

The explanation given so far is complete except for the issue of deciding when a step is taking place. We have observed that steps begin with a sharp acceleration upward. At least, that is the case when walking forward or backward. When walking slowly sideways a person may only raise their foot off the ground slightly and then move horizontally. Our system has a hand coded automaton to track a step, driven mostly by vertical acceleration and experimentally determined thresholds. When there has been a short vertical acceleration upward, integration begins. Integration is stopped just before the foot hits the ground. The sharp and fluctuating acceleration values observed after that time are not used. When there has been no vertical acceleration for a short time, gravity estimation for the next step can begin. The automaton checks that the sequence of times and accelerations observed is consistent with stepping and abandons tracking of a step when unexpected inputs are observed, so that position integration is not done when movement is not as expected. We have observed that it detects steps in steady forward walking with 99% accuracy. Results with horizontal movement are poor (< 50%).

The display phone (in the headset) is configured as a WiFi hotspot. Ankle tracking phones are connected to the hotspot and send changes in integrated position using TCP messages in real time. There is a possibility that message aggregation might cause lag, and it may be preferable to use UDP datagrams instead, but we have not investigated the issue yet. There is a lag in onset of movement detection and transmission caused by the vertical acceleration detection requirement of the step detection automaton. After that, response time depends on data transmission time and the responsiveness of the game engine and display.

Data received from the ankle phones is used to drive player movement in a UE4 game. We have coded a module to establish network connection with phones and pass that data into the game. There are trade-offs in applying movement to players. Locations can be directly changed on each frame of game animation, giving smooth movement with little lag. However this relinquishes the option of integration with character walking animation and game physics simulation. Our current system applies movement increment 'requests' which cause animation and can be redirected on collisions. This requires buffering of received position changes and can introduce both lag and inaccuracy in position change. We have yet to investigate proper integration of our step detection with game walking animation.

Issues with the system at present include difficulty in detecting sideways steps, drift in horizontal direction, and possibly lag caused by the step detection automaton and integration into the game system. We are experimenting with the use of compass sensors for improving accuracy of horizontal direction tracking. At present the system does not have safety features. As users are walking blindly about in real space it is necessary to have an observer watching to ensure that they are not getting physically close to the edge of a physical playing area. In addition our practical experiments have used a virtual play space with clear boundaries that is small in comparison to the physical space available and have been of short enough duration to be certain that position drift could not lead users into danger.

4 Results

We [9] have tested the system with 8 participants in on a rectangular virtual environment with a position grid marked on the virtual ground, a number of signposts of different kinds and a small ramp/bridge construction. In reality participants were walking on a large sports ground that was flat and without obstacles, and large enough that they were not in danger of reaching the edge. The experience was that participants were able to successfully move as requested in the space, and found the experience pleasant. It was interesting to observe that they started tentatively but were soon moving confidently.

References

1. McCarthy, Steve: The VR Glossary. http://www.vrglossary.org/glossary/locomotion/, last accessed 2019/5/6.
2. Wikipaedia: List of Oculus Rift Games. https://en.wikipedia.org/wiki/List_of_Oculus_Rift_games, last accessed 2019/5/6.
3. Razzaque, S., Kohn, Z., & Whitton, M. C.: Redirected walking. In: Proceedings of EUROGRAPHICS vol. 9, pp. 105–106. Blackwell (2001).
4. Zero Latency web site describing commercial system. https://zerolatencyvr.com/, last accessed 2019/5/7.
5. Darken, R. P., Cockayne, W. R., & Carmein, D. The omni-directional treadmill: a locomotion device for virtual worlds. In Proceedings of the 10th annual ACM symposium on user interface software and technology (pp. 213–221). ACM, Banff (1997).
6. Medina, E., Fruland, R., & Weghorst, S. VIRTUSPHERE: Walking in a human size VR "hamster ball". In Proceedings of the Human Factors

and Ergonomics Society Annual Meeting, vol. 52, no. 27, pp. 2102–2106). SAGE Publications, Los Vegas (2008)
7. Virtuix Omni, https://www.virtuix.com/, last accessed 2019/5/6.
8. Google Daydream: https://vr.google.com/daydream/, last accessed 2019/6/7
9. Xiangyan Gao: Virtual Reality Free Walking Development. University of Waikato, COMP591 Dissertation (2018)

Motion analysis for identification of overused body segments: the packaging task in industry 4.0

Brenda E. Olivas Padilla, Alina Glushkova
and Sotiris Manitsaris

Centre for Robotics, MINES ParisTech, PSL Université Paris, France
brenda-elizabeth.olivas_padilla@minesparistech.fr,
alina.glushkova@minesparistech.fr, sotiris.manitsaris@minesparistech.fr

Abstract

This work presents a statistical analysis of professional gestures from house-hold appliances manufacturing. The goal is to investigate the hypothesis that some body segments are more involved than others in professional gestures and present thus higher ergonomic risk. The gestures were recorded with a full body Inertial Measurement Unit (IMU) suit and represented with rotations of each segment. Data dimensions have been reduced with principal component analysis (PCA), permitting us to reveal hidden correlations between the body segments and to extract the ones with the highest variance. This work aims at detecting among numerous upper body segments, which are the ones that are overused and consequently, which is the minimum number of segments that is sufficient to represent our dataset for ergonomic analysis. To validate the results, Hidden Markov Models (HMMs) based recognition method has been

---

How to cite this book chapter:
Olivas Padilla, B.E., Glushkova, A. and Manitsaris, S. 2020. Motion analysis for
identification of overused body segments: the packaging task in industry 4.0. In:
Loizides, F., Winckler, M., Chatterjee, U., Abdelnour-Nocera, J. and Parmaxi, A.
(eds.) *Human Computer Interaction and Emerging Technologies: Adjunct
Proceedings from the INTERACT 2019 Workshops*. Pp. 349–354. Cardiff: Cardiff
University Press. DOI: https://doi.org/10.18573/book3.as. License: CC-BY 4.0.

used and trained only with the segments from the PCA. The recognition accuracy of 95.71% was achieved confirming this hypothesis.

Keywords

Motion analysis · gesture recognition · PCA · ergonomics

1 Introduction

In industrial context, worker's health is directly linked to company's productivity. Ergonomists apply various methods to assess professional postures and gestures and to prevent Musculo-Skeletal Disorders (MSD). Most of these methods are based on observations and a qualitative posture evaluation [1]. One of the most used methods is RULA where the positions of individual body segments are observed and the more there is a deviation from the neutral posture the higher score, which represents the level of MSD risk [2]. The use of motion capture (mocap) technology may bring a significant added value to this analysis and complete it with parameters such as precise information about movement's biomechanics. However, the data provided by mocap may be too complex and in some cases redundant for ergonomic analysis. In this work our goal is to validate that only few body segments form groups of potentially overused body parts. Similar studies of body segments categorisation have been done in the field of expressive gestures [3], but also of handicraft movements [4]. The conclusion from this analysis could be used to define the minimum necessary number of segments to be recorded and analysed.

2 Method

The dataset used for the analysis has been captured with an Inertial Measurement Unit (IMU) full body suit from Nansense Inc. [5] under real conditions in a factory. One worker was recorded performing the packaging task, that consists of grasping boxes of TVs from a conveyor and placing them on a palette in 4 different levels. Each level includes 8 boxes of TVs. Once the worker completed one level, he moved to the next one until finishing the palette with the 4th level. The suit is composed of 52 sensors placed throughout the body. Through the inverse kinematics solver provided by Nansense Studio, the body segments' rotations (Euler angle) on 3 axes X, Y and Z were computed. Fig. 1 illustrates the worker placing a box on the 4th level.

This study was focused only on the upper body of the worker excluding the fingers recorded with the gloves. The dataset included rotations on 3 XYZ axis from 17 sensors resulting in 51 variables in total. This dataset was separated into 4 subsets corresponding to the 4 levels. Each of the subsets included thus

a)   b)

Fig. 1: (a) Visualisation from Nansense Studio. (b) The real gesture of the worker.

the gestures of grasping and placing a box on the corresponding level (from 1st to 4th) while repeating the procedure 8 times (for 8 boxes).

2.1 Dimension reduction with PCA

Before applying principal component analysis (PCA), Factor Analysis has been used to preprocess and fuse the 3 axes rotations from 17 sensors to facilitate the interpretation of the results and to have one variable per sensor. The weights of each XYZ variable have been calculated, and each rotation has been multiplied by its weight and divided by the sum of the weights, as explained in [4]. Resulting in 17 variables per set instead of 51. To check data validity and adequacy, Barlett test of Sphericity and the Kaiser-Meyer-Olkin Measure of Sampling Adequacy (MSA) have been done. These tests permit us to discard the variables that have insufficient loadings. Such as Right Forearm/Arm/Hand and Head from the second subset, and only Right Forearm/Arm from the third. PCA with Varimax orthogonal rotation has been thus applied to each one of the four resulting subsets. Two components (C1 and C2) were extracted per each subset representing above the 83,78% of the total variance. In Table 1 the 7 variables with the highest eigenvalues from each component are shown in decreasing order according to the mean through the 4 subsets.

By analysing the PCA results, a different group of variables can be detected in each component. In C1, the spine and shoulders, which are generally linked to the back, result from having the highest eigenvalues, unlike C2 where the highest were the variables related to the arms. These body segments identified appear to be consistent with the body segments that, according to the RULA, mainly cause the high ergonomic risk of the gesture. These are the back and arms, segments that have the highest score in RULA. From each component, only the variables that had the highest mean eigenvalues per body segment were

Table 1: Eigenvalues from C1 and C2.

Component	Segment	Level 1	Level 2	Level 3	Level 4	Mea n
	Spine 1	**0.938**	**0.976**	**0.950**	**0.981**	0.96 1
	Spine 2	0.933	0.976	0.954	0.980	0.96 0
	Spine 3	0.936	0.975	0.952	0.968	0.95 8
C1	**Right Shoulder**	**0.952**	**0.975**	**0.952**	**0.945**	0.95 6
	Right Shoulder 2	0.962	0.956	0.937	0.949	0.95 1
	Spine	0.925	0.953	0.951	0.971	0.95 0
	Left Shoulder	**0.936**	**0.965**	**0.944**	**0.952**	0.94 9
	Left Hand	0.786	**0.928**	**0.786**	0.471	0.74 3
	Left Forearm	**0.809**	**0.914**	0.588	0.320	0.65 8
	Left Arm	0.759	0.402	0.337	0.689	0.54 7
C2	**Right Forearm**	**0.858**	0.000	0.000	**0.929**	0.44 7
	Neck	0.424	0.288	0.273	0.398	0.34 6
	Right Arm	0.453	0.000	0.000	**0.928**	0.34 5
	Head	0.597	0.000	−0.005	0.629	0.30 5

chosen for gesture recognition. For example, as the back has more than three variables covering the same body segment (Spine, Spine 1, Spine 2, Spine 3), Spine 1 was selected since it had the highest mean eigenvalues.

2.2 Gesture recognition with hidden Markov models

For gesture recognition Hidden Markov Models (HMMs) has proved to be a prominent tool [4]; hence it was used for this study. The XYZ rotations of the variables from C1 and C2, highlighted in Table 1, were used separately for the gesture recognition. HMMs were trained with 4 classes where each class corresponded to the gesture of placing the box on 1 of the 4 levels of the palette. Therefore, the dataset used in this section has 4 classes for 4 levels of the palette and 8 repetitions per class.

3 Results

To evaluate the proposed method, the dataset was split in an 80% training set – 20% test set to estimate the accuracy of the gesture/level recognition. This evaluation was repeated 10 times taking in each a different training set and test set, as the samples were selected randomly in each iteration. The results showed 81.43% of accuracy for the C1 variables and 95.71% for the C2. Consequently, the use of the 4 variables contained in C2 are sufficient to recognise high ergonomic risk gestures, only 2 gestures from Level 3 and 1 from Level 4 were misclassified.

4 Conclusion

In an industrial context, workers perform complex professional gestures that contain essential information about ergonomic risks. In this work we formulate the hypothesis that some body segments are more involved than others in "packaging" professional gestures and they present thus a higher risk of injury. PCA underlined some groups of variables that corresponded to the ones with the highest RULA (back and arms) score. When those variables were used separately for gesture recognition, a better accuracy was achieved with the variables of C2 confirming that these variables seem to be the ones that represent the best our data. Being able to identify those segments could be interesting for a more fast and efficient ergonomic analysis of worker's gestures. At the same time, since the use of full-body mocap suit in industrial context has several difficulties, this analysis could contribute to the identification of the minimum number of segments to record by using more acceptable technologies such as a smartphone (for the back) or a smartwatch (for the arms). To generalise these first results the future work would consist of performing a similar analysis on a bigger dataset including recordings from more than one worker as well as on different types of features.

Acknowledgments

The research leading to these results has received funding by the EU Horizon 2020 Research and Innovation Programme under grant agreement No. 820767, project CoLLaboratE. We want to acknowledge the Arçelik factory for their support in this work.

References

1. Takala, E.-P., Pehkonen, I., Forsman, M., Hansson, G.-Å., Mathiassen, S.E., Neumann, W.P., Sjøgaard, G., Veiersted, K.B., Westgaard, R.H., Winkel, J.: Systematic evaluation of observational methods assessing biomechanical exposures at work. 36, 3–24 (2018). https://doi.org/10.5271/sjweh.2876.
2. Berlin, C., Adams, C.: Ergonomics Evaluation Methods. In: Production Ergonomics: Designing Work Systems to Support Optimal Human Performance. pp. 139–160. Ubiquity Press, London (2017). https://doi.org/https://doi.org/10.5334/bbe.h.

3. Glowinski, D., Dael, N., Camurri, A., Volpe, G., Mortillaro, M., Scherer, K.: Toward a Minimal Representation of Affective Gestures. IEEE Trans. Affect. Comput. 2, 106–118 (2011). https://doi.org/10.1109/T-AFFC.2011.7.
4. Volioti, C., Manitsaris, S., Manitsaris, A.: Offline statistical analysis of gestural skills in pottery interaction. In: MOCO'14. pp. 172–173. ACM (2014).
5. Nansense Inc. (2019) Biomed. https://www.nansense.com/suits/ Accessed 6 June 2019.

Mirror-mirror on the screen am I the most aligned than I have ever been?

Katerina El Raheb[*,†], Marina Stergiou[*,†],
Akrivi Katifori[*,†] and Yannis Ioannidis[*,†]

[*]Athena Research Center
[†]National and Kapodistrian University of Athens, Athens, Greece
kelraheb@di.uoa.gr, mstergiou@di.uoa.gr, vivi@di.uoa.gr, yannis@di.uoa.gr

Abstract

Recent progress in motion sensing, combined with the advanced visualization, augmented reality technologies and related movement computing research, open a great range of opportunities in realtime embodied learning applied to motion domains such as dance, sports, rehabilitation, fitness and well-being. In particular, low-end devices such as Kinect, have been used recently in a variety of domains that extend the paradigm of Augmented Mirror for dance self-training. In this paper we discuss the advantages and disadvantages of these paradigms and settings based on literature research, our previous work in WhoLoDancE project and reflection through an ongoing design process and prototyping of learning experiences related to dance. We focus on identified challenges through a user-centered and interdisciplinary lens with the belief that focusing on particular aspects of movement, guided by the practice itself can lead to more meaningful experiences for self-training.

How to cite this book chapter:
El Raheb, K., Stergiou, M., Katifori, A. and Ioannidis. Y. 2020. Mirror-mirror on the screen am I the most aligned than I have ever been? In: Loizides, F., Winckler, M., Chatterjee, U., Abdelnour-Nocera, J. and Parmaxi, A. (eds.) *Human Computer Interaction and Emerging Technologies: Adjunct Proceedings from the INTERACT 2019 Workshops.* Pp. 355–360. Cardiff: Cardiff University Press. DOI: https://doi.org/10.18573/book3.at. License: CC-BY 4.0.

Keywords

Technology Enhanced Learning · Dance · Movement Analysis and Interaction · Human Computer Interaction · Embodied Learning

1 Making the best out of Augmented Mirror for Dance Learning

In this work, we focus on the advantages and limitations of the augmented mirror setting, using depth cameras such as Kinect [1, 8–12, 18, 21] or regular cameras [13, 19]. In addition, although the goal is different, dance learning experiences design can benefit from existing guidelines in movement based games [14]. As we describe in [4, 6], designing an effective system for dance or embodied training poses a number of HCI and computational challenges. These include identifying the ideal devices and strategies for capturing movement and processing real-time data to provide appropriate feedback. We argue that there is not one solution to fit all and that the possible answers are highly related not only to the devices used but also to the movement domain, dance genre and particular learning objectives.

Comparing to a regular mirror, the setting of the Augmented Mirror presents several advantages, such as providing feedback on what can be enhanced in terms of technique or body posture, as if seen from a different spatial perspective [10, 21] or different time [13]. Similar solutions have been applied for capturing and evaluating effectively the posture of piano performers [16]. In addition, the Augmented Mirror set is simple, low cost, and the mover does not have to wear any special devices. One of the risks however, is that the mover can become more focused on the screen rather than on the embodied experience [14] – A critique that is also valid when using a physical mirror in dance practice. In this work we examine the main characteristics that contribute to the optimum efficiency of the Augmented Mirror for dance learning.

1.1 Conceptual Frameworks and ontologies

The three year EU funded project WhoLoDancE, engaged a group of experts, representatives of four dance genres (Ballet, Contemporary, Greek Folk, Flamenco) [17], in co-design sessions. The question of what to measure and how for evaluating the learners performance was persistent in the design process. As a result, we proposed a conceptual framework [2, 7] that focuses on different Movement Principles, i.e. aspects such as symmetry, balance, alignment, that a student might need to focus on independently of the dance genre. Camurri [3], present the different levels of features and categorises them based on how much processing or complexity they need in comparison to raw data from different sensors. This categorisation not only suggests that some aspects are harder to compute (e.g., qualitative characteristics, vs. posture or velocity), but also that not all devices are appropriate for capturing some of these features in the first place. For example, optical motion capture, depth and direct cameras cannot directly measure the pressure on the floor, and therefore evaluate effectively weight transfer on the feet. We argue that conceptual frameworks as well as ontologies about the devices [23], and/or domain knowledge of the application dance genre, can effectively guide the design of augmented mirror experiences for learning through expressing categories and rules related to movement performance and structure.

1.2 Measuring technique vs. comparing with expert dancers

The augmented mirror paradigm using Kinect for evaluating students performance can be used in dance in two ways: one is to compare the overall performance and closeness of positions and motions in relation to a stored ideal performance [1, 9]. The other is to define particular rules and patterns focusing on specific aspects e.g, calculate the posture deviation through defining e.g torso misalignment or rotation to the pelvis rotation and compare with the ideal range [10, 21]. Although most of the systems that use the first approach provide specific feedback on body parts, this might not be very accurate due to differences between human bodies, and learning objectives that are aligned with the dance system of teaching and practicing. Nevertheless, creating a repository of movement is expensive in cost and time and poses the constraint of capturing students, and teachers' movement with the same precision. On the other hand, one can still be correct in terms of relations and proportions according to what the technique suggests,being within this correct range even if they adopt this correctness for their own body shape and abilities. This approach might be more appropriate as body analogies can differ. Each body is different and it should be compared with its own ideal posture, not with somebody else, especially if the low end device does not allow for such precision in motion capture.

1.3 Mapping of movement practice with limitations of the set-up and hardware

Not surprisingly, most of the aforementioned efforts, target ballet [10–13, 18, 21–22,], a dance genre that requires precision of the shape and posture of the body and has a specific movement vocabulary and terminology suggesting clear known positions and transitions, and rules. It is also traditionally taught in front of the mirror. In addition, conceptual frameworks and ontologies of the movement genre as the one we have developed in our previous work [5] is extended to categorise parts of the syllabus that can benefit of similar exercises.

For example, a ballet dancer can still be performing a good developpé (slow extension of the leg) and be correct, having the spine vertical, and the pelvis aligned, even if they are not still able to extend as high as a professional dancer. In addition the posture might still be correct in terms of technique even if the mover chooses a different posture for the arms or even different directions for the leg extension.

1.4 Feedback: Focus on one aspect at a time

While early attempts use the method of alignment of the positions and motion and evaluate accuracy overall [1, 9], recent research has shown that evaluating the overall similarity compared to a teachers or professionals standard might have several implications that relate to both the evaluation and comparison itself, as well as to the provision of effective feedback [20, 22]. This approach, allows the user to focus on a particular aspect, without cognitive overload and frustration, focus research on particular means of feedback, and overcome the limitations of technology. With the appropriate mapping we can turn the limitations of a technology into an advantage [14]. Trajkova [22] in her evaluation on particular feedback (visual, verbal, emojis) involving 16 novices and 16 advanced ballet students, concludes that providing particular feedback on aspects e.g., focus either on one aspect of movement alignment or one body part is much more effective. Taking into account basic usability principles [15], it is important for the mover to understand what the system measures and what to improve. Knudsen [10] presents an effective system focusing on one dance genre, ballet, one exercise and one objective of learning and self-improvement, in this case alignment providing audio-visual feedback.

2 Conclusion

Evaluating one's movement in dance using low-end devices is a challenging task. The skilled dancer focuses on so many aspects of the shape and quality of the movement simultaneously, without thinking. Nevertheless, the limitation of not evaluating all aspects at once can become a strength from an educational perspective, especially for beginners and amateurs. Building on the idea of less-is-more and informing the design by the concepts and rules of the dance technique, low-end devices and the paradigm of the augmented mirror can create effective scenarios of learning applications.

In this paper based on a) a literature survey of the relevant research that use the augmented mirror paradigm, b) the reflection on the users needs that emerged throughout the WhoLoDancE project and the development of conceptual framework, we summarize some best practices for designing and developing such applications. Currently our application, integrates a variety of modes for practicing alignment, directionality, and other aspects related to dance exercises providing feedback both in abstract manner and through score.

References

1. Alexiadis, D.S., Kelly, P., Daras, P., O'Connor, N.E., Boubekeur, T., Moussa, M.B.: Evaluating a dancer's performance using kinect-based skeleton tracking. ACM Int. Conf. Multimed. pp. 659–662 (2011). https://doi.org/10.1145/2072298.2072412, http://dl.acm.org/citation.cfm?doid=2072298.2072412

2. Camurri, A., El Raheb, K., Even-Zohar, O., Ioannidis, Y., Markatzi, A., Matos, J.M., Morley-Fletcher, E., Palacio, P., Romero, M., Sarti, A., et al.: Wholodance: Towards a methodology for selecting motion capture data across different dance learning practice. In: 3rd International Symposium on Movement and Computing (2016)

3. Camurri, A., Volpe, G., Piana, S., Mancini, M., Niewiadomski, R., Ferrari, N., Canepa, C.: The Dancer in the Eye. Proc. 3rd Int. Symp. Mov. Comput. – MOCO '16. pp. 1–7 (2016). https://doi.org/10.1145/2948910.2948927, http://dl.acm.org/citation.cfm?doid=2948910.2948927

4. El Raheb, K., Katifori, A., Ioannidis, Y.E.: Hci challenges in dance education. ICST Trans. Ambient Systems 3(9), e7 (2016)

5. El Raheb, K., Papapetrou, N., Katifori, V., Ioannidis, Y.: Balonse: Ballet ontology for annotating and searching video performances. In: 3rd International Symposium on Movement and Computing (2016)

6. El Raheb, K., Stergiou, M., Katifori, A., Ioannidis, Y.: Dance interactive learning systems: A study on interaction workflow and teaching approaches. ACM Computing Surveys (2019)

7. El Raheb, K., Whatley, S., Camurri, A.: A conceptual framework for creating and analyzing dance learning digital content. In: Proceedings of the 5th International Conference on Movement and Computing. p. 2. ACM (2018)

8. Hong, G.S., Park, S.W., Park, S.H., Nasridinov, A., Park, Y.H.: A ballet posture education using IT techniques. Proc. Sixth Int. Conf. Emerg. Databases Technol. Appl. Theory – EDB '16 (c), 114–116 (2016). https://doi.org/10.1145/3007818.3007840, http://dl.acm.org/citation.cfm?doid=3007818.3007840

9. Kitsikidis, A., Dimitropoulos, K., Douka, S., Grammalidis, N.: Dance Analysis using Multiple Kinect Sensors. VISAPP2014, Lisbon, Port. pp. 789–795 (2014)

10. Knudsen, E.W., Hølledig, M.L., Nielsen, M.J., Petersen, R.K., Bach-Nielsen, S., Zanescu, B.C., Overholt, D., Purwins, H., Helweg, K.: Audio-Visual Feedback for Self-monitoring Posture in Ballet Training. Proc. Int. Conf. New Interfaces Music. Expr. pp. 71–76 (2017), http://www.nime.org/proceedings/2017/nime2017 paper0015.pdf

11. Kyan, M., Sun, G., Li, H., Zhong, L., Muneesawang, P., Dong, N., Elder, B., Guan, L.: An Approach to Ballet Dance Training through MS Kinect and Visualization in a CAVE Virtual Reality Environment. ACM Trans. Intell. Syst. Technol. **6**(2), 1–37 (2015). https://doi.org/10.1145/2735951, http://dl.acm.org/citation.cfm?id=2753829.2735951
12. Marquardt, Z., Beira, J., Em, N., Paiva, I., Kox, S.: Super mirror: a kinect interface for ballet dancers. In: CHI'12 Extended Abstracts on Human Factors in Computing Systems. pp. 1619–1624. ACM (2012)
13. Molina-tanco, L., García-berdonés, C.: The Delay Mirror: a Technological Innovation Specific to the Dance Studio (2017)
14. Mueller, F., Isbister, K.: Movement-based game guidelines. In: Proceedings of the 32nd annual ACM conference on Human factors in computing systems. pp. 2191–2200. ACM (2014)
15. Nielsen, J.: 10 usability heuristics for user interface design. Nielsen Norman Group **1**(1) (1995)
16. Payeur, P., Nascimento, G.M.G., Beacon, J., Comeau, G., Cretu, A.M., D'Aoust, V., Charpentier, M.A.: Human gesture quantification: An evaluation tool for somatic training and piano performance. 2014 IEEE Int. Symp. Haptic, Audio Vis. Environ. Games, HAVE 2014 – Proc. pp. 100–105 (2014). https://doi.org/10.1109/HAVE.2014.6954339
17. Rizzo, A., El Raheb2, K., Whatley, S., Cisneros, R.M., Zanoni, M., Camurri, A., Viro, V., Matos, J.M., Piana, S., Buccoli, M., et al.: Wholodance: Whole-body interaction learning for dance education
18. Sun, G., Muneesawang, P., Kyan, M., Li, H., Zhong, L., Dong, N., Elder, B., Guan, L.: An advanced computational intelligence system for training of ballet dance in a cave virtual reality environment. Proc. – 2014 IEEE Int. Symp. Multimedia, ISM 2014 (1), 159–166 (2015). https://doi.org/10.1109/ISM.2014.55
19. Toolbox, W.D.: Badco. and danielturing. Transmission in Motion: The Technologizing of Dance p. 118 (2016)
20. Trajkova, M., Cafaro, F.: E-Ballet: Designing for remote ballet learning. Ubi-Comp 2016 Adjun. – Proc. 2016 ACM Int. Jt. Conf. Pervasive Ubiquitous Comput. pp. 213–216 (2016). https://doi.org/10.1145/2968219.2971442
21. Trajkova, M.: Usability Evaluation of Kinect-Based System for Ballet Movements Usability Evaluation of Kinect-Based System for Ballet (June) (2015). https://doi.org/10.13140/RG.2.1.3964.0726
22. Trajkova, M., Cafaro, F.: Takes Tutu to Ballet: Designing Visual and Verbal Feedback for Augmented Mirrors. Proc. ACM Interact. Mob. Wearable Ubiquitous Technol **10**(20), 1–30 (2018). https://doi.org/10.1145/1234, https://doi.org/10.1145/3191770
23. Wikstr, R., Lilius, J., Pegalajar, M.: Understanding Movement and Interaction: an Ontology for Kinect-based 3D Depth Sensors (2013)

Skeleton tracking for serious games and real-time medical diagnosis

Mohamed Adjel[*,†,‡], Antoine Seilles[*], Denis Mottet[†]
and Guillaume Tallon[*]

[*]Euromov, 700 Avenue du Pic Saint-Loup, 34090 Montpellier, France
denis.mottet@umontpellier.fr
[†]NaturalPad, 700 Avenue du Pic Saint-Loup, 34090 Montpellier, France
antoine@naturalpad.fr, guillaume.tallon@naturalpad.fr
[‡]Polytech Marseille, 163 Avenue de Luminy, 13009 Marseille
mohamed-ala-eddine.adjel@etu.univ-amu.fr

Abstract

Physical rehabilitation of people with reduced mobility implies to monitor the movements of the patients during the rehabilitation sessions, so to individualize the therapy patient by patient. A serious-games company, NaturalPad (NP), would like to develop a cheap real-time markerless skeleton tracking device ensuring diagnosis assistance of neuromuscular and articular pathologies among reduced mobility persons such as elderly, post-stroke and persons affected by disability. In this way, the goal of this device is to precisely assess 3D body joints coordinates in real-time, that will be used to format accurate indicators about articular capacities of the patient during a physiotherapy session. These indicators, such as the Range of Motion (ROM) of each articulation, will be printed on a Graphical User Interface (GUI), so the physiotherapist can monitor the

How to cite this book chapter:
Adjel, M., Seilles, A., Mottet, D. and Tallon, G. 2020. Skeleton tracking for serious games and real-time medical diagnosis. In: Loizides, F., Winckler, M., Chatterjee, U., Abdelnour-Nocera, J. and Parmaxi, A. (eds.) *Human Computer Interaction and Emerging Technologies: Adjunct Proceedings from the INTERACT 2019 Workshops.* Pp. 361–368. Cardiff: Cardiff University Press. DOI: https://doi.org/10.18573/book3.au. License: CC-BY 4.0.

evolution of the patients pathologies. After giving details about related studies, we will explicit technological requirements and project constraints. Last we will define a benchmark process of existing skeleton tracking algorithms and cheap motion capture devices. The results will allow us to evaluate if there is an enough accurate camera/algorithm combination to deal with our issues.

Keywords

Real-time skeleton tracking · Medical diagnosis · Joint angles estimation

1 Related works and technological requirements

1.1 Device and algorithm requirements

The Kinect v2[1] and Unity3D[2] are interesting tools to develop real-time interaction games for physical rehabilitation [1–2]. Actually, a lot of movements are supported by NPs serious games platform, such as steps, chest inclination, hands movement and squatting series. We are able to have precise enough skeleton data to improve functional autonomy among older adults [2–3]. Nevertheless, due to Kinect imprecision, we are unable to correctly recognize head inclinations, ankle/chest rotations and center of mass approximation. Moreover, the Kinect skeleton tracking algorithm doesn't take into account osseous and articular constraints of human body, so it's not precise enough for detailed articular angles analysis [2]. Yet, our device must respect skeletal constraints to be used for joints angles assessment.

Thus, the device needs to fulfill 3 technological constraints: 1) being able to handle RGB and/or depth data for real-time interaction in games, 2) being able to extract accurate enough 3D coordinates of the patients articulations to estimate articulations angles for diagnosis purposes, and 3) being sensor agnostic. The combination sensor/algorithm and hardware configuration have to be as cheap as possible, because of commercial constraints. The final device must be easy to set up, thereby the physiotherapist won't have to reconfigure and calibrate the set up between two sessions.

1.2 Clinical uses of depth cameras

Many studies [5–12] have examined the Kinect for assessment and balance control. They indicate that for relatively slow movements, the Kinect can give enough accurate skeleton data to perform dynamic tests as functional reach, sit

---

[1] http://www.arzapstudio.com/kinect-for-windows/.
[2] https://unity.com/.

to stand and timed up and go. Encouraging results also shown that the Kinect sensor can be useful for medical diagnosis and monitoring of patients suffering from Parkinsons, scoliosis and post-stroke diseases [13–15]. However, as we want to estimate articular capacities, were not sure if Kinect is worthwhile given the inaccuracy associated with some of the variables extracted by the sensor [5]. This is particularly true considering the turning movement, as the Kinect cannot accurately record postural movement when the patient performs the turn. Very recent studies [16–19] already worked on medical diagnosis with depth sensors. In [16], a serious games platform is conceived for home-based rehabilitation after the hospitalisation period, with automated evaluation of the patient during the training. Clinical indicators are extracted, such as neglected body areas during session or errors in limbs trajectory. In [16–18] its shown that depth-sensors can be useful for post-stroke rehabilitation serious games and motor function diseases diagnosis among elderly. The study in [19] also demonstrates very encouraging results in clinical data assessment using Intel RealSense depth cameras.

1.3 Joint angles estimation

As a reminder, the device we want to develop should be able to precisely extract 3D coordinates of skeleton joints in real-time, accurately estimate joint angles during a physiotherapy session, and, in the ideal case, during a serious-game session. Several studies [20–23] used markerless motion capture systems to estimate joint angles and compared these values with ground truth to estimate the accuracy of the depth sensor for such task. Studies [20–22] assessed the joint angles estimation accuracy of the Kinect for clinical uses. Marker based motion capture systems were used in [20–21] as ground truth, while [22] used an IMU device. [20] concluded that the Kinect system is not yet suitable for clinical assessments while [21] concluded the opposite. This contrast is explained by the fact that [20] uses a VICON system as ground truth, yet, studies [24–25] shown that there can be interferences between VICON and Kinect that slant the joints coordinates assessment of the Kinect [21] used a jig as guinea pig, instead of real humans, which can distort the results [22] demonstrates that the Kinect is efficient in knee joint angle estimation, which is not sufficient as we want accuracy on all body joints. As far as we know, there is no marker-less device that aims accurately estimating joint angles in real-time to deduce articular capacities of the patient in the context of medical diagnosis support.

1.4 Real-time human pose estimation

Several papers [26–31, 43] tackled the 3D real-time human pose estimation issue. Even if [27] estimates only 2D joint coordinates, we will keep it for our benchmark, for several reasons: 1) It works in real-time on cheap hardware

2) We can deduce 3D coordinates from 2D [32] 3) It uses a monocular RGB camera, which is cheap 4) We want to verify if its accurate for joint angles estimation. We already eliminated [26, 28–31] because of License requirements (cost or lack of documentation). Implementations remaining for the benchmark are [27], Nuitrack, Kinect SDK v2 and Orbbec SDK. First of all, we aim to determine the level of accuracy we can obtain with state-of-the-art real-time skeleton tracking algorithms and a single sensor. We will benchmark different combinations of algorithms/sensors to determine which couple is the best, using the constraints mentioned in 2)a) as criteria to select the best combination camera/algorithm. Then, physiotherapists will assess the clinical relevance of the best combination in selected use cases, for diagnosis and physical rehabilitation.

2 Benchmarking process

For this benchmark, we will test the skeleton tracking algorithms mentioned above and following markerless motion capture devices: Microsoft Kinect v2, Orbbec Astra, Intel RealSense D435i, Regular webcam (for [27]). We will assess the error of pose estimation for each sensor/algorithm combination. To calculate the estimation error for each device, we will use a state of the art motion capture system (VICON, Oxford metrics)[3] as reference system. We will record the movements with the two systems, and will compare the 3D coordinates values given by the VICON with 3D coordinates values given by the tested device/algorithm combination. As mentioned above, the VICON system infrared waves can interfere with markerless sensors. A protocol is defined in [24] to minimize this noise, so we will reduce the number of markers and the distance between Kinect and the volunteer. Then, we will implement the following steps: 1) Collecting skeleton data from Vicon and Tested Camera 2) Synchronize the data in Time, as Vicon and cameras have different frequencies 3) Compute each joints angles thanks to cosines law and calculate the angles assessment error of each camera/algorithm combination 4) Selection of the optimal combination. The last step will consist in comparing the joints angle assessment accuracy of the optimal solution with the accuracy needed by physiotherapists.

3 Further researches

Actually Convolutional Neural Networks (CNNs) are widely used for monocular 3D human pose estimation and show the most accurate results [46]. Nevertheless, both top-down and bottom-up approaches don't take into account the human skeleton constraints. Our approach will consist in using

---

[3] http://www.vicon.com.

Denavit-Hartenberg (D-H) convention to model geometric and kinematic skeleton [45]. Coupled with CNN algorithm we theoretically will be able to have an accurate and constrained skeleton [43] shows we can enhance joints coordinates estimation with integrating skeleton constraints during the training process. Moreover, without going into the algorithm technicalities, we can add human skeleton constraints in two other ways:

- Refine identified human silhouettes (works for top-down approaches) with D-H before recognizing joints on the silhouette
- Refine the pose with D-H after joints coordinates assessment (works for both bottom-up and top-down approaches)

We think both of these refinement steps would enhance accuracy and realism of extracted skeleton coordinates. However, this will have an impact on computational speed that we will have to keep reasonable. Depending on obtained results, we will remove some cost constraints to compute a heavy algorithm on costly hardware device.

References

1. Bakhti K, Mottet D, Mélia G, Laffont I, *Low cost objective diagnosis of learned nonuse of the paretic arm after a stroke using Kinect technology.* Annals of Physical and Rehabilitation Medicine, 58, e11–e12. (2015)
2. Tallon G, Seilles A, Mélia G, Andary S, Di Loreto I, Blain H, *Intérêt du serious game Hammer & Planks pour améliorer lautonomie fonctionnelle chez la personne âgée institutionnalisée.* ICEPS, 19–21 mars, Montpellier (2015)
3. Tallon G, Seilles A, Mélia G, Andary S, Bernard P, Di Loreto I, Blain H. *Effects of the serious game Medimoov on the functional autonomy of institutionalized older adults. Annals of Physical and Rehabilitation Medicine* – Proceedings of the 30th Annual Congress of the French Society of Physical and Rehabilitation Medicine 58, e113e114.(2015)
4. K. Bakhti, I. Laffont, M. Muthalib, J. Froger and D. Mottet, *Kinect-based assessment of proximal arm non-use after a stroke,* (2018)
5. Ross A Clark, F. Mentiplay, E. Hough, Y. Pua, *Three-dimensional cameras and skeleton pose tracking for physical function assessment: A review of uses, validity, current developments and Kinect alternatives,* 2018
6. A. Clark, Y. Pua, K. Fortin, C. Ritchie, E. Webster, L. Denehy, L. Bryant, *Validity of the Microsoft Kinect for assessment of postural control,* (2012)
7. B. Dehbandi, A. Barachant, H. Smeragliuolo, J. Long, S. Bumanlag, V. He, A. Lampe, D. Putrino, *Using data from the Microsoft Kinect 2 to determine postural stability in healthy subjects: A feasibility trial,* (2017)
8. M. Eltoukhy, C. Kuenze, J. Oh, F. Signorile, *Validation of Static and Dynamic Balance Assessment using Microsoft Kinect for Young and Elderly Populations,* (2018)

9. S. Galen, V. Pardo, D. Wyatt, A. Diamond, V. Brodith, A. Pavlov, *Validity of an Interactive Functional Reach Test*, (2015)
10. T. Ramei, Y. Orito, H. Funaya, K. Ikeda, Y. Okada, T. Shibata, *Kinect-based posturography for in-home rehabilitation of balance disorders*, (2015)
11. Y. Yang, F. Pu, Y. Li, S. Li, Y. Fan, D.Li, *Reliability and Validity of Kinect RGB-D Sensor for Assessing Standing Balance*, (2014)
12. A Clark, Y. Pua, C Oliveira, J Bower, T. Rebekah, McGaw, K. Hasanki, F Mentiplay, *Reliability and concurrent validity of the Microsoft Kinect V2 for assessment of standing balance and postural control*, (2015)
13. R. Torres, M. Huerta, R. Clotet, R. Gonzlez, L.E. Snchez, D. Rivas and M. Erazo, *A Kinect Based Approach to Assist in the Diagnosis and Quantification of Parkinsons Disease*, (2016)
14. Vincent Bonnet, Takazumi Yamaguchi, Arnaud Dupeyron, Sebastien Andary, Antoine Seilles, Philippe Fraisse, *Automatic Estimate of Back Anatomical Landmarks and 3D spine curve From a Kinect Sensor*, (2016)
15. Stephanie Vernon, Kade Paterson, Kelly Bower, Jennifer McGinley, Kimberly Miller, Yong-Hao Pua, and Ross A. Clark, *Quantifying individual components of the timed up and go using the kinect in people living with stroke*, (2014)
16. Matteo Morando, Serena Ponte, Elisa Ferrara and Silvana Dellepiane, *Definition of Motion and Biophysical Indicators for Home-Based Rehabilitation through Serious Games*, (2018)
17. Robert J. Dawel, Lei Yu, Sue E. Leurgans, Timothy Truty, Thomas Curran, Jeffrey M. Hausdorff, Markus A. Wimmer, Joel A. Block, David A. Bennett, Aron S. Buchman, *Expanding instrumented gait testing in the community setting: A portable, depth-sensing camera captures joint motion in older adults*, (2019)
18. Mengxuan Ma, Rachel Proffitt, Marjorie Skubic, *Validation of a Kinect V2 based rehabilitation game*, (2018)
19. Francesco Luke Siena, Bill Byrom, Paul Watts & Philip Breedon, *Utilising the Intel RealSense Camera for Measuring Health Outcomes in Clinical Research*, (2018)
20. Shayan Bahadori, Philip Davenport, Tikki Immins & Thomas W. Wainwright, *Validation of joint angle measurements: comparison of a novel low-cost marker-less system with an industry standard marker-based system*, (2019)
21. Anne Schmitz, Mao Ye, Robert Shapiro, Ruigang Yang, Brian Noehren, *Accuracy and repeatability of joint angles measured using a single camera markerless motion capture system*, (2014)
22. Nazeeh Alothmany, Afzal Khan, Majdi Alnowaimi, Ali H. Morfeq, Ehab A Hafez, *Accuracy of joint angles tracking using markerless motion system*, (2014)
23. Franziska Schlagenhauf, Siddarth Sreeram and William Singhose, *Comparison of Kinect and Vicon Motion Capture of Upper-Body Joint Angle Tracking*, (2018)

24. Mreza Naeemabadi, Birthe Dinesen, Ole Kseler Andersen and John Hansen, *Influence of a marker-based motion capture system on the performance of Microsoft Kinect v2 skeleton algorithm*, (2018)

25. MReza Naeemabadi, Birthe Dinesen, Ole Kseler Andersen, John Hansen, *Investigating the impact of a motion capture system on Microsoft Kinect v2 recordings: A caution for using the technologies together*, (2019)

26. Zhe Cao Tomas Simon Shih-En Wei Yaser Sheikh, *OpenPose: Realtime Multi-Person 2D Pose Estimation using Part Affinity Fields*, The Robotics Institute, Carnegie Mellon University, (2017)

27. Daniil Osokin, *Real-time 2D Multi-Person Pose Estimation on CPU: Lightweight OpenPose*, (2018)

28. Muhammed Kocabas, M. Salih Karagoz, Emre Akbas, *MultiPoseNet: Fast Multi-Person Pose Estimation using Pose Residual Network*, (2018)

29. Dushyant Mehta, Srinath Sridhar, Oleksandr Sotnychenko, Helge Rhodin, Mohammad Shafiei, Hans-Peter Seidel, Weipeng Xu, Dan Casas, Christian Theobalt, *VNect: Real-time 3D Human Pose Estimation with a Single RGB camera*, (2017)

30. Hao-Shu Fang, Shuqin Xie, Yu-Wing Tai, Cewu Lu, *RMPE: Regional Multi-Person Pose Estimation*, (2018)

31. Riza Alp Guler, Natalia Neverova, Iasonas Kokkinos, *DensePose: Dense Human Pose Estimation In The Wild*, (2018)

32. Sandika Biswas, Sanjana Sinha, Kavya Gupta and Brojeshwar Bhowmick, *Lifting 2d Human Pose to 3d: A Weakly Supervised Approach*, (2019)

33. Kwok-Yun Yeung, Tsz-Ho Kwok, and Charlie C. L. Wang, *Improved Skeleton Tracking by Duplex Kinects: A Practical Approach for Real-Time Applications*, (2013)

34. Marco Carraro, Matteo Munaro, Jeff Burke and Emanuele Menegatti, *Real-time marker-less multi-person 3D pose estimation in RGB-Depth camera networks*, (2017)

35. Sungphill Moon, Youngbin Park, Dong Wook Ko, Il Hong Suh, *Multiple Kinect Sensor fusion for human skeleton tracking using Kalman Filtering*, (2017)

36. Ziren Wang, Guoliang Liu, Guohui Tian, *Human Skeleton Tracking Using Information Weighted Consensus Filter in Distributed Camera Networks*, (2017)

37. Guoliang Liu, Member, IEEE, Guohui Tian, Junwei Li, Xianglai Zhu, and Ziren Wang, *Human Action Recognition Using a Distributed RGB-Depth Camera Network*, (2018)

38. Sungjin Hong and Yejin Kim, *Dynamic Pose Estimation Using Multiple RGB-D Cameras*, (2018)

39. Madhura P. Pathegama, Dileepa M. Marasinghey, Kanishka Wijayasekaraz, Ishan Karunanayakex, Chamira U. S. Edussooriya, Pujitha Silva k, and Ranga Rodrigo, *Moving Kinect-Based Gait Analysis with Increased Range*, (2018)

40. Filippo Basso, Riccardo Levorato and Emanuele Menegatti, *Online Calibration for Networks of Cameras and Depth Sensors*, (2014)
41. Semih Dinc, Farbod Fahimi, and Ramazan Aygun, *Mirage: an O(n) time analytical solution to 3D camera pose estimation with multi-camera support*, (2017)
42. A. Elhayek, C. Stoll, N. Hasler, K. I. Kim, H.-P. Seidel, C. Theobalt, *Spatio-temporal Motion Tracking with Unsynchronized Cameras*, (2012)
43. David Pavllo, David Grangier, Michael Auli, *QuaterNet: A Quaternion-based Recurrent Model for Human Motion*, (2019)
44. William Dyce, Nancy Rodriguez, Antoine Seilles, Benoit Lange, Sebastien Andary, *Tabu search for human pose recognition*, (2014)
45. Cheng Xu, Jie He, Xiaotong Zhang, Cui Yao, Po-Hsuan Tseng, *Geometrical kinematic modeling on human motion using method of multi-sensor fusion*, (2018)
46. Xiao Sun, Chuankang Li, and Stephen Lin, *An Integral Pose Regression System for the ECCV2018 PoseTrack Challenge*, (2018)

www.ingramcontent.com/pod-product-compliance
Lightning Source LLC
Chambersburg PA
CBHW070347200326
41518CB00012B/2167